TEHRAN

WORLD CITIES SERIES

Edited by
Professor R. J. Johnston and Professor P. L. Knox

Published titles in the series:

Beijing	*Sit*
Birmingham	*Cherry*
Budapest	*Enyedi and Szirmai*
Buenos Aires	*Keeling*
Dublin	*MacLaran*
Glasgow	*Pacione*
Harare	*Rakodi*
Havana	*Segre, Coyula and Scarpaci*
Hong Kong	*Lo*
Lagos	*Peil*
London	*Hebbert*
Mexico City 2nd edition	*Ward*
Paris	*Noin and White*
Rome	*Agnew*
Seoul	*Kim and Choe*
Singapore	*Perry, Kong and Yeoh*
Taipei	*Selya*
Tehran	***Madanipour***
Tokyo 2nd Edition	*Cybriwsky*
Vienna	*Lichtenberger*

Forthcoming titles in the series:

Brussels	*Murphy*
Johannesburg	*Beavon*
Lisbon	*Gaspar and Williams*
Los Angeles	*Keil*
Montreal	*Germain and Rose*
New York	*Smith and Hackworth*
St Petersburg	*Bater*

Other titles are in preparation

TEHRAN

The Making of a Metropolis

ALI MADANIPOUR
Department of Town & Country Planning at the University of Newcastle

JOHN WILEY & SONS
CHICHESTER • NEW YORK • WEINHEIM • BRISBANE • SINGAPORE • TORONTO

Copyright © 1998 by John Wiley & Sons Ltd,
Baffins Lane, Chichester,
West Sussex PO19 1UD, England
National 01243 779777
International (+44) 1243 779777
e-mail (for orders and customer service enquiries): cs-books@wiley.co.uk
Visit our Home Page on http://www.wiley.co.uk or http://www.wiley.com

All Rights Reserved. No part of this publication may be reproduced, stored in a retrieval system, or transmitted, in any form or by any means, electronic, mechanical, photocopying, recording, scanning or otherwise, except under the terms of the Copyright, Designs and Patents Act 1988 or under the terms of a licence issued by the Copyright Licensing Agency, 90 Tottenham Court Road, London, UK W1P 9HE, without the permission in writing of the publisher.

Other Wiley Editorial Offices

John Wiley & Sons, Inc., 605 Third Avenue,
New York, NY 10158-0012, USA

WILEY-VCH Verlag GmbH, Pappelallee 3,
D-69469 Weinheim, Germany

Jacaranda Wiley Ltd, 33 Park Road, Milton,
Queensland 4064, Australia

John Wiley & Sons (Asia) Pte Ltd, 2 Clementi Loop #02-01,
Jin Xing Distripark, Singapore 129809

John Wiley & Sons (Canada) Ltd, 22 Worcester Road,
Rexdale, Ontario M9W 1L1, Canada

Library of Congress Cataloging-in-Publication Data

Madanipour, Ali.
  Tehran : the making of a metropolis / Ali Madanipour.
      p. cm. — (World cities series)
  Includes bibliographical references and index.
  ISBN 0-471-95779-8 (alk. paper)
  1. Urbanization—Iran—Tehran. 2. City planning—Iran—Tehran.
I. Title. II. Series.
HT384.I652T446 1998
307.76'0955'25—dc21   98-15968
                                                                          CIP

British Library Cataloguing in Publication Data

A catalogue record for this book is available from the British Library

ISBN 0-471-95779-8

Typeset in 10/12pt Garamond from author's disks
by Mayhew Typesetting, Rhayader, Powys
Printed and bound in Great Britain by Biddles Ltd, Guildford and King's Lynn

This book is printed on acid-free paper responsibly manufactured from sustainable forestry, in which at least two trees are planted for each one used for paper production.

CONTENTS

Preface	ix

PART ONE: THE RISE OF A METROPOLIS

1 City of Revolutions — 3
A village outside the ancient city of Ray — 3
A walled market town — 4
A capital of the Persian empire — 5
A node in the world market — 8
A revolutionary city: Constitutional Revolution 1906–1911 — 11
The centre of a unified national space: Reza Shah 1925–1941 — 13
A democratic city: the Second World War and beyond, 1941–1953 — 16
A monarch's seat: post-*coup d'état* period: 1953–1963 — 17
A capital of oil: White Revolution and modernization: 1963–1977 — 18
A city of discontented masses: Islamic Revolution and war 1977–1988 — 22
A semi-peripheral world city — 24
Conclusion: from a suburban village to a peripheral metropolis — 25

2 Transformation of the Capital — 28
Emergence of Tehran — 28
Tehran the capital city — 29
The first transformation of the city — 31
The second stage of transformation — 36
The post-war development of the city — 40
Social movements and urban space — 42
Conclusion: the emergence of a new urban morphology — 44

PART TWO: A PROFILE OF THE CONTEMPORARY CITY

3 Urban Economy — 49
Iran's economy — 49
Tehran's economy in the national context — 52
Employment — 54
Sectors of the urban economy — 55

Public and private sector employment	56
Manufacturing	58
Energy	59
Services	60
Wages and prices	61
Conclusion: the largest economic centre in the country	62

4 Urban Management — 64
Urban administration before the Constitutional Revolution	64
Management of Tehran between two revolutions 1906–1979	65
Management of Tehran after the Islamic Revolution	70
Urban management in the 1990s	72
Urban governance	73
Democratic management	76
Financial independence	77
Conclusion: challenges of urban governance	81

5 Urban Society — 82
Demographic change	82
Structure of the population	86
Immigration	87
Family and social transition	91
Individualism	93
Cultural identity in the city of strangers	95
Social polarization and exclusion	99
Conclusion: immigration, difference and social polarization	100

6 Urban Space — 102
Topography	102
Climate	106
The size of the city	109
North–South duality	111
Core–periphery duality	114
Suburban settlements	116
Axiality	117
Street system	119
Land use	122
Building form	123
Conclusion: spatial manifestations of social change	126

7 Urban Problems — 128
Transport	128
Environmental pollution	132
Green space	137

Housing	140
Conservation	144
Conclusion: facing social and environmental problems	145

8 Urban Lives 147
Portraits from a labyrinth 147

PART THREE: SHAPING THE URBAN LANDSCAPE

9 Agents of Transformation 163
Who builds the city?	163
Construction sector and the national economy	165
Key actors in the development industry	167
Relationship between development agencies	172
Tensions of city building: development for use or for exchange	173
Tensions of city building: regulation versus sectoral intervention	176
Conclusion: development agencies and urban transformation	177

10 Building the City: Development Resources 179
Land	179
Financing the urban development process	187
Labour	193
Conclusion: flow of resources into the built environment	197

11 Building the City: Rules and Ideas 199
The city walls of the 1870s	199
The open matrix of the 1930s	201
Foundation of urban planning in the 1960s	205
Tehran municipality's strategic plan in the 1990s	213
Conclusion: rules and ideas that transformed the city	215

12 Inherited Concepts of Space and Political Institutions 218
Political authority and urban structure	218
Citadel and city	219
Axiality and centrality in urban space	223
Nodes of urban space: public squares	226
Intermediate groups	227
Autonomy and urban form	229
Geometrical regularity and rationality	230
Conclusion: power, institutional continuity, and urban form	234

13 Cultural Practices and Urban Form 235
Difference and residential segregation in urban space: neighbourhoods	235

Cultural traditions and urban form 240
Tradition and modernity: cultural challenge and response 245
    Individualism or conformity 247
    Context and modernization 250
    Conclusion: the tension between old and new 252

14 Challenges of the Twenty-first Century   254

Bibliography 258
List of Tables 274
List of Figures 275
Photograph Credits 278
Index 279

PREFACE

Tehran was once called the city of plane trees and it was possible for a traveller to complain about the density of trees and gardens around it, hiding it from visitors (Bell, 1928), who were searching inside these green walls hoping to unveil some remainder of the exotic and sleepy Orient of a magical past. Now, Tehran is a giant metropolis which has devoured its green borders and whose two revolutions and many more upheavals this century have changed the city and shaken the world around it. Nevertheless, it still remains a city hidden from the outside world, enwrapped within what appears to be a new clothing made from a political and ideological fabric. But, we may wonder, does the city reveal itself to its own inhabitants, or are they too visitors, entangled within a labyrinth, a complex web of places, people, and events?

This book has been written for two distinctive but interconnected purposes. First, it is a case study of Tehran, offering detailed information and analysis about an important, but little known, city. As one of the largest cities of the world, Tehran has found international significance for a variety of reasons. The Islamic revolution in Iran toppled the monarchy and threatened the balance of power in the Middle East, the latter reflected in eight years of war with Iraq and in troubled relationships between Islamist movements and political regimes throughout the region. Before these historic events, the establishment of OPEC and the control of oil production, the life blood of industrial economies, had turned Tehran into a decision-making centre with far-reaching economic and political influence. During the cold war, its political status was raised as the administrative centre of a vast country with geopolitical importance. After the retreat of the Soviet Union from Afghanistan, the breakdown of the Soviet bloc, and the liberalization of the Caspian and Central Asian republics, Tehran's political significance has found a new weight within a more fragmented regional power structure. Despite this international significance, with its economic, political, and cultural dimensions, studies on Tehran as a city are rare. There is a wealth of published materials on Iran, which often concentrate on examining the turbulent events of the late 1970s and 1980s. They try to explain the complex social and economic processes that led to (or a few concentrating on what followed) the revolution and war. Many of these studies, which proliferated in the early 1980s, were historical accounts or memoirs of the key actors depicting their perspective of these explosive events. Others were interested in the impact of the revolution on world affairs, through the new role of religion as an emerging cultural and political force and through its impact on the patterns of oil production. None of these studies, however, have concentrated on the urban environment in which these developments took place. This has created a major gap which this book aims to bridge.

Second, the book is concerned with the development of a methodology for understanding cities and their transformation. As such, it is part of a larger project of inquiry into urban socio-spatial change (Healey et al., 1995; Madanipour, 1996a, b; 1997; Madanipour et al., 1998). It sets out to understand the social and psychological significance of space, to explain why a particular urban form is as it is and how it is likely to change. The methodology used here is basically founded on four interrelated notions:

1. That the social and spatial dimensions of a city are closely intertwined.
2. That the study of urban space is best made possible by tracing the process of its development.
3. That the development process, as a social process, is best understood by addressing both individual actions and the structures that frame these actions.
4. That understanding this process will not be complete without addressing the social and physical contexts in which it takes place.

These notions draw upon several key concepts: the assertion that each society produces its own space, and the concept of production of space as a commodity (Lefebvre, 1991); the contentious relationship between exchange value and use value (Logan & Molotch, 1987); the two-sided relationship between structures and agencies in social processes (Giddens, 1984); the necessity of paying attention to political economy analysis as well as to everyday life perspectives and the cultural and aesthetic dimensions of social processes (Habermas, 1987; Lefebvre, 1991); and the tense relationship between reason and subject as a hallmark of the modern period (Taylor, 1989; Touraine, 1995).

With both its purposes, providing information and developing a methodological framework, the book has been written for students and scholars with an interest in the study of cities, from various fields of social sciences and humanities and those with a particular interest in Iran and the Middle East. A case study of Tehran will have some insights to offer to those with an interest in the debates about modernity and globalization. Many around the world today are wary of the globalization process. The way localities feel helpless in the midst of flows of information and resources across the globe, the way decisions about localities are made elsewhere, and the way homogenization of culture may erode local distinctions are among the feared characteristics of the global age. The story of Tehran displays all these and other related features, and as such is a case study of globalization. It shows a gradual integration of the city into the global economy, the impact of this process on the people's lives, and their reactions to it. The story of Tehran tells us how these fears have been present in the city for the last century and a half, how globalization arrived there long before the advent of computers, and how the city has struggled to forge a response.

The story of Tehran is also a case study in the tensions of modernity. The discussions about modernity and postmodernity have been hotly debated in the West in the past 25 years. Tehran's modern history is full of debates about modernity, whether to accept or reject it. Two revolutions are the focal points of these debates. While a revolution at the beginning of the twentieth century strongly promoted modernity, the second revolution towards the end of the century cast serious doubts on many aspects of modernization. Together they are signs of how a city, indeed a country, has struggled to find its place in a global space dominated by powerful players and to find a critical response to the inevitable challenges of modernity.

The book traces the social and physical transformation of Tehran during the last 200 years and how the city has been restructured and reimaged during its process of integration into the world system of capitalist economies as a peripheral centre. It starts by outlining the historic development of the city, followed by a portrait of the contemporary city and a more detailed account of its development. Part One offers a brief account of the general historical contexts in which the contemporary city is rooted. Readers searching for a profile of the contemporary Tehran will find it in Part Two, where social, economic, political, cultural, and spatial aspects of the city and some of its current problems are discussed. Part Three provides a more detailed analysis of the way the urban landscape has been shaped during the last half-century and the way space making works in Tehran. Here, the main emphasis of the study is on urban development processes since the Second World War, with their distinctive combination of agencies, resources, rules, and ideas. The search for the roots of ideas, however, takes us at times back to a distant past or to places that have had an influence on the making of Tehran. Together, the three Parts unveil some of the main characteristics of Tehran and lead the way to a better understanding of the social and environmental contexts of which it is a major constituent part. They also reveal how space making is an integral part of the social processes and how a society shapes its space.

I have tried, as much as possible, to be consistent in translating and recording Iranian years (a solar, hejira calendar with 621 years' difference from the Gregorian calendar), and Iranian names (recording as they are pronounced in a standard Tehrani accent). However, where I have come across a word which already has a recording in the English language, I have used it in that form, rather than relying on its Persian pronunciation. In these cases, therefore, I have used, for example, Azerbaijan, rather than Azarbaiejan, and *qadi*, rather than *ghazi*.

This book draws upon my professional engagement in, and academic research into, the city's urban development process. It also draws upon my personal experiences of growing up in Tehran and witnessing the historic events of revolution and war. There are therefore many sources of information and inspiration in developing the ideas presented here. Acknowledging all these sources would be an impossible task. Specifically, I would like to thank Abdolhussein Abarghouei, Jafar Mojtabavi, Mohammad Mahmoodi, Hamid Zarazvand, and Babak Zirak who helped me with collection of information in Tehran, Mahmood Rahimian and Yaghoub Mousavi for our discussions on the city, Nasrollah Kasraian and Tehran Municipality's Public Relations Office and International Affairs Department for allowing me to use their photographs, Allan Gillard and Patsy Healey for support and help in developing the study in its earlier form, Anthony King for encouraging me to turn it into a book, Anoushiravan Ehteshami, the Series Editors, Paul Knox and Ron Johnston, for their helpful comments on the book draft, and at Wiley, Tristan Palmer, Iain Stevenson, Louise Portsmouth, Ben Mullane and Mandy Collison for their help and support during the project. Continuous support, however, came from Simin and Suroosh, to whom I dedicate this book.

PART ONE

THE RISE OF A METROPOLIS

1

CITY OF REVOLUTIONS

As a city, what are the changes that Tehran has gone through to become what it is now? In a land where most towns and villages have some claim to historical significance, what are the roots of Tehran? What can we find in Tehran's past which would explain its present and point towards its future? How far back do we need to go to find out about Tehran's past? This Part gives an account of the city's history and its social and physical evolution since it became the capital of Iran 200 years ago. This will provide a context in which a more detailed picture of the contemporary city, as offered in Part Two, and the process of urban development which has created the city, as analysed in Part Three, can be better understood.

Chapter 1 looks at the historical stages of Tehran's growth and change. It offers an account of change in Iranian society and its capital city's social environment. The history of Tehran is largely intertwined with the modern history of Iran. As such any account of its evolution will have to be embedded in an account of change in the country as a whole. The chapter investigates, very briefly, the city's past history, particularly the history of the economic, political, and social change since the second half of the nineteenth century. At the risk of oversimplification of complex developments, it helps to understand the societal dynamics which led to the emergence of Tehran as a metropolis. This will be complemented by Chapter 2, in which an account of the evolution of the built environment is outlined.

A VILLAGE OUTSIDE THE ANCIENT CITY OF RAY

A glance at the long history of settlement in this particular area of Iran reveals its strategic importance. Tehran was a village outside the ancient city of Ray, which is now incorporated into the giant metropolis and is often considered as its historical predecessor. The city of Ray, ancient Raga, has been continuously inhabited for more than 6000 years (Semsar, 1986; Kariman, 1971, 1976). According to the Avesta, the sacred book of the Zoroastrians, Ray was the twelfth city in the world to be created by Ahura Mazda, the Good Spirit (Lockhart, 1960). The city was located on the great Khurasan highway, along the southern side of the Elburz mountain range, which has always been the main means of communication between east and west of Iran and a part of the Silk Route. It was one of the major cities of Media in Aryan times; the spring residence of the Parthian kings; and the place from which the last Sassanian king made his final attempt to rally the populace against the advancement of Islam (Lockhart, 1960).

In AD 643 it was occupied by the Arabs who, after a revolt by its inhabitants, almost totally ruined the ancient city and established a new one near by. It became a favourite residence of some early Abbasid caliphs and a frequent residence of the founder of the Seljuk dynasty (Lockhart, 1960). The ancient city of Ray was revitalized by the House of Buwaih (Semsar, 1986). From the eighth to the twelfth centuries it enjoyed prosperity and growth of population, reported to be, not without exaggeration, as large as 8 million (Lockhart, 1960). In this flourishing period, Ray, as the second most important city in the East (Istakhri, in Sykes, 1902), was nicknamed by some as "the world's bride" (Semsar, 1986) or, for its antiquity, *Shaykh al-Bilad* or *Umm al-Bilad* (Dinwari, in Barthold, 1984). In the eleventh century, Ray was the capital of the Seljuk empire by its founder Toghril Beg, before he moved his seat of government to Isfahan (Morgan, 1988: 28, 34).

The factional strife between the religious groups of Hanafis and Shafiis caused the initial deterioration of the city as early as the tenth century (Barthold, 1984). The destruction of Ray was to be completed by the Mogul invasion of the year 1220 from which the city never fully recovered. After this, Ray remained as a major strategic focal point in the military movements across the Iranian plateau but lost its importance as a city. For a while, Varamin, a nearby village and now a city, was gaining regional superiority (Barthold, 1984) before it was time for Tehran to emerge.

A WALLED MARKET TOWN

The name of the village of Tehran was first mentioned in a chronicle in the eleventh century as the birthplace of a well-known scholar (Khatib Baghdadi, in Semsar, 1986). In the twelfth century, it was reported as being prosperous and famous for its pomegranates (Ibn-Balkhi, in Semsar, 1986). In the thirteenth century it was described as a large village located 6 km away from Ray, with underground houses surrounded by a belt of gardens. The village had 12 rival quarters whose people were known for their defiance of the government (Yaqut, in Semsar, 1986). In 1340, Tehran was described as a considerable town with a climate better than, and a produce comparable with, Ray's (Semsar, 1986; Minorsky, 1934). The Spanish ambassador to Timur, Clavijo, described Tehran of 1404 as very large with no walls, well supplied with everything, and delightful (Sykes, 1902; Ferrier, 1986).

The strategic location of Tehran and its gardens attracted the Safavid king, Tahmasb, when visiting the tomb of one of his ancestors in the nearby shrine of Hazrat Abd al-Azim (Vahedi, 1989). In 1553 (AH 961), he built a bazaar and a town wall, which gave Tehran the status of a city. Other Safavid kings added more buildings to the town which gradually grew in importance to become a garrison town, a trading centre and a regional capital and eventually a temporary court. The collapse of the Safavids was followed by a period of economic decline and political decentralization throughout the eighteenth century. In 1760, Karim Khan Zand considered making Tehran his capital city (Minorsky, 1934). This, however, took place at the hands of the next dynasty, the Qajars. In the absence of Ray, Tehran took over, growing from a minor village to a capital city.

A CAPITAL OF THE PERSIAN EMPIRE

It is now more than 200 years that Tehran has been the capital city of Iran. There are some debates about the year in which Tehran became capital. Saidnia (1994) uses the date given in *Mer'at-al-Boldan* (Sunday 11th Jamadi-al-ula AH 1200, the Persian Nowrooz day) as the most accurate and concludes that Tehran became capital on 20 March 1785, which is close to Minorsky's mention of 1786 (1934: 716). Earlier in Iranian history, the seat of government had changed with the change of dynasties. As Lockhart (1960) reminds us, in the last four centuries, Tabriz, Qazvin, Isfahan, Mashhad, Shiraz, and Tehran have all become capital cities. This had given all an opportunity to pull people and resources, to grow in size and importance, to be embellished by magnificent monuments and public buildings, and to become nodes in the country's territorial configuration. Tehran has held this role longer than the others, and in a period in which substantial changes have happened in Iran, changes which have allowed Tehran to grow from a small market town to one of the larger cities of the world.

It was the founder of Qajar dynasty, Agha Muhammad Khan, who decided to choose Tehran as his seat of government. This was a town near enough to the Qajar tribal territories and far enough from previous capitals in which elites loyal to previous rulers could be found. It was also located centrally and strategically enough from which it would be possible to rule a vast country. This strategic and historic importance can be traced back to the ancient city of Ray, and the significance that previous Safavid and Zand rulers had attached to Tehran. Its symbolic location at the foot of the highest peak in the land has also been a contributing factor throughout history (Figure 1.1).

The town's population swelled by the courtiers and soldiers, who in turn attracted more people and a development of trade and industry. In 1796, Olivier reports a population of 15 000, of which 3000 were soldiers (Minorsky, 1934: 717). A reported 12 000 families, probably including traders and artisans, were moved by the Qajar king from Shiraz to Tehran (d'Allemagne in Taleghani, 1992: 4). In 1808, General Gardane estimates a winter population of 50 000, the summers being when the well-off left the city. Several others, including Kinnier (in 1808–9) who estimates a summer population of 10 000, Ouseley (in 1811), and Ker Porter (in 1817) estimate

FIGURE 1.1 Tehran is located at the foot of Mount Damavand, the highest peak in the land

the winter populations of up to 70 000 (Minorsky, 1934: 717–18). The Qajar court and royal bodyguard, it was estimated, constituted 6 per cent of the town's population (Wagstaff, 1985: 207).

In the early years of the establishment of the Qajar dynasty (1779–1925), rapid economic development occurred in Iran. Later in the century, however, the country suffered from depopulation, poverty, and economic exhaustion (Issawi, 1971: 13). In the early nineteenth century, the importance of foreign trade in Iran's economy was considerably diminished. Since the sixteenth century, the new overseas trade route between the Far East and the West had caused a decline in the ancient overland trade route, the Silk Route, of which Iran was a middle point. The east–west trade axis in Iran, which had survived for centuries, was finally scaled off in the early nineteenth century (Avery & Simmons, 1980). The production and export of silk, the major export item of the country, also decreased to very low levels by the middle of the 1860s (Gilbar, 1979).

The great majority of Iran's population, about 80–85 per cent, were engaged in agriculture and rearing of livestock. In the mid-nineteenth century, about 58–59 per cent of Iran's 9 to 10 million population lived in rural settlements (Gilbar, 1976). The basis of the village economy was the production of wheat and barley, the staple food of the people, and a considerable variety of other crops. Animal husbandry, as mainly carried out by the nomadic or semi-nomadic tribes, who constituted a third of the population, was another important basis in the country's economy. When in peace, the relationship between the nomadic tribes and the settled people was based on the exchange of their products (Lambton, 1987: 48–51; Gilbar, 1976).

In the early nineteenth century, Iran's territorial structure, as similar to previous Persian empires, consisted of a collection of loosely connected provinces. Some provinces were ruled by governors appointed by the central government and as such were more or less attached to the centre. Others were under tributaries, remaining autonomous in their affairs and acknowledging the nominal authority of the shah (Lambton, 1987: 42). In any case, the extent of authority of the central government was limited due to the vastness of the country, lack of communication, and the existence of regional power structures of tribal leaders and large landowners. This was coupled with the diversity of communities with different ethnic origins, languages, and religions. These groups constituted relatively self-sufficient, closed economies mostly confined to regional boundaries, because of geographical difficulties as well as social complexities and communal structure. Their limited surplus did not allow the growth of urban centres. Only 8–9 per cent of the population lived in towns of 10 000 or more inhabitants (Gilbar, 1976). The towns were political, administrative, and commercial centres, and the rural areas produced the agricultural products which formed the backbone of the economy. As in the rest of the Middle East, and unlike medieval Europe, towns were part of a rural–urban continuum, in which the mutual relationships favoured urban areas (Hourani, 1970; Cahen, 1970; English, 1966). The basic function of the towns was, thus, not production but control and distribution of regional surplus, which was produced in the countryside, through political power and exchange mechanisms (Amirahmadi & Kiafar, 1987).

Despite its differences from Western feudalism (Katouzian, 1981), this society is loosely called feudal, mainly because of the power being derived from the possession of land, existence of a subject peasantry, fragmentation of authority, and the military character of the ruling class (Lambton, 1987: x–xi). In spite of the existence of socio-economic stratification, the strength of communal bonds prevented the formation of class consciousness and state-wide socio-political classes. The communities, whether tribal, rural, or urban, were almost all similarly organized hierarchically. The rich and poor were tied together especially through tribal lineages, religious sects, regional organizations, and paternalistic sentiments (Abrahamian, 1982). Inherent in the diversity of the communities, whose unit could be a city quarter, a village, a tribal camp, a religious community, or a corporate organization, was the communal conflict between these groups, not dissimilar to the factional strife in feudal Europe of the Middle Ages (Vance, 1977).

The prevalent parochialism and the limited extent of the central government's power over the provinces meant that the role of Tehran as the administrative centre of a fragmented territory was limited. Adverse economic conditions, strong communal and regional bonds, and a very low, and at times negative, rate of population growth created little economic surplus and social mobility. Although Tehran grew substantially after becoming the capital city, it was still in its infancy.

A NODE IN THE WORLD MARKET

This relatively enclosed society was not aware of the challenges that it was to meet later by the encroaching power of the West. This society, which had shown a striking structural continuity throughout its history (Wilber, 1963), underwent a radical change from the nineteenth century, mainly through interaction with the West. Mostly from the middle of the century, a process of transition into capitalism, through participation of Iran in the world commodity exchange, started which was to restructure all of society and its institutions. The main outcomes of this restructuring included an increase in the population of Tehran and its entry into the world market as a peripheral node.

The first motivators of change were political threats and territorial losses (Lambton, 1987). The defeats which were imposed on the Persian empire through wars with Russia in 1813 and 1826 and with Great Britain in 1856–57, led to the contraction of its territory. The military advancement of the two rival powers from the north and the south was followed by their political and economic influence. Foreign trade increased and unequal treaties and concessions gave the foreign traders superiority over their Iranian counterparts (Keddie, 1981). The exemption of the European traders from internal duties and taxes, as against the Iranians who were subjected to numerous arbitrary taxes, opened the Iranian markets to foreign capital and goods. Commercial services were monopolized by the Russians and the British so that a north–south trade axis, as against the then obsolete east–west axis, was developed (Avery & Simmons, 1980). Tehran's strategic location at the intersection of these two axes would give it a natural advantage against its rivals.

The subsistence crops, wheat and barley, were replaced by export crops such as cotton, rice, opium, and fruit (Lambton, 1987; Issawi, 1971). This process resulted in an increase in cultivation and production (Gilbar, 1979). It also led to an increase in the social stratification of the countryside

(Keddie, 1981). The landlords strengthened their hold on the land and, as land became freely alienable, the newly grown merchant class invested in it, resulting in the growth of private ownership. As against this, most peasants lost their traditional land rights and became landless sharecroppers (Keddie in Issawi, 1971). It also deepened the gulf between the rural and urban population (Lambton, 1987), and, through reduction in the production of subsistence crops, helped developing social crises such as bread riots and disasters such as the great countrywide famine of 1869–72 (Keddie, 1981).

During the second half of the nineteenth century, unemployment rose and the proportion of artisans declined in favour of commerce and services (Gilbar, 1976). The locally produced handicrafts were replaced by imported manufactured goods, which was beneficial for merchants and some consumers but detrimental for artisan and trading groups. The latter lost the employment and income which the home industries provided, without being compensated by the development of manufacturing industries (Keddie, 1981; in Issawi, 1971). These developments linked Iran's economy to the global economy so that the worldwide devaluation of silver, the country's currency, or fluctuations in the supply and demand of cash crops now had far-reaching effects on the country's economy (Gilbar, 1979; Avery & Simmons, 1980).

The whole financial system was becoming subjected to foreign capital through loans and banks. The economy was gradually restructured to export raw materials and import manufactured goods. The nascent native bourgeoisie started to invest in farming whose products were in great demand in the world market. This had a disastrous impact on the primitive accumulation of capital and on the character of the national bourgeoisie, putting it in a dependent position (Abdullaev, in Issawi, 1971). The dependent economic relations with the West which resulted are best indicated by the monetary drain it had caused. An overall trade deficit started from the 1860s onwards (Issawi, 1971), especially in the southern areas, which caused an outward drain of money (Avery & Simmons, 1980). In the late nineteenth century, the volume of raw materials which Iran exported was five times larger than that of the imported finished goods, while the price of the latter was three times more than the former (Keddie, in Issawi, 1971). At the turn of the century, the 10 million population of Iran with a net growth rate of under 1 per cent was slightly higher than 50 years before, due to epidemics and famine (Gilbar, 1976).

The relaxation of the old economic structure gave rise to a change in the structure of population. The proportion of nomads reduced to a fourth of the population and the overall percentage of those engaged in the primary sector reduced to 70. Especially from 1870, a marked increase in the urban population occurred to reach 18 per cent of the population in the early 1900s (Gilbar, 1976). This was in line with a greater degree of social and spatial mobility. It took the form of migration from the rural areas and small towns to provincial centres and the capital; international emigration, especially to Russia; and, within Tehran, a level of suburbanization. The first census in 1867 recorded the population of Tehran as 155 736, a tenfold growth since becoming the capital city. It was partly in response to this growth that, as we shall see in the next chapter, the city was extended to accommodate the population expansion. A high proportion of Tehranis were immigrants, as in this year only 26.7% were of Tehrani origins and more than a third were renting, rather than owning, their accommodation. Of the working population 12.3 per cent were soldiers and more than a quarter were servants (Taleghani, 1992: 6–8). This clearly shows the concentration of wealth in the city and its administrative and military character.

In the second half of the nineteenth century, in line with the limited development of regional and national markets and some improvement in communication, a move was made towards political centralization. It extended the authority of the government to the more remote districts (Lambton, 1987: 44). Gradually the "men of the pen" played a more important role in the affairs of the state as compared to the "men of the sword" who formed the dominant group in the earlier part of the century. The former developed a highly centralized and elaborately organized bureaucratic system on the pattern practised by the Seljuk, Ilkhanid, and Safavid empires before them. However, in absence of an effective system of financial control, the high degree of provincial independence remained intact (Lambton, 1987: 216–17).

Central government assumed only basic functions such as defence and the conduct of foreign affairs (Yapp, 1977). In 1900, the annual governmental budget was only about 2 per cent of the GNP, meaning that the influence of the state on the economy was extremely weak (Bharier, 1971: 5). The main purpose of the bureaucracy was collecting taxes to support the army and the royal family. Public works were seldom undertaken. Most of the functions that are considered as governmental, including all levels of education, most forms of judicial and legal activity, and social and charitable services, were carried out by the religious authorities (Keddie, 1981: 29–31). The authority of the state was partly limited by the feudal character of the court. It was also checked by the existence of rivalry: internally between the various groups and communities which constituted the society; and externally between the two major powers of Russia and Britain. The policy of the government in this respect was based on trying to maintain this strife so as to be able to keep the independence of the country and secure its rule over it (Lambton, 1987; Abrahamian, 1982).

The impact of foreign economic and political influence and the subsequent involvement of Iran in international trade as a dependent partner had an instrumental effect on the stratification of society. On the one hand, there were the upper classes of courtiers, merchants, tribal chiefs, and landlords, along with Europeans and religious minorities whose economic importance grew through their connection with Europeans. On the other hand, there were the tribal masses, the landless or nearly landless peasants, and the urban poor along with traditional and religious groups (Lambton, 1987; Abrahamian, 1982; Issawi, 1971).

Although limited in comparison to later periods, the increase in international trade, change in social and economic structure of the country, and the centralization of the state power all meant a greater importance for Tehran. The population of the city and its surrounding area grew to 300 000 by the year 1899 (Taleghani, 1992: 10). Another source in 1900 estimates the city population to be 250 000, with 100 000 more living in its 670 adjoining towns and villages (Minorsky, 1934: 719). At the beginning of the twentieth century, the rapid concentration of population in the capital city was creating a hotbed of tensions which would unfold in a century of social unrest and revolutionary struggle.

A REVOLUTIONARY CITY: CONSTITUTIONAL REVOLUTION 1906–1911

In the last two centuries, the dominant theme of the economic, and social, history of Iran, within a wider Middle Eastern context, has been a "reaction" or a "response" to an "impact" or "challenge" (Issawi, 1982: 1). The latter was put forward by the worldwide expansion of the industrializing, capitalist Europe in search of food, raw materials, markets, and outlets for its energy, capital, and population. As the history of Iran in the present century shows, with two revolutions and two *coups d'état*, the response to this challenge has varied from cautious attempts for reconciliation to total assimilation or rejection.

The modern history of Iran since the beginning of the nineteenth century, therefore, can be seen as a response to the political, economic, and cultural challenges of a domineering West. The response can be analysed in the tensions between three sets of actors with different roles and strategies: modernizers, traditionalists, and the state. The modernizers or reformists, as represented by the secular intelligentsia, have sought to transform the country with the aim of economic, political, and cultural development. The traditionalists or conservatives, as represented by the clergy and the bazaar, have sought to resist this process of reform, which they have thought avoidable, and have demanded that the traditional norms and patterns of life be maintained. At their extremes, the traditionalists have manifested a tendency towards maintaining the feudal–tribal structure and refusing to negotiate with any new development. The extremist modernizers, however, have wanted to move towards total assimilation with the capitalist industrialized countries of the West. The state has often played the role of a mediator between, and making alliances with, these trends (particularly with reformists) and the Western influence. Whenever the reformists and the conservatives have united, they have been able to mobilize masses and achieve major concessions from, or even transformation of, the state. The two peaks of the long history of struggle and tension between these forces are two revolutions, each showing a supremacy of one of these two trends in their alliance against the Western political and economic influence and the state. This sketch, even though brief, shows some of the complexity of these tensions, which have been labelled by some observers as continuity and change (Wilber, 1963), or traditionalism and modernism (Yapp, 1977).

As early as the 1830s both the opposition to the foreign influence and attempts to reform had started. This was a time in which hand-manufacturers and merchants protested against the rising tide of European imports which were ruining their trades (Keddie, 1981). These protests continued throughout the century and some of them, such as the protest against the tobacco concession in 1891–92, became more important. The culmination of this process is manifested in the Constitutional Revolution of 1906. The beginning of the process of reforms in the 1830s is also marked by Prince Abbas Mirza's attempts to modernize the army, after the two Russian wars. The military superiority of Iran's opponents caused the tendency in Iranians of studying the technical achievements, the arts and sciences, and the advantages inherent in the social and economic structure of Europe (Alavi, 1983). The reforms which followed were "from above", usually carried out by the high-ranking officials (Keddie, 1981). Some reforms were supported, or even started, by the shah. The urban improvements under Amir Kabir and the restructuring of Tehran under Nasser al-Din Shah were such reforms. They were among a range of other reforms such as establishing in the capital a secular school, a medical clinic, a central mint, a regular police force, and a municipal service (Abrahamian, 1982: 57).

However, what was detrimental to major reforms was the arbitrary nature of the monarch's power (Yarshater, 1983; Alavi, 1983; Lambton, 1987). The Constitutional Revolution of 1906 aimed to replace this arbitrary rule with the rule of law (Katouzian, 1995), checking the royal absolute power by setting up a national assembly with the power of controlling the state. This was performed by a major alliance of liberal reformers, clergy, merchants, traders, students, workers, and radical members of secret societies (Afary, 1994). They fought against the foreign political and economic influence and against a weak and dependent government. The main site of this battle was Tehran, where the most important achievements of the revolution, a constitution and a parliament, were shaped by an urban social movement.

In the early twentieth century, the long-standing discontent with government mismanagement and foreign influence, which had reduced Iran to a buffer state (McLean, 1979), together with a deepened economic crisis led to the Constitutional Revolution of 1906. However, the decline in the authority of the central government which followed, economic dependence, and the outbreak of the First World War debilitated the economy and increased foreign intervention. This is especially shown in two ill-fated international agreements: the 1907 Anglo-Russian agreement which was to divide Iran into spheres of influence and the 1919 Anglo-Iranian agreement which was to practise tight control over the country by the British empire in the aftermath of the Bolshevik Revolution which had removed the Russians from the scene for a while.

The impact of these periods of political and economic instability was a stagnation of urban development. Nevertheless, the demand for reform, which characterized this period, was such that the incoming political structure was forced to undertake another major programme for the transformation of the city.

THE CENTRE OF A UNIFIED NATIONAL SPACE: REZA SHAH 1925–1941

The First World War and its associated events brought about new circumstances. These included the advent of socialist revolution in Russia, which renounced all the previous economic claims over Iran, and the post-war financial difficulties of the British empire, which prevented any direct intervention (Olson, 1980). An atmosphere was created in which the integrative nationalism (Abrahamian, 1980), which had started to develop since 1890 (Cottam, 1964), could grow. What was required for a full transition into capitalist development was the destruction of feudal dispersion and the surviving medieval partition, which had proved to be difficult in the hands of the Qajar feudal aristocracy (Abdullaev, in Issawi, 1971). The change of dynasty from Qajar to Pahlavi (1925–79), which followed the 1921 coup by Reza Khan, highlights this stage in transition.

The immediate task of Reza Shah was centralization of government and consolidation of his power, which were carried out by the creation of a new army, a reorganized government bureaucracy, and a court patronage (Abrahamian, 1982: 136–7). Whereas the court turned into a wealthy landed military complex, the army and the bureaucracy provided the basis for the growth of an urban middle class living in the capital and the large cities. This was a modern middle class which was culturally and economically intertwined with the new regime. The drive for the increase in the power of government, however, had adverse implications for the political and social freedoms achieved by the Constitutional Revolution. The elections of the national assembly were manipulated, opposition parties, religious leaders, radical and liberal movements were persecuted and suppressed. The 1920s and 1930s saw the increasing intervention of the state in economic affairs. The state established monopolies on many goods and tried to take full control of foreign trade.

Serious efforts were made to improve communication. The first major railway in the country, the Trans-Iranian Railway, was constructed, linking the Persian Gulf to the Caspian Sea. The tolls and road taxes were abolished and, under a road development plan, 14 000 miles of new roads were built by the end of the 1930s. Together with the rapid import of vehicles, up to the annual average of 3000 in the mid-1930s, the travel times were cut and the inland freight rates fell (Bharier, 1971). The reduction in the cost of transport made it easier to export bulky agricultural items such as cotton, wool, raisins, and hides, earning the foreign exchange which could be used in the industrialization programmes (Clawson, 1993). The improvement of communications linked the regions and opened up the country for the internal trade and movement of imports. Military mobility was increased so that the regional movements and power structures were suppressed and the strength and dominance of the central government established. The transportation network enabled the nationalist government to try to integrate the diverse communities into a unified nation and to overcome the existing factionalism.

The state paid little or no attention to the agricultural sector which employed the great majority of the workforce and whose products were sufficient to meet domestic needs. The importance of the agricultural sector in the country's economy, which contributed 80–90 per cent of GNP at the turn of the century, declined to about 50 per cent by 1950. Despite changes in the type of crops, for example curbing the production of opium and increasing tea and sugar, the structure of agricultural production remained basically unaltered (Bharier, 1971). The attempts which were made to change the land tenure system resulted in the acquisition of vast areas by the shah or large landlords, reducing the peasant ownership of land to a minimum (Issawi, 1971; Keddie, 1981).

As against the neglect of agriculture, a major move was made towards industrialization. By the end of the 1930s, 20 per cent of the general budget was allocated to manufacturing industry. By 1947, the contribution of the industrial sector to GNP rose to about 5 per cent (Bharier, 1971). The government was envisaged as a prime mover encouraging private enterprise by import duty protection, industrial credits, and facilities for the importation of productive equipment. By 1950, the public sector covered 15 per cent of the enterprises employing 32.5 per cent of the total number of workers, the rest covered by the private sector (Grunwald & Ronall, 1975). With the main stress being put on large industries, especially sugar, textiles, glass, matches, and cement, the small industries which were involved in simple processing of agricultural products apparently suffered. The number of small industries, which had proliferated earlier in the large cities, had reached 5000 in Tehran by 1928, employing 15 000 workers, before their decline in the next decade (Bharier, 1971). The number of industrial concerns increased from 38 in 1931 to 635 in 1945, of which 378 were concentrated in Tehran (Grunwald & Ronall, 1975), this centre of decision-making and the largest market of the country. Most of the concerns were situated in the south of the city, which was gradually gaining the character of an industrial zone. This was accentuated by accommodating the living places of the newly born industrial working class in this area. In this way, the industrialization and its associated new social groups were finding geographical expression. It sustained and accelerated the basic polarization of the city structure which had started in the nineteenth century.

Foreign trade expanded and new foreign partners, the USA and later Germany, were sought to balance the power between the old rivals (Knapp, 1977). The withdrawal of the government from its attempt to nationalize foreign trade proved the strength of the merchants. In this period, merchant capital, which had strong Western ties, continued to be the dominant form of capital (Keddie, 1981). However, excluding oil exports, foreign trade still showed a regular deficit. When the increasing oil revenue was included, the deficit ceased after 1921 (Bharier, 1971). The oil industry, which developed in an enclave, was run by the Anglo-Persian Oil Company, which was based on a concession obtained by W. D'Arcy for 60 years' exploration, exploitation, and export. The royalty it paid to the government, 16 per cent of the profit, formed only 10 per cent of the country's general budget in the mid-1920s. After the 1933 agreement, which followed the cancellation of the concession by the government in 1932, the royalty increased and the proportion of the oil revenue in the budget increased to about 25 per cent by the end of the decade (Bharier, 1971).

Reza Shah implemented reforms which had remained ill-fated in the previous century. For him, as for many reformers in the late nineteenth century, modernization was associated with Westernization, his long-range goal being "to rebuild Iran in the image of the West" (Abrahamian, 1982: 140). His ambition was to transform a multi-ethnic empire into a unified nation state. The past was associated with administrative inefficiency, tribal anarchy, clerical authority, and social heterogeneity. This was to be replaced by a future marked by cultural uniformity, political conformity, and ethnic homogeneity (Abrahamian, 1982: 140–9). Some of his reforms were far-reaching, such as secularization of educational and judicial systems, reorganization of the military and administration, and introduction of new financial and fiscal systems. Others, however, remained superficial, as exemplified by the forceful replacing of traditional ethnic and religious clothes with European-style dress in 1928 (Abrahamian, 1982). Another example of such symbolic, Western-style change was decorating the new streets and squares of Tehran and other towns and cities with his own statues.

The improvement of transport led to the relative prevention of local famines and, consequently, the rate of population growth rose from under 1 to 1.5 per cent. The proportion of the urban population, however, remained static, at about 20 per cent, for the first third of the century. It was in the mid-1930s that, as a result of intensified rural–urban migration, the annual rate of population growth in urban areas reached 2.3 per cent as compared to 1.3 per cent in rural areas (Bharier, 1971: 23–8). The city became a scene and a symbol of the transformation of the country (Ehlers & Floor, 1993). Centralization of administration, expansion of bureaucracy, development of a transport network, and the integration of the regions into a national market were coupled with more attention being paid to towns and cities. These were nodes in the emerging national political and economic space. Through them the state could exert its power and could control the countryside. Breaking the old regionalism, unification of the national space, and the increased strength of the state all meant that cities and among them Tehran were to become ever more important. By 1940, 58.5 per cent of all domestic capital investment was made in Tehran (Keddie, 1981: 102), which attracted more and more immigrants to the capital. According to the first official census by the municipality in 1922, Tehran had a population of 210 000. The second census of this kind in 1932 shows a population of 310 000, which grew to 540 000 in 1939. This growth continued, especially as a result of the destructive impact of the Second World War on the countryside, to 700 000 in 1941 and 880 000 in 1946 (Taleghani, 1992: 10–14; Vezarat-e Barnameh, 1987a).

A DEMOCRATIC CITY: THE SECOND WORLD WAR AND BEYOND, 1941–1953

The outbreak of the Second World War and the occupation of Iran by the Allies in 1941 led to the abdication of Reza Shah, who had developed close ties with Germany in his latter years of rule, in favour of his son Muhammad Reza. The relaxation of political suppression gave rise to a revival of free press, trade unions, and rival political parties, which lasted for 12 years. The explosion of free and democratic activities in Tehran changed the face of the capital.

The presence of the Allied forces had an enormous impact on the distribution of supply, which led to famine in some areas, and to an increasing inflation in others. The cost-of-living index rose from 100 in 1939 to 757 in 1944 (Keddie, 1981: 116). This was beneficial for those middle and upper classes who dealt with goods or credit, and detrimental to lower classes and those on fixed incomes. The new circumstances hit government revenue and caused the deterioration of industries.

Many of the forcefully settled nomadic tribes began to move again. Large numbers of peasants migrated to the cities and towns, as they were impoverished by debt and inflation and high interest rates as well as the rising power of landlords, who were heavily represented in the government, and new private landowners. They constituted the urban unemployed and a growing working class employed in railways, construction, oil industry, the growing private sector industries, and the newly privatized state factories.

The demands of the Allied forces for urban goods and services, expansion of professions, and continued growth of the army, gendarmerie, and bureaucracy stimulated urbanization. This was followed by a boom in residential buildings especially between 1945 and 1949 (Bharier, 1971) as well as a growing density in the cities. By 1951, the urban population increased to 4.9 million or 30.4 per cent of the total population. Within a decade, Tehran's population doubled to pass the level of 1 million (Vezarat-e Barnameh, 1987a). The residential boom was the first of successive waves of speculative land and property development which have characterized the post-war production of the urban fabric in Tehran. It was a direct result of the bases founded in the two stages of spatial transformation, which had incorporated the production of space into the emerging capitalist mode of production.

This period ended with the nationalization of the oil industry by Mossadegh's nationalist government in 1951. It led to an international economic blockade of the country and finally the collapse of the government in 1953 by an American-supported *coup d'état* in favour of the shah to safeguard the exportation of oil.

A MONARCH'S SEAT: POST-COUP D'ÉTAT PERIOD: 1953–1963

The post-war period marked the beginning of an era in which a new rivalry between the great powers, the United States and the Soviet Union, dominated the foreign relations of Iran. The 1953 coup was a focal point in which the United States, whose influence had grown since the war through economic advisers and military missions and aids, became the dominant foreign power in Iran. The decade which followed witnessed the consolidation of the shah's power through suppression of the opposition, firm control of elections, setting up a secret police, and expansion of armed forces. The foundations of a royal dictatorship were laid which was to last for 25 years.

In 1954, a new oil concession was granted on the basis of 50–50 profit-sharing between the government of Iran and a consortium of major European and American oil companies. The share of the latter rose to 40 per cent, to be equal to that of the Anglo-Iranian Oil Company which was renamed British Petroleum. As a result of the new agreement, the oil revenue increased from $20.7m. in 1954 to $90.2m. in 1955 and to $380m. in 1963 (Razzaghi, 1988: 454–8, 485).

From the mid-1950s, the state started an industrialization drive, the basic policy of which was to encourage private investment, both domestic and foreign, for developing import-substituting industries. There were no stress on export promotion or considerations of employment in these modern capital-intensive industries. Also no relationship between these and the agricultural sector was envisaged. As a result, manufacturing industries grew significantly, with an increase in the number of industrial enterprises and the production indices of most of Iran's major commodities. Most of the plants were located in Tehran and its environs so that, in 1960, this area accounted for 30 per cent of all new establishments (Bharier, 1971: 185–9). In 1956, the population of Tehran had risen to 1.56 million, constituting 26.2 per cent of the country's urban population (Vezarat-e Barnameh, 1987a). In this year, 20.1 per cent of the workforce were employed by industry, as compared to 56.3 per cent in agriculture and 23.6 in services (Razzaghi, 1988: 117).

The rise in oil revenue and the increasing rate of population growth and immigration to cities led to a further expansion of the capital city. In the 1950s, speculative development, which had been started in the early post-war years, found even larger scales. The rising numbers of cars and buses allowed the urban fabric to spread freely across the surrounding countryside.

To finance the escalating military expenditure and the ambitious development plans, the government had to rely on heavy borrowing from abroad. The conditions of the International Monetary Fund to protect the value of currency and pressure from the Kennedy administration to carry out liberal reforms destabilized the regime (Bharier, 1971; Abrahamian, 1982). Consequently, the period between 1960 and 1963 saw an economic crisis, a degree of political freedom, the beginning of a major land reform, and a popular revolt which was a rehearsal for a revolution 15 years later.

A CAPITAL OF OIL: WHITE REVOLUTION AND MODERNIZATION: 1963–1977

This period witnessed a major step towards the development of a market economy by removing the pre-capitalist barriers to it and attempting to strengthen a weak private sector. This was carried out by the state whose autocratic nature and monopoly control of the ever-increasing oil revenue tended to create a state capitalism (Keddie, 1981: 160). The land reform of 1962, the three phases of which were officially completed by 1971, has been seen as the intervention of the state to encourage the capitalist transformation of the Iranian countryside (Halliday, 1979). It was the backbone of what was declared as a White Revolution. By then, about 70 per cent of the fertile agricultural land was owned or controlled by a small number of large absentee landowners and was cultivated on the basis of the small-holdings of crop-sharing peasants (Bharier, 1971). In the land reform programme, this system of ownership and production, which was considered as a barrier to both development and the central government control of the countryside, was largely dismantled.

According to the reform, large landowners had to sell, or lease, their agricultural property, in excess of a certain amount, through the state, to the sharecropping peasants who worked on the same land and had some cultivating rights. However, this programme did not include the rural wage earners, about 40 per cent of the cultivating villagers (Keddie, 1981). Also the nationalization of pastures took away the tribal control of pastureland and, subsequently, the nomads, being deprived of their livelihood, were forced to settle. Instead, from the late 1960s, the government economic and technical aid and encouragement favoured a small number of large agricultural units, farm co-operatives, and agribusinesses run by domestic and multinational corporations.

The process of land reform encouraged the old magnates to be incorporated more into the urban and rural bourgeoisie. The unequal distribution of land created a rural middle class. It also gave impetus to those who had received insufficient or no land to migrate to the cities. The percentage of employment in the primary sector fell to 46.2 per cent in 1966 and to 34 per cent in 1976. The number of nomadic tribes was reduced to only 1 per cent of the population (or 7 per cent according to another definition). Migration to cities increased so that, between 1966 and 1976, the population of the 20 largest cities grew 67 per cent (Razzaghi, 1988: 69–126).

By undermining the old feudal magnates, a power vacuum was created in which the political support by, and the total control of, the countryside was taken over by the state. However, it proved to be an economic failure. An increase in production took place which was the result of an increase in area of cultivation (Bharier, 1971). However, the rate of increase of agricultural production was below the rate of increase of population and far below the rising demand for consumption stimulated by the oil revenue, which led to an ever-increasing rise in the import of food (Halliday, 1979: 127). The contribution of the agricultural sector to GNP declined once again, from 33 per cent in 1959 to only 25 per cent in the late 1960s (Bharier, 1971).

Oil revenues increased as a result of the renegotiation of the 1954 agreement with the international consortium and the dramatic price rise of 1973. It rose from $482m. in 1964 to about $20.7 bn in 1977 (Razzaghi, 1988: 485). An effect of the boom was an increase in the dependency of the economy on oil and, through it, on the advanced industrialized countries of the West. The oil contribution rose from 17 per cent of GNP in 1967–68 to 38 per cent in 1977–78, and accounted for 77 per cent of government revenue and 87 per cent of foreign exchange earnings in 1977 (Halliday, 1979: 138–9).

From the mid-1960s a major industrial growth, at an average annual rate of 15 per cent until 1975, was taking place. Development plans concentrated on producing consumer goods for the internal market and encouraging the growth of basic and intermediary industries. By 1977, there were 250 000 manufacturing establishments, of which 6000 were employing 10 or more, with a total employment of an estimated 2.5 million people (Halliday, 1979: 148). From 1966, the proportion of employment in industry rose from

27.1 to 34.2 per cent (Razzaghi, 1988: 117). The share of manufacturing in GNP rose to 17 per cent in 1977 (Abrahamian, 1982: 430).

Unemployment rose gradually to 10.2 per cent in 1976. The number of employers, which had grown from 1.16 per cent in 1956 to 2.9 per cent in 1971, fell to 2.1 per cent in 1976 due to the accumulation of capital in fewer hands and expansion of monopolization. During this period, the urban-based employers grew from 51.5 to 78 per cent. Along with rural–urban migration, other forms of employment also increased in favour of the cities. The proportion of self-employed, i.e. independent workers without employees, fell from 43.2 per cent in 1956 to 32 per cent in 1976. The number of employees grew from 44.3 per cent in 1956 to 54 per cent in 1976. In this period, there was a fall in private sector employment, from 36.9 to 34.9 per cent, and a dramatic increase in public sector employment, from 7.9 to 19 per cent (Razzaghi, 1988: 110–11).

As a result of investment in health care facilities, most of them concentrated in cities, the population grew from 25.8 million in 1966 to 33.7 million in 1976, the urbanized population from 39.1 to 47.1 per cent. In this period, Tehran grew from 2.98 million to 4.59 million (Razzaghi, 1988; Vezarat-e Barnameh, 1987a). Tehran became the largest concentration of economic enterprises as well as the largest market in the country. It extracted money and people from all around the country, creating large surpluses of capital and labour which needed to be absorbed, increasingly by being channelled into the built environment. In the mid-1970s Tehran accounted for 72 per cent of migration between provinces and 44 per cent of that between urban areas. It accommodated 13.3 per cent of the whole population and 28.6 per cent of urban population, producing half the GNP (excluding oil revenue); 40 per cent of all the national investments, and 60 per cent of industrial investments were made in Tehran which housed 40 per cent of large industrial concerns; 40 per cent employment in retail and 60 per cent in wholesale activities; 35 per cent of the banks with 75 per cent of deposits, and 41 per cent of insurance companies were concentrated in Tehran; 84 per cent of housing loans were allocated in the capital whose share of all construction investments was 47.2 per cent. Tehran was also a concentration of 56.8 per cent of all hospital beds, 57 per cent of physicians, and 55 per cent of students; 57 per cent of university graduation, 64.1 per cent of newspaper distribution, and 68 per cent of vehicle registrations were made in Tehran (Shahrdari-e Tehran, 1978). The urban fabric of Tehran grew faster than ever before. During the period 1967–80, the number of dwellings grew two and a half times. The new developments, supported by the oil boom of the 1970s, were built in different forms, from low rise to high rise and from single developments to large new towns, constituting a complex and ever-expanding metropolis.

Despite the dramatic growth of GNP, from about US$200 per capita in the early 1960s to about US$1000 in real terms in the late 1970s, the income gap widened due to the government policies (Keddie, 1981). The large and increasing disparities by region and class are reflected in the patterns of consumption and income. Whereas 32.5 per cent of the total consumption was accounted for by the highest 10 per cent of families in income scale, only 2.5 per cent was accounted for by the lowest 10 per cent. The divide between classes and between urban and rural areas is shown in the wide discrepancy between the income of the upper-level urban households and other households, a ratio of 6:1 on a per capita basis for lower urban households, and 11:1 for rural households. The capital city accommodated most of the higher-income households. Per capita income in Tehran was 45 per cent higher than in other large cities and 70 per cent higher than in small towns (Looney, 1975: 3). It was the deterioration of income distribution and the widening social divide that was a major contributing factor to the widespread discontent of the late 1970s (Looney, 1982).

Four classes are identified as forming the urban population of Iran by the mid-1970s (Abrahamian, 1982). An upper class of not more than 1000 families included royal and aristocratic families and entrepreneurs. They not only owned many of the large commercial farms but also some 85 per cent of major private firms involved in banking, manufacturing, foreign trade, insurance, and urban construction. The propertied middle class, with bazaar community at its core and urban entrepreneurs and clergy at its sides, constituted a traditional force which had preserved much of its power. Half of the country's handicraft production, two-thirds of its retail trade, and three-quarters of its wholesale trade were controlled by the bazaars. The salaried middle class, whose number had doubled within 20 years, included civil servants, teachers and school administrators, engineers, managers, and white-collar workers. The working class, including rural and industrial wage earners, together with the impoverished urban poor, constituted 34 per cent of the labour force by the mid-1970s, as compared to 16 per cent in the 1940s.

The fact that the state was the recipient of oil income, i.e. the major source of funds, and, accordingly, the major distributor of it, gave it a far-reaching place in the economy, somewhat similar to other oil economies (e.g. Gilbert & Healey, 1985). Together with support from its international allies, this allowed the state to practise the utmost degree of political control over the population (Halliday, 1979). In the 1970s, the Iranian state was characterized as being a royal dictatorship, dependent on support from the advanced capitalist countries, which was promoting the growth of capitalist social relations and the expansion of productive forces along capitalist lines (Halliday, 1979: 38–65). The form of this dictatorship was, however, unique in that it "combined the vigorous promotion of capitalist development with a fully constituted monarchist regime" (p. 56), a fundamentally anti-capitalist form of political structure.

The period 1963–77 saw an expansion of economic activities and a deliberate underdevelopment of the political system (Abrahamian, 1982:

427). The gulf between the two became so wide that an economic crisis, resulting from a fall in oil revenue, was able to provoke a revolution which dismantled the whole political apparatus and shook the socio-economic structure. Once again, as in the revolution of 1906, the authoritarian regime was swept aside by a class alliance which saw it as an obstacle to political development and unable to cope with the complexities of socio-economic development (Graham, 1979).

A CITY OF DISCONTENTED MASSES: ISLAMIC REVOLUTION AND WAR 1977–1988

The year 1979 was the culmination of a two-year period in which millions of demonstrators occupied the streets of Tehran and other large cities, putting an end to monarchy in Iran. In analysing this revolution, the literature shows a general tendency to identify single causes for the mobilization of the masses and their discontent. Many Western observers have agreed with a cultural explanation: that the revolution was a traditionalist challenge to a forced and rapid modernization by the Pahlavi regime. Others, however, have tried to offer political and economic explanations as well (Parsa, 1989; Amirahmadi, 1990; Afshar, 1985; Abrahamian, 1993). Some have seen the revolution as the result of a tension between economic development and political underdevelopment, where the middle classes have sought a more active participation in the political scene. Some have seen it as the reaction of the local bourgeoisie to the stifling intervention of the state and the international capital in an uneven market-place. Conspiracy theorists have blamed the Western powers for being instrumental in the downfall of a too proud monarch. Others see the revolution as the triumph of a mass movement by the uprooted and disgruntled immigrants who had been concentrated in Tehran and other large cities. There is no doubt that there are elements of truth in all these explanations. What all shades of opinion agree upon is that the revolution was a coalition of various groups with different interests and backgrounds. What brought these groups together was a complex combination of various causes. We will have to search for the causes of the revolution in a combination of political, economic, and cultural tensions between the state, the extraterritorial forces, and the populace. A new generation of scholars are developing more complex and comparative analyses of the Iranian revolution. Foran (1994: xvi), for example, convincingly argues that the revolution, as the latest in a long line of Iranian social movements this century, should be studied "at the intersection of the mixed results of the shah's model of capitalist industrialization in a dependent and authoritarian context, the diverse political [and] cultural responses to this experience articulated by secular and religious opponents, and the fortuitous opportunity afforded by an economic downturn and perceived pressures for reform emanating from the United States in the late 1970s".

The charismatic leader of the revolution, Ayatollah Khomeini, who had been a witness to and a critic of the Constitutional Revolution and an active opponent of the White Revolution, wanted to ensure a traditionalist revival, as represented by the doctrine of the rule of clergy (Saffari, 1993), and the use of religious rather than secular laws. In the massive revolutionary alliance which had brought most urban groups together, this doctrine was combined with a liberal reformist idea of parliamentary republicanism, and with radical anti-capitalist mottoes of the left. As in other revolutions, the alliance of the elite was soon broken, resulting in massive purges, arrests, and executions. However, the combination of these narratives, the radicalism of which had mobilized masses, was more difficult to dismantle. The combination of two parallel systems with two different natures, the rule of clergy and parliamentary republicanism, has created constant tensions, which can be observed in many spheres of political processes.

The revolution which established the Islamic Republic in 1979 aimed at restoring the political, economic, and cultural independence, which was eroded through further integration of the country into the world market. This was to be gained through reducing the dependence on oil revenue, giving priority to agriculture, encouraging the rural economy to prevent further urbanization, democratizing the political arena, decentralizing the administrative system, and reducing social polarization. Nationalization of banks and large companies accompanied the revolutionary government's preference for small-scale private enterprise. However, the war which was imposed on Iran in the aftermath of the revolution had disastrous social and economic effects. In 1980, fearful that revolutionary tides would engulf neighbouring countries, the expansionist Iraqi army invaded Iran and started a bloody and futile war (similar to the one it waged later against Kuwait), which lasted for eight years and inflicted huge damage upon both countries. In its two-hundredth birthday as capital in 1985, as Saidnia (1994) reminds us, Tehran was under Iraqi air attack and suffering from terrorist explosions, in which hundreds were killed and some areas of the city destroyed or damaged.

Just before the end of the war in 1988, a picture of Iran's social and economic scene, as depicted by the Amendment to the First Development Plan of Islamic Republic of Iran (Vezarat-e Barnameh, 1987b), tells a troubled story. It recounts an increased rate of population growth, 3.1 per cent annually as against 2.7 in the late 1970s, which, without respective expansion of the economy, had led to impoverishment of large sections of the population. The problems which the country was facing included lack of new investment in agriculture and industry, deterioration of infrastructure, high inflation, increased dependency upon oil revenue, a large budget deficit, and various administrative, legal, and executive obstacles. The declining oil revenue was being spent on imports of consumer products, raw, intermediary, and capital goods for assemblage industries, skilled workers, and modern technology, not to mention weapons. Low productivity, underutilization of industrial capacity, and unemployment of 19 per cent were among other problems. Even though a reduction in social polarization had occurred, 10 million people were identified as facing substantial deprivation. As against them there were about 100 000 households who controlled much of the surplus through trade and speculation.

The private sector grew considerably, to the extent that it controlled a turnover three times the size of the annual governmental budget. During 1976–86, the service sector expanded considerably to account for 45.4 per cent of employment. As compared to that, there was stagnation or decline in agriculture, whose share fell from 34 to 29.1 per cent, and in industry, from 34.2 to 25.5 per cent (Razzaghi, 1988: 111–17). Revolutionary rhetoric, war, economic instability, relaxation of political authority, and the continuation of a centralized administrative system stimulated urbanization further to increase the total urban population to 26.9 million or 54.4 per cent in 1986. In 1982, 25 per cent of the urban population lived in one city, Tehran, 45 per cent in 6 cities, 66.5 per cent in 33 cities of 100 000 inhabitants and more. In the same year, the density of Tehran province was 15 times that of the national average and 107 times that of Semnan province (Razzaghi, 1988: 92).

In 1986, the population of Tehran increased to 6.02 million (Markaz-e Amar, 1987a). Even though the proportion of its population to the total urban population had started to decline gradually from the 1960s, from 30.4 per cent in 1966 to 23.2 per cent in 1986, its suburbs grew very rapidly. Between 1976 and 1982, the suburban cities of Karaj and Islamshahr were the fastest growing cities of Iran with annual growth rates of 16.7 and 13.9 per cent respectively (Razzaghi, 1988: 93). In 1986, with its suburbs, Tehran formed an urban region of nearly 8 million inhabitants or about 30 per cent of the country's urban population. Only within the space of a decade, 1976–86, this urban region received 3 million more people. By 1991, the city's population had reached 6.5 million within an urban region of 9.1 million (Markaz-e Motale'at, 1994). By the year 2010, it is expected to have a population of 15–27 million (Hesamian, 1987; Vezarat-e Barnameh, 1987a).

A SEMI-PERIPHERAL WORLD CITY

The death of Ayatollah Khomeini in 1989 and the end of the war with Iraq in 1988 signified the end of the revolutionary period and the beginning of normalization in Iran (Ehteshami, 1995). Normalization has partly meant a new centralization of power (Milani, 1993), which would follow a troubled route back to the world market-place and to establish new relationships with the main players in the global economy. A full return to the world market appears an inevitable direction to move in, as the economy is largely dependent on oil. Its internal clashes of power and ideology, however, have resulted in a continuation of challenges against the West, which has made this return problematic. These can be seen in cultural challenges against the West, as represented by the Salman Rushdie affair, and in political challenges, as reflected by the Israeli Prime Minister calling Tehran a "capital of terror" (*The Guardian*, 14 March 1996: 13). At the same time, the overwhelming majority of the Iranians who elected the moderate President Khatami in May 1997 have shown that their priority is a return to normality.

Tehran may lack the normal concentration of headquarters of the multinational corporations, which characterize world cities. It is, however, a centre of some political, economic, and cultural influence. Tehran's control of huge oil reserves and its political and cultural influence in the Middle East and Central Asia have given it the status of a semi-peripheral world city. The reconfiguration of the major world powers and their spheres of influence have had major implications for Tehran and its role in the global and regional scenes. Early in the century, the rise of the Soviet Union and the end of rivalry between Great Britain and Russia had had a direct impact on Iran. The demise of the Soviet Union and the end of its rivalry with the United States has now had a major impact on Iran. The political and economic fragmentation of the Soviet Union and the disappearance of the Iron Curtain from the north of Iran have given Tehran a more important regional role. Iran competes with Pakistan and Turkey to establish links with, and win influence in, the war-torn and impoverished countries of Central Asia and the Caucasus. It competes with Saudi Arabia in the Persian Gulf and the Middle East for similar reasons. As the West-centred world system, which was formed after the sixteenth century, is being transformed in a global economy, Tehran is trying to re-create, and claim its place in, the ancient Silk Route, connecting the Middle East and Central Asia with the rising Eastern Asian economies. Inside Tehran, however, as the resources have dwindled and the population has grown, social polarization and environmental problems have threatened the inhabitants of a city who remember a century of instability and unrest in search of a more sustainable set of relationships.

In the rest of this book, we shall outline a more detailed picture of this semi-peripheral world city in terms of its economy, administration, society, space, and the problems its inhabitants are facing, and how it has evolved to become what it is today.

CONCLUSION: FROM A SUBURBAN VILLAGE TO A PERIPHERAL METROPOLIS

Within two centuries, Tehran has grown from a small town of 15 000 to one of the larger cities of the world. Its strategic location, on the main trading routes, and its symbolic location, at the foot of the highest mountain in the land, made Tehran, like its predecessor Ray, a focal point in a vast country. Iran's integration into the world economy, through commodification of agriculture and the establishment of the oil industry, has made its administrative centre a site of mediation, a bridge between the country and the rest of the world. Tehran has housed an increasingly centralized power structure which has stood on the ruins of feudal economies of fragmented regions. It stood at the centre of a unified space of a national market, in which people and resources grew detached from localities. Tehran gained from this social and spatial mobility of a growing population, becoming a site for the concentration of power, money, and people. The pace and dimensions of these concentrations, however, have created constant tensions, within them, between them, and with the outside world. A century of social movements, revolutions, and wars is a vivid witness to the intensity of these tensions.

The predominant theme in the modern history of Tehran has been a fundamental, all-embracing change. The historic developments in Iran from the nineteenth century show a dramatic transition from a feudal, or pre-capitalist social formation to a capitalist one (Halliday, 1979; Razzaghi, 1988). The immediate consequence of this transition has been a conflict between the pressures of the incoming political economy and the resistance of the outgoing one. This dichotomy and conflict have been coupled with the political and economic polarization which the market economy has created, resulting in tensions and imbalances, miseries and fortunes. The history of these tensions is manifest in the history of Tehran, whose pace and dimensions of change have left its inhabitants and managers feeling ever more out of control in the face of change.

Economically, the restructuring of agriculture in the nineteenth century and the increasing oil revenue in the twentieth have integrated Iran's economy firmly into the world market. From a closed, self-reliant economy, it changed into one based on the export of raw materials and import of manufactured goods, technology, and increasingly foodstuff. Through commodification of agricultural produce, land and labour became market commodities. The restructuring of agriculture to enter the world market and the land reform were the major processes through which old structures were broken down, freeing capital and labour to concentrate in urban areas. This was eased by the improvement of communication and development of regional and national markets. With an increasing oil revenue and population, the surplus of capital and labour was to be absorbed by expansion of manufacturing industry. This was a task the failure of which led to the growth of the service sector.

Politically, the international challenge, which gradually annexed the country into the world market, was to remain a vital element in safeguarding Iran's position in the global economy. As a scene of rivalry between, and sometimes collaboration of, the great powers of the time, Iran witnessed occupations, *coups d'état*, and unequal international agreements. Tehran became the site of an often weak government mediating between these international challenges and the internal pressures from below.

Internally, the political process has been one of centralization. The state had to overcome feudal economic and political disintegration, and to respond to an international challenge to its authority. As a result, a move towards centralization started from the second half of the nineteenth century which has continued ever since to expand the government's authority across the country into various spheres of life. This has been reflected in a change of dynasty and two *coups d'état* as well as numerous smaller regional conflicts. The strength of the government, supported by its increasing monopolization of the oil revenue, implied that it could intervene to foster social and economic change with actions such as land reform, industrialization drives, and improvement in transport and communication. Contradictory to this process of centralization has been the struggle for individual political and economic freedom which is fundamental to a market economy. The outcome of this struggle has been reflected in two revolutions and numerous protest movements, often occurring in Tehran and other major cities.

Socially, the parochialist, communal structure of society was dismantled to be replaced by one in which the relationships were to be defined by individuals' access to money. It was at once a drive for homogeneity of population, in which loyalty to the nation substituted for loyalty to the community, and an inevitable social polarization, which stemmed from uneven access to money and power. These developments have been directly or indirectly reflected in national and urban space. In the next chapter, we shall follow the evolution of the built environment in Tehran and how it has been in line with these societal transformations.

2

TRANSFORMATION OF THE CAPITAL

The major political, economic, and cultural changes that Iran has undergone were largely taking place in Tehran and other major cities. As such, Tehran's urban space is a manifestation of, and one of the conditions for, these changes. In this chapter we look at the evolution of Tehran's built environment, putting forward a historical context for an analysis of the contemporary urban environment. We concentrate on the development of the built space since the second half of the nineteenth century in its main stages of transformation in the 1860s/1870s, in the 1930s, and the urban expansion after the Second World War. Before that, however, a brief account of the emergence of Tehran as a city and some of the limited information which is available from that period are given.

EMERGENCE OF TEHRAN

For many visitors, the "crowning glory" of Tehran has been Mount Damavand, the highest in the land and the source of many ancient legends. According to Curzon, "What Fujiyama is to the Japanese, Damavand is to the Persian landscape. Both are ever-present, aerial and superb. Both have left an enduring mark upon the legends of their countries" (quoted in Ross, 1931: 79). It is on the southern slopes of this mountain and others in the Alburz chain that the city of Tehran has been located and has spread in all directions.

The earliest information about Tehran's built environment is given by the famous geographer Yaqut in the thirteenth century, that it had 12 quarters with underground houses and a ring of gardens (Semsar, 1986). Minorsky concludes from Yaqut's account that the town must have grown from the south to the north, towards the mountains, and that the oldest parts of the town are in the Ghar quarter in the south of the present-day city (1934: 717). In 1404, it had grown in size but still was not important enough to be walled (Sykes, 1902). The walls that the Safavid king, Tahmasb, built around Tehran in 1553 (AH 961), were 6000 steps in circuit with 114 towers, on the pattern of the 114 Sura of the Qur'ān, with four gates and a moat (Semsar, 1986). Like other Persian towns (Barthold, 1984), Tehran had a square shape with four gates opened on its four sides. In this respect, it was not unlike the city of Ray, its predecessor. Ray consisted of a citadel (*quhandezh*), an inner town (*sharestan*), and an outer town (*rabaz*). The citadel was located on a steep hill with a view over the entire city (Ibn Rusta, in Barthold, 1984). The city was a square in shape, its sides reported to be from 6 to 9 km (Maqdisi & Istakhri, in Barthold, 1984). As in other commercial and manufacturing towns in the Islamic period, the *rabad*, wherein the bazaars were situated, became the focus of life, causing the inhabitants to abandon both the citadel and the inner town in the tenth century and to shift to the outer town (Barthold, 1984; Istakhri, 1961).

Shah Tahmasb's successors added more buildings to this growing town. After his 1589 stay in Tehran, Shah Abbas built a *chahar-bagh* (four gardens) and a *chenarestan* (plane grove) in the northern part of the town. This area was later separated from the rest of the town by walls to become a citadel (*Arg*) (Zaka, 1970; Minorsky, 1934). Tehran was described by Pietro della Valle in 1618 as "a large city . . . but not well peopled, nor containing many houses, the gardens being extremely large, and producing abundance of fruit of various descriptions" (Curzon, 1892: 301–2). He admired the city for its lofty plane trees shading the streets which were watered by considerable streamlets. However, "excepting these", he added, "Teheran possesses nothing, not even a single building worthy of notice". Sir Thomas Herbert in 1627 referred to the 3000 houses built by mud brick and to the residence of the governor and the partly roofed bazaar (Curzon, 1892: 302).

Tehran grew to become a temporary court of the Safavid kings and a palace was built in the citadel by Shah Suleiman (Zaka, 1970). Another gate to the north of the city, the Arg or later Dowlat gate, was opened by the Afghan invaders in the eighteenth century to provide a secure exit without passing through the town. After the Safavids, Karim Khan Zand added to the buildings of the Arg and fortified it with walls and a moat (Zaka, 1970; Najmi, 1984).

TEHRAN THE CAPITAL CITY

Tehran was chosen by Agha Muhammad Khan, the founder of the Qajar dynasty, as the capital of Iran in 1785–76 (AH 1200), mainly due to its central position and its vicinity to the tribal territories of the Qajars (Lockhart, 1960). On becoming the capital, the city started to flourish. In 1796, according to Olivier, the city of 15 000 inhabitants was a square of little more than 3 km, of which only a half was built upon (Minorsky, 1934: 717). Within the space of little more than a decade, there were about 50 000 people living in 12 000 houses (Gardanne; Morier; Ouseley, in Curzon, 1892). In 1811, Ouseley counted 30 mosques and colleges and 300 baths for a city of 40 000–60 000 (Minorsky, 1934: 718). The second Qajar ruler, Fath Ali Shah (1834–48), tried to embellish the capital by constructing palaces and mosques (Hillenbrand, 1986a; Lockhart, 1960). Under his successor, Muhammad Shah, a sixth gate was opened to the city.

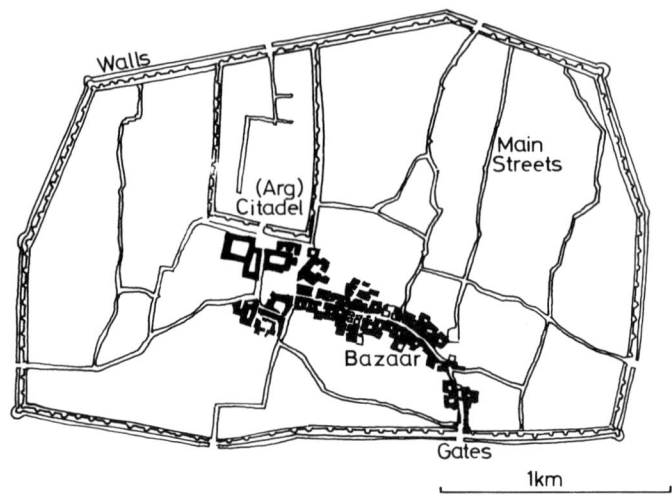

FIGURE 2.1 Tehran in 1858 had an axial layout and a functional structure

The structure of the city, an area of about 4 km² enclosed within the Safavid walls of 1553 (Kariman, 1976: 223, 298), comprised a citadel on the northern side, which was connected to the southern gate of Hazrat Abd al-Azim through the axis of the bazaar. To this axis were attached the Friday and Shah mosques. The rest of the town, in the form of four residential quarters, was clustered around this axis (Figure 2.1). This was an axial spatial structure with a clear functional organization: a political authority (royal compound), an economic centre (bazaar), a religious focus (Friday mosque), and living places of the townspeople (four quarters).

The surrounding walls of the city formed a polygon, opened by six gates, and enclosed by a moat. The mud city wall, ruined in parts, was 6 m high and flanked by circular towers, and was defended by a moat 12 m wide and 6–9 m deep (Curzon, 1892). The rectangular citadel also had walls and moats of its own.

Two neighbouring urban squares formed the main foci of the city structure: the Maydan-e Arg (Citadel Square), immediately inside the citadel as its entrance, and the Sabzeh Maydan (Herbs Market) (Browne, 1926), or market square, immediately outside the citadel, as the main entrance to the bazaar. These two squares, which were connected by the citadel's gate and a wooden bridge over the citadel's moat, were the converging point of the citadel and the bazaar and the meeting place of the townspeople with each other and with the ruling authorities. The citadel square was enclosed within the walls of the citadel whose arcades housed the artillery personnel. The square had four gates on its four sides and a number of cannons in the middle signified royal supremacy (Zaka, 1970). The market square, however, which was more accessible to the public, was generally known as the main city square.

The four living quarters, which represented a parochial social structure, were not physically separated from each other. Each of them had a main thoroughfare which led to the main axis of the city, the bazaar, through several minor squares. These urban arteries found more and more commercial character by approaching the bazaar, eventually becoming a branch of it, a *bazaarcheh*, a small bazaar (Faghih, 1988). In 1852, each of the living quarters, had, on average, 1900 houses, 645 shops (apart from the main bazaar), 36 public baths, and 35 mosques, a *madraseh* (religious school), and a *takyeh* (place of religious ceremony). Each quarter housed a mixture of lower and higher social classes (Ettehadieh, 1983).

The appearance of the Qajars' capital was not impressive for many travellers who compared it with the glories of the Safavid capital, Isfahan, or with the Victorian splendour of European capitals (de Planhol, 1968). In 1838, Fraser was disappointed by the absence of domes in Tehran, as compared to other cities of Iran (Minorsky, 1934: 718). Its location in the hollow of a plain, its dense fabric, its narrow, twisting, dusty streets and, apart from the citadel, its unpretentious buildings (Curzon, 1892), with flat roofs and blank façades (Pollock, in Semsar, 1986), are all features of the city, which have been described in negative tones.

THE FIRST TRANSFORMATION OF THE CITY

Despite heavy loss of life after the outbreaks of cholera in 1846 and 1852, the population of Tehran grew and the city spread beyond the limits of its physical boundary. In the late 1860s, the extramural inhabitants formed a tenth of its population (Ettehadieh, 1983). It was partly due to this factor and the development pressure from inside that the city underwent radical transformations.

The first attempts to transform the old city were made during the long reign of Nasser al-Din Shah (1848–96). The resulting changes in the city structure were so dramatic that, according to an observer, "the visitors in the first half of this [nineteenth] century would barely recognise it", featuring what was regarded as the second stage of a "twofold renaissance", the first one when Tehran became a capital city (Curzon, 1892: 300). The process of change, which embraced the whole city, started from the royal compound, by the reformist vizier Amir Kabir, by restoring its walls, improving its streets for the movement of vehicles (Najmi, 1984), and laying out a new, large square, Tup-Khaneh. The two main squares were also improved and beautified (Zaka, 1970; Najmi, 1984).

However, these minor improvements were only a prelude to the major changes of 1868, the focal point for the transformation of Tehran, when the shah decided to expand the city (Figure 2.2). By this time, Tehran, with its

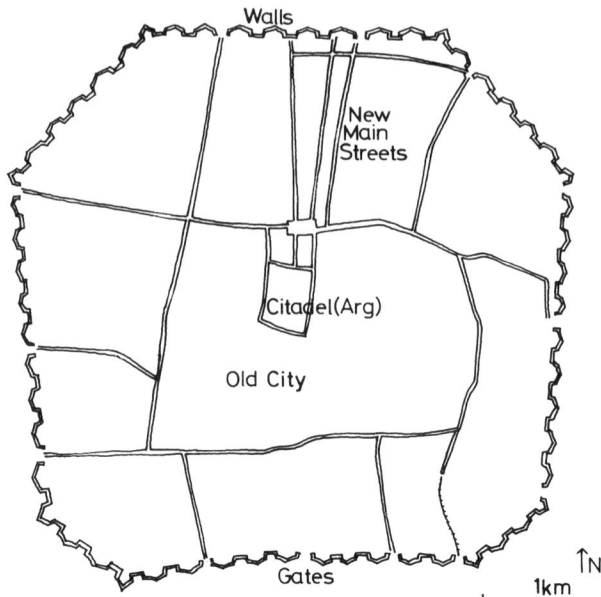

FIGURE 2.2 Tehran in 1890, after its first transformation which lay the foundations of a socio-spatial divide

150 000 population, had reached its limits of development within the old walls. A number of gardens and residences had started to grow outside the city walls. Mostowfi al-Mamalek, the grand vizier, and Mirza Issa, the minister for the capital, who were ordered by the shah to prepare plans for the expansion, set up a team headed by General Bohler, a French teacher in Dar al-Fonun, the institute of technology. The new plan of the city was a perfect octagon, enclosed by moats and walls, with 58 spearhead-shaped bastions, which were pierced with 12 gates (Zaka, 1970; Alemi, 1985).

The construction started in 1868 (AH 1284) and was not completed until twelve years later (Zaka, 1970). Even the famine of 1871 did not stop the construction work (Curzon, 1892). The old walls were pulled down and the moat filled. The new moat and walls, at a distance of 1.6 km from the old walls (Curzon, 1892), were built, which included the recently developed suburbs. The circumvallated city of about 18 km² was now four and a half times the size of the old city (Kariman, 1976: 223, 298). The 12 new gates on 4 sides were monumental structures decorated with glazing tiles, although they were not comparable to the quality of the Safavid models (Ross, 1931: 78). The rampart and fosse, which were not equipped with cannons, were regarded as having little or no defensive value (Curzon, 1892).

This first expansion of the city, like most of the subsequent phases of its development, was mostly northward. The filled moats around the citadel were turned into new avenues and a new focus was created for the city in the form of a new square, Tup-Khaneh, which was attached to the northern boundary of the royal compound. This was a large quadrangle enclosed with two-storey arches which housed, in the ground floor, the cannons and, in the upper floor, the artillery staff. This square was the converging point of six new, wide streets each with a gate, decorated with glazed tiles, at its entry to the square. The most important building flanking the Tup-Khaneh square was the Imperial Bank of Persia. This was a new economic institution with international connections, as compared to the traditional economic institution of the bazaar whose entrance flanked the old market square. To the north of the Tup-Khaneh square were located the new quarters which were the houses of the aristocracy and the embassies, delegations, and residences of Europeans. In and around the new square, especially to the north, new institutions were built. Apart from the bank, there were hotels, European shops, an institute of technology, a hospital, and a telegraph house.

Urban transformation in Tehran not only helped in establishing the national and international importance of the capital, but also had immediate economic and social impacts by providing a new source of revenue for the government. The inclusion of the newly developed suburban areas within the city walls extended the basis of the "gate tax" which the government charged (Curzon, 1892). The construction activities attracted large numbers of unskilled workers from the surrounding countryside (Gilbar, 1976) who came to live in the southern areas of the city. They formed the lowest stratum of society and had an intensifying impact on social and spatial stratification of the city. Following the gradual disintegration of communal bonds and beginning of the formation of new social classes, especially in urban areas, the space was to be transformed accordingly. The 1868 reform of Tehran's physical structure partly aimed to accommodate this new, polarizing social structure by the expansion of the city and creation of new, upper-class quarters. In the new urban structure the upper and lower classes were housed separately in the northern and the southern parts of the city. A process of spatial segregation of social classes started which was to constitute the most important feature of the city ever since.

The increase in the degree of centralization of political power and expansion of bureaucracy, limited though it was, is reflected in the government's ability to undertake such tasks as a major urban development scheme in Tehran. In spatial terms, the growing power of the state is reflected in the new spatial structure of Tehran. The intermediary role of the monarchy, between internal factions and external threats, was therefore reflected in the spatial structure of the city both before and after the transformation. Within the new walls, a new urban structure emerged whose geographical centrepiece was the royal compound (Scarce, 1983). It was different from the old structure in which this compound was located on the northern side of the city. The royal compound, which used to be connected to the city by a sequence of two squares, found two more points of contact. However, the importance of the third square, Shams al-Emareh, was later reduced, leaving the two squares, to the north and south of the citadel, as the focal points of the urban space. Therefore, this created a bipolar urban structure with a dual morphology: the old square surrounded by the old, traditional institutions housed in old parts of the town; and the new square surrounded by new institutions housed in newly developed areas. This bipolarity of the city was the first manifestation of what came to be an ever-enduring north–south divide. As opposed to the old urban structure with a highly specialized land-use pattern, the new urban structure provided, and it was intensified later, the basis of a mixture of uses along the new street frontages.

The nature of squares did not change as compared to the new approach to the streets. Compared to the narrow, twisting streets which, when they became main arteries like bazaars, were partly roofed, the new streets were wide, straight, and unroofed (Figure 2.3). However, they were not yet forming a network of streets connecting to the points of entry to the city. Only 7 of the 12 gates were linked up with the newly laid streets (Faghih, 1988). Since the new city boundaries were planned to allow for future developments and expansion, there was vacant land between the walls and the urban fabric, which seemed so unpleasant to some observers (Sykes, 1902: 178). Even after these transformations, the city's appearance failed to attract European visitors. The most imposing building of the capital was the mosque of Sepahsalar, which was finished in 1890 (Figure 2.4). Nevertheless, there was no "fine public building", as the main beauty of the city was in the large private houses and their gardens (Minorsky, 1934: 718).

A number of the new streets, Nasseriyeh, Lalehzar, Ala-al-Dowleh, came to be known as the most attractive places for the townspeople. These were comparatively wide streets which were cobbled; with separated pavements lined with trees watered with streamlets; and flanked with one- or two-storey buildings of shops and houses.

Even after the erection of the new city walls, suburban gardens and villages, especially towards the north of the city, were being developed outside the walls as the summer retreats of the wealthy. The green belt of the gardens around the city was so dense that travellers described Tehran as a city within a forest (Bell, 1928) or "a city of mud in an oasis of plane trees" (Arnold, in Graham, 1979: 22). Some of the gardens, like Yousefabad and Behjatabad, were within a short walking distance from the walls (Browne, 1926: 95), which subsequently became new neighbourhoods. The existence of a moat and walls around the city created a more visible, clear-cut case of marginalization. As Shahri (1978) shows, many marginal groups were housed in the moat areas. The marginal space of the moat appeared a natural breeding ground for marginal and often excluded groups, from

FIGURE 2.3   Nasseriyeh was one of the new, wide streets that surrounded the royal compound, which included Shams al-Emareh Palace

dervishes and gypsies to thieves and prostitutes. Further development of the city, however, changed all this.

The city grew rapidly during the next decades. However, this expansion, which was on the urban fringe, did not extend beyond the walls and moats (Farmanfarmaian & Gruen, 1968). By the turn of the century, the number of houses doubled and commercial activities flourished. In 1902, the numbers of caravanserais was two and a half times and shops four times those of 50 years earlier. Parallel to it, a secular trend was reflected in the decreasing number of religious institutions (Ettehadieh, 1983). In these developments, Tehran found an increasing commercial importance, as reflected in the considerable increase in the number of traders and shopkeepers in the city (Ettehadieh, 1983). This, which in turn attracted more people to the capital, was not due to its industries or agricultural production, but to its location along the main internal trade routes and the presence in it of the royal court (Issawi, 1971).

FIGURE 2.4 Sepahsalar (now Motahari) mosque used to be regarded as Tehran's most imposing building

The commodification of agricultural land and produce was the first step taken towards the development of a market economy and integration into the world market. It was not surprising that this process was soon extended to the urban space. The first transformation of Tehran's urban fabric in the nineteenth century should be seen in this light. The city was reshaped by opening up the urban structure to the emerging social relations. Nevertheless, this was a modest step when compared to the second phase of transformation in the twentieth century, which aimed at the creation and improvement of infrastructures.

THE SECOND STAGE OF TRANSFORMATION

The population of Tehran grew threefold during the nineteenth century to reach an estimated 150 000 in 1910 (Ettehadieh, 1983). The population density increased from 43.5 persons per hectare in 1883 to 65.5 in 1891,

80.5 in 1922, and 105 in 1932. During the inter-war period, its population rose to about 0.7 million (Vezarat-e Barnameh, 1987a). This growth in population and density meant new pressures for urban development and expansion. The second major attempt to reform the city was made in the 1930s, during the reign of Reza Shah, which was more vigorous in its implementation and more far-reaching in its scope. Whereas the first phase in the 1860s and 1870s was limited to the creation of new city walls and quarters, the second phase, through large redevelopment schemes, was an attempt to change the morphology of the entire urban area. From "an Oriental city, without good communications and with but few amenities", it was commented, Tehran was being "radically re-planned and re-built" (Lockhart, 1939: 11). This was a treatment that was, according to Elwell-Sutton (1941: 108), "quite ruthless".

The 12 gates of the city, together with numerous other buildings, were destroyed during the mayoralty of General Karim Bouzarjomehri in 1930 for "modernization of the city" (Zaka, 1970: 16). As with the first stage, the route of the moats and walls provided the space for constructing wide boulevards. Apart from these, new streets were built, cutting through the old fabric of the city, which was regarded as a group of "squalid and congested areas" (Lockhart, 1960: 7). The result was, as shown in the 1937 map of the city (Figure 2.5), a transport network (Faghih, 1988), 218 km long (Farmanfarmaian & Gruen, 1968). In this redevelopment of large parts of the city fabric, it was the outward appearances that were given priority, with carefully planned streets and imposing buildings. Infrastructures such as water and electricity were to be provided later (Elwell-Sutton, 1941: 108–9).

The royal compound was fragmented, its buildings redeveloped, to be replaced by a new government quarter, mainly Ministries of Justice and Finance. The buildings which survived were turned into other uses, like the Golestan Palace which became a museum (Figure 2.6). With the pressure put on the traditional institutions such as the bazaar, retailers were encouraged to move to the new street frontages and abandon the old streets of the bazaar, which were threatened by redevelopment as not being accessible by car. The new streets were cobbled and intersected at right angles, with monuments and fountains at many crossroads (Lockhart, 1960; Wilber, 1986). The streets became the main channels of transportation and the squares became traffic circles, as distinct from the older squares and streets which were the places of communication for pedestrians.

Two more important streets, Shah-Reza (now Enghelab) and Pahlavi (now Vali Asr), both named after the ruler, eventually formed the main east–west and north–south axes of the city structure. The latter was more than 20 km long which started from the railway station in the south, linked to the new Trans-Iranian network. It passed Kakh-e-Marmar (Marble Palace), which was built by the shah in 1925 as the place of receptions and official functions.

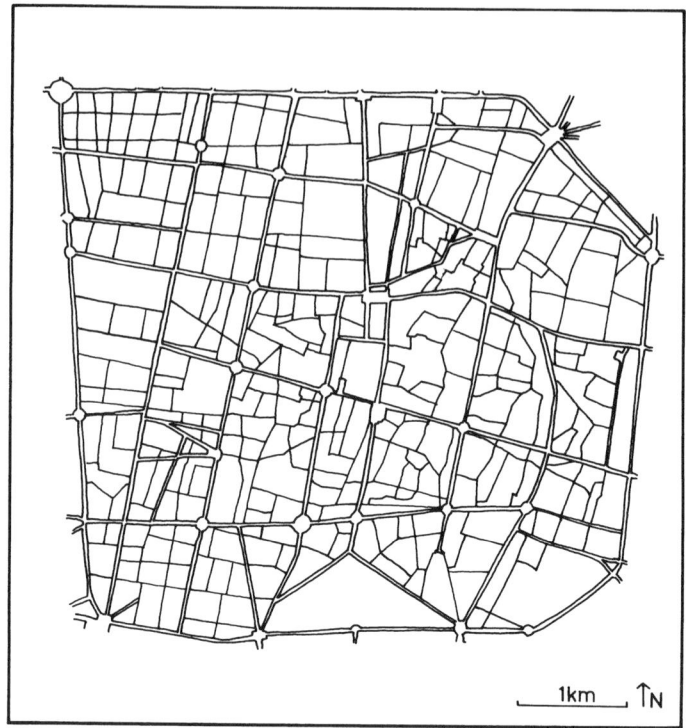

FIGURE 2.5 Tehran in 1937, after the second transformation which turned it into an open matrix

Around this palace were built a number of minor palaces as the private residences of the royal family. Other high-ranking officials were also gathered around the palaces, later supported by military bases and government offices (Saidi Rezvani, 1992). The Pahlavi avenue, lined with trees, finally ended at the foot of the Alburz mountain, in the northernmost part of the present city, where another palace compound, Sa'dabad, was developed (Wilber, 1986; Lockhart, 1960; Falamaki, 1988). The other avenue, Shah-Reza, which was built on the filled northern moat, was an east–west axis which intersected Pahlavi at right angles and along it were erected new institutions such as the Tehran University.

All the property in a large quarter of the old town, Sangeladj, neighbouring the citadel from the west, was bought and razed to the ground to set up a stock exchange and the related economic institutions. But this project was stopped due to the beginning of the Second World War. The High Technical Council of the city suggested developing a new residential quarter instead. This quarter, it was argued, was to serve as the living place of the inhabitants of another old quarter which in turn would undergo complete

FIGURE 2.6 Golestan Palace is now a museum

redevelopment (Azhdari, 1964). Eventually, the area was, according to the decision of the Parliament, turned into the central park of the city.

The process of suburbanization which had started in the second half of the nineteenth century with the building of large extramural gardens by the aristocracy, intensified after the First World War. The merchants and the tradesmen, who would continue working in the bazaar, moved their residences out from there to the northern and western suburban areas which had better climates. This led to a deterioration of the old fabric (Motamani, 1964), which has been a feature of the central and southern parts of the city up to the present day. The destruction of the walls in 1930 was in fact to lift the physical barriers to the intensifying urban development process. By 1929, the city was already 24 km^2, implying that a third of the urban fabric was built beyond the walls. After the filling of the moats by 1934, Tehran had an area of 46 km^2 (Kariman, 1976: 298).

Reza Shah established a transportation network to unify and control the national territory. A network of transportation with similar aims was developed in Tehran: to ease military movement throughout the city to support the increasing strength of the government; to change the city into an open matrix for easy movement of goods and capital; and to overcome the existing feudal factionalism by linking the separate residential quarters and imposing a framework on them, a unified space to encourage homogenization. By imposing a new road system, wide, tree-lined streets intersecting at right angles, upon the old urban fabric, it modified the urban space in accordance with the demands for higher mobility. It was partly to break down the existing social structure, its communal heterogeneity housed in a quarter system, that a network of new streets was laid out to cut across many urban areas around the country (Clarke & Clark, 1969; English, 1966; Clarke, 1963), including the all-important capital city. Factionalism which was identified with regional differences and power structures as well as by segregated urban quarters was thus to be overcome by the imposition of a framework on the urban fabric to create physical, as well as social, homogeneity.

Despite the fact that the commodification of urban space had started with the first transformation of the city, it was the second which opened up the whole fabric, extending the market economy into the urban space and setting the pattern for the future. The massive scale of urban development in this phase, which transformed the urban fabric in a radical way, distinguishes it from the previous phase. It served to absorb the surpluses of capital and labour, which had resulted from political and economic reorganization. It also built the foundations of a new land and property market, which was to flourish especially in the period of the relaxation of controls after the Second World War.

THE POST-WAR DEVELOPMENT OF THE CITY

The post-Second World War development of Tehran was very rapid and uncontrolled. Within 45 years after 1941, its population grew 8.6 times and its area 12 times. It took the form of free expansion of the city into the surrounding land and the growth of suburban villages and satellite towns, which have been gradually integrating into the urban fabric by new waves of expansion and development (Figure 2.7). The form of the built-up areas now seems to be a radial expansion of a core across the outgoing roads, especially on the west side, to constitute an ever-growing metropolis. The rapid and unprecedented growth of the city caused the disappearance of the suburban and intra-urban gardens, which were subdivided and built over. The control over post-war development was absent to the extent that a deputy mayor of Tehran in 1962 commented that in this city "the buildings and townlets have been developed by whoever has wanted in whatever way and wherever they have wanted". The result of this was that Tehran was "in fact a number of towns connected to each other in an inappropriate way" (Nafisi, 1964: 426).

The segregation of the suburban settlements from each other, was due to, and provided for, the geographical segregation of the social classes. Different social groups found spatial arrangements based on, and enhancing, a north–south divide. This structural characteristic of Tehran's urban form, which was partly rooted in the first transformation of the urban fabric, was enhanced further. In Tehran it was now possible to see "a social gradient on

TRANSFORMATION OF THE CAPITAL / 41

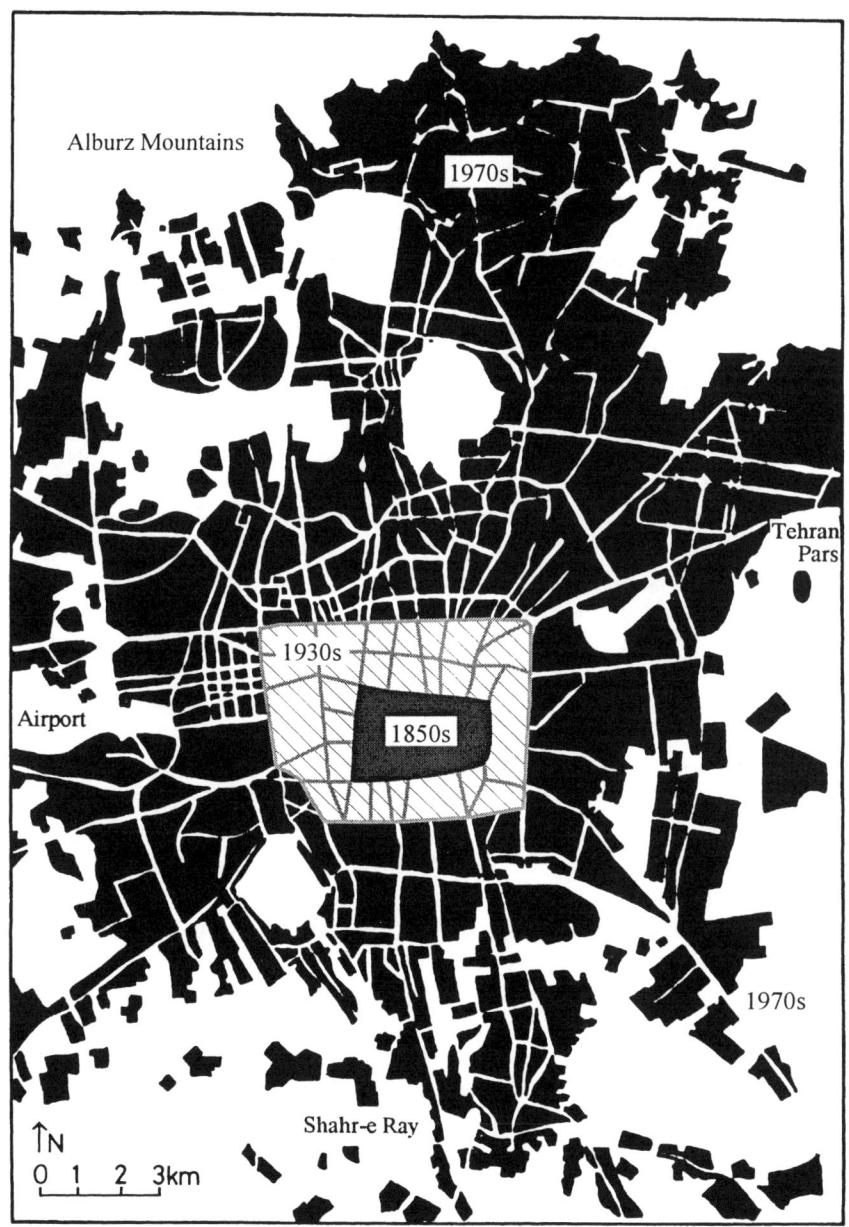

FIGURE 2.7 The city expanded in all directions

the grand scale . . . on the ground" (Costello, 1977: 99). The density in the southern areas reached a peak of 610 persons per hectare in 1956 as compared to the northern areas which always remained low (Farmanfarmaian & Gruen, 1968). Variations within this duality, however, occurred according to the ethnic and cultural varieties of the social structure.

Many of the suburban townlets, such as Shahrara, were developed on purely speculative bases to respond to the high demand for housing in the rapidly growing capital. Others, such as Yousefabad and Narmak, were provided by the public sector for the increasing numbers of civil servants. Whatever the way in which these settlements were developed, they suffered from poor services (Golestani, 1964; Badi', 1964). Inside the settlements, town centres gradually developed in the form of high streets, or at the intersection of the main streets, which were usually providing very basic services. For most of the required services, however, they had to rely on the city centre.

During three decades, the size of the physical fabric of Tehran grew fourfold to reach 180 km^2 in the mid-1960s (Farmanfarmaian & Gruen, 1968). Its population rose even faster, to reach 1.5 million in 1956 and about 3 million in 1966. By 1976, the population increased to 4.5 million in a city of 250 km^2. During the next decade, another 1.5 million were added to the population of Tehran and, with the extension of municipal boundaries, its size more than doubled (Vezarat-e Barnameh, 1987a). The pace of urban development can be traced in the fact that in 1980 about 60 per cent of the dwellings had been built during the space of the previous 13 years (Markaz-e Amar, 1981).

In the mid-1960s, about 40 per cent of the urban area was occupied by residential use. Next to it was the transportation network with about 27 per cent. Two other land-consuming uses were government institutions and industries, each with 10 per cent of the urban area. Trades were housed in 4 per cent and the rest was for other uses such as health, education and recreation (Farmanfarmaian & Gruen, 1968). In the southern parts of the city, the majority of small industrial establishments, which formed 96 per cent of all the industries, were spread and mixed with residential areas. Large industries, which constituted only 4 per cent of industrial establishments but employed 66 per cent of the industrial workforce, were mostly located in the west and south-west along the routes to the nearby city of Karaj. We will come back to this post-war transformation, when the bulk of the contemporary city has been built, in Chapter 6, where we look at the spatial qualities of the city today, and in Part Three, where we look at the development process which produced this urban fabric.

SOCIAL MOVEMENTS AND URBAN SPACE

We have seen how in the course of 100 turbulent years, several social movements have been staged in the city, of which two are widely known as revolutions. It is very interesting to see how urban space was used in these movements and whether the transformation of urban space in earlier periods had any relationship with these movements.

A brief review of a year and a half of events which culminated in the Constitutional Revolution of 1906 reveals a fascinating connection between space and social movement. One of the early events which mobilized masses was an opposition to an urban development project in Tehran. A derelict cemetery and seminary was bought by a Russian bank for redevelopment. A major cleric, who eventually became one of the leaders of the revolution, objected to this development on religious grounds, a public objection which led to the demolition of the half-built building (Kasravi Tabrizi, 1965; Kermani, 1967).

The history of the revolution shows how the urban space was the site of contest between the government and the revolutionaries. The spatial behaviour of the two sides shows how the unfolding of the revolution took place first in private and then public places. The revolutionaries first gathered in secret in some homes, and then publicly in public spaces, especially in the Friday mosque. The initial reaction of the government was to expel some of the revolutionaries from Tehran and then to group soldiers in the streets and city squares, attacking the revolutionaries. To prevent bloodshed, the revolutionaries then took refuge in religious sanctuaries of Hazrat Abd al-Azim and in Qom, as well as in the British Embassy (Kasravi Tabrizi, 1965). In these events, the centre of activities was around the focal points of the old city structure: the Friday mosque and the bazaar. The new, upper-class quarters are understandably absent from the reports.

One of the nodes which developed during the Constitutional Revolution and remained a sensitive place for more than two generations was the site of the national assembly and the square which was developed in front of it, Baharestan Square (Figure 2.8). It was a major site of public gathering and has witnessed many battles between demonstrating groups and government troops (Shahri, 1978: 204). In the short season of political freedom which followed the Second World War, Baharestan was always a focal point.

The new nodes and axes that the inter-war redevelopments and the postwar expansions of the city created were often showpieces of the state, many embellished by the rulers' statutes. These public spaces staged symbols of power, which is why at the time of the Islamic Revolution they became sites of contest for millions of demonstrators who brought down these statues and claimed the public spaces of the city as their own. The main east–west axis of the city, which was renamed Enghleab (Revolution) Avenue, was the main site in which these millions moved. Shahyad, a brand new showcase square at the western entrance to the city, was at one end of this axis and provided a major open space for revolutionaries. The first major clash between people and state took place in the streets around Zhaleh Square.

FIGURE 2.8 Baharestan Square today, where the memories of the Constitutional Revolution and many political activities afterwards linger on

Because of the large number of casualties, revolutionaries immediately renamed it Shohada (Martyrs') Square and its name entered the chants of the later demonstrations (Figure 2.9). In both revolutions and other major unrests of the last century, public spaces of Tehran and other large cities of the country have been the scenes on which the battles for power and emancipation have been staged. Whoever could be in charge of the public sphere was in charge of the country. The contest over, and the domination of, the public spaces of the city was the embodiment of the revolution: in a sense, this *was* the revolution.

CONCLUSION: THE EMERGENCE OF A NEW URBAN MORPHOLOGY

The built environment of Tehran has changed considerably since becoming the capital of Iran more than 200 years ago. Two stages of radical transformation, in the 1860s/1870s and in the 1930s, have been carried out by the authorities to allow for the constant growth of population, for the increased demand for mobility, and for reimaging a capital city which became a bridge to the world market. The most dramatic expansion was to take place after the Second World War, which gave the city the dimensions of a large metropolis. In this way, the built environment of the city was a comprehensive reflection of the stages of transition through which urban and national communities were passing.

FIGURE 2.9 Shohada (Martyrs') Square was the site of the first major clash between the people and the state in the Islamic Revolution

The cultural stratification, in which modern and traditional elites separated, and the economic stratification, in which rich and poor split, were all rooted in the first transformation of the city and found spatial manifestations afterwards. The response to the challenge of the West came in tensions and transformations of the social world, resulting in integration into the world economy. The same happened, in parallel, in the transformation of the physical world, where, as we shall see in Chapter 6 and in Part Three, the overall spatial structure, as well as the patterns of streets and squares, land use, and building form all changed. We shall also see how the production of the urban space has been a significant part of the country's economic life and how it has been closely associated with tensions in social life. In this Part, we have briefly outlined the historical evolution of the city in social and spatial dimensions. This has provided us with some background information which we need to analyse, in some more detail in Part Two, the main features of the contemporary city.

PART TWO

A PROFILE OF THE CONTEMPORARY CITY

3

URBAN ECONOMY

After all these turbulent historical changes that the city has gone through, what are its contours today? How does its economy work and what is its livelihood based on? How do people live their lives and relate to each other? How is the city managed? How is its space organized? What sort of problems does it suffer from? In this Part, we portray the main characteristics of the contemporary city. When seen together, Chapters 3–8 offer a range of perspectives into the city life and environment, looking at the economy, the administration, the society and culture, the space, and some of the main problems of the metropolis.

Chapter 3 starts from the picture of Iran's economy and evaluates the role of Tehran in this scene. It then outlines the shape of employment in the urban economy and its main industrial and service sectors, followed by a look at wages and prices. Other related discussions about the economy, such as those on population, urban land and property, and urban development process will follow in Chapters 5 and 7 and in Part Three.

IRAN'S ECONOMY

Compared to historical, literary, and social analyses, there is surprisingly little research into Iran's economy. In particular the impact of the revolution on the economic configuration of the country has been little understood. We know that almost the entire political and economic elite were swept aside by the tide of the revolution. However, many radical commentators have argued, from the first days after the collapse of the monarchy, that the new, lower-middle-class leadership was unable to lead a thorough economic and social transformation. The idea that the Iranian revolution was a political, rather than economic and social, revolution, is still being echoed by observers (Ehteshami, 1995; Amirahmadi, 1990). The grand coalition that made the revolution happen had a united aim of challenging the shah. Apart from this, there was disagreement on almost everything. Although the leadership internalized the narratives of many radical groups to lead the revolutionary sentiments, the different nature of various groups and their varying degrees of radicalism soon resulted in factional strife. Together with external pressures, this proved to be a major obstacle to any constructive use of the huge emotional and intellectual energy that the revolution had amassed and mobilized.

With an estimated 92.86 billion barrels at the beginning of 1995, Iran owns 9.3 per cent of the world reserves of crude oil. Its natural gas reserves, at 2 billion m³, are second only to the former USSR. Despite the intentions of the revolution to reduce the reliance on oil, it is still the main source of income for the country. The production of crude oil, which averaged at more than 5 million barrels a day (mb/d) in the 1970s, remained below 3 mb/d in the 1980s, before a rise in the 1990s of up to nearly 4 mb/d in 1993. The deterioration of the crude oil market, the long war with Iraq, and the competition with other members of OPEC, the oil-producing countries' cartel, have all exerted various forms of constraint upon the economy (EIU, 1995: 29–30).

The picture of Iran's unsettled economy in the 1980s can only be understood in the context of a revolution and a war. The revolutionary pressure to restructure the economy by radical undertakings, the flight of capital and trained workforce, and an eight-year war with Iraq all brought underinvestment and economic instability, high inflation, high unemployment, and deterioration of the physical stock. This was worsened by two major shocks when the country's foreign exchange earnings dramatically dropped: in 1980 when the annual oil revenue was cut from $19 186m. to $13 286m., and the oil price crash of 1986 when the oil revenue fell from $15 590m. to $6261m. (EIU, 1995: 17). As a result, the real growth rate of GNP per capita in the period 1985–94 has fallen by 1 per cent and inflation has risen by an average of 22 per cent (World Bank, 1995: 18).

As against this picture, the post-1989 government led the way out of the revolutionary phase by introducing liberal economic reforms. The end of the war had been followed by popular expectations of the end of austerity measures and a better standard of living. This was a time when the post-revolutionary government had to deliver its long-awaited promises. The Islamic Republic had rejected the West and East and had declared its aim of creating a new economic model, one that was neither capitalist nor socialist (*na sharghi, na gharbi, jomhoori-e eslami*). A decade after the revolution, there was an obvious gap between the optimistic visions of revolutionary masses and the reality (Amirahmadi, 1990). President Rafsanjani's government outlined a reform programme whose main features were moving towards an open market economy, through liberalization and injection of resources. Alongside the reform, monetary policy was emphasized in the regulation of the relations between economic variables and to compensate for some of the consequences of economic restructuring (Central Bank, 1993: 7). Ehteshami (1995: 104) identifies 11 elements in the reform agenda:

> "1. Privatization of industry, mines and other industrial and non-industrial productive activities.
> 2. Deregulation of economic activity and of banking and financial services.
> 3. Activation, expansion and modernization of the Tehran stock exchange.

4. Encouragement of inward direct foreign investment.
5. Foreign borrowing.
6. Establishment of free trade zones across the country.
7. Devaluation of the rial.
8. Gradual reduction of subsidies.
9. Liberalization of trade and returning it to the private sector.
10. Freeing of prices; and . . .
11. Return of exiled capital and (not inconsiderable) expertise."

Economic policies such as deregulation and privatization were being promoted in the 1980s in Britain and the United States, and became the main features of numerous liberalizing economies across the globe. For Iran, however, this has meant a reversal of many revolutionary trends, finding a path back to the world market, which inevitably has some common features with the economic forms and practices whose rejection was an essential feature of the revolution. The implications of accumulating foreign debt to more than $US20bn in 1993 (EIU, 1995: 47) have included an awareness of the inherent political restrictions arising from a full participation in the world market. The continuation of the revolutionary fervour, however, has made this return problematic, creating new political factions and therefore new tensions.

The vulnerability of the economy to external factors and the falling oil revenue have led to an encouragement of exports, rather than import substitution favoured by the shah. The oil boom and industrialization drive had left the agriculture sector deeply damaged. One of the main aims of the post-revolutionary government has been to support and revitalize this sector, aiming to encourage self-sufficiency in food, to reduce reliance on oil exports, and to stop migration into urban areas. The expectations of this policy have been further strengthened by a decline in oil revenues and opening up of new markets in Central Asia and the EU for exporting agricultural products. The sector has been supported by setting up an organization of volunteers, Jahad-e Sazandegi. The policies concerning guaranteed purchase, establishment of co-operatives, extension of banking facilities at preferential rates, and subsidizing agricultural inputs have been in place (Central Bank, 1993: 21). As a result of these and other initiatives, such as the encouragement of traditional methods of farming, between 1979 and 1993 agricultural outputs have quadrupled (EIU, 1995: 23). The share of agriculture in the GDP increased to 26.9 per cent in 1992 (Central Bank, 1993: 12), to almost the same level as in 1959, although it fell again in 1993 to 21 per cent (The World Bank, 1995: 18).

One of the main consequences of the country's downward economic trends has been a now chronic slide of the rial, the Iranian currency, from IR70 to $US1 in the late 1970s to the official rate of IR1750 in 1995 (*Ettela'at International*, 14 December 1995: 2). At the same time, the value of the currency in the black market has been far less than this, at IR3020 in 1995

FIGURE 3.1 Tehran is the largest concentration of wealth in the country (Modarres motorway)

(ibid.), continuing its slide down to IR4300 in July 1996 (*Ettela'at International*, 2 July 1996: 2), and further down afterwards. One of the main aims of the government's economic reform has been unification and rationalization of the multi-tier exchange system (Central Bank, 1993), an attempt which has not yet succeeded.

TEHRAN'S ECONOMY IN THE NATIONAL CONTEXT

Tehran is the largest concentration of all forms of economic activity in the country (Figure 3.1). The roots of economic concentration in Tehran can be traced back to the time when it was chosen as the capital city. This became particularly important with several developments: the entry of Iran into the world market, which gave Tehran the role of a mediator and a bridge between the country and the rest of the world; the formation of a national market and unification of the national space, in which Tehran's centrality enabled it to extract capital and labour from around the country; the move towards the centralization of political power, which made Tehran a more powerful place in the national landscape; and the ever-increasing reliance on oil, which concentrated the decision making about the most important sector of the economy in fewer hands, increasingly based in Tehran.

The predominance of oil in Iran has given the state a strong role in the national economy. The monopoly of production and export of oil, which accounts for 80 per cent of foreign exchange income, and the distribution of these resources have ensured the state's powerful presence in the economic scene. Even after the 1979 revolution, which challenged this presence, the concentration of power in the government's hands has grown, through nationalization of banking, insurance, large industries, and major parts of foreign trade. As before the revolution, the state prepares and implements five-year development plans in which the utilization of oil revenues and other credits is managed. The latest plan, the second in the Islamic Republic, covers the period 1995–2000 and aims to expand employment and reduce the dependency on oil (EIU, 1995).

The crucial role of the government in the economic scene has made its seat Tehran a site of concentration of economic activity and the largest market in the country. The relationship between Tehran's growth and its concentration of political and economic power is widely known (Khalili Araghi, 1988; Rafiei, 1991; Ahsan, 1995). In 1991, Tehran's province (Ostan) had a population of 9.98 million, 18 per cent of the country's population (Markaz-e Amar, 1996a: 38). However, it has had larger shares of employment in industry and services: 30 per cent of the country's employment in manufacturing industry; 24 per cent of water, electricity, and gas; 29 per cent of wholesale, retail, restaurants and hotels; 26 per cent of transport, communication, and warehousing; 44 per cent of financial services, insurance, property, legal and trade services; and 24 per cent of public, social, and personal services. Tehran had 26 per cent of scientific and specialist jobs; 48 per cent of high-ranking bureaucrats; 34 per cent of clerical workers; 30 per cent of retail and trade workers; 26 per cent of service workers; and 23 per cent of transport and production unit workers. While only 17 per cent of those employed in the private sector were based in Tehran, the employers and wage earners had a larger share than independent and family workers. There were 31 per cent of private sector employers and 26 per cent of wage earners in Tehran, as compared to only 12.5 per cent of independent workers and 2.5 per cent of unwaged family workers (Markaz-e Amar, 1996a: 67–70). In 1994, Tehran accounted for 25 per cent of all the country's hotel rooms (p. 277), 56 per cent of all new vehicle registrations (p. 297), 46 per cent of all flight destinations (p. 308), 35 per cent of all telephone lines (p. 332), 24 per cent of all electricity consumption (p. 198), 26 per cent of all water consumption (p. 186), 23.5 per cent of all physicians (1992 figures, p. 481), and 32 per cent of all university students (p. 471). When compared to all urban areas, Tehran has an older population, with higher rates of economic activity and lower unemployment. With 20.3 per cent of the country's urban population, Tehran has 21.6 per cent of those aged 10 and over, 22 per cent of the economically active, 23 per cent of the employed, and only 14 per cent of the unemployed in all urban areas (*Hamshahri*, 16 November 1995: 12). All these concentrations, developed as a result of long-term trends of economic and political concentration, have made Tehran a dynamic centre as well as a giant head on the weak shoulders of a developing economy.

EMPLOYMENT

In 1991, Tehran had an unemployment rate of 6.6 per cent, a figure much lower than the 10.4 per cent for all urban areas in the same year (Markaz-e Motale'at, 1995: 55) and 12.1 per cent for rural areas (Markaz-e Amar, 1996a: 61). It is a marked improvement when compared to the city's 16.2 and 14.3 per cent rates of unemployment in 1980 and 1986, in the midst of revolution and war (Markaz-e Motale'at, 1995: 56).

To have a more accurate picture of employment in Tehran, however, we need to look at some other figures at the same time. The age groups of 10–64-year-olds form 71.6 per cent of the city's population. (It should be noted that the 10–14-year-olds are included in Iran's statistics, despite the fact that only 2 per cent of this group were economically active in 1991.) Only 38 per cent of people in these age groups are economically active, i.e. employed or seeking employment. The rest of the population in these age groups are students, housewives, those with earnings but without employment, and those legally prohibited from work (pp. 37–8). Out of a 1.86 million economically active population in 1991, 1.73 million were in employment, hence the figure of 6.6 per cent unemployment. When seen in the context of the city's 6.5 million population, however, there is only one in four in employment. The rest are either too young (36.8 per cent below 15 in 1991; p. 26), or are outside paid employment (only 9.8 per cent of women are indicated as economically active, p. 61). Women's rate of unemployment (12.2 per cent) has been more than twice that of men (5.8 per cent) (p. 61). Other patterns of employment include a high rate of youth unemployment and a not inconsiderable rate of activity for men over 65. The highest rate of unemployment (20 per cent) is among the 15–19 age group, as compared to the lowest (2.2 per cent) in the 40–44 age group (p. 61). The rapid population growth has meant entry of the young into the labour market faster than the development of employment capacity, a factor which has contributed to the destabilization of all recent governments regardless of their ideology and performance. In the same year, there was a 38.8 per cent rate of activity for men over 65, of whom 83.1 per cent were in employment. This indicates an absence of pensions and support mechanisms to allow them to retire, as well as the existence of employment opportunities for this group. Even when there are pension provisions, high inflation has eroded the purchasing power of the retired. Compared to the figures from the 1970s, when the economy was in much better shape, it becomes clear that these trends have been long term. The 1976 figures for high youth unemployment (12.9 per cent for 15–19-year-olds), low rate of paid economic activity for women (9.9 per cent), and active participation of men over 65 (38.5 per cent) are quite comparable to these current trends (p. 58). Furthermore, these trends in Tehran are comparable to other urban areas of the country (p. 64). Even though unemployment has fallen in the country as a whole, from 11.1 per cent in 1991 (Markaz-e Amar, 1996a: 61) to 9.8 per cent in 1994 (Markaz-e Amar, 1996b: 12), more than a quarter of those seeking employment in 1994 have been unemployed for more than four years (p. 16).

As these patterns of employment show, middle-aged men are the main breadwinners, supporting a young population in growing households. The economy has not absorbed women and has found it difficult to provide opportunities for the young. The elderly have to be supported by their children or have to work to support themselves. In the absence of adequate social welfare provisions, it is the household which is the main support structure to cope with these shortcomings. The recent dramatic events combined with historical insecurity have ensured that the household remains the basic unit of the economy and the main coping mechanism for confronting economic difficulty.

SECTORS OF THE URBAN ECONOMY

In 1986, from a total of 1.3 million firms in Iran, 21 per cent were based in Tehran. The largest share (45.3 per cent) were engaged in wholesale or retail activities (Figure 3.2), the rest in manufacturing industry (24.2 per cent) and services (17.6 per cent). Most firms were very small in size: 44.1 per cent with only one worker and 37.4 per cent with two to five workers. When compared to other urban areas, however, Tehrani firms were larger and more involved in industrial activities (Markaz-e Motale'at, 1995: 89). In addition to this information about the firms, we have to rely on employment figures to understand the structure of the urban economy in Tehran. In the absence of other forms of information consistently available across all sectors of the urban economy, it is only employment statistics which we can use to acquire a knowledge of the overall economic structure in the city. Although relatively detailed information is available on agriculture and manufacturing industry, little is published on services, which make up the bulk of the urban economy.

In 1991, the largest employment categories in Tehran were social and personal services (35.7 per cent of jobs), followed by manufacturing (22.2

FIGURE 3.2 Tehran's old bazaar is still a centre of the city's wholesale and retail activities (Hajeb al-Dowleh Arcade)

per cent) and sales (15.6 per cent). Transport, construction, and financial services have together absorbed 19 per cent of the workforce (Markaz-e Motale'at, 1995: 69). When grouped together under the three main sectors of the economy, services account for almost two-thirds of the workforce, and another third employed in industrial activities, with less than 1 per cent employed in agriculture (Table 3.1).

PUBLIC AND PRIVATE SECTOR EMPLOYMENT

The revolutionary government's nationalization of private firms and the advent of war led to a growth of the public sector, especially in Tehran. While the public sector employed 39.2 per cent of Tehranis in 1976, it grew to employ 47.1 per cent in 1991. The same growth occurred in all other urban areas, from 34.2 to 44 per cent (Markaz-e Motale'at, 1995: 98). The end of the Iran Iraq war and the liberalizing policies of the post-war

TABLE 3.1 Employment in the main sectors of Tehran's economy (%)

Sector	1976	1980	1986	1991
Manufacturing, mining, construction, and utilities	32.78	35.48	26.56	31.05
Services	64.22	63.51	67.86	63.51
Agriculture	0.94	0.84	0.88	0.71
Other	2.08	0.18	4.68	4.72
Total (%)	100	100	100	100
Total (number)	1 288 912	1 357 797	1 433 807	1 739 960

Source: Markaz-e Motale'at (1995: 77–80).

government have caused the revival of many private sector activities. Despite this, the unprecedented growth of the public sector and the massive concentration of government employees in Tehran and other cities are a major legacy of the revolution and war, one which the government feels the need to tackle but is unable to do so for political reasons. The fact that almost half the population of the capital depend on employment in the public sector gives the state mass support as well as heavy obligations to meet. The public sector offers women employment opportunities unavailable elsewhere. In Tehran, 77.2 per cent of working women (74 per cent in all urban areas) are employed in the public sector (p. 99). The configuration of the private sector is such that 10 per cent are employers, 43 per cent wage earners, and 46 per cent are independent workers (p. 100).

After the major programmes of nationalization in the aftermath of the revolution, and during the long war with Iraq, the state was expanding its sphere of activities. It was involved in production and distribution of goods, property and other services, currency control and distribution, pricing goods and services, control of foreign trade, industries, insurance companies, banks, mines, radio and television, air travel, shipping, post and telecommunications, railways, hospitals, universities, etc. This increased the number of public sector employees substantially. There was little participation and investment from the private sector due to a general lack of security and trust. Furthermore, in these very difficult times, the state was considered to be responsible for supporting as many people as possible by providing employment and subsidies. During the period of the first post-revolutionary five-year development plan, the economic and administrative efficiency and productivity of public organizations became a major problem. The plan had predicted an annual reduction of 4 per cent in the number of public sector employees at all levels. In practice, however, the reduction in public sector employment during the five years of the plan amounted to only 2 per cent. Indeed, the management level has grown so that the number of deputy ministers has increased by 11.3 per cent and department directors by 3.3 per cent (*Hamshahri*, 26 October 1995: 5). Nevertheless, the restructuring of public sector employment is again a major task in the second development plan. It is thought to be an inevitable undertaking due to dwindling oil revenues, leading the government to believe that liberal reforms are the only way forward.

MANUFACTURING

The shape of manufacturing industry in Iran is largely formed of small units (96.6 per cent with nine or fewer workers), mainly engaged in textiles, clothing, and leather (36.1 per cent of the units), metal machinery and equipment (21.3 per cent of the units), and food, beverages, and tobacco (19.8 per cent of the units) (Markaz-e Amar, 1993: 1). Despite the prevalence of small units in the economy, large units with 50 or more workers have a significant role in industrial production and employment. In 1988, these units employed 34.2 per cent of the industrial workforce, paid 64.7 per cent of the wages in the sector, and generated IR1229.8bn or 45.1 per cent of all industrial added value (Markaz-e Amar, 1993: 2–5). Tehran is the largest industrial pole in the country, a fact that all the indicators clearly show (Kharrat Zebardast & Moezzeddin, 1992). Apart from basic metal processing, Tehran province has the highest concentration of all other forms of manufacturing activity (Markaz-e Motale'at, 1995: 143).

In 1986, out of 67 000 industrial units in Tehran, 37.9 per cent were engaged in textiles, clothing, and leather, 25.7 per cent in metal machinery and equipment, 11 per cent in wood and wooden products, and 9.9 per cent in food, beverages, and tobacco (Markaz-e Motale'at, 1995: 91). In 1991, manufacturing accounted for 22.2 per cent of employment in Tehran. One-third of Tehran's industrial workforce was employed in metal machinery and equipment, 29.9 per cent in textiles, and the rest, in order of their size, were in wood, chemicals, mining, paper, and basic metals (Markaz-e Motale'at, 1995: 108).

In 1993, Tehran province housed 1751 industrial units with 10 or more workers, i.e. 32.9 per cent of all such units with 34.9 per cent of their employees in the country. The second such concentration was in Isfahan with only 9.1 per cent of the units (Markaz-e Amar, 1995: 13–14). These units in Tehran, as in the rest of the country, have been largely (84 per cent) under private sector control (p. 110). Employing more than 213 000 workers (p. 111), Tehrani units paid the highest salaries in the country (p. 123). As the trends after the end of the war with Iraq show, there has been a considerable increase in investment and added value but only a modest increase in the number of workers in large industrial units, showing the underutilization of their capacities during the war (Markaz-e Motale'at, 1995: 115). In 1993 in Iran, the large industrial units have been mainly engaged in mining (34.9 per cent, excluding oil and coal), metal machinery and equipment (16.9 per cent), and food (16.9 per cent) (Markaz e Amar, 1995:

13).The pattern of concentration of large industrial units in Tehran shows that in the food industry, 40.7 per cent of all workers with 44 per cent of added value were based in Tehran (Markaz-e Motale'at, 1995: 116, 118). The figures for the other main groups of industrial activity in which Tehran's large units have a considerable share are: textiles with 27.8 per cent of workers and 25.1 per cent of added value, chemicals with 50.2 per cent of workers and 49 per cent of added value, and metal machinery and equipment with 48.7 per cent of workers and 62.6 per cent of added value (Markaz-e Motale'at, 1995: 117–20).

Despite various policies to prevent further concentration of industrial activity in Tehran, in 1994 there were 2113 permissions issued for the establishment of new industries in the province, i.e. 24 per cent of all such permissions in the country (Markaz-e Amar, 1996a: 163). In 1993, IR322bn, or a quarter of all investment in such units, were invested in large industrial units in Tehran (Markaz-e Amar, 1996a: 173).

Traditional handicraft goods occupy an important place in the national economy, as exemplified by the $US1.38 billion value of carpet exports in 1993/94 (EIU, 1995: 35). Craftspersons, however, are mostly based in rural areas. In 1994, of 1.1 million households which were engaged in some form of manufacturing in their homes, 90.6 per cent were producing carpets and related products. Only 5 per cent of these households, however, were based in Tehran province (Markaz-e Amar, 1996c: 30–1).

ENERGY

In the 1970s, the growth of demand for electricity led to frequent power shortages, at times shown as power cuts in peak times. With the advent of the war in 1980, power shortage became a part of urban life, as all the city's lights in public places were switched off at night. Power cuts were reduced after the end of the war as a result of efforts to increase electricity production in the country by a quarter between 1990 and 1994 (Markaz-e Amar, 1996a: 189). Tehran's regional electricity company produces the majority of its output from hydroelectric generators located in the mountains to the north of the city (pp. 191–2). The company's 2.7 million customers are mainly domestic users (84 per cent), followed by commercial (12 per cent) and public sector (3 per cent) customers. After domestic consumption (40 per cent of consumption), electricity is mainly used by industrial concerns (26 per cent of consumption), followed by commercial (23 per cent) and public sector (7 per cent) use (pp. 196–8). Tehran's refinery is the second largest producer of oil products (p. 144) and Tehran region is the largest consumer of these products. Along with an increase in production, the number of domestic and commercial consumers of natural gas in Tehran has risen by more than 2.5 times in the period 1990–94 (p. 150).

SERVICES

We have seen that two-thirds of employment in Tehran is in the service sector. Iran's Statistical Centre (Markaz-e Amar-e Iran) provides information about the four groups of activity which make up the service sector. The largest number of firms in this sector, and in the city as a whole, belongs to the trade and catering group. In 1986, there were 126 692 such units (45.3 per cent of all firms) in Tehran. The majority of these firms (87 945) were retail units (Markaz-e Motale'at, 1995: 92). In retail, 63.4 per cent of the units have only one worker and a further 27.7 per cent have two to five workers. This predominance of small firms in retail is in line with the structure of the trade and catering group as a whole, in which 58.9 per cent of firms have one worker and 31.8 per cent two to five workers. A similar pattern signifies the structure of firms in all sectors of the economy in Tehran, where 85.6 per cent of firms employ five or fewer workers (p. 92).

The pattern of employment in the service sector, however, does not correspond with the number of firms. The largest share of employment in services is in public, social, and personal services, a group of activities which accounted for more than 622 000 employees, or 35.7 per cent of all employment in Tehran in 1991. Within it, the largest subgroup is public services and security, which employs 275 000 (44.3 per cent), followed by 222 000 in social services (32.7 per cent). The other considerable subgroup here is personal and domestic services which employ 97 000 (15.7 per cent). The early attempts of the post-revolutionary government somewhat reduced the number of those engaged in this group. This trend, however, was soon reversed and the group continued to grow, reaching a peak in the middle of the war in 1986.

This group of activities has offered women relatively more opportunities for work, as 72.5 per cent of working women are employed in the service sector, as compared to 30.9 per cent of men (Markaz-e Motale'at, 1995: 71–2). Young men also find more work in social and personal services, as 43.8 per cent of 15–19-year-olds and 41.7 per cent of 20–24-year-olds were employed here. From the 25-year-old age group, however, the percentage drops to 28.6 (p. 80).

The picture that emerges from a brief look at the service sector shows three sets of activity: retail, security and public services, and social services, which account for 735 143 jobs, i.e. 42.2 per cent of all jobs in Tehran. It is perhaps mostly in these activities that disguised unemployment and the informal economy can be found.

Services, especially casual and low-paid jobs, are seen in Iran as unproductive and a major weakness of the economy. The foreign exchange earned through the export of oil is used to buy goods and services from other countries. The goods go through many hands to reach the consumer, a process lengthened and intensified when there is a shortage of foreign currency, as has been the case since the 1980s. There is an increasing demand for goods that are too few and too expensive. On the other hand, the government has been subsidizing many goods and services, especially during the war. The ground, therefore, is fertile for speculation and profiteering and a black market to be based on the exchange of imported and subsidized goods. At the same time this allows an informal economy to exist where, in the absence of a welfare state, the unemployed and the underemployed can survive by engaging in petty trading, casual services, and moonlighting.

WAGES AND PRICES

A recent poll found that Tehranis consider inflation and the high cost of living to be the most important problem for the city. In their view, the solution lies in price control, stricter punishment for profiteers, and an increase in domestic production of goods and services (*Hamshahri*, 14 March 1996: 2). In 1994/95, the average annual earnings of a household in Tehran province was IR7.3m., which has been much less than its annual expenditure at IR8.2m. Although the earnings of Tehrani households were 27.5 per cent higher than the average for all urban households in the country, their expenditure was 31.8 per cent higher. Foodstuffs formed a major part of household expenditure (28 per cent in Tehran) with meat the most expensive item on the menu, costing almost a quarter of food expenditure. Another 25 per cent of household expenditure was devoted to housing. The rest was spent on clothes, furniture, transport and communication, health care, education and leisure (Markaz-e Amar, 1996d: 54–61).

Between 1993/94 and 1994/95, annual household expenditure rose by 35.3 per cent, while the average income only rose by 29.5 per cent (Markaz-e Amar, 1996d: 15–19). As the index of consumer prices shows (Table 3.2), there has been a continuous growth of prices after the revolution, which has had a major impact on the purchasing power of households and has led to a decline in their living standards. Especially after the war, when economic reforms removed many subsidies, price inflation has increased more rapidly. The price of some basic foodstuffs rose by two or three times in spring 1995 and inflation was estimated at 58.8 per cent in May that year (EIU, 1995: 22). The consumer prices which had increased more in Tehran in 1994/95 were health care (4.5 times since 1990), food (2.7 times), and transport and communication (2.7 times) (Markaz-e Amar, 1996a: 590). As the monthly monitor of consumer prices shows (Markaz-e Amar, 1996e–h), basic consumer items have continued to rise dramatically. This has increased impoverishment and social polarization to a large degree, as earnings grow more slowly and are therefore unable to meet the needs of households and individuals.

TABLE 3.2 Retail price index for goods and services in Tehran (1990=100)

1976	1980	1986	1990	1991	1992	1993	1994
9.9	21.7	44.8	100	122.3	152.1	187.5	251.8

Source: Markaz-e Amar (1996a: 594).

CONCLUSION: THE LARGEST ECONOMIC CENTRE IN THE COUNTRY

Tehran is the largest economic agglomeration in Iran. Its economy is to a large extent based on managing the national economy, a fact shown in that almost half the working population in the capital is employed by the public sector. The national economy is in turn largely dependent on oil production and export, as Iran holds huge reserves of oil and gas. Tehran plays a unique role in the national economy. The concentration of most forms of economic activity has historically followed its administrative supremacy over the rest of a vast country. The state, which controls the oil industry and channels its revenue into the economy, has attracted the country's largest grouping of industrial and service activities located within the country's largest market. As the war, revolution, and external pressures have had an impact on the oil economy, the country has gone through a very difficult period since the end of the 1970s. Although Tehran has been less exposed to some of the major problems of the war, such as invasion and displacement, it has suffered considerably from disinvestment, unemployment, and high inflation. At the end of the war and with the passage from the revolutionary to a normalization phase, the government introduced liberal economic reforms to revitalize the economy and reintegrate it into the world economy. The reforms, however, have removed the subsidies which protected the poor, have accumulated sizeable foreign debts, and have been unable to curb the high inflation rate.

Tehrani firms are mostly small, mainly engaged in trade, manufacturing, and services. Large industrial units, however, have a major role in manufacturing. Two-thirds of working Tehranis are engaged in services and the rest in manufacturing, mining, construction, and public utilities. More than one-fifth of the workforce is employed in manufacturing industry, involved in textiles, food, and metal machinery and equipment. In services, three sets of activities stand out: retail, public services and security, and social services, which together account for more than one-third of all employment in Tehran. Compared to other urban areas in Iran, the capital city has an older population, lower unemployment, and higher rates of economic activity. The official unemployment rate of 6.6 per cent in 1991, however, conceals an employment configuration in which women and the young have limited access to jobs while many older men have to work. It also conceals many types of disguised unemployment and casual work, such as selling cigarettes in the streets, as retail or various forms of services. If Tehran's economy cannot diversify, its future will be, like its recent past, dependent on the fortunes of the national government, itself dependent on the volatile fluctuations of the price of oil in the global market.

4

URBAN MANAGEMENT

In this chapter we look at how the city is managed and at the nature and role of the Tehran municipality. We trace the historical development of the modern municipality and concentrate on its current state of affairs. We shall see how the problem of establishing an efficient and democratic urban management has been a central concern in the city, creating constant tensions between democratic forces and the central government's tendency to monopolize power.

URBAN ADMINISTRATION BEFORE THE CONSTITUTIONAL REVOLUTION

Until the end of the nineteenth century, in Iran as elsewhere in the Middle East, the executive head of the town was a prince or, more often, a military man appointed by him as the governor, with unrestricted duties and prerogatives except sitting in judgement in the religious court. Most of the town business, however, was passed on to the governor's assistants, *qadi* and *muhtasib*, whom he had the privilege to appoint (von Grunebaum, 1981: 151). The office of legal secretary to the governor developed to be the theoretically independent office of *qadi* as one of the most vigorous institutions in Islamic society. Nevertheless, he did not control the criminal justice, police, and taxation (Schacht, 1970). The *qadi* was the trustee of the pious foundations who provided the maintenance of mosques, seminaries, and miscellaneous public services such as fountains or hospitals, and could become the actual regent of the town (von Grunebaum, 1981: 151).

An official was responsible for trade and local commerce, concerned with honesty in manufacture and selling, protection of the client from fraud, and of the manufacturer from competition. At first known as the "head of the suq", he was later given the more religious title of *muhtasib*, the officer responsible for promoting good and to repressing evil by concerning himself with all questions of public morals, the behaviour of non-Muslims and women, the observance of ritual obligations, and the rules of professional ethics (Cahen, 1970: 529). Thus the position of *muhtasib* was the embodiment of a fusion of two concerns: that of *ulama*, the clergy, for moral order and that of the state for fiscal interests (Lapidus, 1967: 98). The *muhtasib* was delegated with some of the governor's judicial powers. He was the most important cog in the administration of any town, authorized to punish trespassers on the spot, but not to deal with statutory penalties of the *shari'a*, the Islamic law. His duties included some form of development control such as dealing with complaints about the encroachment on a neighbour's boundary or extension of beams beyond the outside wall as well as supply of water and repair of city walls (Mawardi, in von Grunebaum, 1981: 153). The *muhtasib* selected assistants from each craft or trade as their overseers, to be the agents of the state in levying taxes. They were advisers to the *muhtasib* on the conditions of trade and the market, responsible for watching craftsmen execute their duties assigned by the government, such as making provision for auxiliary military service and ceremonial occasions (Lapidus, 1967). The powers of the *muhtasib* in Iran remained unchanged until the seventeenth century when some of his functions were taken over by the *darugheh*. The office of *muhtasib* disappeared in some cities in the nineteenth century (Lambton, 1980: 13–14).

In Iran, a hierarchy of *kalantar* and *kadkhuda* was in charge of the cities from the sixteenth and seventeenth centuries onwards. The *kalantar*, who was appointed by the government, was in charge of the *kadkhudas* of the wards and the affairs of the corporate organizations of crafts and trades. The *kadkhuda*, who was appointed by the *kalantar*, needed the support of the inhabitants of the ward and was a linking agent between the government and the townspeople. As the duties of the *kalantar* were partly transferred to the *darugheh*, his office died out towards the end of the nineteenth century. The *darugheh* and his subordinates, *farrash* and *gazmeh*, constituted a kind of police system in the nineteenth century, dealing especially with the settlement of disputes in the bazaar (Lambton, 1980: 10–15).

Until towards the end of the nineteenth century, the cities were run by the governor and his judicial and administrative assistants. In Tehran, an attempt to create a co-ordinated city management in 1874, in which city assemblies were composed of government officials and distinguished citizens, was aborted a year later when these assemblies were disbanded (Clark, 1981). In line with the first phase of the transformation of Tehran, a municipal institution called the "Ehtesabiyeh" was established. It was formed of two departments, Ehtesab and Tanzif. The former dealt with policing and the latter with waste disposal and water distribution (Shahrdari-e Tehran, 1985).

MANAGEMENT OF TEHRAN BETWEEN TWO REVOLUTIONS 1906–1979

The constitutional revolutionaries were eager to establish the rule of law in the country. That is why in 1907, the first Parliament after the revolution passed a Baladiyeh Act for the establishment of modern municipalities.

According to this Act, cities were to be run by a municipality under the control of a council of elected representatives (Mozayeni, 1974;Vezarat-e Maskan, 1977). The council members were to be elected for four years and their leader, who carried the traditional title of *kalantar*, now the equivalent of a mayor, was also in charge of the municipality. The mayor and three others appointed by the council were the main members of the municipal organization. The main aim of the Parliament in the establishment of municipalities was "to protect the interests of cities and to respond to the needs of the citizens" (*Bulletin*, No. 19, Day 1372: 26). Municipal duties were wide-ranging, including the management of the city's assets, control over distribution of food and water, establishment of hospitals and pharmacies, street cleaning, town planning, fire fighting, promotion of cultural activities by building libraries, museums and conservation of historical buildings, and the promotion of trade through development of markets and exhibitions. The municipality's sole income, however, was the gate tax charged from the carts and beasts of burden entering the city (Shahrdari-e Tehran, 1985). City council decisions were to be approved by the governor. In case of dispute, the minister for internal affairs or Parliament were to arbitrate. The Tehran municipality was therefore to be established as a relatively autonomous organization (*Hamshahri*, 25 January 1996: 2–4). The first Baladiyeh in Tehran was established in 1910 under Dr Khalil Khan A'zam al-Dowleh (Saghafi). This was not, however, based on the Act, as no city council had yet been formed (*Bulletin*, No. 19, Day 1372: 26–31). As with the rest of the democratic aspirations of the revolutionary parliamentarians, municipal autonomy was first watered down and then removed altogether.

In 1930, this municipal Act was replaced by another which eroded the relative autonomy of municipalities and turned them into local agencies of central government (*Hamshahri*, 25 January 1996: 2–4). From these early stages, the Ministry of the Interior became the main actor in establishing municipalities, in appointing their management, and in controlling their affairs, a situation which has essentially remained unchanged until now. The first attempt to create an autonomous urban government was therefore only partly implemented. With the accession to the throne of Reza Shah, who suppressed political freedom and built up a strong central government, a new municipal law was devised. Now the municipality was an institution entirely dependent on central government. Mayors were installed by the Ministry of the Interior and the city councils found the role of advisory groups whose main decisions had to be approved by the ministry (Vezarat-e Maskan, 1977: 44). Townspeople could elect five times the required number of representatives, from whom the government would choose and appoint the members of the council. Thus in 1930, the city of Tehran had for the first time a city council. The leader of the council, the mayor appointed by the Ministry of the Interior, was General Karim Agha

Khan Bouzarjomehri (*Bulletin*, No. 19, Day 1372: 26–31). It was in this period that radical transformations of the city (as we saw in Chapter 2) took place.

The attachment of municipalities to the central government was a part of Reza Shah's drive to centralize political power. After his demise in the Second World War, which led to a renaissance of democratic forces, municipalities once again became the focus of attention. The third municipal Act was approved in 1949, which returned to the municipalities a degree of legal autonomy. The 1949 Act uses the term Shahrdari (a Persian term) to replace Baladiyeh (an Arabic term) for municipality. The main purpose for municipalities was to provide the people of towns and cities with their general needs and amenities (*Bulletin*, No. 19, Day 1372: 26–31). City councils were to be elected by citizens for a period of four years and had wide-ranging powers in the management of the city. The mayor was to be appointed by the Ministry of the Interior from three candidates put forward by the city council (Vezarat-e Maskan, 1977; *Bulletin*, No. 19, Day 1372: 26–31). The councils had the right to legislate, devise local taxes, engage in a degree of urban management, and become relatively independent from the Ministry of the Interior. Three years later under the premiership of Dr Mossadegh, this law was amended to provide municipalities with more independence and limit their relationship with the Ministry of the Interior. The members of the city councils (30 in Tehran) were elected from city wards to have a more direct relationship with their constituencies. The councillors could appoint or sack the mayor, and were allowed to have control over municipalities' financial and administrative affairs. The municipal duties remained much the same as the 1949 Act had defined (*Bulletin*, No. 19, Day 1372: 26–31). With these changes, the 1952 Act, with its later amendments in 1955, 1966, and 1976, have formed the basis of the current municipal practices. The current municipal law is in fact based on the frameworks devised in 1952 and the 1976 provisions (*Hamshahri*, 25 January 1996: 2–4) (Figure 4.1).

Two years after the 1953 monarchist coup which brought Muhammad Reza Shah back to power, a watered-down version of the 1952 law was confirmed as the Municipality Act (Vezarat-e Maskan, 1977). The city councils were granted more power in the selection of the mayor. However, the influence of central government in local affairs was reasserted and expanded through financial and administrative controls. Furthermore, council members no longer represented city wards. With major amendments in 1966, this law has continued to form the legal basis of municipalities even after the Islamic revolution of 1979. According to the 1966 amendments, members of the city council could not become mayor. On the other hand, the amendments made the government's rights to dissolve the city councils conditional upon the approval of a legislative–executive committee. Inability of a city council to elect a mayor could lead to dissolution of the

FIGURE 4.1 Before its demolition to ease traffic, the Tehran municipality building flanked the city's central square (Tup-Khaneh, now Imam Khomeini Square)

council (*Hamshahri*, 25 January 1996: 2–4). In spite of the legal provisions, a considerable level of urban autonomy never came into being. In practice, city councils were rarely formed or, if they were, hardly had a real authority. According to the 1966 law, the mayor of Tehran was required to have royal approval. This implied that none of the 30 members of the city council could have effective control over the mayor who was installed by the Ministry of the Interior and was backed by the shah. The last city council elections in Tehran took place in 1976, which was abolished by the demise of monarchy and its constitution in 1979.

In 1968, a major piece of legislation, the Urban Development and Renewal Act, enabled the municipality to implement Tehran's Comprehensive Plan. The plan, which was eventually approved in 1970 by the city council and the High Council for Town Planning and Architecture, defined two boundaries for the city: an existing boundary and a 25-year expansion area. As the municipal structure had developed to deliver urban services, the municipality was made responsible for the implementation of the plan within the existing boundary. A new organization, called the Supervisory Council for the Expansion of Tehran, was set up to control the 25-year expansion area. The council was chaired by the prime minister and involved a number of government ministers who had an interest in the development of the areas around Tehran. It made policies regarding urban development and provision of infrastructure and services. The municipality was in turn responsible for enforcing development policies, including the demolition of illegal developments at a time of phenomenal growth for the city. The Tehran municipality continued to be financially dependent on the central government and shared the management of the city with the High Council for Town Planning and Architecture and with the Supervisory Council for the Expansion of Tehran, as well as with several government organizations. The municipality, however, was strengthened by several developments. The mayor was chosen as secretary of the Supervisory Council and therefore had a major role in policy making beyond the municipality's existing boundaries. The organization chart of the municipality in the 1970s shows a complex bureaucratic structure with several departments including: finance and administration, urban affairs, social affairs, planning, and technical.

In all these stages of legal provision and change, the struggle to establish a democratically elected local government distinctive from the central power can be clearly seen. The debate was also centred on the relationship between city council, the mayor, and the municipality as the constituent parts of the municipal government. What has remained outside the discussions, however, has been the limited range of issues in which a municipal government is allowed to engage. In all these pieces of legislation, the duties of the local government are limited to mostly physical development and provision of urban utilities (*Hamshahri*, 25 January 1996: 2–4).

The main features of urban management in Tehran in the period between the two revolutions can be summarized as:

1. Increasing organizational complexity, through which the municipality grew to be a large bureaucratic structure.
2. Increasing technical abilities.
3. Lack of democratic accountability (except for infrequent and at times controversial city council elections), which has been an outcome of the central government's grip on power.
4. Lack of financial autonomy, as the municipal budget was prepared by the central government.
5. Lack of administrative autonomy, even when legal provision was made.
6. A range of activities limited to the provision of basic urban services and infrastructure. Planning only focused on physical development and was not to deal with social, cultural, and economic issues.
7. Lack of centralized and co-ordinated management of urban affairs, as the city was being managed by several ministries, public organizations, and the municipality.
8. Lack of power for long-term planning.
9. Limited area of authority, as the municipality had to focus on the city and not on the urban region or the dependent metropolitan areas.

In other words, in all these years the municipality has been an agency of the central government set up to deliver some services in particular urban areas. It has increasingly become more complex with more technical ability to deliver these services. It has not, however, evolved to be a democratic organization for urban management, as it lacks both democratic legitimacy and management powers to perform in this way. These are the shortcomings mostly identifiable even after a revolution with far-reaching claims for democracy and public participation.

MANAGEMENT OF TEHRAN AFTER THE ISLAMIC REVOLUTION

The Islamic Revolution, which was the result of mass protests and mobilizations, brought forward a new, widespread demand for democratic governance. As always, however, the main battles were fought around national politics as performed in the capital and other large cities. The issue of urban government itself has been less emphasized either by popular demand or by the new authorities. Urban management has continued to be seen as service delivery. The necessity of a more democratic governance, however, has been increasingly felt, even by the authorities whose resources are scarcer than before.

After the revolution in 1979, new forms of management emerged in the Tehran municipality, as in many other public institutions. Its management was now formed of management councils for finance and administration, welfare, urban services, research units, traffic and planning, and urban districts. The urban area was subdivided into metropolitan districts, each with their own mayor and municipality. Now, for the first time, with the expansion of the city's boundaries, the number of municipalities in the metropolitan districts rose from 12 to 20 (Figure 4.2).

The revolution's new constitution asked for Islamic city councils to be set up. This, however, has not yet been implemented nearly two decades after the revolution. Instead, a temporary city council was formed by the members of the municipality and the Ministry of the Interior. The revolution inherited an administrative system which has continued to be essentially centralized. The organization of the Tehran municipality has expanded with the expansion of the city. It is now formed of a central municipality and a group of 20 municipalities each in charge of one of the 20 areas of the city. The major constituent parts of its IR29.1bn income in 1985 were property tax, fines on illegal developments, car tax, driving fines, and gate tax (Shahrdari-e Tehran, 1985).

In the 1980s, the main parts of the municipality which dealt with urban development were three departments. The Urban Services Department included offices for planning, urban services, development, and green space throughout the 20 areas of the city. This department also includes offices for

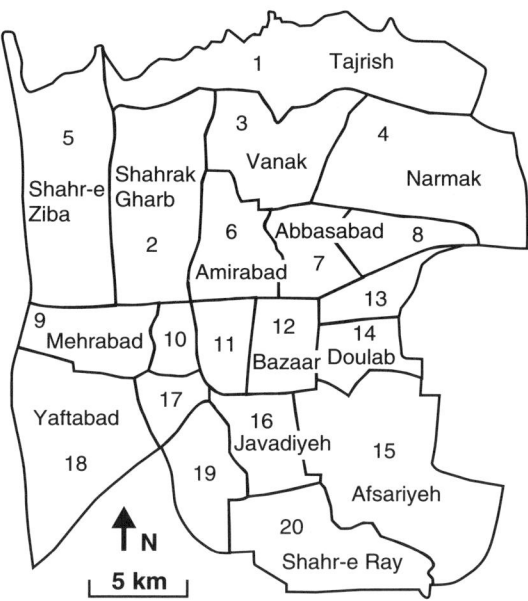

FIGURE 4.2 The city is now divided into 20 districts each managed by a municipality

parks, environmental improvements, vegetable markets, the High Council for Resettlement of Squatters (Gowd), opening up of blocked rights of way, and a number of other offices less related to urban space. The Development and Technical Department included a series of offices for development and redevelopment and road building. The Urban Transportation Department covered the offices for traffic, terminals, metro, bus, and taxis (Shahrdari-e Tehran, 1985). In 1988, the municipality was divided into seven departments: finance and administration, technical and development, city planning and architecture, planning and co-ordination, urban services, and district affairs.

The main features of urban management in this period are essentially similar to those of the pre-revolutionary period in the 1970s. The organization of the municipality has continued to be ever more complex with more technical abilities. Its financial dependence and lack of democratic participation also remained intact. The municipality was limited to deal with certain functions in a limited area, and as such did not deal with issues of urban management in the whole of the metropolitan area (*Hamshahri*, 25 January 1996: 2–4). When comparing urban management before and after the Islamic revolution, it may be surprising to see a large degree of legal and administrative continuity. After all, the 1906 revolution had introduced new, radical ideas that, although partially implemented, formed the basis of urban management in the twentieth century. This time, however, the legal foundations of municipal government were mainly developed before the 1979 revolution. Also, the practices of urban management, in undermining local democracy and deliberate neglect of city councils, show a consistency uninterrupted by the advent of the revolution.

URBAN MANAGEMENT IN THE 1990S

The year 1990 appears to be a turning point for the Tehran municipality. The drive for liberal reforms, that had started with the end of the war and the establishment of a new government, was now to be extended to city management in the capital. A new mayor, a powerful figure who had shown success in running the historic city of Isfahan, was appointed. The new mayor's strategy was to move towards financial and administrative independence for the municipality. This created support as well as criticism due to some controversial means with which some forms of self-reliance were achieved. After the election of a new national government in May 1997, these criticisms led to the brief arrest of several district mayors and the mayor himself, charged with embezzlement of public funds. The controversy continued as the supporters of the mayor argued that these arrests and accusations were made for political reasons by conservatives who wanted to undermine the new, reform-minded administration.

The main features of city management in this period have been summarized as:

1. A programme of privatization of some of the municipal services started, services which were delivered by organizations in charge of recycling, statistics, information and computer services, cemetery, fire brigade, fruit and vegetable markets, motor vehicles, environmental improvement, parks, supervision of taxis, transport and traffic control, abattoirs and cold stores, and terminals.
2. A new wave of major urban development projects has been implemented, including roads and parks.
3. Questions of sustainability, environmental quality, and accessibility have been introduced.
4. The municipality has become more engaged in social and cultural issues. A new department has been set up to deal with the establishment of cultural centres, public libraries, sports centres, entertainment and tourist facilities.
5. The necessity of long-term planning for dealing with urban problems has been stressed.
6. In a short period of time the municipality has become financially independent.

7. The mayor of Tehran has been given a more powerful presence in the political scene, to the extent that he attends cabinet meetings as an observer.
8. The municipality has continued to establish new commercial units, such as chain stores and fruit and vegetable markets (*Hamshahri*, 25 January 1996: 2–4).

The Tehran municipality has been engaged in the collection of information and development of a municipal plan for the period 1996–2001 (Shahrdari-e Tehran, 1996a). The plan identifies the main areas of strength and weakness in the municipality. The plan's vision of Tehran for 2001 is to move towards creating a city of six distinctive qualities: a clean city, whose environmental problems have been tackled; a moving city, whose traffic problems have been addressed; a green city, whose trees and parks make it a more beautiful and healthy place; a city with a rich culture, where cultural facilities are numerous; a dynamic city, whose operations are smooth; and a city with a traditional and modern physical fabric. We shall return to these themes in Chapters 6 and 7.

The central management issues that the Tehran municipality is facing are largely similar to those of the past. These are at the same time the main challenges for any future urban management in the metropolis. If properly addressed, municipal strength in these areas would enable the urban managers to tackle the major problems of the city. They can be classified as challenges of urban governance, municipal finances, and democratic management.

URBAN GOVERNANCE

In Iran, the administration of the country is based on sectoral management. Local branches of different ministries, therefore, are engaged in development and delivery of services and deal with major urban and national problems in their own capacities. A local organization such as a municipality finds it very difficult to cross the divide between these different public agencies. The overlap of issues and interests between local public agencies and the municipality often leads to a confusion of responsibilities, especially undermining the municipality's role (Shahrdari-e Tehran, 1996a: 47).

The city of Tehran is run by a central municipality overseeing 20 district municipalities. Each district is further divided into subdistricts, of which there are 118 in total. Districts are run by district mayors who are supported by a number of advisors and deputies. In 1993, the 20 districts employed 4442 white-collar workers (Markaz-e Motale'at, 1995: 13) and a larger, unspecified number of blue-collar workers.

Tehran municipality's range of activities fall into three categories: administrative services, urban services, and urban development. Administrative services deal with revenue, renewal tax, and organizational issues. Urban services deal with keeping the city clean, environmental maintenance and improvement, fire fighting and security, traffic, urban transport, social services and distribution of drinking water. The urban development functions include development planning, development and improvement of infrastructures such as water, sewerage and transport systems and of sports, entertainment, cultural, and tourist facilities. Some of the municipal duties that have now been transferred to other organizations include health control and combating contagious diseases, price control, supervision of weight and other standards, and preparation of trade regulations.

Other public organizations that share in Tehran's governance and in delivery of urban services include a range of ministries, each dealing with different and at times overlapping issues. The Ministry of the Interior deals with the establishment and abolition of municipalities, the election and abolition of city councils, determining the municipal boundaries, and supervising the implementation of town planning rules and regulations. It also deals with register offices and religious endowments, each with a role in the land and property development process. In housing and urban development schemes, several organizations may be involved. The urban land organization (Ministry of Housing and Urban Development) or the religious endowment organization (Ministry of the Interior) provide land for housing and urban services. The housing unit (Ministry of Housing and Urban Development) prepares land for future development. The technical unit (Ministry of Housing) develops buildings and other facilities where finance comes from the country's development budget. The Ministry of Housing and Urban Development deals with the preparation of development plans and supervises their implementation. The Plan and Budget Organization provides the budget for the preparation of development plans, for urban development schemes, for land acquisition, and for municipal development programmes. The Ministry of Economic Affairs collects the municipal taxes and delivers them to the municipality. The Ministry of Trade sets and controls prices. The Ministry of Energy runs the water, electricity, and sewerage systems. The Ministry of Posts, Telegraphs, and Telephones delivers telecommunication services. The Oil Ministry provides natural gas. A range of social services is provided by the Ministries of Education (educational services), Ministry of Higher Education (higher education), Ministry of Health (health care), the physical education organization (sports services), the security services (security), Ministry of Islamic Guidance (cultural and religious services), the environmental protection organization (combating air pollution), and the civilian defence organization (relief for sudden disasters) (*Hamshahri*, 22 February 1996: 6–7). This vertical intervention in urban development and management is often in contrast to the municipal responsibility of managing the city at a horizontal level.

Tehran is the seat of the national government. The country's spiritual leader, the president, Parliament, and all the ministries are based in Tehran.

Before them, the shah, the court, the foreign dignitaries, and all the state apparatus were based in Tehran. This has traditionally created a massive concentration of the country's elite in Tehran, powerful figures who would have an interest and an influence in the affairs of the city. There are official and informal channels through which the national government and their local agencies intervene in the governance of the city. As we have seen in Chapter 3, the presence of the national government has led to almost half of those working in Tehran being employed in the public sector. The concentration of public sector employees in the city makes its social and economic life closely tied to variations in public sector management and finances.

The city's management, therefore, suffers from a multiplicity of agencies and the absence of an authority which can be in charge of managing the city with an overall perspective and responsibility. The municipality has been seen as a branch of central government responsible for delivering some services. Another hindrance to the authority of Tehran's municipality is its limited spatial domain of activities. Most of the recent growth of the metropolis lies beyond the official boundaries of the city, outside the municipality's jurisdiction. This limitation means suburban developments, some of which can have a major impact on the metropolis, will remain outside an effective, overall management.

Between the Constitutional Revolution of 1906 and the year 1994, 570 municipalities have been established in Iran, signifying a substantial growth of urbanization and a need for modern urban management structures (*Bulletin*, No. 35, 5th Khordad 1374: 19–21). The history of modern municipalities in Iran, as best exemplified in Tehran, shows a constant struggle between democratic aspirations for local autonomy and central government's assertion of its powers. As Tehran has grown in size and importance, the prospect of a democratically elected mayor has become ever more daunting for the central government. Tehran's municipality now seeks more legal and administrative autonomy after it has achieved financial independence. It seeks more powers and an integrated approach to the metropolitan area. This can be seen from the pages of the municipality's publications. This may create efficiencies which have not been achieved so far. It will be more rational for the big city region to be regarded as a complex set of interrelated urban areas, rather than a collection of disjointed entities. The major challenge, however, for both the central government and the municipality will be a move towards local democracy in which Tehrani citizens can take a more active role in the management of their city. Without such participation, more powers for the municipality may create a more overwhelming hurdle for the citizens to overcome. Public participation at all levels of urban management will be the only way to ensure an urban government that the citizens can own and support. So far, the modern history of the city has shown an endless, and as yet unsuccessful, battle for democratic governance.

DEMOCRATIC MANAGEMENT

One of the main features of the revolution was the neighbourhood-level mobilization of Tehranis in their challenge to the outgoing regime. Neighbourhood groups organized themselves to protect their areas and later, during the war with Iraq, to ensure a fair supply of food. It would be natural to expect such grassroots level of public participation in urban affairs to develop into a genuine local democracy. The revolutionary council approved the local councils law in 1979 (*Bulletin*, No. 19, Day 1372: 26–31). In 1982, the first post-revolutionary Parliament devised a system of democratic councils for the country. With enthusiasm similar to that of the constitutional revolutionaries before them, the Islamic revolutionaries proposed a complete set of Islamic councils at all levels: from villages and rural districts to towns, cities, counties, and regions. With similar fate, however, the councils have mostly remained on paper. The Act was amended in 1986 and 1991. The fourth Parliament rejected councils above the level of cities, i.e. county councils and regional councils. Meanwhile, the establishment of city councils has not been pursued with any vigour. At the moment, it is still the Ministry of Interior which, according to a 1994 amendment, acts on behalf of the city councils.

The law defines the main duties of the city councils as: electing a mayor for a four-year period; approving the naming and renaming of streets, squares, and places; approving the price of services provided by the municipality and its related organizations; approving the price of transport in the city; devising the regulations regarding the establishment and management of the public markets; supervising the management and maintenance of the municipality's property and belongings; public approval of the municipality's budget every six months; approval of the municipality's loans; approval of the property deals in which the municipality is involved; approval of the amount and any change to local taxes; supervision of health inspection in the city; supervision of theatres, cinemas and other such services run by the public or private sectors; supervision of cemeteries and related services; devising regulations and supervision of canals and ditches for utilities; supervision of the implementation of the construction and expansion of roads, streets, squares, open spaces, and public utilities (*Hamshahri*, 25 January 1996: 5–6). These duties and areas of involvement are essentially similar to the pre-revolutionary practices and duties. What was new after the revolution was some expansion of duties and powers of the councils. These included: identifying shortages in social, cultural, educational, economic, health care, and welfare provisions, and preparing plans to tackle these problems; collaboration with government organizations; planning for public participation in delivery of social, economic, developmental, cultural, and welfare services; promoting private sector participation in the establishment of cultural, entertainment, and sports facilities; and initiating the establishment of social and cultural organizations. Some of the duties of the city councils have now been removed from their agendas, such as dealing with water, electricity, hospitals, and trade disputes (*Hamshahri*, 25 January 1996: 5–6).

Despite the claims of the revolutionary government in ending the authoritarian rule of its predecessors, the last city council in Tehran was formed in the 1970s and was abolished by the revolution, which has not yet established one. The post-revolutionary governments have failed to accept a democratic system of urban management, in which the municipality derives its legitimacy and powers from the citizens rather than from central government. There are, however, mounting pressures to do so. The boom period of oil economies has been replaced by a period of structural adjustment, in which subsidies are cut and therefore a less secure state will have to rely more on the citizens for sharing the costs, responsibilities, and blame. As Richards (1995: 56) argues, in the Middle East

> ". . . coping with the challenges of the food, jobs, and investment will require greater integration into the international economy; such economic changes imply enlarging the role of the private sector, widening the scope of the rule of law, and more generally restructuring the state's relationship with its citizens. In short, expanded political participation will be a necessary tool in the struggle to forge a successful 'Arab', 'Turkish', or 'Iranian' capitalism in the information age."

It is partly in response to these pressures that the Iranian government has moved along the route of reintegration into the world economy through economic liberalization, a route which will inevitably require a larger degree of political freedom and democratic accountability. It also partly explains why there are pressures from inside the Tehran municipality for democratic legitimacy and for a wider legal and spatial mandate. In urban management, if the municipality wishes to attract more investment from the private sector, as we will see in the next section, there will be a real need for realization of the revolution's democratic aspirations.

FINANCIAL INDEPENDENCE

In the 1990s, the Tehran municipality has become financially independent, with an income growing between 1992 and 1995 at an average annual rate of 32 per cent (Shahrdari-e Tehran, 1996a: 39). This has reversed the long trend of reliance on central government for financial support. However, the move to financial self-reliance, which has concentrated on generating and collecting more revenue from a variety of sources, has been a controversial process. The municipality has adopted entrepreneurial approaches to delivery of goods and services, bringing about rising revenues. On the one hand, the pressure to pay more taxes and the entrepreneurial approaches to urban management have led to wide-ranging public criticism of the municipality. On the other, the considerable increase in municipal activities, especially in infrastructure development and environmental improvement of the city, have attracted support from citizens.

In 1987, the municipal revenue in Tehran comprised four main categories: income from the public sector (11.3 per cent), municipal taxes (63.4 per cent), sale of goods and services (0.36 per cent), and sale of property (24.8 per cent), all amounting to a total of IR41.2bn (Markaz-e Amar, 1990: 3). Municipal expenses, however, were IR43.8bn, formed of personnel (61.4 per cent), administration expenses (11.5 per cent), investment (21.6 per cent), and transfers (5.3 per cent) (pp. 24–5). By 1992, the municipal budget had risen to IR400bn. Only two years after the appointment of the new mayor, the municipal budget had increased five times (*Ettela'at*, 4 October 1992: 5 & 10). By 1993, this had gone up to IR700bn (*Bulletin*, No. 28, Mehr 1373: 28). This rapid rise reflects a high inflation rate, as well as rising municipal revenue and a new trend of paying attention to the capital city.

In the aftermath of the revolution, there was a negative attitude towards investment in Tehran. It was thought that Tehran had had more than its fair share of the country's resources. The concentration of wealth in Tehran had been parallel with, and a cause of, the deterioration of small towns and villages. A revolutionary government, therefore, would not continue to spend on the wealthy parts of the country and would create a balance in favour of the more deprived and disadvantaged provinces. So started a period of deliberate discrimination against Tehran, exacerbated by the advent of a long war. A decade of underinvestment and neglect, however, had to come to an end. There was the political realization that the people of Tehran had been one of the main forces behind the revolution, and at the end of the war they expected to see a positive change. Furthermore, the capital of a revolutionary government which aspired to impress the world had to be a showcase. The new mayor's drive for environmental improvement and development in infrastructure should be partly seen in this light.

In the drive for maximization of revenue, many services and parts of the municipality were privatized. This has changed the nature and character of their services and their efficiency in delivery of services. Some previously municipal departments now act as private contractors to deliver the same services. These contractors have reduced their costs and have renegotiated municipal duties. An example is the case of the vehicle services organization, which undertakes collection and disposal of refuse. In 1994, this agency received IR500m. from the district municipalities for its services. In 1995, the agency successfully argued that collection of waste from hospitals, hotels, and public buildings was not part of its duties and that these organizations had to collect and dispose of their waste themselves. As a result, the year 1995 witnessed a revenue of IR1.2bn from these organizations for these services. Furthermore, the agency made IR1.8bn by reorganizing the operational system and restructuring the workforce. For example, the workforce collecting refuse from hospitals was reduced from 300 workers and 100 vans to 16 workers and 8 lorries (*Bulletin*, No. 35, 5th Khordad 1374: 36). These and similar measures have proved controversial in a post-revolutionary atmosphere. The most controversial move towards maximization of revenue has perhaps been the approach to urban development projects, where the main source of municipal income lies. In 1995, 84.33 per cent of all municipal earnings were from land and property taxes, showing an annual growth of 36 per cent since 1992 (Shahrdari-e Tehran, 1996a: 38–9).

The population growth, the recycling of oil revenue in urban land, and the pressure for development create higher land prices and therefore higher densities in Tehran. At the same time, town planning regulations in Tehran have traditionally controlled density and have required a certain amount of open space in new developments. The prospect of high rent value of properties has been so attractive, however, that constant pressure exists to build above the permitted levels. In response to this tension and the pressure for high residential densities, the municipality has decided to allow excess development for a fee. It allows substantial extensions to low-density buildings or sells the rights to build high to developers who build high-rise, luxury apartment buildings. At times, the municipality itself enters a partnership with private developers and generates revenue from the sale of these luxury flats. However, a number of problems arise, which are often controversial and have caused strong public opposition. These include undermining the planning law by the authority in charge of implementing it; increasing the density of the neighbourhoods without corresponding improvement in infrastructure and parking facilities; loss of green and open spaces; and infringing on neighbours' privacy. These concerns have led to a demand from the municipality to enforce a height limit of four to six storeys in the city.

The municipality also develops retail and office complexes, as exemplified by the Golbarg development in district 8, a six-storey development of 4740 m^2 including offices, shops, and parking (*Bulletin*, No. 37, 5th Mordad 1374: 39). A major entrepreneurial exercise by the municipality has been the Navab project. Navab was a wide street developed before the revolution. The municipality had planned to extend the street, which meant cutting through some old dense fabric of the town, linking the street to the network of roads in west Tehran. As this was a costly exercise, the municipality intended to attract private capital by promising an annual rate of return much higher than the banks offered at the time. This was, however, strongly criticized and subsequently abandoned. In late 1994, the municipality issued a bond to finance the project, which included commercial property and retail development. The project was very attractive to investors, as it

FIGURE 4.3 Financial dependence on property development makes the municipality vulnerable

promised a 20 per cent annual return in the early stages. Within six days, IR250bn worth of shares were sold and the financing of the project secured (EIU, 1995: 42–3). The first phase of the scheme was completed by June 1997, a scheme in which 4000 decaying dwellings in the densest part of the city were replaced by 6000 new dwellings. The success of the scheme has encouraged the municipality to talk about a 20-year programme, which would redevelop the urban fabric south of Enghelab Street (*Ettela'at*, 8 June 1997: 1). Other means of investment, such as sharing with Iranian and foreign banks, have also been used in the municipality's development projects (*Bulletin*, No. 28, Mehr 1373: 26).

The heavy reliance of municipal finances on land and property development, however, makes the municipality vulnerable to changes in the property market (Figure 4.3). A slowdown in the market would substantially reduce the city's revenues. Furthermore, high inflation and increasing impoverishment of the citizenry mean a rising public inability to pay the costs of urban management. The municipality therefore wishes to have access to the added value created as a result of its development projects (Shahrdari-e Tehran, 1996a: 46–7). It also tries to diversify its sources of income.

The municipal policy for revenue generation has included a focus on retailing. The municipality has become a major retailer of foodstuffs through the establishment of fruit and vegetable markets. A typical market is Ekhtiyariyeh in district 3, which was established in spring 1995 with an area of 2500 m^2 with 28 retail units selling fruit, vegetables, meat and dairy products. By 1995, there were 40 markets in Tehran daily selling 9000 t of agricultural produce (*Bulletin*, No. 35, 5th Khordad 1374: 40). The markets sell their goods at prices 20–30 per cent below those of other retailers, and hence are visited by 750 000 shoppers every day (*Bulletin*, No. 35, 5th Khordad 1374: 36–7). Attention has also been given to a plan to use the municipal parks for growing and export of flowers and related products. At an international flower show in Tehran in 1992, the mayor of Tehran expressed his intention to increase the share of Iran from a mere US$0.5m. in a global market for flowers worth US$100bn (*Bulletin*, No. 1, Khordad 1371: 11–12). This could generate hard currency and be used for the environmental improvements in the city.

CONCLUSION: CHALLENGES OF URBAN GOVERNANCE

The constitutional revolutionaries set up the foundations for modern municipalities to replace the old forms of urban administration which had been practised for centuries. Throughout the twentieth century, democratic pressures for public participation in urban management have always had to confront the central government's assertion of its power and control. After many waves of legislation, an independent local government has not yet been established in Tehran, or any other urban area in Iran. Economic pressures on the municipality to become financially independent, however, are now leading to recognition of the demand for more political freedom and public participation. The Tehran municipality, which is often seen as responsible for delivering urban services within limited official boundaries, realizes that the tasks of managing a metropolis are very complex. What is required is a coherent approach to the urban region and an institutional arrangement for the clarification of responsibilities between horizontal and vertical intervention in city management, as performed by the municipality and other public agencies involved in managing the city. Municipal endeavours to gain financial independence have proved to be very successful, but controversial, as well as vulnerable to fluctuations of land and property markets and to the political struggles of opposing factions. It is only through democratic legitimacy that municipal government can find the necessary mandate and power, and the political and economic support of the citizens.

5

URBAN SOCIETY

In this chapter, we briefly look at the size and growth patterns of population. We then look at how immigration is a major factor in the social life of the city. We trace the society in transition, as evident in family structure, the rise of individualism, and the questions of cultural identity, social polarization, and social exclusion in the city. These closely relate to the discussions of urban problems, such as unemployment, housing and environmental quality addressed in Chapters 3 and 7.

DEMOGRAPHIC CHANGE

Tehran is the largest concentration of people in Iran and one of the largest cities in the world. In 1991, the city of Tehran had a population of 6 475 527 (Markaz-e Motale'at, 1994: 2), accounting for more than a fifth of the country's urban population. This figure, however, only refers to the 20 districts within the official boundaries of the city. A more accurate figure for the population of Tehran's metropolitan region would include, as the 1992 comprehensive plan studies suggest, the number of inhabitants of the counties with close economic ties with Tehran. For example, in 1983, the headquarters of 75.9 per cent of the firms in Varamin and 63.6 per cent of those in Karaj were based in Tehran. There are seven such counties (*shahrestan*): Tehran, Ray, Karaj, Savejbolagh, Shahryar, Shemiranat, and Varamin, which together in 1991 had a population of 9 140 239 (Markaz-e Motale'at, 1994: 6–11). This included 2.6 million inhabitants of the metropolitan region who were living outside the administrative boundaries of the city. In 1991, the population of Tehran Province (*Ostan*), the official administrative region of which Tehran city is a part, was 9.98 million (Markaz-e Amar, 1996a: 38). This grew at an annual rate of 2 per cent to 11.1 million in 1996. This was slightly above the national population growth rate, which has slowed down to 1.81 in the period 1986–96 (*Ettela'at*, 13 January 1997 and 29 May 1997).

As we saw in Part One, the growth of population in Tehran started with its selection as the capital of the Persian empire two centuries ago, bringing the court, the military, and the government offices to the city. The predominance of the state apparatus in Tehran has continued to this day, as we saw in Chapter 3, in that almost half of the working population in Tehran are employed in the public sector. We also saw that Tehran has the

TABLE 5.1 Tehran's population between the first and the last census, 1867–1991

Year	Population
1867	155 736
1891	160 000
1922	210 000
1932	310 139
1937	425 000
1939	540 087
1940	700 000
1946	880 000
1956	1 512 082
1966	2 719 730
1976	4 530 223
1980	5 443 721
1986	6 042 584
1991	6 475 527

Sources: Taleghani (1992: 3–14); Markaz-e Motale'at (1994: 19).

largest concentration of wealth in the country. This massive concentration of wealth and power has attracted a constant flow of population from around the country to Tehran. Between the first census in 1867 and 1991, the population of Tehran has grown more than 40 times (Table 5.1).

This growth has been accompanied by a growth of the city's boundaries, from the fixed physical boundaries in the form of walls and moats to lines on the map, when these boundaries became entirely administrative. As the population has grown, it has become more difficult to establish the accurate number of Tehranis and the pattern of population change. Nevertheless, it is possible to see, in the context of the general population rise, that the growth rate of the population of the urban region has started to decline since the 1950s and 1960s. In the city, the intensity of population growth peaked in the 1950s, to reach 6.68 per cent per year (Khatam, 1993: 106) and has been consistently declining ever since. The decline in growth has been faster especially since 1980, reaching the lowest level for the past century to an annual 1.4 per cent in the early 1990s (Figure 5.1).

This slowdown in the growth of population in the city, however, has been in parallel with an initial process of growth in the suburbs. Between 1956 and 1966, 2 towns and 132 villages were absorbed into the city of Tehran (Markaz-e Motale'at, 1994: 22). The population of some towns in Tehran county (*shahrestan*) grew many times, as in Rajaiishahr, which increased from 8332 in 1956 to 16 362 in 1991, and in Islamshahr, which grew from 36 976 to 230 183 in the same period (p. 15). The population of the suburbs continued to grow at very high rates to reach an annual peak of 10.28 per

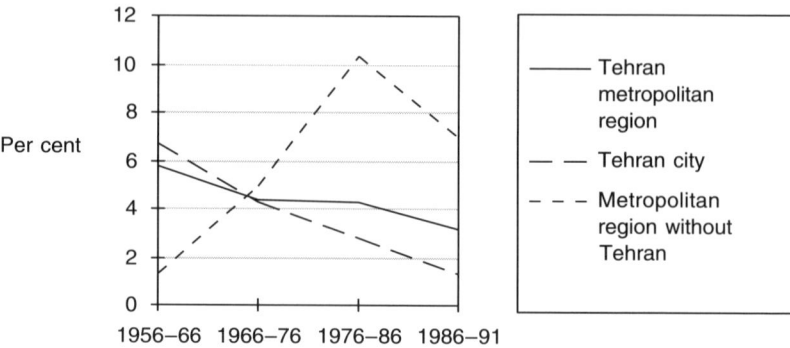

FIGURE 5.1 Annual rate of population growth 1956–91. Ever since the mid-1950s, the rate of population growth in Tehran has been declining

TABLE 5.2 Annual growth rate of population, 1956–91

	Tehran metropolitan region	Tehran city	Metropolitan region without Tehran
1956–66	5.78	6.68	1.32
1966–76	4.37	4.27	4.95
1976–86	4.27	2.82	10.28
1986–91	3.20	1.31	7.00

Source: Khatam (1993: 106).

cent in the decade after the 1976 census. From 1986 onwards, however, it has started to slow down (Table 5.2) (Khatam, 1993: 106). In 1991, of the 9.1 million population of the Tehran region, 1.2 million lived in rural areas and small towns and settlements (Markaz-e Motale'at, 1994: 15).

Inside the city of Tehran, there has been a process of decentralization and suburbanization. Many central districts have started to lose population and outer districts to grow (Figure 5.2). The highest loss has come in the central bazaar area, the traditional business district, which in the period 1980–91 lost population at an annual rate of 3 per cent (Markaz-e Motale'at, 1994: 26).

The pattern of population change in Tehran, therefore, shows at least three distinctive trends:

1. The continuing growth of population in the metropolitan region. This has been due to the reasons already mentioned. The capital city has been the administrative centre of a large, increasingly bureaucratic state and the largest job market in the country.

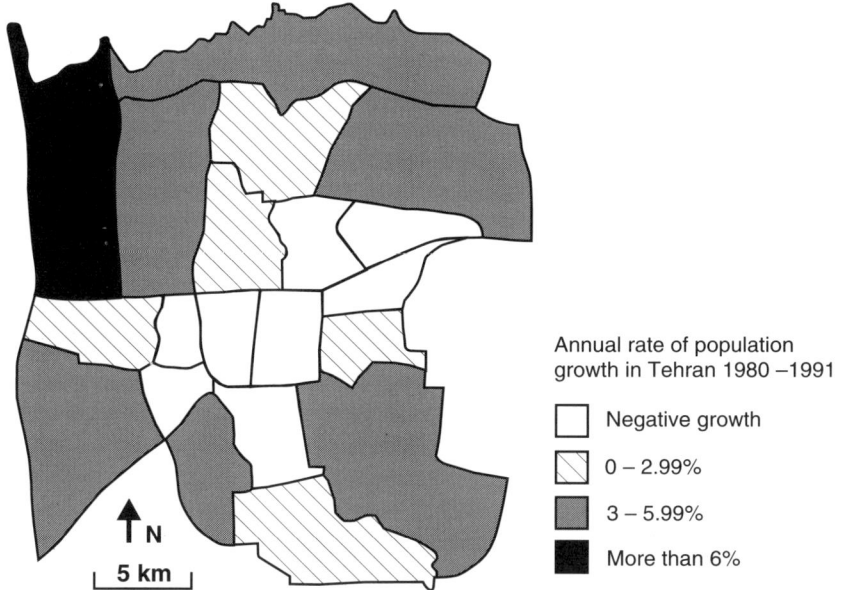

FIGURE 5.2 Annual rate of population growth 1980–91. Many central districts have started to lose population while outer districts have grown

2. The slowdown in the growth of the urban region. This is a trend comparable to that in many other large urban areas in the developing world (Khatam, 1993). In Tehran, it could be attributed to a variety of factors with negative impact on the process of immigration: the rising cost of living in the capital, which will be even more acute with the pressure for further removal of subsidies; the scarcity of jobs in the city whose economy has suffered from the revolution and the war; increased congestion and high densities, with their economic, social, and environmental consequences; some success on the part of policies controlling the concentration of industrial activity in the area; and the growth of other urban areas in the country, which has created a slightly more balanced urban system.
3. The process of suburbanization. The population of the central areas has decreased and the outer areas have grown. The deterioration of the physical fabric and quality of the environment, as well as the encroachment of business activities into residential areas, have had major impacts on the life of the city. Policies such as traffic restrictions in central areas and change of administrative boundaries of the city, both introduced in the aftermath of the Islamic revolution, have encouraged the process of suburbanization and the decline of inner areas. Suburbanization continues to be the main form of population change and

can have a considerable impact on the future of the city. Through this process, as we shall see in Chapter 6, social polarization has intensified, as most new immigrants from the central areas or from outside the metropolitan region are attracted to these outer towns and settlements.

STRUCTURE OF THE POPULATION

As a destination for immigrants from around the country, the male population in Tehran has historically been rising faster than the female population. The difference, however, has never been very substantial, as their families have joined the male workers later. In 1956, 52.9 per cent of Tehranis were men, which changed to a more balanced figure of 51.6 per cent in 1991, comparable to the national figure of 51.5 per cent (Markaz-e Motale'at, 1994: 30–1; Taleghani, 1992: 24). Inside Tehran, there is a spatial differentiation in gender, where the more mature areas in the centre have better gender balances than the areas on the fast-growing fringes, where men are in the majority (Markaz-e Motale'at, 1994: 33–4).

In comparison with the rest of the country, Tehran has an older population (Taleghani, 1992). Nevertheless, the population of Tehran is very young. In 1991, half of Tehranis were younger than 22.3 years (Markaz-e Motale'at, 1994: 83). This is despite the fact that the trend in the last 30 years shows a move towards maturity of population (Table 5.3). This age structure reflects high birth rates, especially among recent immigrants from rural areas. The age groups show a clear spatial differentiation in the city. The central and northern areas (such as districts 3, 6, 11) have older populations than the peripheral areas (such as districts 15, 18, 19) (Figure 5.3). The youngest are the population of district 19, a poor district in the south of the city, where half the inhabitants are younger than 16.7 years (Markaz-e Motale'at, 1994: 83).

The advent of the Islamic revolution and the war had a major impact on the birth rates of the city for over a decade. Birth figures jumped from 144 341 in 1978 to 211 517 in 1979, i.e. a rise of one-third in a year. This rise continued and peaked in 1983, at the height of the war, when it started to decline. From 1991 the number of births in the city has been smaller than pre-revolution figures (Markaz-e Motale'at, 1994: 146).

The rate of literacy in Tehran has risen over the years, to reach 87.9 per cent of those aged six years and older in 1991. Two patterns of differentiation can be detected: men are more educated than women, as literacy among men reaches 91.04 per cent compared to 84.6 per cent for women. Also the poorer areas in the southern outskirts of the city are less educated and have higher rates of illiteracy (Markaz-e Motale'at, 1994: 118) (Figure 5.4).

Tehran has an essentially Muslim population (98 per cent), with Christian (1.2 per cent), Jewish (0.3 per cent), Zoroastrian (0.3 per cent) and other (0.2 per cent) religious minorities (Markaz-e Motale'at, 1994: 121).

TABLE 5.3 The change in the main age groups, 1966–91

Year	Main age groups (%)		
	0–14	15–64	65+
1966	41	56	3
1976	36.8	59.9	3.3
1986	37.4	59.2	3.4
1991	36.3	59.9	3.8

Source: Markaz-e Motale'at (1994: 35).

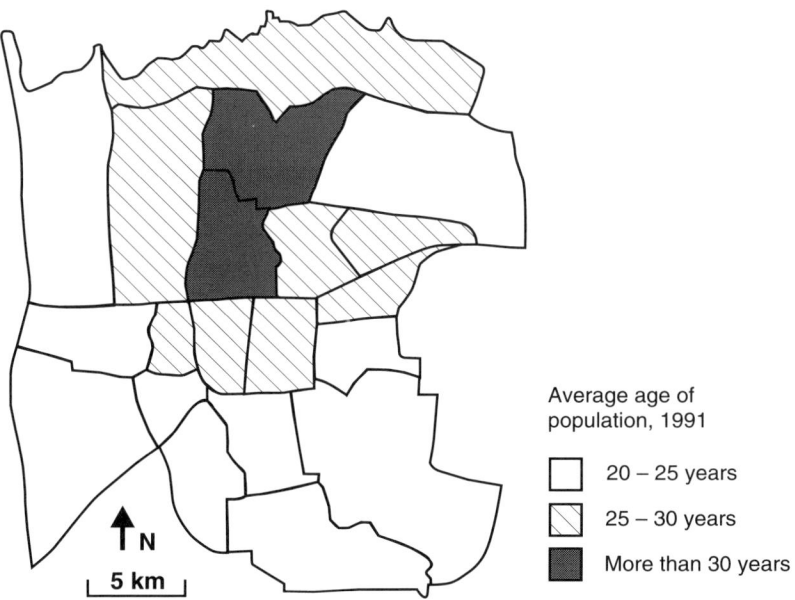

FIGURE 5.3 Average age of population, 1991. The central and northern districts have older populations than the peripheral areas

IMMIGRATION

The growth of Tehran from a small town 200 years ago into a metropolitan region has been largely based on immigration. As it has grown it has also annexed the surrounding towns and villages. The great majority of today's Tehranis have roots in other parts of the country. The further back in time we go, the larger the proportion of the Tehranis born outside Tehran. In 1986, around one-third of Tehran's population were born elsewhere.

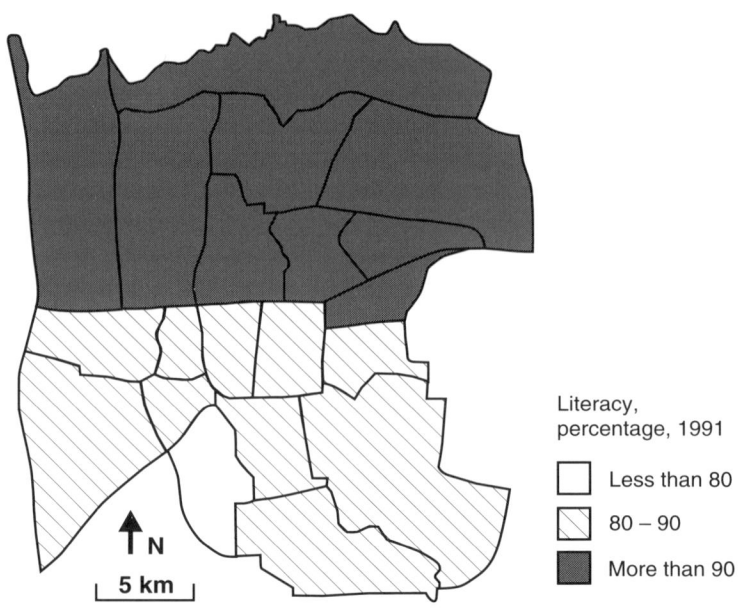

FIGURE 5.4 Literacy, 1991 (per cent). There is a clear north–south divide

Twenty years earlier, this figure was around 45 per cent (Taleghani, 1992: 120). In 1867, 73 per cent of the city's population were born outside the capital (Taleghani, 1992: 8).

Out of choice or despair, different waves of migration have had different reasons and circumstances. In the 1920s and 1930s, the centralization of power and the expansion of the military and bureaucracy pulled more and more people to the capital. A period of economic growth in the 1960s attracted a large number of people. This paralleled the destruction of the traditional agrarian relationships in the countryside and the drive for industrialization, where most industries were based in Tehran. The oil boom, especially in the 1970s, meant a rapid growth in the construction industry, where new crowds were drawn to the city for building work. In the aftermath of the Islamic revolution, the promises of the revolutionary government of free or low-cost utilities and housing were another major factor in immigration. Then came the war in the south-west of Iran, from which many fled to large cities away from the war front, including Tehran.

Immigrants have come from all across the country. In general, however, the central and northern parts, which have historically been wealthier and more densely populated, have sent more immigrants. In 1867, Isfahanis and Azeris were the largest groups of immigrants in Tehran. In the decade ending in 1986, from the 500 000 arrivals in the city, Azeris were still the

TABLE 5.4 The main reasons for, and the conditions before, immigration

Main reason for immigration	Total (%)	Conditions before migration (%)		
		Employed	Unemployed	Non-active
Higher income	22.35	33.83	18.33	12.7
Friends and relatives	6.76	8.48	5.79	3.9
Better opportunities	4.64	6.71	3.70	1.14
Looking for work	18.47	15.73	58.69	3.5
Following family	43.43	2.75	13.49	78.76
Job transfer	4.35	7.72		
Total	100	100	100	100

Source: Taleghani (1992: 130).

largest group (21 per cent from east Azerbaijan), followed by those from around Tehran province (9.2 per cent). A considerable number came from Khuzestan (7 per cent), fleeing the war and destruction imposed on them by the expansionist Iraqi president, Saddam Hussein. Immigrants from other countries were also a considerable group (9.2 per cent), including Afghanis fleeing the Soviet occupation and civil war and Iraqis of Iranian descent deported by their own government (Taleghani, 1992: 129). Between 1986 and 1991, of almost 1 million immigrants to Tehran province, immigrants from other countries continued to form a sizeable group (7 per cent). The main group (79 per cent), however, came from other provinces of Iran. Some were also migrating within the province (13 per cent) (Markaz-e Amar, 1996a: 44).

Most immigrants have come to the city for economic reasons. Research in 1985 showed the main reasons for, and the employment pattern of, immigrants to Tehran in that year (Table 5.4). When including the households who have followed family members to the city, more than three-quarters of the immigrants indicated the search for better employment prospects as their main reason. Statistics show a large degree of success for these groups. Of those immigrating to the city in the period 1986–91, only 1.7 per cent (of 10-year-olds and above) were unemployed and seeking employment. What the figures do not tell, however, is the type of jobs they have found, jobs which may include casual work such as street vending and windscreen cleaning.

Immigrants are often young. Between 1986 and 1991, around 250 000 immigrants arrived in the city, of which more than 80 per cent were in the 6–36-year-old age group. Men in the 20–24-year age group are the largest category of immigrants. In 1991, 55.5 per cent of immigrants were men (Markaz-e Motale'at, 1994: 154–5). Historically men have come first, paving the way to bring their families or start new families. The very high proportion of women among the immigrants shows widespread immigration of

FIGURE 5.5 Tea houses provide a focal point in social networks and job markets for new immigrants

households. There is a tendency to find housing near friends and relatives from the same village or town, the network which would have been instrumental in coming to Tehran in the first place and one which could continue to act as a support mechanism. Through these networks, and due to higher mobility of immigrants and cheap transport, ties with the home towns and villages remain strong. This is especially the case for construction workers who, due to the seasonal nature of their work, can spend several months in their native towns and villages (Figure 5.5).

A pattern in the period 1986–91, which contradicts historical trends, is the relatively high proportion of literacy among immigrants (87.4 per cent of six-year-olds and above). This is partly due to the large number of children of school age among the immigrant households (more than a quarter of 10-year-olds and above) (Markaz-e Motale'at, 1994: 163–6). It also contradicts the stereotypical image of illiterate peasants arriving in the metropolis from their distant villages, as depicted for years by the more settled immigrants who make up Tehran's population.

Tehran has always been a recipient of immigrants. Between 1981 and 1986, however, almost 500 000 people left the city (Markaz-e Motale'at, 1994: 152). This is partly due to the impact of revolution and war, when large numbers of emigrants left Tehran for other countries. It is also due to a process of suburbanization. The rate of immigration to the city has been declining, as many immigrants are not able to afford to live in the city and have settled in the outlying towns and villages. The impact of rationing during the war should also be taken into account, as it prevented new immigrants from settling in the city, who in turn settled in suburban locations.

As these figures show, the city of Tehran is founded on immigration. People from around the country, and to a limited degree from other countries, have come together in a relatively short period of time to constitute a gigantic metropolis. This can offer us a significant insight into urban society and the transitions in institutions and social relations in the city. Ever larger numbers of people, who have been uprooted from their previous social contexts, have created a new social world, one in which their previous habits, social norms and beliefs would only be partially recognized. This agglomeration of individuals and households with different ethnic origins, languages and dialects, and histories, has created a constant turmoil, a fast-changing environment in which old institutions have either evolved or collapsed and been replaced with new ones. The Iranian revolutions should be seen in this light, as they are caused by, and cause further, fluidity of social norms. One of the main outcomes of this social and spatial change has been a move towards individualism. The process of urban change brought with it a commodification of social relations and an emergent individualism, as individuals were no longer embedded in, and therefore constrained by, their social and environmental contexts. In spite of this trend, however, the family has remained strong.

FAMILY AND SOCIAL TRANSITION

The family continues to be a strong social and economic unit, despite the major changes that it has gone through. The main trend in Tehran, as elsewhere in urban areas, has been a decline of extended families in favour of nuclear families. As the economic base of the metropolitan household is no longer agriculture, the economic necessity of large, extended families has declined. Furthermore, the migrant, often young, families have historically left the older generation behind in their towns and villages. Intentionally or unintentionally, the modernizing governments have been promoting nuclearization of the family by all sorts of measures such as housing policy, and the wartime rationing book, among others. The high land prices have also led to the development of smaller and smaller dwellings. In this process of nuclearization, the size of the family has decreased, the age of marriage has increased, and the divorce rate has risen.

Traditionally, one of the reasons for high birth rates has been early marriages. The years 1956–76 witnessed a gradual increase in the marriage age among men and women, partly due to the immigration of men to the city, but also due to more involvement in education, unemployment, housing shortage, and the high cost of living. After the Islamic revolution, despite a continuation of these problems, the number of marriages

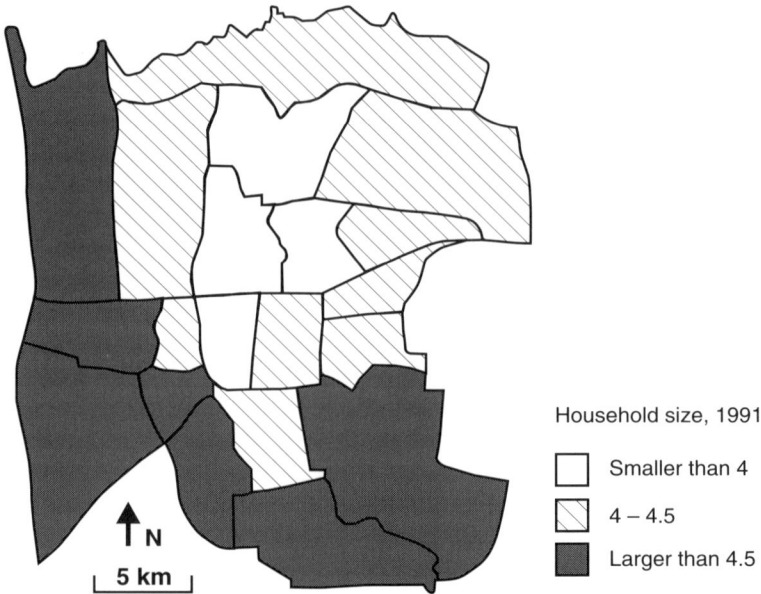

FIGURE 5.6 Household size, 1991. Central and northern districts have smaller households

increased and the average age of marriage went down, mainly for social and cultural reasons (Taleghani, 1992: 28–9). The average age for the first marriage, however, has continued to rise overall, especially in the late 1980s, to reach 24.4 for men and 21 for women in the 1990s (Markaz-e Motale'at, 1994: 106).

Divorce has a low rate. In 1994, there was one divorce for every eight marriages in the urban areas of Tehran province (*Ostan*). This, however, was much higher than the average for the country as a whole in the same year, with one divorce for every 14 marriages (Markaz-e Amar, 1996a: 48).

The largest category of households in Tehran is four-person households (22.4 per cent), followed by five-person (17.9 per cent) and three-person households (17.3 per cent) (Markaz-e Motale'at, 1994: 94). The average size of households in Tehran has become smaller over the years, from 4.9 in 1966 to 4.3 in 1991. Tehrani households are smaller than the average in the country as a whole, which was 4.89 in 1993 (Markaz-e Amar, 1994: 28). Inside the city in 1991, the middle-class areas, such as district 3, had an even smaller household size of 3.6, while the poorer district 19 on the southern outskirts of the city had a household size of 5.2 (Markaz-e Motale'at, 1994: 99) (Figure 5.6).

Despite these changes, family and kinship remain essentially strong, especially as supporting networks which allow individuals to cope with hardships of immigration, unemployment, and through various stages of life. Where the family is engaged in a collective enterprise such as a family business, it has a range of support opportunities to offer, especially to the young. For the wage earners, however, it is less possible to be of direct help unless they have access to networks through which they can find support and employment for the needy members of the family and kin and for newcomers to the labour market.

In addition to economic support, family and kinship are a meeting place, where socialization of the young and marriage are facilitated. By the 1970s, new centres for socialization, such as youth clubs, had been set up for the young and were being especially used by the middle classes. The advent of the revolution dismantled some of these centres and introduced strict rules of conduct in the relationship between young men and women. Although it opened up other avenues, such as mosques and other nuclei of political and social activities, socialization of the young remained under severe constraint. That is partly why a new emphasis was put on the family and kinship as the centres for socialization. The demands of a large metropolis, however, will not be met through these limited networks alone. As a result, the municipality of Tehran has been pursuing a policy of setting up new youth clubs and cultural centres as sites for the socialization of the young.

The height of the revolution was a period of intense politicization of households and of pluralism of political views and loyalties. But when the Islamic Republic became established, suppression of the opposition factions and parties began. Families were explicitly asked to surrender their members if they opposed the state. This caused open strife between many families, at times even leading to the execution of those arrested. In a country whose long history has witnessed constant insecurity and instability, blood ties have always been the strongest and surest ones to rely on. This was, however, an invitation to replace blood loyalty with a religious and political loyalty. In other words, collective loyalty of the revolution was taking precedence over family and group loyalty. After two decades, the intensity of the moment, and with it the collective loyalties, have faded away. The family has survived this threat, but what has also emerged from the ashes of collective emotions is a rising tide of individualism.

INDIVIDUALISM

Development of individualism, as associated with the emergence of the bourgeoisie in the West in the modern period, was almost absent in most parts of the world, including Iran, where society has historically prevailed and subordinated individuals. Ahmadi & Ahmadi (1995) argue that in Iran, the strong influence of mysticism, with its doctrine of unity of existence, has been instrumental in the non-development of the concept of the individual. They argue that the separation in Western thought between self and other has been absent from Iranian thought, whose mystical traditions have promoted a unification of self and other. Together with other factors, such as the "divine" nature of Islamic law and the persistence of despotism in the political sphere, this has led to a tendency towards conformity, rather than individuality, among Iranians. This conformity, they argue, is not an inevitable consequence of long-term instability. Conformity is especially apparent in the value given to "the collective man" (Ahmadi & Ahmadi, 1995: 398), where "an anonymous social force" (p. 396) has a strong authority over the lives of individuals.

While there is some value in this analysis of the systems of Iranian thought, we need to be aware of two points. First, that mysticism has been present in most Indo-European cultures, but it has not prevented the growth of individualism among some of them. Furthermore, the absence of humanist individualism is not confined to Iran and can be found in many parts of the world where mysticism has not been so influential in shaping cultural traditions. Second, we should note an emerging individualism in Iranian society, as manifest in Tehran, which could be a threat to its already fragmented social fabric. In a city with a large population of immigrants, who are no longer deeply rooted in a traditional socio-spatial context, the presence of a collective man and of an anonymous social force is much less felt. The social systems that are in operation are far more flexible and formless than those in towns and villages and of the cities of the past. Now social and spatial mobility means a weakening of social norms and social control of individuals. It is because of this transformation of social norms that the Islamic state felt the need to patrol the streets of Tehran to ensure conformity with Islamic rules of conduct. Earlier this century, there would have been less need for such transparent control as the social norms were effectively strong. It is true that at the time of revolution there was a strong sense of collectivity among the urban masses. This was, however, a short-lived feeling, giving place to, as before the revolution, economic individuality and instrumental rationality. It is important to note, however, that this individualism has not been translated into philosophical and political individualism. In the West, it can be argued, the influx of immigrants to the cities during the nineteenth century brought anonymity and weakening of social norms, as *Gesellschaften* emerged as opposed to *Gemeinschaften*. The Western tradition of humanism, however, had endorsed the development of political and philosophical individualism, which eventually led to democratic institutions and redefined social relations. In Iran, the existence of a split between economic and political individualism has created an environment in which social relations are associated with ambiguity and tension. It is common practice to act according to instrumental rationality of economic transactions: entering a free and mostly under-regulated market as an individual in pursuit of economic gains. It is not, however, common practice to enter the arena of decision making as an individual, despite a degree of political freedom which has been introduced after the revolution. The revolutionary movement can be seen as a major attempt to close this gap. Its outcome, however, shows a continued tension between a tendency to re-create the strong social norms of the past, which subordinated the individual, and the reality of social and economic practices, where individuals have an increasingly stronger presence.

Economic individualism in Iran is the outcome of the introduction of monetary relationships into an agrarian society since the nineteenth century. The commodification of social relations has freed many peasants from their attachment to localities and to land. As a result, large groups of individuals have migrated into cities in search of a better life promised by the oil economy. The absence of a humanist tradition, however, has prevented a cultural development of individualism. A paradoxical development after the Islamic revolution has been, on the one hand, setting up a republic and encouraging people to vote, which is based on the assumptions of individualism. On the other hand, the revolutionary ideologues have fiercely challenged Western humanism and its associated individualism, as it questions religious dogma. This shows the contradiction between humanism, with its belief in the individual, which in the West led to liberal democratic government, and the rule of the clergy, which is based on the assumption that individuals are in need of clerical supervision and control.

This combination appears to delay further the possibility of bridging the gap between economic and political individualism. The daily practices of Iran's market economy, however, show a move towards, rather than away from, individualism. If anything, the urban society of immigrants, especially in large cities like Tehran, is in danger of being driven by excessive self-interest and by egotistic behaviour, and therefore threatened by a fragmentation of social relations. It is to counter this danger that the narratives of nationalism and religious populism have been employed during the course of the twentieth century.

CULTURAL IDENTITY IN THE CITY OF STRANGERS

For those who are used to their daily routines in the city, it may seem to be a coherent place. They feel they know all its corners and it has lost its mysteries for them. But it is "their routines" and "their corners" that they are aware of. They are, or become, unaware of the plurality of the social worlds that make the city. This is a fragmented social world with a very weak public sphere. Tehran is a city of strangers. The Islamic revolution was one of the rare moments in recent history that brought these strangers together and forged a collective, but temporary, identity. It was, however, an identity based on negation. When the object of anger, the monarchy, was removed, this collective identity began to be dismantled. The city became, once again, a city of strangers, in a synthesis that was even more fragmented than before. The collective actions of the revolutionary years had developed a sense of optimism and an explosion of confidence, so essential in social development. As confidence and esteem evaporate in the face of mounting economic and social problems, pessimism once again sets in. Pessimism may have been a weapon helping the Iranian culture to survive through the ages, but now it causes further social fragmentation.

Tehran's urban society is an agglomeration of immigrants. It is a mirror of the country as a whole, as Iran is a multi-ethnic and multi-lingual country, where Kurds, Azeris, Turkmans, Arabs, Lurs, and Baluchis, among others, form large ethnic minorities. Even among the Persians, the dominant ethnic and linguistic group, there is a wide variety of accents and dialects. They all live in a vast territory with different historic and environmental specificities. As these groups have come together in Tehran, they have created a mosaic of diverse backgrounds and identities, but one dominated by the official Persian language and culture. For years, the Persians, and among them the Tehranis, have made jokes about the peoples of the provinces. These narratives of humiliation, often against the people of the Caspian coast and the Azeris, relatively prosperous regions with dense populations, have been cultural weapons in the historical competition that has shaped Iran. In different historical periods, different cities have become the capital of the country and have come to dominate politically and culturally. The last 200 years have been Tehran's turn to claim supremacy, specifically strengthened by the establishment of a unified national space under the Pahlavis. The Persian language and the Tehrani accent thus became a unifying standard imposed on other groups through mass media and education.

The prevalence of the Persian culture and language in Iran is not accidental. Ever since the migration of the Indo-Europeans into the Iranian plateau, and especially after the establishment of the Persian empire 2500 years ago, the Persian language and culture have been the dominant force in this part of the world. There have been many peaceful or forced exchanges with other civilizations of the East and West. The most notable conquests which had major impacts on the Persian culture were Greeks, Arabs, and Moguls. Also, exchanges with Romans, Ottomans, and the modern West have all been significant. The Persian language evolved through these phases but always survived and re-emerged, creating a rich literature, whose influence spread in all directions. This high culture, as exemplified by the poets Ferdowsi, Hafez, Sa'di, and Mowlavi, among others, has deep roots in society and is still a potent force. It has also lived all the time alongside other languages and cultures, some of which have come to rule Iran. For example, the Qajar tribes, who chose Tehran as their capital, were Turkish speakers. Yet they were absorbed into the Persian culture and language, like many others before them. It is only in the modern era, however, that the idea of imposing an official religion and an official language on the non-Persians has emerged. In the sixteenth century, the

Safavid kings imposed Shi'ism as the official religion of Iran and, in the twentieth century, the Pahlavi kings prevented other ethnic groups from publishing and being educated in their own languages.

This forced denial of difference, which was an official cultural policy in the Pahlavi period and was part of the narratives of nationalism, as implemented by an authoritarian regime. Its aim was to create a unified nation state as opposed to a multi-ethnic empire. It therefore manufactured and emphasized "national" rather than ethnic or religious identities. The idea of Iran as a political concept dates back to the first half of the third century. But this was a time when the primary element of "Iranian" identity was loyalty to the ruler, which was later displaced by loyalty to religion (Frye, 1993). The new form of Iranian identity was developed during the second half of the nineteenth century by modern intellectuals whose battle with political and religious absolutism culminated in the Constitutional Revolution (Ashraf, 1993). Transformed by the Pahlavi kings, the notion of national identity became a strait-jacket to undermine any manifestation of difference in a highly diverse country. They saw it as essential to move towards centralization of power and unification of the economic and political diversities of a country which was leaving feudal fragmentation behind. This nationalism therefore appeared to dismiss the possibility of various ethnic and linguistic groups living together peacefully within the same political boundary. One of the main threats of Iran's last monarch was that he saw himself as a unifying element for the multiplicity of groups who constitute Iran and that his departure would lead to the fragmentation of the country along ethnic lines. In an era of the rise of national identities, as best manifest in the Kurdish struggle for autonomy and independence, this centrifugal tendency has been a real threat for the Iranian government. The post-revolutionary government initially replaced the secular, nationalist narratives of the Pahlavis with a religious internationalism. The Shi'ite emphasis of the religious leaders, their involvement in Iranian politics, and the international pressures on Iran, however, meant a shift to religious nationalism, but one which alienates, as under the shah, the Sunni, non-Persian speakers. Rather than democratically emerging, through the establishment of a civil society and the promotion of citizenship, social integration has been forceful and authoritarian, relying on nationality and religion, whose often narrow definitions act as exclusionary rather than integrative factors. This is why difference has always been feared by the politicians. The rapid pace with which strangers have come together in Tehran, and the absence of a public sphere in which they could explore and shape new social relationships, have kept the city of strangers fragmented and always explosive.

Tehran, therefore, both before and after the revolution, has been seen as a melting pot, rather than a mosaic of difference. In the battle of status, which signifies all social strata from the poor to the rich, being an immigrant is something to escape from. Being born in Tehran is traded in this battle as

FIGURE 5.7 Tup-Khaneh (Imam Khomeini) Square, "the best known destination for any stranger"

some valuable weapon against those who are from the provinces. The emphasis on the Persian language and the Tehrani accent is ever present. The Tehrani accent becomes the standard means of communication which the immigrants wish to acquire. Mojabi (1993) explains how in and around the old squares such as Tup-Khaneh, "the best known destination for any stranger" (p. 160) (Figure 5.7), and Enghelab, which is now the main gate of entry into the city, new immigrants can be heard in their diversity of dialects and accents. Soon, however, they find out that their accent is a cause of discrimination and disadvantage. To compensate for this, they train themselves in the capital's accent, as heard on the radio, television, and in cinemas. By learning "a fake voice which is nobody's voice" (p. 163), Mojabi argues, they are distanced from their origins. Furthermore, communication through fake voices collapses, as they have no mastery of this fake language. There is no direct relationship between the concepts, developed and nurtured in a variety of languages, dialects, and accents, and the fake means of communication. This is a gap which leads to alienation and a collapse of communication.

There have been, at the same time, attempts to make sense of this diversity and to make the best of the pluralism of the city, as best exemplified by the optimistic evaluation of difference in the film *White Balloon*. However, the large number of immigrants in the city frightens many established, middle-class Tehranis, who see these strangers as a source of evil. Fear of disorder and of loss of identity are recurring themes in today's debates (Aslani, 1992; Daneshvar, 1994). We hear frequently that the city lacks identity, and that it is a victim of the diversity of cultures which meet in the city (Mousavi, 1992). Immigrants are blamed for turning the city into a large village, as they are not familiar with what is referred to as urban culture (*Bulletin*, No. 3, Mordad 1371: 7–10) and therefore are a liability for the city as a whole. The city is simply dismissed as a malignant tumour, rather than a human settlement, and that this tumour will eventually cause a painful death (Teymouri, 1992). The municipality's campaign for building public libraries and cultural centres is partly meant to "raise" the standards of urban culture by providing cultural, sport, and leisure facilities for a young urban population (Ardalan, 1995a). In the absence of other channels of socialization apart from family and kinship, social integration is in need of such support. The development of these centres, however, is by no means uncontroversial, as they stand in competition with the more traditional centres of mosques and local militias. The elitism of the upper social groups, who look down upon the new arrivals and wish to educate them, is a sign and a cause of more deeply rooted divides.

SOCIAL POLARIZATION AND EXCLUSION

Urban society in Tehran is deeply polarized. As will be shown in Chapter 6, this has found a clear spatial manifestation, where the north of the city is where the rich and upper middle classes live and the south the poor and the marginal. The immigrants who enter the city find a place in the city or on the peripheries, depending on their social networks and available resources.

The oil boom of the 1960s and 1970s had massively increased the resources available to Iranian society, and in particular Tehranis who controlled much of this income. There was, however, a major divide in terms of access to these earnings. While large groups of immigrants would populate the city, fleeing rural poverty in the hope of a decent life, a minority of Tehranis were becoming extremely affluent. A well-known advertising campaign by Iran's national airline used to invite potential passengers to wake up in Tehran but have breakfast in Paris or London. The rich were acquiring real estate and shares in international markets, while the poor were living in shanty towns on the margins of the city. The cultural divide was also becoming unbridgeable. While annual art festivals, such as the one in Shiraz, would gather together an international elite of the art scene, large parts of the population were alienated from the cultural products offered in these events. Politically, the majority of the population were excluded from any decision making by an authoritarian and often corrupt government.

It was in reaction to this severe combination of political, economic, and cultural polarization that the protest movements and ultimately the revolution took shape. What became the Islamic revolution occurred because a coalition of most shades of political opinion took to the streets, demanding a share in decision making, a better distribution of wealth, and the right not to be alienated in their own cultural sphere.

The outcome of almost two decades of revolutionary rule, however, has not offered a remedy for these ills. In the revolution, political power was seized by the participation of the public and a system of voting was introduced. In practice, however, the governance system has deliberately excluded many political groups. One of the key themes that made President Khatami so popular with the voters was his discussion of the need for development of a civil society. In the cultural arena, the popular culture, with its strong traditional and religious overtones, has been revived and has taken centre stage. This, however, has excluded any other form of cultural expression and dialogue. It appears to be suspicious of any change, wishing, nostalgically and even romantically, to re-create a golden past which might never have existed. Furthermore, it is under threat from mounting economic and social pressures. While some improvement in the political and cultural scenes is identifiable, the economic prospects have become much worse. The economic, and subsequently social, polarization has intensified. The revolution, the war with Iraq, American economic sanctions, the fall in oil income, a weak economy, and high inflation have all led to a substantial impoverishment of the masses, while a new minority of affluent groups has emerged. The impoverished masses, who were the backbone of the revolution and the war, find themselves at a loss. The massive and increasing foreign debts mean that even hope in the future is being mortgaged to current economic failure. These are signs of more instability for a society whose revolutionary heritage constantly reminds it that nothing is immutable.

CONCLUSION: IMMIGRATION, DIFFERENCE AND SOCIAL POLARIZATION

The population of Tehran has grown to be a city of 6.5 million set in a metropolitan province of 11.1 million. This growth, which started when Tehran became the capital, has continued to this day, although there is a slowdown in population growth. As opposed to the decay in inner-city populations, suburbs have grown, either as a result of the outmigration of the city inhabitants in search of better environmental quality, or of those forced to live on the margins of the city due to high living costs. The Tehrani population is young. Its family structure has changed to become smaller and less stable. But it is still a quite strong social and economic unit which, together with the wider network of the kinship, protects its members against the threats of the big city.

The population of Tehran has mainly grown through attracting immigrants, surplus populations of the provinces looking for work and better living conditions. This has uprooted households and individuals from their social contexts and, together with commodification of social relations, has promoted a degree of individualism in economic relationships. Political and cultural individualism, as supported through the establishment of a public sphere and civil society, has lagged behind. The cultural identity of the city of strangers has therefore been in a state of tension, as the city has had to absorb a constant flow of immigrants from around the country and from abroad. Social exclusion in economic, political, and cultural areas is detectable, as access to resources, to decision making, and to common narratives are often limited. Social exclusion and polarization have found a spatial manifestation in the form of a north–south divide.

From outside, post-revolutionary Iranian society has been interpreted as a traditional society challenging the disruptions of an imposed modernization process. The problem with this interpretation is that it takes society as a static entity which is acting in self-defence. In complete contrast, Iranian society, before and especially during and after the revolution, has been a fast-changing, dynamic social environment. When we observe society from the inside, we find a constant tension between rival narratives, all attempting to make sense of, and control, a highly volatile set of circumstances. A very young population is likely to move in any direction, as it is not yet well connected to the collective narratives and memories. The governments' inherent political and economic weakness has left the rulers defenceless, hence encouraging them to turn to authoritarian practices. After the revolution, it became common among the new wave of dissidents to expect another revolution to happen, rectifying the mistakes of the existing one. A society which has experienced two revolutions and many more upheavals is likely to look at social norms and practices at best as temporary, leaving the social world and the political authorities in a constant crisis of legitimacy. The young population, fluctuation of the oil price in the global market, the short history of the republican government, its expanding but still limited authority, a weak public sphere, and many new and changing institutions all signify the continuation of a fluidity of social processes which can easily turn into a new flood.

6

URBAN SPACE

In this chapter we look at some of the characteristics of the natural space in which Tehran has been developed. Then we focus on the city's spatial structure: how land use is broadly organized and how the social space of the city is therefore stratified. Finally, we will look at the details of urban space, the way the morphology of street pattern and building form has changed over time. Together, they offer an understanding of the space of the city. Many of the characteristics of the urban space that are introduced here will be analysed in more detail in Part Three, which traces the urban development process. The next chapter will also deal with some urban problems with direct spatial significance, such as housing and transport.

TOPOGRAPHY

The gigantic metropolis is scattered across a large area. The natural space which it has occupied and transformed has had a major influence on the qualities of urban space through its distinctive topography. Iran has been generally likened to a bowl, with a highland interior, much of it with an altitude of more than 1000 m above sea-level, surrounded by an outer rim (Fisher, 1968). This rim is formed of high and prominent mountain chains, also extensive in ground area, in the north and west, and of narrower and lower ones in the east and south. Because of the aridity of the central highlands, with two large deserts in the middle, most of the towns and villages are situated along the northern mountain range of Alburz and the western chain of Zagros. Here factors such as availability of water, arable land, safety, and a more moderate climate have made the foot of the mountains favourable for settlement.

The Alburz chain, which runs from north-west to north-east with an average width of about 100 km, is unusually high, appearing as an almost continuous wall from both sides (Fisher, 1968). Approximately in its centre lies Mount Damavand, 5678 m high, Iran's greatest peak and higher than any other summit to the west of it in Asia or in Europe. Because of its restricted width, the mountain chain is extremely steep, especially on the northern slopes which rise directly from the coastal plain of the Caspian, which lies at or just below sea-level. This relative difference is reduced on the southern side due to the great altitude of the inner plateau, where the land surface drops more gradually by shallow terraces and low bluffs to the flat wastes of Kavir.

The city of Tehran is located on these southern slopes of the Alburz chain (Figure 6.1), not far from the Damavand ridge, as the summit can be seen from the city on clear days. Directly 20 km to the north lies the To-Chal ridge, 3933 m high, which dominates the city (Lockhart, 1960). To the south, Tehran stretches to Kavir, the central desert of Iran. The centre of the city is on longitude 51° 26' E and latitude 35° 41' N (Kariman, 1976: 8).

The northernmost limit of the city, as established by the municipality, is the contour of 1800 m above sea-level. When compared to the height of 1160 m on its southeastern border, it shows a difference of more than 640 m between the two furthest points of the city. The difference increases as we approach the desert on the southern outskirts of the city, about 30 km away from the northern heights. This dramatic difference in height has had significant impacts on the characteristics of urban space in Tehran.

The wall of mountains has limited the growth of the city in the north and, to a lesser extent, in the east. To the south, the desert is a barrier to expansion, although less definitive than the mountains. It is on the western side of the city that there has been no natural barrier and the built environment has gradually stretched towards the city of Karaj, 40 km away, which has become one of the most rapidly growing suburbs of the capital.

The north–south slope, on which the city is built, has provided a natural setting in which the process of social stratification has taken a particular shape. The north has been traditionally associated with privileges such as a better supply of water, a higher defensive value, a visual dominance over the south and the countryside, and a better climate. Given the scale of the old city, it appears that these privileges have been instrumental in the location of the citadel in the northern side of the city. They were enjoyed by Tehran itself as a northern suburb of the ancient city of Ray. From the early nineteenth century, some of the villages to the north of Tehran, now incorporated into the urban fabric, became the summer retreats of royal and aristocratic families and, later, major foreign embassies. This set a pattern which became a widespread phenomenon, as those who could afford to choose where to live gradually moved out to the north. The south remained for those whose freedom of choice was more limited.

The presence of a wall of mountains at the northern end of the city and the downward slope make possible a sense of orientation which in many areas of the city can be strongly felt. Since the street system had been adjusted to the slope and the mountains, nearly all the north–south streets can be distinguished as being on the slope with a view of the snow-covered mountains of the north. The slope therefore gives the city traveller a clear sense of orientation: ascending when moving to the north and descending when moving to the south (Figure 6.2).

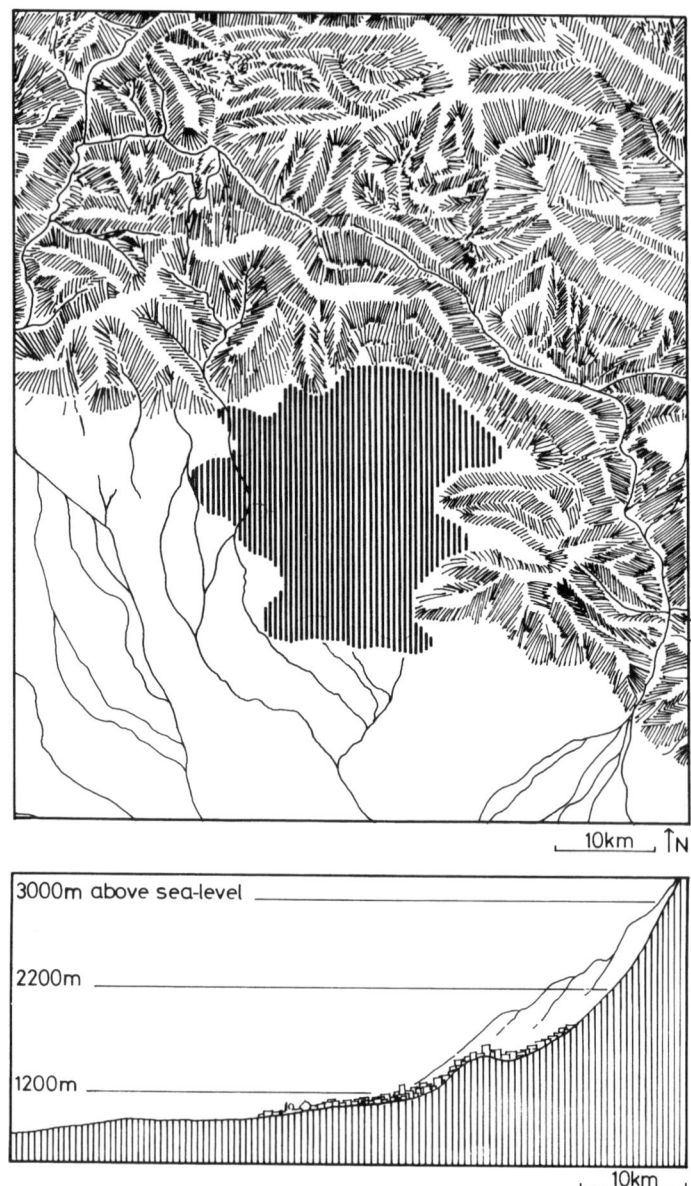

FIGURE 6.1 Tehran sits on the southern slopes of the Alburz mountain range

FIGURE 6.2 The street system is adjusted to the landform (Africa Avenue)

The difference in the height of the northern and southern areas has made possible a degree of visibility over the city. From many northern vantage points, vast areas in the central and southern city are visible, while some of the southern parts have a glimpse of the north. This has always given the north a sense of visual (and social) superiority, a sense which is now seriously limited due to the smog which prevents any panoramic views over the city. The existence of hilltops and valleys in the north and flat land in the south has led to the emergence of a dual typology of skyline. Whereas the north, with its varied topography and the relative wealth of its inhabitants, has a diversity in its skyline, the southern skyline is less diverse and more monotonous. An exception to this is the old fabrics in Tehran and Shahr-e Ray, where the domes and minarets of the mosques and shrines create a skyline of more diversity and richness. Another impact of topography on urban form, coupled with the rapid and uneven expansion of the city, is a degree of inconsistency in urban fabric, where many land plots are left undeveloped. A number of sites have been regarded as inappropriate or very expensive to be developed, while others await development some time in the future.

Located at the foot of the Alburz chain of mountains, Tehran is vulnerable to the flow of the excess water of the heavy rains which sometimes, in the form of floods, attack the city. A number of canals and seasonal rivers, called *maseel*, have traditionally channelled this excess water away from built-up areas. Since the *maseels* have been used to safeguard the city from flood, they are not usually found in the older areas near the city centre and the south. The route of these canals and rivers, especially the larger ones, has been effective in defining limits to the development of the urban fabric. In the built-up areas which developed around the suburban villages and along the main arteries, the *maseel* played an important role as the physical boundaries of growth, creating gaps in the urban fabric. However, in some areas they were filled and developed by speculators, which has caused major disasters. These disasters, with few exceptions such as the major flood of the summer of 1987 in the north city, have always hit the poor neighbourhoods of the south. These southern neighbourhoods have also suffered from the problems of sewage disposal and water distribution, where the general slope has favoured the north. In Chapter 7, we will see how these problems have had major social and environmental consequences.

CLIMATE

Like most parts of Iran, Tehran has a hot arid climate. The Alburz mountain range separates it from the Caspian Sea, the most humid area of Iran with up to 1950 mm annual precipitation (Ganji, 1968). In Tehran, the annual average temperature is 17°C, with an average temperature of 22.6°C in summer and 11.5°C in winter. The extremes of temperature can reach a maximum of 44°C in summer and a minimum of −14.8°C in winter. Throughout the year, there is an average precipitation of 229 mm and an average 51 days of frost (Markaz-e Amar, 1986a: 11).

The juxtaposition of high mountains and desert has created a diversity of climatic conditions in the metropolis, which is revealed by looking at 1970 climatic data from three stations across the slope (IMO, 1974). In Sa'dabad Palace, the northernmost station with a latitude of 35° 48' N and a height of 1700 m above sea-level, there was a total annual precipitation of 309.5 mm and 88 days with temperatures below freezing. The mean daily temperature was 26.1°C in August and 1.2°C in January. Further down in the south city centre, in Park-e Shahr station located in the old core, with a latitude of 35° 41' N and a height of 1210 m, the annual rainfall totalled 157.6 mm with 45 days below freezing, both figures nearly half those of Sa'dabad. Here the mean daily temperatures of January and August were 3.6°C and 28.1°C, both higher than Sa'dabad. The precipitation figure again dramatically changes at Varamin station, beyond the southernmost areas of Tehran and on the edge of the desert. At a latitude of 35°C 19' N and a height of 1000 m, the total annual rainfall was only 86.7 mm, 55 days below freezing, and daily means of 3.9°C in January and 28.8°C in July.

This climatic change has been very important in determining both social and physical characteristics of the urban space (Figure 6.3). The northern area, because of its cooler summers, has been traditionally preferred by the better-off as their summer residence. With an increase in mobility

FIGURE 6.3 The better climate of the northern foothills has attracted the better-off

and availability of fuel, it became their permanent living place, from which they commute to the city centre. This has been reflected in the large plots of land and the large number of trees in the northern areas. In contrast, the proximity of the south to the desert brings with it hotter and dustier summers. Here the smaller land plots are more densely built and the presence of green space is rare.

The layout of old Tehran was strongly adapted to climatic conditions and shared its basic features with many other cities of Iran and the Middle East. It has been argued that the marked uniformity in urban areas of these hot arid zones is due to the significance of climatic factors in their urban forms. This has been best characterized by two features: narrow, twisting streets, and large open courtyards and internal gardens. The narrow streets served as reservoirs of cool, fresh air. The courtyards, with their closed vistas, performed the same function by retaining any cool air that may be deposited during the night (Fathy, 1986: 64). High walls and deep courtyards were used to enhance this cooling process (Tavassoli, 1982). The old urban fabric in Tehran was built as compactly as possible, to reduce the surfaces in direct contact with sunlight and to increase the shaded surfaces. The streets were narrow and twisting with overhangs to create as much shadow as possible. However, the new urban fabric is marked by wide streets and an absence of central courtyards. In the morphology of the new public spaces which have emerged, climatic rationality was rarely used as a leading guide. This loss of environmental awareness and predominance of other factors in the making of urban space can also be seen in the choice of building materials and form, although to a lesser extent.

If the change in street dimensions and form was not a climatic necessity, the orientation of the dwellings, and subsequently the street pattern, has incorporated a level of environmental rationality. The wind direction and the sun are both contributing factors in determining the orientation of buildings and street patterns. According to the process of absorption or loss of heat by the great mass of the Alburz range, the air circulation in Tehran is dominated by currents which move from the mountains to the valleys or vice versa (de Planhol, 1968: 454–5). This has set the desirable orientation of the buildings along the north–south axis so as to exploit the much-needed freshness of the air currents during the long summer. If the buildings were slightly turned towards the south-west, as many traditional structures did, they could also benefit from the strong western and south-western winds (Rahbari, 1986), which entered the region due to the absence of natural barriers.

Choosing the general north–south orientation is consistent with the fact that the main façades should be facing south to maximize exposure to the winter sun. A combination of these two shows the climatic necessity of the north–south orientation of dwellings. In the old, large courtyard houses, the northern and southern parts of the building were devoted to winter and summer use respectively. When the morphology of land plots changed into geometrical regularity of new land subdivisions, this migratory system within the house was abandoned. In spite of the loss of the central courtyard as an island of cool fresh air, the new building form has retained some climatic awareness. The building is often located in the northern part of the plot, which made better use of the winter sun. This was the basic unit of the gridiron pattern of streets, which was set in the 1930s and was the basis of future developments.

Every single building modifies the climate around it by affecting the radiation regime of adjacent areas and by interfering with the wind pattern (Gates, 1972). An urban fabric, as a group of buildings and activities, has a considerable impact on the climate to the extent that it can assume equal importance with regional factors or the influence of topography in controlling local climate. In other words, "the cities create their own climate" (Smith, 1975: 48). By replacing vegetation with large areas of concrete and brick, the natural radiation balance is disturbed, the wind pattern is limited, and the water vapour balance is upset (Munn, 1966). In the city, therefore, radiation, relative humidity, and wind speed fall, as opposed to the increase in temperature, clouds and rainfall, and especially contaminants such as dust particles and carbon dioxide (Peterson, 1969). The rapid expansion of Tehran has had enormous effects on its climatic conditions. The pressure for development, and the lack or the weakness of environmental control, resulted in the disappearance of large gardens and farms to be replaced by high-density residential areas, creating a city with strikingly limited green space. The immediate impact of the climatic change on urban form has been reflected in the drive for further suburbanization. Through generating atmospheric pollution, this has enhanced and indeed intensified, the north–south structural divide.

THE SIZE OF THE CITY

The first important dimension of Tehran's urban form which requires explanation is the size of the city, now accommodating more than 6.5 million people in some 600 km^2 (Figure 6.4). The main reason for this large size is the rapid and disproportionate growth of Tehran since it became the capital city of Iran 200 years ago: its population has grown 400 times, its area 142.5 times, and its density 2.8 times. The living place of almost a fifth of the country's urban population, Tehran is much larger than any of the secondary cities of Iran. Excluding its suburbs, this is a city which extends over some 600 km^2 to include all the previously separate settlements and suburban villages. It now extends from the foot of the mountains in the north to the edge of the desert in the south, embracing both Shemiran and Ray. Including its suburbs, this is a vast conglomeration which stretches beyond municipal boundaries, especially towards the west where there has been no natural limits to its development, to be nearly linked with the suburban city of Karaj 40 km away.

This can be explained by the political, economic, and cultural transformation of Iran, which has caused a considerable change in demographic patterns and its geographical distribution. The transformation process started with the military and economic advancement of the rival international powers of the nineteenth century into Iran. This led to the restructuring of agriculture, the main basis of the economy, to substitute cash crops for subsistence crops, resulting in commodification of agricultural land and produce. The improvements in communication and sanitary conditions were followed by an increased rate of population growth.

Ultimately, commodification of agriculture, increase in foreign trade, and demographic change caused the creation of surpluses of capital and labour to be absorbed in the development of urban areas. These surpluses continued to grow even faster after major developments in the twentieth century, such as the discovery and exploitation of oil, which created an increasingly large revenue, and the land reform, which undermined the old landlords and gave rise to the migration of rural populations. The drive for industrialization and the growth of the tertiary sector, which accompanied the blight of agriculture, were among other major factors which made urban areas the recipients of massive immigration from rural areas.

Parallel with this economic restructuring, which gradually integrated Iran's economy into the world's capitalist economy, was political centralization.

FIGURE 6.4 Tehran's urban fabric

Resulting from the international challenge of the great powers to the sovereignty of the state and from the demand of the emerging capitalist economy to develop regional and national markets, an increasingly centralizing government emerged. The government, which was an intermediary agency between the rival factions of a parochialist social structure, rose to become the sole dominant force, mostly through the dismantling of those social factions and the political opposition, as well as through its monopoly over oil as the main source of revenue.

The direct outcome of these processes of political centralization and economic transformation was the emergence of Tehran as the largest concentration of wealth and population. It was the seat of this centralized power, the ruler, the army, and the bureaucracy. It was, therefore, capable of extracting the surpluses of capital and labour from other parts of the country. A major part of these surpluses were switched into the production of the built environment, hence a growth in the size of the urban fabric and a considerable expansion of the construction industry, both giving rise to further immigration. Through this circular process, there has been a general increase in land prices and, as accompanied by planning rules and regulations, an intensified use of land and a rising density. The availability of new means of transport and cheap fuel, which has followed these earlier phases of growth, has spread the overcrowded city in all directions.

NORTH–SOUTH DUALITY

There is a clear north–south divide in the urban structure. The northern half of the city, where the middle and upper classes live, is distinguished by a wide range of social and physical privileges over the southern half. The north has tree-lined streets with larger houses, lower densities, higher land prices, smaller households, higher rates of literacy and employment, higher concentrations of modern facilities and amenities, and more green space (Figures 6.5 and 6.6). With a more diverse skyline and a degree of visual supremacy over the south, the north enjoys a more moderate climate and is a safer place as regards floods, underground sewage, and atmospheric pollution. In earlier periods, the privileges of the north included a better water supply and a higher defensive value. Because of these privileges, and enhancing them, was the location of the citadel and, later the palace complexes, in the northernmost areas of the city. The south, however, lies at the opposite end of the spectrum in relation to these characteristics. In short, the affluent north and the poor south are separated by a wide social and physical gap.

This duality has replaced an early nineteenth-century urban structure in which, with the exception of the royal compound, rich and poor lived together within four distinctive urban quarters. However, the first transformation of Tehran, beginning in 1868, laid the foundations of a bipolar

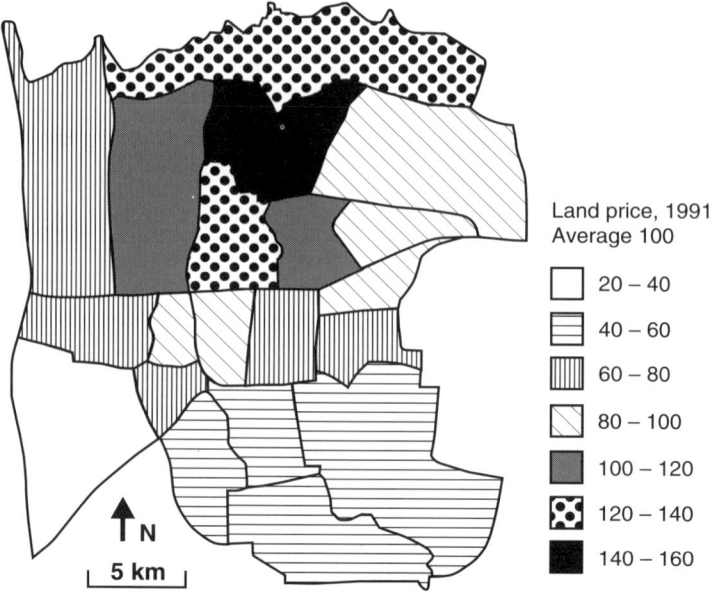

FIGURE 6.5 Land prices in the north and south show a sharp contrast (1991, average 100)

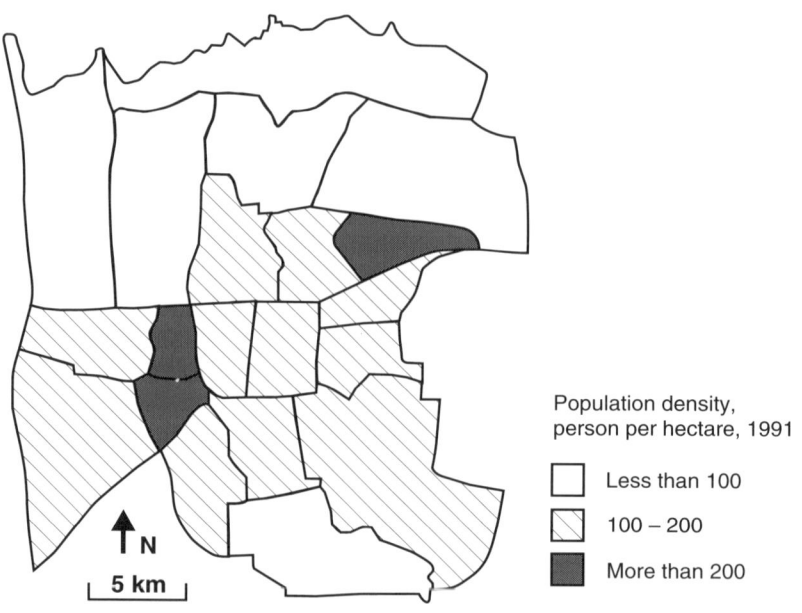

FIGURE 6.6 Population density is higher in the central and southern districts (1991, people per hectare)

city by expanding the urban fabric through the addition of new, upper-class quarters. The bipolarity of urban fabric was the spatial manifestation of the emerging social stratification, which in turn was associated with the integration of the country into the world capitalist market. The urban structure which developed afterwards has kept this bipolarity ever since.

The second transformation of Tehran, in the 1930s, was also an outcome of social stratification, as well as giving impetus to furthering that process. Both of these phases were carried out by the largest and most powerful development agency, the government. The urban fabric was opened up to support the new social and economic relations of an emerging market economy, by easing the movement of capital, goods, and services and by increasing the controllability of the townspeople by the centralizing government.

After the establishment of the spatial divide, it has been enhanced and reproduced through a range of activities. A land and property price mechanism has institutionalized the difference between urban areas. Supporting this spatial stratification were a new planning system, devised in the 1960s, and the patterns of distribution of development resources. The factors which prevented large sections of the population from gaining access to land and property and enhanced the spatial divide included: the rising prices of building materials; the higher increase in wages in the construction industry; the rising immigration of the unskilled workers and the skills gap; and the policies of the banks and financial institutions, which favoured middle- and higher-income groups. This spatial divide has been tightly related to the reproduction of the social divide ever since. The supremacy of the north has been institutionalized through its physical qualities, such as its better climate, and through its socially constructed qualities, such as the fact that the investment in land is potentially higher there. The widespread use of cars and the opening up of the urban fabric gave a freedom of choice and movement to those who had access to money to separate themselves from those who were deprived of this access. The former were, therefore, capable of manifesting the geographical expression of a social and economic phenomenon (Figure 6.7).

This pattern of north–south segregation reflects the wage stratifications of a society in which the relationships are now increasingly defined according to the access of individuals to money, as distinct from the earlier periods when communal bonds were far more important, as reflected in the factionalism of the social structure and urban space. The communal bonds which made the urban quarters relatively coherent physical and social entities were gradually substituted by the individualism which was the outcome of the increasing prevalence of the money economy. This debased the social rationality of the members of these communities to be undermined by the instrumental rationality of the individuals. Nevertheless, some of these communal bonds have survived and have found spatial

FIGURE 6.7 Higher densities and lower quality of environment in the southern parts of the city

manifestations, although with diminishing importance. These are reflected in the more or less distinguishable residential areas of the ethnic and religious minorities as well as of the different lifestyles produced by the clash of modernity and traditionalism. This created a secular space in the north, in line with the incoming social environment, leaving the religious institutions for the south, where the previous social habits and beliefs have continued to exist. Also distinguishable are the rural settlements which have been absorbed by the expanding city while retaining many of their characteristics.

Despite some early attempts by the revolutionary government, the north–south divide has continued as the main feature of the city's spatial structure. There may have been some degree of success in changing the secular character of the north. But the intensified social polarization which has followed the revolution and the war has operated to maintain the social and physical divide which is so clearly visible in Tehran.

CORE–PERIPHERY DUALITY

There is a recognizable difference between the core and periphery of the city. The central areas, comprising the old city and its northward expansion between 1868 and the Second World War, are where most of the business activities and services are concentrated. Next to these areas are the intermediate areas characterized by the prevalence of residential uses. Enclosing these two are the peripheral areas with their lower densities and rates of activities, and their higher rates of growth. The only exception to this concentric pattern has been an increase in density in some southern areas, where the model is modified by the impact of the north–south divide. The city, therefore, shows a combination of the three classical models of urban structure: it has a concentric as well as a sectoral structure, and has become multinuclear after the annexation of surrounding settlements.

The concentric pattern has resulted from three distinct, but interrelated, processes: the historically established character of the central bazaar, the rapid outward expansion of the urban fabric, and the competition for sites within this urban development process.

From 1553, when Tehran was for the first time circumvallated and emerged as a city, to 1868, when these walls were replaced by the new, outlying city walls, the urban fabric had grown slowly, especially before Tehran was selected as the capital in 1786. During this period of growth, the pattern of the central bazaar of the city, similar to other cities of the Middle East, was developed. The main commercial and industrial activities were concentrated along the streets of the central bazaar. This created a centrality in urban structure, which was inherited and transformed by the next stages of urban development. During the second half of the nineteenth century and the first half of the twentieth, the size of the city grew fast. Yet it was the inter-war destruction of the city walls, the improvement in communication, and the increase in the use of vehicles which gave rise to the unprecedented suburbanization after the Second World War. This was a process encouraged and supported by the state through its policies of decentralization and growth management.

Developed by the private sector on a speculative basis, most of the post-Second World War suburban developments focused on housing. The pace of urban development was so fast that the provision of public facilities and infrastructure could not keep up with the needs of the new areas, which partly explains why so few facilities are found in these dormitory suburbs. The old city, with its limited facilities, had to provide the infrastructure and services for an ever-increasing population. The planning system, with its policy of containment of growth within the five-year boundary, also contributed to further concentration of facilities in the centre.

In this context of rapid, outward expansion of the physical fabric, competition between individuals for sites has been introduced mainly through the extension of commodity relations to urban space by the commodification of urban land. Development agencies, increasingly with the purpose of exchange, as distinct from the predominant purpose of use, have been involved in the production of space. In this process, they have been competing for desirable locations, which has been reflected in the land price mechanism. Their competition for sites was eased by the opening up of the urban fabric, the imposition of the new road system upon the old city by the public development agencies. The outcome of this competition has been a concentration of facilities and services in the central areas, enhancing the pattern of the central bazaar in the heart of the city. The central areas have been desirable for the competing agencies because of their higher level of accessibility and the wider geographical area they serve, as compared to the peripheries which would only provide services on a more local basis. Combined with the historical pattern of the central bazaar, these two processes of outward expansion and the competition for the centrally located sites have resulted in an urban structure which has a distinguishable core–periphery relationship. This also explains the land-use pattern of the quarters in the central areas, where economic activities have been rapidly increasing. They have encroached upon the residential areas, pushing them towards peripheries or containing them inside the centres of urban blocks.

Nevertheless, after the initial stages of concentration in the central areas, there has emerged a growing decentralization and suburbanization process, as encouraged by both public and private agencies. This has been through rules and regulations, such as the policies of the Tehran Comprehensive Plan and also the revolutionary government's traffic management programmes which aimed at reducing the density and congestion of the central areas. These measures have led to deterioration of environmental quality in the central areas and the gradual development of peripheral subcentres.

SUBURBAN SETTLEMENTS

The spread of satellite settlements around the urban fabric is another major characteristic of Tehran's urban form. It is essentially the general pattern which the process of suburbanization has taken. The main reasons for the development of suburban settlements are the growing number of immigrants who cannot live in the city or those migrating out of the city to find better living standards (Mousavi, 1998). This has resulted in the concentration of new urban development in the existing suburban villages and towns and also in new settlements.

The rural settlements around Tehran, which have been engulfed by its expanding fabric or are still separate from it, are the main nuclei of most new suburbs, which have developed through the gradual addition of new built-up areas. The growing size of the development agencies has brought a drive towards the production of larger developments in search of larger profits. Whereas small development agencies are only capable of infill development or gradual additions to the urban fringe, large agencies have been able to produce new towns and townlets around the city. These were made possible with the increasing availability of credit, as the surplus of oil revenue was switched to the construction sector by banks and financial institutions. The organization of these large development agencies also benefited from the surplus of labour, as provided by the rapid population growth and the blight of agriculture by the government. In addition to the more formal channels and agencies, informal networks and procedures have been involved in the development of suburban settlements, often consisting of squatters or the poor neighbourhoods of the south.

AXIALITY

Another characteristic of Tehran's urban structure has been its axiality: there is a central axis linking the south-centre to the northernmost areas, along which most of the facilities and amenities are located and the land prices are at their peak. There is also a secondary, east–west axis which intersects at right angles with the main axis. The major squares along these two main axes of the urban structure are the city's focal points and have the highest land prices. The primary axis is formed of a number of north–south streets, among which a high street, Vali Asr, predominates. Similarly, the secondary axis centres on a single street, Enghelab (Figure 6.8).

Although there is not enough evidence to find the reasons for this axiality, we can put forward three possible explanations: we can argue that the axiality is the outcome of the combination of other main characteristics of the urban structure, that it is a result of the historical power relations in society, and that the axiality of urban structure is a historical concept of space in Iran.

The main central axis may be seen as the outcome of a combination of the north–south and the core–periphery relations. The concentric urban structure which results from a core–periphery relationship has been affected here by the north–south divide. The economic and social dominance of the north, as established during the historic process of urban development, has caused a modification of the city centre. The elongated form of the city centre, therefore, has resulted from two sets of formative forces: on the one hand, the old bazaar, the opening up of the urban fabric, and the competition for sites within urban space have intensified the use of central areas. On the other hand, a northwards movement of the city, which polarized the urban structure, has caused a northwards extension of the city centre. The divide between north and south has created a border area, as represented by the secondary axis which is also a major part of the city centre linking the main roads out towards east and west (Figure 6.9).

The second explanation for the axiality is provided by power relations, namely the relationship between the ruler and the ruled. We may argue that in a society with a millennia-old heritage of despotic rule, the position, and hence the location, of the ruler is significant in affecting the urban structure, as best shown by the distinctiveness of the citadel and the city in the old spatial relations. Along the main route to the seat of the shahs, which started at the main gate of the city, were concentrated the main economic activities, facilities, and services. This implies the intermediary role and the dominance of the ruler in daily life and the attempts of the development agencies to

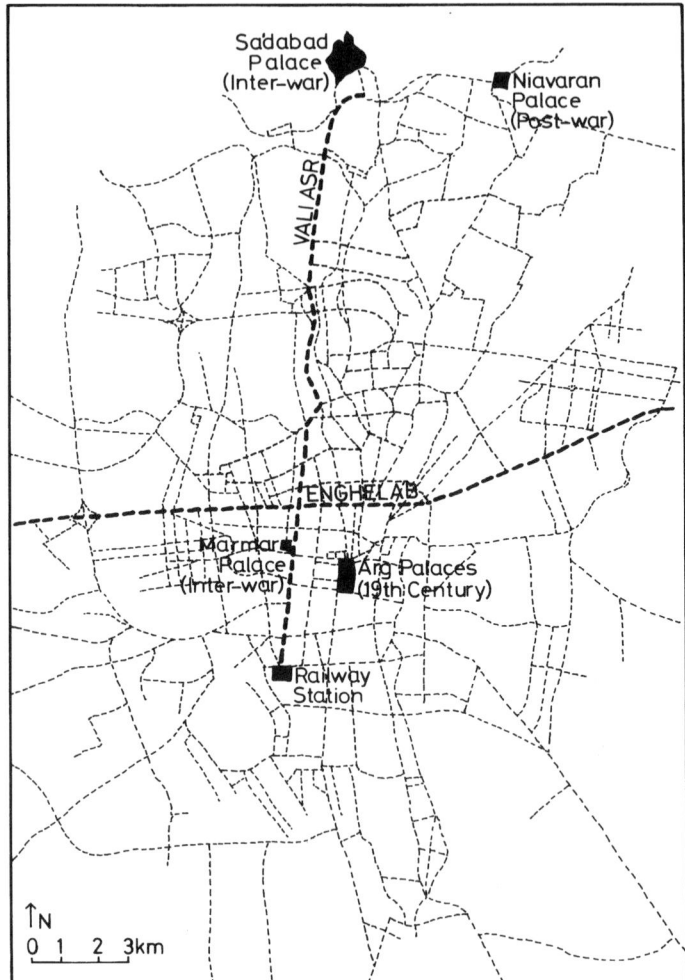

FIGURE 6.8 Two main axes can be identified in the spatial structure of the city

adapt themselves to this framework while being aware of other social and economic structures. This has been a characteristic of Tehran both in the nineteenth century and in the twentieth, when, until the Islamic revolution, the dramatic social and economic transformations of society had left the institution of executive monarchy almost intact.

The third explanation may be seen in close relation to the second. It is another historic precedence for axiality, which is traceable at least for 2500 years in Iran: the pattern of intersecting main axes leading to four gates on four sides. This is a symbolic pattern which, in geometric or irregular forms, has survived in collective memory throughout history and has been used in

FIGURE 6.9 Enghelab (formerly Shah-Reza) Avenue is the main east–west axis of the city

urban forms as well as in gardens and smaller-scale developments. We will return to these themes in Chapters 12 and 13.

STREET SYSTEM

The change in the street system, from traditional to modern, is another characteristic of Tehran's urban form. The traditional system, based on pedestrian movement, was a hierarchical distribution pattern of narrow, twisting, partly roofed streets leading to culs-de-sac which ended in groups of buildings (Figure 6.10). The spine of this pattern was a local high street, a bazaar. Upon this pattern, which had evolved over long periods of time according to strong social and environmental rationalities, was imposed an orthogonal network of roads, gradually eliminating the culs-de-sac. The new network was an open matrix which would ease the flow of people and resources into the urban space. With the change of movement from pedestrian to vehicular, the gridiron was meant to maximize mobility and accessibility, hence the disappearance of the culs-de-sac (Figure 6.11). With the introduction of the motor car and the rise in its ownership, the urban form has been transformed to be adapted to this technological innovation

FIGURE 6.10 The narrow, twisting streets leading to culs-de-sac were an integral part of the old urban fabric

which has been increasingly determining the size and pattern of urban streets and squares.

The state, through direct intervention or through the regulatory framework of the planning system, was capable and willing to tear down the old urban fabric and impose a new order on the city. This was carried out through physical surgery of the urban fabric by an increasingly bureaucratic municipal organization which, without any degree of autonomy and in the absence of general democratic procedures, was acting on behalf of the central power. By opening up the urban fabric, which eased the movement of troops, the sovereignty of the government over the people of the capital city was to be secured. It was to create a unified, homogeneous space to overcome the divide between urban quarters and their factionalism, in line with the emerging integrative nationalism. On the other hand, this open matrix was providing a basis on which a new social stratification, as associated with the incoming economic relationships, could find geographical expression.

URBAN SPACE / **121**

Oudlajan

Baharestan

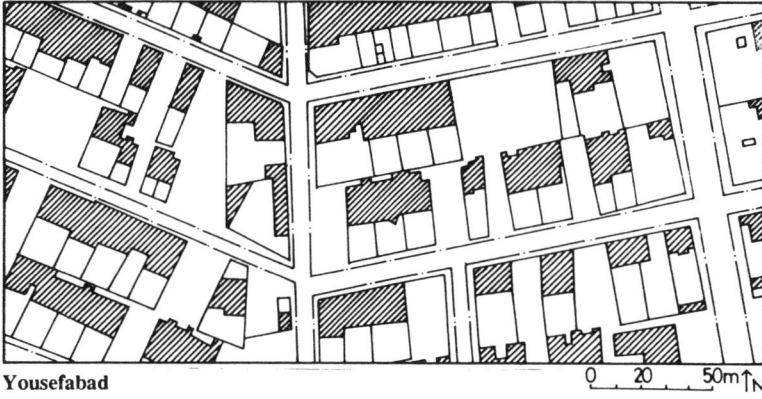
Yousefabad

FIGURE 6.11 Evolution of the street system, from a hierarchy of narrow, twisting streets to a network of wide, straight roads

The form and orientation of the new street system were rationalized according to natural, technological, economic, and cultural considerations. The topography of Tehran, which is based on a north–south slope, and the earlier water distribution system of *qanats* and canals, which works with the topography, have set the pattern of a gridiron based on a north–south orientation. This is supported by the desirability of the winter sun in the south, the wind direction across the slope, and the orientation of the prayers towards Mecca in the south-west. Although rational in these respects, the new street pattern has not found the level of the social and environmental rationality of the old street system. The latter evolved over long periods of time, taking advantage of the natural environmental qualities of the area and devising a clear relationship between public, semi-public, and private realms, all manifested in the street system. It was based on the disposition of the units of social and productive forces as distinct from the imposition of theoretical systems upon the structures. On the other hand, the new urban space has been increasingly rationalized according to the new instrumental rationality which has been an expression of the emerging individualism.

The new street system has resulted from a transformation process, whose major objectives included the creation of images of modernity, images of the West borrowed along with the goods, ideas, and appearances. The new forms were borrowed from the Renaissance ideal cities, from the transformations of Paris, from the inter-war developments of Germany, from the Modern Movement in architecture and from the post-war developments in Britain and the USA. These were images to match, to ease, and to generate the new social and economic system which emerged after military defeat and the economic incompetence of Iran in its nineteenth-century contacts with the West. Thus the new streets which were imposed upon the old city were in line with the new social, economic, cultural, and administrative institutions. In borrowing from the West, although approaches such as redevelopment of large parts of the urban fabric were used, some of the main purposes of the original schemes were not followed, mainly due to the difference in societal circumstances and in the concern for imagery. The concepts of space which were used had, therefore, both material bases in their association with societal processes and conceptual bases in relation to the importance of imagery to signify modernity. We will discuss these ideas further in Part Three.

LAND USE

While land use across the city is mixed, residential use is dominant in the northern and eastern quarters, industrial use in the west and south-west, and commercial and office use in the central quarters (Figure 6.12). Non-residential use in the old, central neighbourhoods is concentrated along the edges, gradually penetrating towards the centre of urban blocks, where residential use is dominant. In contrast with this, in the new, peripheral quarters, is the development of local high streets in the middle of the quarters, a pattern similar to the structure of old cities and quarters before recent transformations. This phenomenon may be explained by the general core–periphery relation of the urban structure and by the importance of the new street system. The prevalence of mixed use, however, is explained by the pace of development and the ways in which it has been encouraged or discouraged.

The mixture of uses, as distinct from the traditional urban structure in which some form of zoning was at work, has emerged as the government encouraged commercial uses to spread out of the central bazaar to support the newly laid out street network. This was mainly due to the political motivation of the state to dismantle the monopoly of the bazaar merchants over economic space and activities. It was also due to the limited capacity of the bazaar to accommodate new businesses, hindering competition for sites in the city. This also stemmed from the rapid development of the urban fabric in the absence of any form of communal consensus or effective planning system. Even when the latter, with its proposals for zoning, was established, the limited powers of municipalities curbed the adequacy of planning control to enforce these proposals, resulting in the development of mixed use areas.

With the growth in the size of the city, the centre has witnessed an expansion of activities. The concentration of non-residential activities in the central areas of the city, as referred to in the discussion of core–periphery relations, has been the driving force in the encroachment of these activities into surrounding residential areas. The pattern of land use in the old urban quarters has, therefore, changed in response to this process of expansion.

The imposition of the new street system upon the old urban structure and the encouragement from the government that the new, street-based businesses compete with the old bazaar are the main reasons why the edges of urban blocks are occupied by small firms and shops. The hearts of the superblocks, due to their limited accessibility, have remained residential. The similarity between the high streets of the new, peripheral neighbourhoods and the local bazaars of the old, pre-transformation urban neighbourhoods suggests a similarity between their development processes: the gradual emergence of a local centre in the middle of the residential areas, where accessibility is highest. Peripheral neighbourhoods have not been under pressure from commercial development, whereas the central areas have witnessed the encroachment of business activities.

BUILDING FORM

In parallel with other changes in urban space, there has been a change in building form: from one- or two-storey, inward-looking, courtyard buildings

124 / TEHRAN

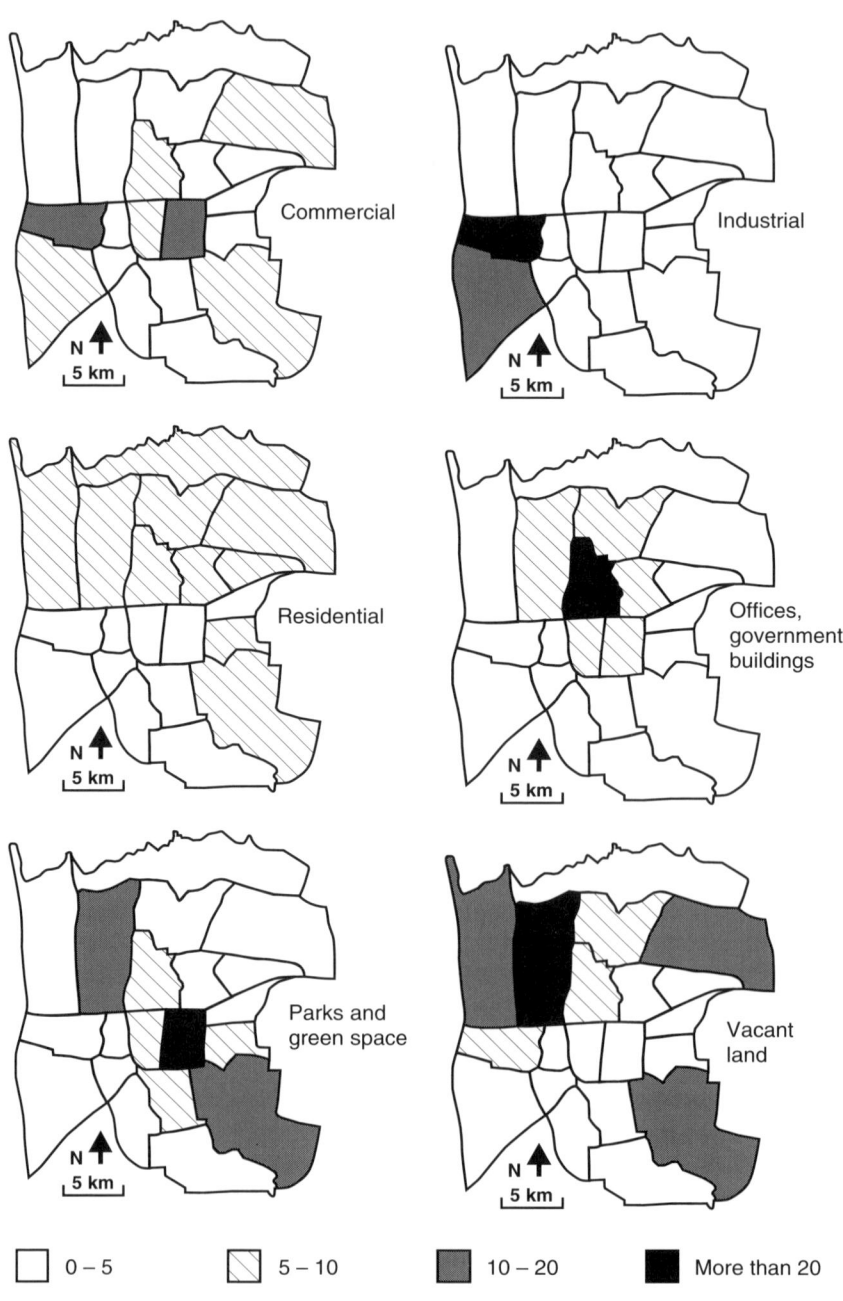

FIGURE 6.12 Distribution of land use shows a degree of specialization in the urban space (1992, per cent)

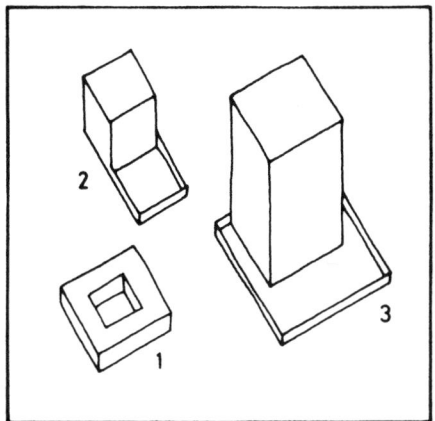

FIGURE 6.13   The changing pattern of building form, from (1) an inward-looking, low-rise courtyard house to (2) an outward-looking, medium-rise house with a courtyard, to (3) high-rise apartment buildings

to higher, extroverted buildings, although still enclosed within walled courtyards (Figures 6.13–6.15). The change in building form has been largely associated with the change in the street system. The explanation lies in the patterns of production and exchange of space, the images involved, and the patterns of continuity which have resisted change.

The new building form was partly an outcome of the new system of land subdivision, the rationalization and standardization of the size and shape of land parcels which was consistent with the orthogonal blocks and streets. This allowed the emerging urban middle classes to afford housing and landowners and speculators to maximize their profits. The successive waves of monopolization and release of land, by aristocracy, government, and speculators, had made the land into a commodity, turning a natural resource into a financial asset.

With the increasing availability of finance, banks and financial institutions facilitated the flow of money from the public to private sector through construction, and encouraged private developers to invest in larger-scale projects: large housing estates and high-rise buildings. The developers grew larger and used new construction technologies to develop expensive land at higher densities. Supply of labour and the patterns of production and distribution of building materials had to be adjusted to this process, although their fluctuations have had a clear impact on the quality of the outcome. The development of the new building form was, like the new street pattern, a part of a package of goods, ideas, and images imported from the West. This has been exemplified in the widespread use of pitched

FIGURE 6.14 The courtyard houses of the old core have been neglected

roofs for a while, which have now remained in use in luxury developments as a sign of prestige. These images of modernity, however, were confronted by some cultural patterns which have resisted change. The need for security and privacy, as enhanced by Islamic traditions, caused the retention of the walled courtyard. The orientation of the buildings was also largely determined by those affecting the orientation of the street system. Availability of building materials has influenced the external façades. The general external modesty of the buildings has stemmed from social and religious norms and a need for security. This modesty, however, has been increasingly undermined by the demand for spatial expression of individualism.

CONCLUSION: SPATIAL MANIFESTATIONS OF SOCIAL CHANGE

Urban space in Tehran is a clear manifestation of social change. The city's social and spatial structure has been influenced by its location between a high mountain range and a large desert. As society has stratified, this topographical and climatic differentiation has been employed to signify the social stratification. The city is characterized by a divide between the affluent north at the foot of the mountains and a disadvantaged south on the margins of the desert. As the city has grown and competition for accessible sites has intensified, a concentric pattern of growth is identifiable, where the core is distinguishable by a concentration of business activities and the periphery by

FIGURE 6.15 The increasingly dominant building form in the city

the predominance of residential use, which on the outskirts takes the shape of small settlements and new towns. The spatial structure is also characterized by two main axes in the east–west and north–south directions.

At more detailed levels, the street system has changed from a hierarchical distributional system of narrow, winding roads to an orthogonal system of wide streets and motorways. The land-use pattern is signified by a concentration of business activities in the city centre, mainly on the edges of the urban blocks, leaving the core of these blocks and the peripheral neighbourhoods to residential use. Building form shows a transition from low-rise, inward-looking, courtyard houses to medium to high-rise outward-looking apartments, although the walled courtyard has kept its significance. In Part Three, we will explore further the processes that have shaped the city in this way.

7

URBAN PROBLEMS

In previous chapters, we have identified some of the major social, political, and economic problems of the city. In this chapter we outline some of its most important problems in transport, housing, environmental degradation, loss of green space, and loss of historic buildings. These are problems which have often attracted most attention from the authorities and have had a direct impact on the quality of environment and living experience in the city.

A recent poll asked Tehranis about the main problems of their city. They answered, in order of importance, high inflation and high cost of living, traffic, environmental pollution, housing, and overcrowding. When asked about what they considered to be attributes of an ideal environment, most men wanted an easy flow of traffic, followed by good sports and entertainment facilities, good weather, cleanliness, optimum population density, and good urban utilities. For women, the most important criterion was to have a clean city, followed by good weather, good social relations, good sports and entertainment facilities, optimum population density, and green space (*Hamshahri*, 14 March 1996: 2–3).

TRANSPORT

Traffic is a major problem in Tehran (Figure 7.1). After high inflation, many Tehranis consider traffic to be the most important problem of the city. They see the solution as lying in better transport planning, co-ordinated intervention by the state, and banning older vehicles from the city (*Hamshahri*, 14 March 1996: 2–3). Traffic congestion, lack of sufficient parking space, and erratic driving habits are all putting great strain on everyday life. Pedestrians and the disabled, as well as drivers and passengers, find it difficult to move around the city (Toumeh, 1994). The average speed of everyday trips in the city is 18 km/h (Ardalan, 1992a). In 1994, it was estimated that there were 11.5 million daily journeys in the city, with an average of 1.6 passengers per journey. Around 40 per cent of these journeys were by private vehicles and the rest by public transport (including buses, minibuses, taxis, and unlicensed taxis). Almost a quarter of all trips were made by bus, followed by 22 per cent by licensed and unlicensed taxis (Shahrdari-e Tehran, 1996a: 118–20). Around 10 per cent of the trips were made by minibus, operating in almost the same way as taxis, carrying

FIGURE 7.1 Traffic is a major problem in the city

passengers along the main arteries but not to their final destinations. The only vehicles carrying passengers to their requested destinations are airport taxis and telephone-operating taxis. This type of use of the different modes of transport and the malfunctioning of other transport-related facilities have been identified by the director of Tehran municipality's centre for transport studies as one of the main sources of the problem. The planning regulations demand that all new buildings provide off-street parking provision. However, many garages have been converted into living or commercial spaces, and as a result, cars are parked on the streets. In the absence of an underground railway system, buses operate as if they were metro lines, serving long-distance routes. Taxis, instead, operate as buses, in that they operate only along the main arteries. The primary network of motorways, which were constructed to ease the flow of traffic, have been turned into secondary roads. For example, Resalat motorway has become an urban street, as shops and other land uses have developed alongside the motorway (Ardalan, 1992a).

The number of private cars was estimated to be 425 000 in 1985, which was 80 per cent more than other urban areas of the country, reflecting the high concentration of vehicles in Tehran (Farmand & Rafiei, 1991). More recent studies show the number of private vehicles to be 750 000 motor cars and 300 000 motor cycles (Shahrdari-e Tehran, 1996a: 121), showing a rate of one motor car for every two Tehrani households. The fall in car production and imports, which occurred as a result of war and revolution, halted the rising number of cars in Tehran and other urban areas. Even so, the high density of activities in the central areas of the city has led to severe traffic congestion.

The pressure on the city centre and the heavy traffic congestion it created led to a radical undertaking in the aftermath of the revolution. Special traffic restrictions were imposed on around 22 km^2 in the city centre, where on weekdays private vehicles are not allowed in. Although this scheme has been moderately successful in easing the city centre's traffic, it can be identified as one of the causes of decentralization of activities and people and contributing to the decay of the central areas.

Public transport was first introduced in Tehran in 1919, when a Belgian company started a carriage service on four routes. Buses came into use from the 1930s, operating on eight routes with no predetermined terminals and stops. The number of private bus companies grew until 1956, when the first public bus company was established, following a 1952 law by Parliament. The company was associated with the municipality and started its services on one route and with 1 rial tickets. The company grew considerably so that by 1988, its 2000 buses served 1.7 million passengers a day. After the increase of its fleet to 3200 buses in 1989, the number of passengers rose to 3.5 million a day in the early 1990s (Ardalan, 1992b). More recent figures show that buses account for 23 per cent of all the 11.5 million intra-urban daily trips, followed by taxis with 22 per cent and minibuses with 10 per cent of daily trips (Shahrdari-e Tehran, 1996a: 118–21).The 1989 changes also decentralized the operations to 6 districts with 151 routes, and reduced the length of the routes for a faster and more flexible service. Despite its large number of passengers, the very cheap ticket prices have caused a substantial budget deficit for the company. Ticket prices covered only 10 per cent of the company's IR110bn expenditure in 1992. To run this public service, therefore, the Tehran municipality allocates around 10 per cent of its income to bus services. Old buses with diesel engines are a constant source of public complaints and anxiety about air pollution. Although the company claims that its diesel fleet accounts for only 1.5 per cent of the city's air pollution, it has started distributing diesel buses around the city to help in relieving the centre from its worsening air pollution. In doing so, most have been sent to the southern parts of the city, the explanation being that these buses cannot cope with the steep slopes of the northern city. This, however, has created controversy as it is seen to increase pollution in the poorer districts for the benefit of the more affluent parts (Ardalan, 1992b). A major initiative in the 1990s has been the introduction of electric buses which should contribute towards a healthier environment (*Bulletin*, No. 6, Aban 1371).

One of the main solutions to the traffic problems of the city has been the development of a metro system. This project had started in the 1970s, but suffered a setback in the 1980s. The work started again in the mid-1980s, but huge financial and technological problems have been the cause of very slow progress. The French company, which had designed and had started to implement the project in the 1970s, had envisaged seven routes with a total length of 146 km of urban railway network. The work has now concentrated on only two main routes along the main north–south and east–west axes of the city (Rahimi Farzan, 1991).

Increasingly, there have been attempts to systematically collect traffic data, to use closed circuit television cameras at major intersections to monitor and control the traffic flow, and to prepare a long-term traffic plan (Ardalan, 1992a). In 1992, the Tehran municipality established a centre for the study of transport problems in Tehran. The centre started a research programme to collect and analyse data and to prepare plans for the city's transport. The last major study of Tehran's transport had been undertaken in the late 1960s. The idea of developing long-term transport plans for the capital had been discussed but postponed due to the advent of revolution and the war with Iraq. In 1995, the centre published a five-year plan for improving traffic conditions in Tehran and started working on its long-term plan. The five-year plan promotes the management of the demand for journeys, management of the traffic system, completion of the motorway network, revision of public transport provisions, and management of land use. These include encouraging the reduction of the length and number of journeys, relieving the pressure in rush hours through the management of working hours, co-ordinating the traffic light systems, the design of intersections, and the decentralization of some of the major land users, such as the fruit and vegetable market and the Friday prayers (*Bulletin*, No. 37, 5th Mordad 1374: 28–9). These points have been fed into the Tehran municipality's strategic plan for the year 2001 (Tehran 80). This plan's main priorities include improvement of the public transport system, co-ordination between the metro and existing public transport, encouraging private sector investment in the provision of transport and parking facilities, continued construction of the urban motorway network (from the existing 210 to 380 km), improvement of the main road junctions, educating the public to achieve better driving, improvement and use of information and research, and emphasis on the environmental impact of transport (Shardari-e Tehran, 1996a: 134) (Figure 7.2).

Tehran is connected to the other cities of the country by three coach terminals, a railway station, and an airport. The three coach terminals are located on the margins of the city on the east, west, and south and account for around 130 000 daily arrivals to the city. Next is the airport with more than 25 000 daily arrivals and the last major port of entry into the city is the railway station with around 18 000 arrivals (Shardari-e Tehran, 1996a: 125). The outdated and inefficient railway system is not heavily used by passengers. It is now being promoted more for goods transport, as its main rivals, coach and air travel, are proving more popular and efficient. Tehran is the hub of air traffic in Iran. Before the revolution, it was also a major stop

FIGURE 7.2 The urban motorway network continues to be the centre of attention

in international east–west flights, a position it lost due to the war and instabilities of the 1980s. The main airport of the city was Mehrabad, located in the west. The growth of Tehran, however, has now engulfed the airport, limiting its capacity to be modernized and expanded, especially in the context of a rapid rise in demand. Proximity to high mountains, the dual military and civilian use of the airport, its noise, proximity to security zones inside the city, electronic interference from industrial installations near by, and the outdated layout of the airport have all led to the development of a new, large airport in the south of the city (Kaviani, 1988).

ENVIRONMENTAL POLLUTION

Tehran suffers from mounting environmental problems and water, air, land, and noise pollution. Tehran has been listed as one of the most polluted cities in the world. The presence of an estimated 1.1 million motor vehicles,

FIGURE 7.3 The city suffers from atmospheric pollution for most of the year

which produce 70 per cent of the air pollution, together with household fuel and industries in the south have been the causal factors. These are coupled with high pressure and the encapsulating effect of the mountains. For two-thirds of the year, the city suffers from inversion. The hot air creates a dome at the height of 350–400 m above the city, trapping the cold air and the polluting emissions inside it. For most of the year, therefore, pollutants are present in the atmosphere at high rates and threaten the health of the citizens (Figure 7.3). The main sources of air pollution are fossil fuels, as the city consumes daily 7 million litres of petrol, 1.5 million litres of diesel, and more than 20 million m^3 of natural gas. Unleaded petrol is rarely available and the amount of sulphur in diesel is far more than international standards. Around 83 per cent of motor vehicles have been in use for more than seven years. Their age and dated technology have created major obstacles for the control of air pollution in the city. The city has a considerable concentration of industries, which are mostly unregulated in terms of their generation of environmental pollutants.

Despite a rising awareness of the environmental problems in the city, there is an absence of information on the amount and source of pollutants. A 1987 study showed that in a day on average 3211 t of carbon monoxide, 470 t of hydrocarbons, 151 t of nitrogen oxides, 73 t of sulphur dioxide, and 33 t of suspended particles were released into Tehran's atmosphere. Most of these exceed the safe levels set by the World Health Organization. For example, the amount of carbon monoxide in central Tehran has been recorded as 80 ppm or four times its safe levels. Research in more recent years has shown that dust particles are three times, sulphur dioxide twice, and lead three to seven times the safe levels (Shahrdari-e Tehran, 1996a; Vahedi, 1989; Bahram Soltani, 1994; *Hamshahri*, 8 August 1993: 7).

The high altitude of Tehran and the wall of mountains to the north and east have created problems with natural ventilation. The local winds are often not strong enough to circulate the air. Around 70 per cent of the winds in Tehran have speeds below 6 knots and have little impact on air circulation in large built-up areas. Only 30 per cent of the winds, which usually blow in spring, late summer and early autumn, have speeds of more than 10 knots and can clear the air (Vahedi, 1989). The problem, however, is that the major winds blow from the west, south, and south-east, where most of the industries are located. Rather than cleaning the air, they can pollute the air further. Only the winds from the northern mountains, with their limited impact, blow in the right direction (Bahram Soltani, 1994).

The city's topography has helped to cause an unequal distribution of pollution. As an indication of this inequality between north and south, the gradient impact of pollution on trees and their associated diseases might be traced throughout the city. The location and height of the north have given it the privilege of being at a relatively safe distance from the smog which dominates the city for most of the year. The lower densities and the mountain winds are other factors in diminishing pollution there. As against this, the centre, especially the south centre, and the south, are the most polluted areas of Tehran as a result of high residential densities and concentration of commercial and industrial activities, enhanced by its topographical circumstances. The dome of hot air which rises above the centre attracts the polluted air from other quarters of the city.

As well as being a threat to life, air pollution is a cause of cultural and behavioural change. The high level of pollution has created circumstances in which none of the traditional environmental solutions which utilized the climatic circumstances would function. Sleeping on the roofs becomes inconvenient, the courtyard ceases to be a welcomed outdoor living place, its vegetation cannot survive in the polluted air, and its polluted pool is unable to generate freshness. Instead, the use of electrical ventilation and cooling systems have rapidly increased.

There have been many attempts to fight against air pollution. However, their effectiveness has been minimized by the increasing concentration of people and activities in the central areas of the capital city. From the 1960s, legislation has limited the location of new industries to outside a radius of 120 km from Tehran. Other policies have included provision of parks inside the city, major tree-planting schemes in the west and south, and encouragement of the use of gas as household fuel, to replace kerosene. The new traffic arrangements after the revolution, preventing private cars from entering the city centre, although aimed at improving the traffic, was helpful in reducing pollution. Tehran municipality's strategic plan identifies a "clean city" as one of its goals and introduces a range of initiatives and policies. These include setting targets for reducing the pollutants and promoting the expansion of public transport, restriction and monitoring of emissions, more reliance on natural gas consumption, management of land use, relocation of industries, and environmental education and research (Shahrdari-e Tehran, 1996a).

Tehran is far from any major river and has to rely on water supplies located at a distance from the city. Its shortage of water was known soon after it became the capital of the country when its population began to grow. Earlier, a 52 km canal was built to bring water from the Karaj river in the west (*Hamshahri*, 14 March 1996: 4). Before the 1960s, the city was still relying on this canal and the traditional man-made underground streams (*qanats*). In 1964, a major dam was built on the Karaj river to direct more water to the city. As the Karaj water was not sufficient for the growing metropolis, another dam (Latian) on the river Jajrood in the north-east supplemented the water supplies to the capital. Both dams, however, have caused considerable damage to the agriculture of their areas. A third dam on the river Lar in Mazandaran, north of the Alburz mountains by the Caspian Sea, was built to direct more water to Tehran from this major agricultural province. Studies have also been undertaken to redirect water from the river Taleghan to the city. With its endless thirst and its irrational and wasteful use of water in a hot, arid climate, therefore, the city has deprived many rural areas of their source of vitality and has endangered their livelihood. The negative impact of these projects on the city itself has also been considerable. Geologically the Tehran plain is likened to a bowl, limited in the north by high mountains and in the south by the hills of Kahrizak. The underground water tables in the plain are fed by water from the Alburz chain of mountains, which permitted the development of the old *qanats*. The injection of water from these rivers to the plain, which is being consumed at the rate of 25 m^3/s, has caused the rise of underground water tables. As there is no sewage collection and processing system in the city, cesspools are the main form of water disposal, which usually filter and pass the water to the underground tables. The result is an alarming rise in underground water levels, in some areas by 7 m in only four years. At the same time, the underground water resources are being contaminated, as the pressure on these cesspools is increased. The result of the rise and pollution of underground water tables can be seen in the outpouring of polluted water in the poor districts of the south, damaging buildings, the environment, agricultural activities, and creating marshlands in Gharchak and Varamin (Vahedi, 1989). As the city continues to rely on the underground water tables for around 20 per cent of its water needs, the problem is becoming even more acute (Shahrdari-e Tehran, 1996a: 95). After almost three decades of commissioning studies for a sewerage system, the first phase of a sewerage system is being built.

The absence of a sewage collection system and the inability of the underground tables to absorb more water have also caused problems for managing surface water. As a small town, Tehran had a system of open streams, which watered rows of trees and created freshness and pleasant views. A canal system led the water to houses, where it could be stored for consumption. Excess rain-water was either channelled away from the built-up areas to the southern deserts by some natural canals or was absorbed on the surface and enriched the underground water tables. With the growth of the city, however, all this has changed. The flood relief canals have been either filled and built upon by speculators, or are being used as open sewage systems by industries. The open streams and canals have become major environmental threats, as some people dump their rubbish in them, polluting the streams and blocking the tunnels and passageways. These reach disaster dimensions in the southern districts, where the pressure on relief canals increases, causing floods of polluted water (*Hamshahri*, 14 March 1996: 4–5). Water pollution has led to, and is coupled with, contamination of land. There is no clear information on this issue in Tehran, but it is believed that industrial activities and water pollution have caused considerable land contamination (Shahrdari-e Tehran, 1996a; Behazin, 1994). Tehranis also suffer from noise pollution, mainly resulting from traffic, industrial activities, the airport, construction activities, as well as street vendors, all resulting from high densities of population (Behazin, 1994).

The amount of waste in Tehran has been growing by 10 per cent a year between 1981 and 1994. Until the late 1980s, two waste dumps in Kahrizak and Abali were used. The Abali dump in the north-eastern mountains, however, had become a major threat to the environment. Its 15 lakes of liquid waste had been controlled by several dams. Some years ago, when one of the dams broke and liquid waste found its way into the nearby Jajrood river, the disaster struck and the river's fish died. These lakes have now been dried and replaced by 100 ha of trees. Another frequent occurrence in the Abali dump were the fires started by chemical interactions in the waste, which at times had to be controlled by the fire brigade. With the closure of the Abali dump, Kahrizak has become the only place for receiving the city's waste from several major collection points. Each day, 6000 t of waste are carried to Kahrizak, which until 1991 were disposed of in open dumps, attracting some 2000 people who would search the rubbish for reusable items. Since the introduction of a major improvement scheme in 1992, however, the waste in Kahrizak is being buried. Some attempts have been made to recycle the waste. Three-quarters of it is organic materials, followed by paper (8.3 per cent) and plastics (4.8 per cent). A major problem in waste disposal is the amount of rubble that is being produced as a result of redevelopment. Although most buildings are relatively new, the pressure for new space has led to a vertical expansion of the city, redeveloping existing buildings for building at higher densities. Seven

FIGURE 7.4 Urban development has destroyed the city's green spaces

million tonnes of rubble are thus produced annually which need to be disposed of (Shahrdari-e Tehran, 1996a; *Bulletin*, No. 3, Mordad 1371: 7–9).

GREEN SPACE

Tehran was once known as the city of plane trees. Visitors to the city found it engulfed in gardens and trees. In its rapid growth, however, it has lost many of these gardens, an issue which has become ever more serious as environmental problems mount. The traditional houses with their courtyards provided much of the green space of the city. Now, higher land prices, higher densities, higher price of water, and a changing lifestyle of living in flats have all rendered the provision and maintenance of private green spaces ever more difficult (Figure 7.4).

The necessity of protection and preservation of trees and vegetation has a very long history in this hot, dry land. From ancient times, gardens have been a sacred part of the Persian psyche, as evident from the rituals of the Zoroastrians and their legacy in the culture today. The English word "paradise" has its roots in ancient Persian, where it meant "garden". The new era of development and change, however, has undermined these ancient sensitivities which appeared to have only mythical value but in fact were environmentally quite rational. Such realization is gradually coming to the fore, as the natural environment continues to suffer.

The growth of population in the country has brought substantial pressures on the natural environment. As the forests were under threat, they were nationalized in 1962 and strict laws were passed in 1967 to protect trees. A 1973 law promoted the maintenance and development of green space and protection of trees. Without the municipality's permission, no trees could be removed from the urban areas. In practice, however, urban trees in Tehran continued to disappear at a fast rate, as the city was expanding restlessly outside the municipal jurisdiction. As the land prices rose, old gardens and parks were being destroyed to give way to lucrative, high-density residential developments. In 1980, the revolutionary council passed a law for development and maintenance of urban green space, asking the Tehran municipality to prepare a framework for its implementation. All the urban trees were given identity plaques, they were protected from felling without municipal permission, and all the green spaces larger than 500 m^2 became protected by law from conversion to residential use (*Bulletin*, No. 13, Tir 1372: 28–9). It was felt important that not only the trees in public places be protected but also the private trees and gardens should be preserved. The 1980 law was similar to that of 1973, but applied now to an enlarged municipal jurisdiction (Ardalan, 1995b).

Despite protective legislation, the process of urban development has continued to destroy green space in its expansion. One of the shortcomings of the legislation is that it sets the limit of 500 m^2, so that the smaller gardens can be converted without permission. Also the landowners are allowed to fell diseased and dead trees. Many landowners and speculative developers have used these routes to destroy trees, first by not watering them and then arguing that they are dead and need to be felled.

The main solution for Tehran's environmental problems has been seen to be removing the pollutants and replacing them with oxygen produced by expansion of the city's green space. Yet the new residential developments by the private sector, and the sectoral nature of the public sector intervention have undermined green space by giving priority to the development projects rather than environmental protection. Solutions for the city's traffic problems, for example, are developed just to ease the flow of traffic, without taking into account their impact on green spaces and on the environmental quality as a whole.

The acute shortage of green space in the city has forced the municipality to take a number of initiatives in the 1990s. In 1990, a unit was established to identify and monitor the city's large gardens. In five years, the unit has identified 28 million m^2 of large green spaces, mostly located in areas 1, 2, 3, 5, 18, and 20 (Ardalan, 1995b) (Figure 7.5). It was decided that up to a radius of 20 km, Tehran should be surrounded by green space. Tehran municipality, therefore, has concentrated on development of parks on the urban peripheries. Between 1991 and 1993, 4000 ha of green space were developed on the urban fringe, despite the serious limitations caused by water shortages (*Bulletin*, No. 13, Tir 1372: 36–41). Furthermore, many small parks and playgrounds were developed across the city. The rapid

FIGURE 7.5 Some gardens have survived in the northern suburbs

growth of the city has often been inconsistent, leaving many gaps in the urban fabric. Land plots are left undeveloped here and there because of lack of resources, the absence of owners, and the particular difficulties of developing the site such as awkward topography or shape. One of the initiatives of the Tehran municipality in the 1990s was to convert many of these residual parts of urban space to green spaces.

The municipality, however, is being criticized for allowing the old trees to be cut down for new development, while developing these small parks (Aslani, 1993). This is especially the case for district 1, at the foot of the northern mountains, which has the largest concentration of gardens in the city. This has attracted a development pressure in the area, where many luxury high-rise residential developments have mushroomed in recent years. Despite the reassurances of the area's municipality that these developments are not destroying the gardens, there is no doubt that the increase in residential density will put pressure on these vulnerable assets of the city.

Nevertheless, the Tehran municipality's campaign to improve the quality of the environment has won international recognition. Its efforts to reduce carbon monoxide emissions have earned it United Nations support. In the restricted traffic zones of the city centre, mandatory emission inspections are enforced. Some 1500 buses have been converted from diesel fuel to compressed natural gas. Also the green space per person has been radically improved, from 2.5 to 10 m^2 in 1993. For these reasons, in the United Nations 1996 Conference on Human Settlements (Habitat II), Tehran was identified as one of the 25 best practice cities highlighted for use as models for future programmes in cities world-wide (United Nations, 1996).

Creating a "green city" is another goal of the Tehran municipality's strategic plan, which admits there are major obstacles in the way. It aims to acquire 4800 ha of military sites in the city for conversion into parks, and also to complete the green belt with an area of 3000 ha of green space. The long-term plan for the city's green spaces aims to use non-drinking water and to introduce a more diverse range of plant species (Shahrdari-e Tehran, 1996a).

HOUSING

The constant flow of immigrants into Tehran and the natural growth of its population have created historically increasing demands for housing. Another pressure on housing has come from a change in the pattern of household structure, from the extended families of the nineteenth century to the nuclear families of the twentieth, which has meant a demand for more dwellings for the same number of people. This demand has also been triggered by increasing living standards and rising expectations. The provision of housing has generally improved over the years. For example, between 1966 and 1986 in Tehran province, the number of households per dwelling fell from 1.57 to 1.17. There was also a sharp reduction in the number of persons per room, from 2.04 to 1.41 (Abedin Dorkoosh, 1993: 145). In 1976, around 30 per cent of all the dwellings in the city had multi-occupancy, which were reduced to 14 per cent in 1986 (Rafiei, 1989: 6).

Between the 1960s and 1980s, the quality of buildings also improved: whereas in 1966, one-third of urban housing in Iran was built of durable materials, in 1986 two-thirds were recorded in this category (Abedin Dorkoosh, 1993: 146). In 1966, most of the housing stock in Tehran was new, with 60 per cent built since the mid-1950s. Nevertheless, only three-quarters of the city's dwellings were considered to be built of durable building materials such as brick, steel, and concrete. By 1986, the quality of housing stock had improved considerably. In this year, two-thirds of the stock was built after the mid-1960s, while only 6.8 per cent were recorded as being built of non-durable building materials (Rafiei, 1989: 7–8). Despite these improvements in the quantity and quality of housing in Tehran, the cost of housing and its proportion of household expenditure have risen dramatically. From 1969 to 1988, housing expenditure rose from 18 to 27 per cent of an urban household's monthly expenditure (Abedin Dorkoosh, 1993: 138). Land prices in Tehran are so high (on average up to 2.3 times that of other large cities such as Mashhad, Shiraz, and Isfahan) that minor price reductions have no, or even a negative, impact on affordability. In the early 1990s, there was a fall in the growth of land prices as a result of a general economic slowdown. As a result, the cost of rented accommodation increased considerably, as the supply of dwellings for sale was reduced in the hope of recovery (Vezarat-e Maskan, 1992).

There are 654 000 dwellings in Tehran, covering an area of 120 km^2 or about one-fifth of the urban area (Shahrdari-e Tehran, 1996a: 123). The form of dwelling which the population has historically preferred is the single family house. In the nineteenth century this was predominantly single-storey courtyard housing. The continued pressure on urban space from rising numbers of population, and the introduction of Western dwelling types of two-storey terraced houses and multi-storey flats, have led to a new housing morphology. Dwellings are generally smaller and a culture of living in flats has developed. The large, old-style courtyard houses in central areas have been used for multi-occupancy renting. At the same time, additional floors have been added to the newer terraced houses, providing flats which could be a source of income for the family or accommodation for the household's offspring. Large apartment buildings have also been developed to cater for the middle- and upper-income groups. The continuously rising land prices have led to ever-increasing residential densities and rising housing prices. In parallel, dwellings are now smaller. The average dwelling in the mid-1980s was an owner-occupied house with an age of slightly more than 10 years, with 117 m^2 consisting of 3.6 rooms (including the kitchen), housing a household with a size of 5.2 (Rafiei, 1989: 9).

The pattern of home ownership has varied over the years. In 1883, about 90 per cent of Tehrani households owned their dwellings. With the rising tide of immigration, this was reduced to only a half in the 1950s and 1960s. From then on, with the booming oil economy, the number of home-owners has increased to reach two-thirds in 1986. In this year, 25 per cent of the households lived in privately rented accommodation and the rest (12.2 per cent) in housing provided by the public or large employers (Taleghani, 1990: 179). The highest proportion of households in rented accommodation was in district 12, where the central bazaar is located and where old houses have either been turned into businesses and warehouses or to multiple occupancy for immigrant workers (p. 180). In the 1960s, a clear divide could be traced in the quality of rented and owned accommodation. While most of the home-owners in 1966 lived in dwellings with three or more rooms, most of the renters lived in dwellings with just one room. The situation, however, has generally improved as the 1980 census in Tehran showed an increase in the number of rooms in rented accommodation (p. 181).

The city's clear social divide, however, continues to be visible in housing conditions (Figure 7.6). A combination of qualitative and quantitative indicators shows that central and western parts of the city enjoy better housing conditions than the southern parts (Rafiei, 1989: 21–5). Abedin Dorkoosh (1991: 42) shows an interesting relationship between housing prices in the

142 / TEHRAN

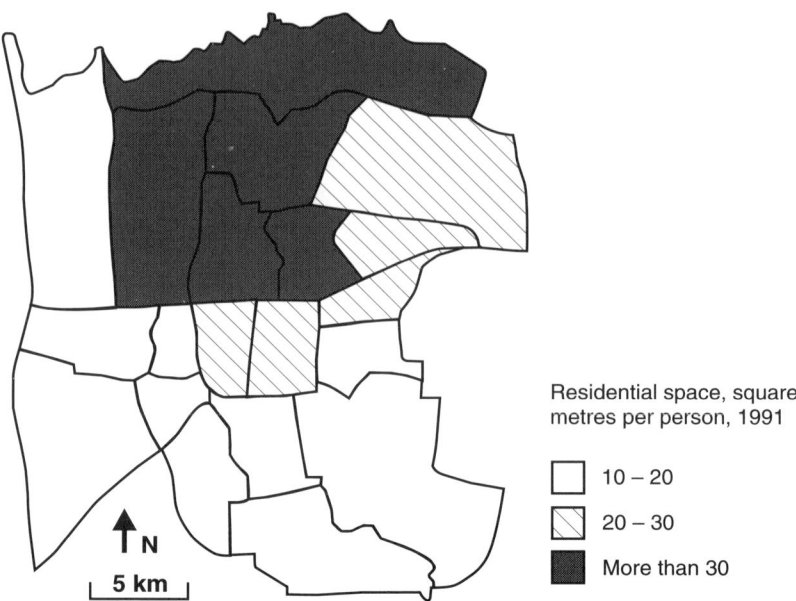

FIGURE 7.6 Housing conditions are poorer in the south and west (residential space, square metres per person, 1991)

northern city, the city centre, and the rest of the city. According to him, in the affluent north the prices increase as you move away from the city centre. In contrast, in other parts of the city prices fall with distance from the city centre. This shows the higher mobility and spatial freedom in the north and spatial dependency in the south, signifying the deep social divide in the city.

Clear symptoms of the social divide in the city can be seen in concentrations of squatters and shanty towns. Tehran has never suffered from the large-scale development of shanty towns seen in some other large cities in developing countries. New settlements sprang up around the city on lands which had not been owned by anyone, as historically the absence of water and cultivable land had left them unoccupied. According to Islamic rules, whoever developed an unclaimed piece of land could claim its ownership. As the city grew, more and more parts of the surrounding land were claimed by speculators and the countryside became a valuable commodity. The continuing flow of immigration into the city and the rising cost of land, however, meant that access to land for housing was becoming ever more restricted for the poor. The result has been squatter residential areas. In a study of 25 such areas, Piran (1988) shows that they may be a grouping of a few or of several hundred households. Some of the dwellings are built of pieces of wood, metal, and plastic, with very small rooms, suffering from sanitary problems, lack of natural light, electricity, water, and waste disposal. Their populations are often rural immigrants and have an uneasy relationship with the residential areas around them. Unemployment, debt, crime, and drug dealing are known in some areas. Many are engaged in casual employment and street vending, which make them very vulnerable. The municipal authorities, both before and after the revolution, have attempted to evacuate these squatter areas, which has at times led to violent clashes between the residents and the police. These pockets of extreme disadvantage and social exclusion are scattered around the south and east and mostly, although not all, around the margins of the city.

The role of the government in housing provision has been reduced substantially in the last two decades. According to the minister of housing and urban development, the share of investment by the public sector in housing fell from 24 per cent in 1974 to only 2 per cent in 1991 (*Ettela'at*, 2 November 1992: 11). The government, however, had a direct impact on a major slump in the property market in the early 1990s. As the economy was suffering from high inflation, the government limited the credits to the development industry and raised the interest rates to the level of 16 per cent. This was to reduce the amount of money in circulation. Its impact on the housing market, however, was devastating, as the investors turned to banks rather than property which historically had been the most reliable investment in volatile and inflationary market conditions (*Ettela'at*, 13 June 1995: 5). From the mid-1990s, however, the housing market has experienced a revival.

The second five-year development plan of Iran promotes a more active role for the government in housing provision. The plan concentrates on a better distribution of resources across the country and on promoting new development. The number of new residential units would increase through promotion of mass production, which now accounts for only 8 per cent of housing production. According to the minister, reducing the size of dwellings and using industrial production methods would lead to a substantial rise in the number of residential units (*Abadi*, No. 13, Summer 1373: 56–8). Alongside reduction in the average size of the dwellings, efforts will be made to reduce the average cost of development and increase the life cycle of the new units. The five-year plan outlines a mixture of different forms of investment. Around 5 per cent of new residential units in the plan period will be built by public sector agencies. The government will subsidize 30 per cent of urban housing units through low interest rates and other incentives. These are units which in return will have to take into account the new housing standards set by the Ministry of Housing and Urban Development. The government will enter into partnerships with banks and public sector agencies for social housing, which will account for 16 per cent of the new units and will be built at minimum standards. The rest of the housing production (58 per cent of the dwellings in urban areas) will be entirely built by the private sector without any support from the government. Apart from the normal planning controls, these will not have to comply with any restrictions on the size or methods of production. To cater for the demand, the plan promotes the provision of privately rented accommodation and production of mass housing and new town development, encourages the removal of legal obstacles, supports the developers and housing co-operatives, and provides investment in the regeneration of decayed urban areas (*Abadi*, No. 13, Summer 1373: 59–61).

CONSERVATION

As we have seen in Part One, Tehran was expanded by two major schemes in the nineteenth and twentieth centuries. These allowed the city to grow and accommodate its ever-increasing population. At the same time, these schemes and the post-war development of the city undermined the old core and introduced a modernist and utilitarian approach to the old fabric of the city. The old core is now only a very small part (around 4 per cent) of the sprawling metropolis and is suffering from decay and lack of maintenance (Figure 7.7).

Praise of the new and disregard of the old have dominated the twentieth-century attitudes towards the built environment. Old buildings are easily pulled down as land prices go up and the gap between exchange value and use value widens. The Islamic revolution witnessed serious threats to and even demolition of several ancient monuments around the country, either on the basis of hostility towards the past monarchies or on the basis of a utilitarian tendency. The latter tendency was exemplified in the enlargement of a mosque to accommodate larger crowds without regard to the fact that it was built 1000 years ago and has enormous historical and cultural value. This tendency, which in its extreme forms touched on vandalism, was soon controlled as a result of pressure by the conservationists. It appears to be in sharp contrast with the values of a revolution whose stated aims were to revive tradition and to contradict the disenchantments of modernism. Yet these sensitivities, which were manifest in the area of cultural and religious norms and behaviour, were hardly extended to dealing with the built environment (Madanipour, 1995). This can also be observed in dealing with political institutions. After all, the revolution uprooted a very traditional institution, the monarchy, and replaced it with a very modern one, the republic. As such it has continued the modernist tradition of recent history, despite its traditionalist appearance.

Tehran's old core continues to be neglected, as it is seen to be outdated and dilapidated. Only 38 buildings in the city are listed and a further 12 are in the process of being protected. The bazaar and Oudlajan districts have been identified as having 5000 buildings of historical and architectural merit,

FIGURE 7.7 The old buildings suffer from decay and lack of maintenance

although no specific action is being taken to protect them (Shahrdari-e Tehran, 1996a: 242). Conservationists argue that the conservation of the old core would give the city a degree of historic continuity and can be used to promote cultural activities (Safamanesh, 1993, 1994; Safamanesh & Monadizadeh, 1993). However, rather than protecting the city centre, the municipality's policy of decentralization of activities could be a further blow to the old core by depriving it of some of its means of livelihood (Shahrdari-e Tehran, 1996a). Elsewhere in the city, especially in the northern areas, historic gardens and buildings are under threat from development pressure. It is partly this absence of continuity in the built environment that has given rise to frequent complaints about the loss of identity in Tehran.

CONCLUSION: FACING SOCIAL AND ENVIRONMENTAL PROBLEMS

As one of the largest cities of the world, Tehran suffers from acute problems. Providing housing for an increasing population has proved to be a major problem, despite the high rate of space production by the public and private sectors and the general improvement in the quality of housing. Easing the movement of goods and people across the city is another major challenge. In the process of building roads and houses, however, the old fabric of the city has been consistently neglected or damaged. Worst of all is the environmental pollution which seriously threatens the health of the citizens. There are some positive signs that these problems are being dealt with, as is evident from the municipality's efforts in introducing environmentally friendly technologies and increasing the city's green space, which have won the city international attention. Without substantial efforts to solve these huge problems, the next generation of Tehranis will live in far worse social and environmental conditions.

8

URBAN LIVES

How can we acquire a complete profile of the city? Is it at all possible to arrive at such a picture? Whichever approach we take to the city, we see a different scene. Whoever we talk to will tell us a different story. Do we dismiss these stories as "subjective" and try to build up a completely "objective" model of reality? But we know that even this objective story is a narrative told from a perspective, embedded in a set of contexts and experiences. We know that what is epistemically objective can be ontologically subjective (Searle, 1995). So far, we have looked at the patterns of the city's economy, its society, the way it is managed, the way its space is organized, and some of the problems it is facing. We have drawn a sketch of the city along these lines and have provided some details, to render a more accurate picture of the city. Whatever we do, however, will not capture a complete portrait of the city in its rich diversity and complexity of meaning.

Like any other social world, the city of Tehran is a dense tapestry of relationships and meanings, developed and constantly changed by its millions of inhabitants in their daily lives. In order to develop our profile of the city further, we could leave our reliance on documents aside, at least for a short while, and listen to some of the stories of these individuals, in the hope that they would give us a taste of what life looks like in the city, but with the knowledge that there is no end to the diversity of these stories and that each can fill many books. How a century of turbulent change, and the places and events recounted in this book, have been intertwined with people's lives. How they have experienced pleasure and pain in the city and how they have attributed meaning to these events and places. Here are some scenes (Figures 8.1–8.7) and a handful of possible monologues from among millions of Tehrani voices.

PORTRAITS FROM A LABYRINTH

I A Construction Worker from Oudlajan

I am a young man. I used to be a teacher in Kabul, Afghanistan, but had to run away because of the civil war in my country. Here I have had to work as a construction worker. It is very hard and nothing in my previous life had prepared me for this job. I wish I could go back to Kabul and live an ordinary, more dignified life. But things are worse back home, with all the

FIGURE 8.1   Nine in the morning at Imam Hussein Square, the eastern gate to the city

continuous fighting. Here some people don't like Afghanis. They think we take work opportunities away from the locals and get paid less for the same work. None of them appreciate that we get paid less for often harder jobs, which even Iranian workers are not prepared to do, like digging and cleaning the sewage wells. Sometimes when I go to the street corner, where we are picked up by the clients, we get jeered by the Iranian workers who were more expensive and could not find a job. Others think we are too violent, that on the evidence of only a few incidents, often among ourselves.

I live with six other Afghani workers in a small section of an old, crumbling house in the middle of Tehran. It is awful to live like that, but I have no other alternative. These houses look a bit like some places in Afghanistan. Some parts of Tehran have huge buildings with fancy shapes I had only seen in the movies. One good thing about being in the middle of the city is that a lot of things happen here. Our rent is low and we are together. There are so many people from everywhere that nobody bothers us about our documents. I don't wear my traditional costumes so that I don't stand out in the street. If I don't get a job for a day, I just wander around in the city centre, looking at thousands of passers-by and at the street vendors, shops, and places. I can get some rest in a mosque or go to one of many cinemas near by. I like these cinemas, although in this country they don't show many Indian films, which are very popular back home.

Despite all this, for me Tehran is an alien place. I am Shiite and my mother tongue is Persian, the same as most people here. Even my Dari

FIGURE 8.2 Despite their name, coffee houses (*ghahveh khaneh*) serve tea

accent is not a problem because many people have different accents here. There are some Iranian people who don't even speak Persian. But these don't make me feel at home. Things are very different here and I am not comfortable with most things. My jobs don't last long and I have to look for new ones. I know some friends who work in a neighbourhood on the outskirts of the city, where many new buildings are being built. They live on the site and if I am desperate I can go and stay with them. But this line of work cannot go on for ever. I wish to get married and start a family, but there are no prospects. Most Afghanis who have come to Iran are men and I don't know any local people. I have not heard from my parents for a while, that is ever since one of my clan came over and said they were quite well but suffering from the civil war.

II A Domestic Worker from Gharchak

I am a middle-aged woman, living in Gharchak, in the southern outskirts of Tehran. I go out to the city every day, working as a domestic helper,

FIGURE 8.3 An Achaemenian pillar in Iran Bastan Museum

cleaning, washing, cooking, etc. I am originally from a village in Khurasan. My husband did not own agricultural land and there was nothing to do in the village apart from working on other people's land. He thought it'd be better to do the same in Tehran and earn much more. Therefore, we moved to Tehran, where we had some relatives who had come before. My husband learned to work as a plasterer. He was often violent and was addicted to drugs. He was killed in an accident on the construction site. Without him, I have had to bring up our eight children on my own. I had rented a room in Afsariyeh, south-west city. Life in that house was really difficult. Several families lived there each in one room round a courtyard. In our village, houses are much more spacious and you don't have strangers as house mates. But here, with so many people in a house, things were too bad. One of my daughters who was often ill had to fast during the month of Ramadan because of pressure from neighbours. They were very nosy. Thank God we are out of that house now. My elder son managed to buy a piece of land in Gharchak and with the help of his cousins built a home for us. My two sons were little at the time of the revolution. They loved Imam Khomeini and both joined the volunteers on the war front as soon as they were old enough to be accepted. One of my sons has stayed with the revolutionary guards.

I take a bus to the city every day. All my time in this city I have had to travel to various places, where my clients live. I have had a few good clients for many years. They appreciate that a trustworthy domestic helper is not easy to find. Before the revolution, it was easier to find work. People even imported domestic help from the Philippines. I rarely go back to my village. There is nothing there for me. I left when I was very young and my children are now my most important relatives. I have always had to work to earn my living and support my children. I have had some help from various people, like some of my clients, for my children. But that was never enough. God knows how I got used to this huge city, which has no beginning and no end, after coming from our little village. My husband was not much of a support and I had to start working from very early on. I am not sure how long I can continue working. My children have grown up and now I go and stay with them once in a while. But I still have to rely on myself, although I am not as strong as I used to be. Two of my children live in Mashhad, a city I love. I have gone there a few times to visit. My eldest daughter lives there with her family. Her husband is a relative from our village. They and their children are very kind to me. Also I can go to the Imam Reza's shrine to pray, with its large golden dome and many grand halls. I have often wished to be able to live in Mashhad.

III A Housewife from Amiriyeh

I am a middle-aged housewife, living with my husband in Amiriyeh in the south of Tehran. We are both originally from Shiraz and came to Tehran many years ago. When our children were still young, we used to go back to Shiraz every summer. We go back rarely now, as the children are no longer interested, fewer of our close relatives are alive or live there, and travelling is not easy after all. We have lived in this house for nearly 30 years. My two youngest children were born here. I go out of the house every day, for shopping. I know all the shopkeepers in our street and they know me. In the past, they were more friendly and looked after us. Nowadays they seem to have so many customers that they don't care much about any of them. At the time of the war rations, the butcher and the grocer and many others all felt like God on earth. I'm glad those war days are gone. The city would go completely dark and you could hear these missiles landing in and around the city. One fell not very far from here. You keep your nerves for the first few, but afterwards you get seriously worried, although I believe in fate and used to think that if I was destined to be hit by one of Saddam's missiles, I would be hit no matter what I do to prevent it. Many families I know have suffered in some way, or have lost one or more members in the years of revolution and war. The war days are gone now but most subsidies are also gone. Everything is now far more expensive and it is very difficult for us to afford a decent standard of living.

The city has become much noisier and dirtier. We used to sleep on our roof in the summer, enjoying the cool breeze from the mountains. Now if we sleep outside, in the morning our sheets will have become dirty with chunks of soot. I constantly wash and clean everything, but can't do much about our carpets and walls, which get dirty very quickly after each cleaning and redecorating. Our little pool in the courtyard is now almost always dirty, even the day after we have changed the water. Only a few years ago, the water would stay clean much longer.

My children have all grown up and live and work in different parts of Tehran. They come and visit most weekends, on Fridays. The only time I go out of this neighbourhood is to visit them or our relatives. Once I knew almost everyone who lived in this street. Now very few of them have remained. Most people we used to know have moved out to other parts of the city, many to the north. Some of their children have gone overseas. We used to have a colonel and a judge as neighbours. Their houses had large gardens and old trees. Now those large houses are mostly gone. One household has sold its courtyard, to be turned into a new house. Another has been completely redeveloped. All the houses used to be one or two storeys high. From our rooftop, we could see a number of beautiful domes and minarets and many trees. Now our views are blocked by taller and taller buildings, all apartments. That is why we now have more neighbours and more cars parked on the street. Now our neighbours are lower down the social scale, small shopkeepers and minor government employees. We don't know many of them and have no relationships with them. My children insist that we should sell and go to some better place in the north of the city. I have refused to go. I still feel more comfortable here. I can walk to all the shops and every kind of shop is near by. Elsewhere, shops may be far away. Basically, I don't like to leave this neighbourhood. I like my home. It is not the best in the world but I like it. I know all the routines and places of the neighbourhood as well. I don't want to have to learn to live in a new place.

IV An Office Worker from Yousefabad

I am a young single man. I work in an office and live on my own in my apartment in the upper floor of my parents' house, although I rely heavily on my mother's cooking. I drive to work every day, which takes me half an hour. I normally avoid being an example of the donkey's theorem. A donkey walks the shortest possible distance between two points: from where it is to where the food lies. I try to use a different route every day,

FIGURE 8.4 The fruit market in Amin al-Sultan Square

just to make it a bit more interesting. Some routes are more congested than others. On some winter days the travel time can easily double.

I have heard some of my friends complaining that Tehran has no identity, that it is a grey and uninteresting place. I don't really think so. I think Tehran, like every other city, has its interesting and uninteresting places. Some people talk about how neighbours don't know each other and how the city alienates people. I have to say, I don't want to know my neighbours and don't want them to know me. I want to come and go freely as I wish. It is worse after the revolution, as there are more restrictions on personal freedom and it is as if you are always being watched. You always have to have a good excuse for what you do.

If you ask me, people in Tehran have no real attachment to their neighbourhoods. They are constantly moving and changing their places. I now live in Yousefabad and may go to Shemiran if I find a good apartment, although I will have a problem persuading my parents. Admittedly, some areas have specific characters. In particular some Armenian areas have a very nice, almost European feeling. There is always a lovely smell of coffee in the air. I go to Café Naderi for a cup of coffee any time I pass by, especially in the summer evenings when you can sit outside in its cool garden. I've heard that in the past, that is before the revolution, they used to have live bands in summer evenings. I love summer evenings in the city, in the wide pavements of Naderi Street, or Vali Asr Street north of Vali Asr Square, or the Tajrish area. The sun is setting so the weather is not as hot, but you still have the daylight of the long summer days. People have come out of their homes for a walk, or for shopping, or are going back home from work. All the shops are open and everything seems to be very relaxed.

Summer evenings are nice even in the old neighbourhoods, although not much of them is left now. The voice of the muezzin is echoed in the roofed streets of the bazaar, or the narrow streets of residential areas, where you find people have sprayed water in front of their doors to make them cool and inviting. People also water their plants and trees inside their courtyards, which helps to cool the air, although every year at the beginning of the summer there is constant warning about the dangers of water shortage. There is another warning at the beginning of each summer: about women's dress. Many women find it really difficult to cover themselves fully in the heat of the summer and this as you know is against the Islamic codes.

Pavements are not particularly inviting in the winter, especially in the east–west streets where the ice and snow remain on the ground throughout the season. I love walking. I have visited most major cities in Iran and a few abroad. I walk in the city without a map, hoping to explore some nice corners and interesting places. The old cities of central Iran with their narrow, twisting streets are a wonderful place to do that. Tehran has its own spots. When I get tired, I go to a coffee house (which is where they serve tea really, but the name is from before the nineteenth century when we were still coffee drinkers), drink tea, smoke a hookah, and start moving again. On Friday mornings I go with some friends for a walk in the mountains north of Tehran. We go there very early in the morning, before it gets too hot or too busy. We walk all the way up to a nice coffee house, where we eat a fabulous breakfast and look over the city from some distance. We come back before most people have even woken up. Some friends have asked me to go to ski with them further north, where there are very good pistes. I always say yes, I'd come next time.

V A University Student from Pasdaran

I am a young woman. I was born in Tehran and have lived here all my life. I have just started at the university, which is in the middle of the city, which means I have to take a bus every day from my home in Pasdaran, in the north of the city. This is a big change for me. Before this, I just walked every day to my high school. I had to study very hard to pass the universities' entrance test, in which hundreds of thousands across the country participate. It is very competitive and you have to work really hard to get in, unless you are in some sort of privileged position of having fought or lost a close relative in the war. That is why I have not been doing much else or going anywhere. My only entertainment has been going to the movies with friends from school or going out with my parents visiting our relatives or occasionally going to a restaurant. The highlight of the year is usually the

FIGURE 8.5 A shop in the coppersmiths market

Persian New Year at the beginning of spring, when we visit friends and relatives and they visit us. Oh yes, and we sometimes go to the Caspian Sea in the summers, which I like very much, although I hate swimming with my clothes on.

At high school my movements were very limited and I didn't know much of the city. Now I have to move around on my own and it is both exciting and a bit scary. Buses are convenient, as men and women are separated on them. The women's section is always quieter than the men's, I guess because women don't go out as much. At school we were all girls but here at the university there are boys too, although our contacts with them are rather limited. There are also strict rules about our dress. My mother and I wear scarves only when we go outside, not in front of friends and family.

I intend to finish university and then find work, because I want to be independent. After that I will think about marriage. My parents are very good and don't try to persuade me to marry as soon as possible, as some parents do.

The university is in a large site in the middle of the city. There are many bookshops in front of the main entrance and I take a walk there any time that I can, both for trying to find the books I need and for fun. Just next to the university is Enghelab Square, which is always very busy. It is always full of buses, taxis, cars, and crowds of people moving in all directions. There are all sorts of people there. That is why I try to avoid it if I can. My brother says Tehran has become like a big village, because there are so many rural people in the city. He says they come to the city and ruin the character of the place, since they do not know how to behave and live in a city. He says all these peasants should be sent back to their villages. I find my brother's views on this too harsh.

VI   A Cobbler from Shush Square

I am a middle-aged man. I have a small shop in the south of the city, working on my own as a cobbler. I have a large family, living in a small house near by. We have been in this house for many years. I walk to my shop every day. I come home for a lunch break and some rest. Apart from my shop and my home, I rarely go elsewhere. My earnings are rather limited, but I have no complaints. What I earn is destined for me, no matter what I do. That is why I am so content. If I find myself wanting something, I say to myself, "This is the material self and has to be controlled." Somebody asked a Sufi, "Where do you stand in this world?" He answered, "Nothing happens in this world without my consent, not even a leaf falling off a tree." He was asked, "How can you make such a claim?" He answered, "Because I am completely happy with all the events in the world, as I know that God is in charge." I am not concerned with material well-being. Some devout people are very interested in appearances and the procedures of religion. I am more interested in what lies behind words and appearances, and try to see through them.

My eldest son wants to get married. This is why he has been pushing to redevelop our house. Previously, it was a one-storey house with a small courtyard. Our kitchen was in the basement, but washing and a lot of other household tasks were done in the courtyard. Now, he has pulled down the old house and has built a three-storey building, with one separate apartment on each floor. He and his bride will occupy the top floor. I don't mind these changes. It would be very difficult for him to afford buying a place elsewhere and it is good for us in that the family stays together, although we can't provide enough space for all our children to stay with us after getting married.

Some days, especially Mondays and Thursdays, I have some visitors here at home. They are from all walks of life and often come to recharge their

FIGURE 8.6 Dizin ski slopes are not far from the city

spiritual batteries. We drink tea, smoke cigarettes, talk, and read classical Persian poetry, whose major works are often inspired by mysticism.

VII A Public Sector Employee from Karaj

I am a public sector employee, living with my wife and three children in our home in a township near Karaj, in the western suburbs of Tehran. I have to commute to Tehran every day, which means spending a long time on the road, waiting for and on the bus. My income is so low that I am constantly under stress with worry. I feel very ashamed in front of my family, as I can't provide a decent standard of living for them. My children are still young and have many needs that I am unable to meet. This is why I am very unhappy, but I don't know what to do. This is a problem of people on fixed incomes who get squeezed when prices go up like this. Traders and businessmen just adjust their charges. We are stuck. Some of

FIGURE 8.7 The 13th day of the Persian New Year (Nowrooz) is spent outdoors

my friends moonlight, mainly running a taxi service with their car. Others spend all their time buying subsidized goods and then selling them on the black market. Some even resort to corruption. None of these options is open to me.

We managed to buy this house with a lot of problems, saving for a long time, selling my wife's jewellery, and borrowing from our relatives. We ran out of money in the middle of construction, so we had to postpone some of the work, including the façade, which is now left in rough brick. I hope to finish the work in the future whenever I can afford it. A lot of other buildings in this township are in this state of half-completion. We used to rent a small flat in the south of the city but moved out here to have a place of our own. We could not afford to buy a place inside Tehran. There are many others in this township who are like us. Others are newcomers from towns and villages.

I would say people here are more friendly to each other than where we were in the city. Many are from the same town or village and stick to each other for support. But there are many problems here in this township: the school is not good, our streets are not paved, our electricity connections are erratic, and we don't have a park. Luxuries such as telephones are out of the question. There are only a few shops catering for a large number of people. We have to queue for everything. My wife spends most of her time in queues to buy our basic needs.

I have heard that people kill themselves and their children out of desperation. Sometimes I feel that I am on the verge of doing just that, although my religious beliefs prevent me from committing a sin like that. But what can I do? I feel very old, tired and hopeless.

VIII A Retired Civil Servant from Elahiyeh

I am a retired man, living in Elahiyeh, north city. I used to be a senior civil servant before the revolution. After all those years of working, my pension is ridiculously small, only enough to cover my telephone bill. I wonder how some people can live on their pensions. Luckily I have some real estate in Tehran and on the Caspian coast, which help me earn a living. My house is large, to be honest too large for me and my wife. Our two children live in California. Last time we were out there to visit them, my wife was keen to see if we could stay there, to be near them. We reckoned if we sold this house, we could buy a good house over there and put some money in the bank to keep us going. I can easily sell this house for 1 million US dollars. But we both thought it would be hard for us to live in another country at our age. Our children go to work and we are not sure how much time they could spend with us. Moreover, our standard of life here is definitely better, despite all the problems of the past 20 years. We have a gardener and a cleaner, which I am not sure I can afford over there. Some of my contemporaries who fled the country have lived comfortably in the West. Others have had quite a miserable time. I think I am better off staying here in these last days of my life and I can be properly buried.

Most days I go out for a walk in the park or visit my friends. I enjoy reading history, especially of the nineteenth century, which is a fascinating period of our history. Some of my friends think we are still under the spell of the conspiracies which were shaped against us in the nineteenth century. Before it was banned, we had a satellite dish installed, which was very entertaining, with many channels showing good movies and news. Some people have now hidden their satellite dish inside their houses. I decided it wasn't worth the consequences. I rarely go to the city, as the air is so polluted. Some days children and the elderly are specifically asked to stay at home. Our part of the city has been a very good neighbourhood for many years. Houses are all large, with good-sized courtyards and gardens. But these days things are changing, with high-rise buildings cropping up everywhere. Just imagine next door a large garden disappears and you are confronted with all these new flats looking into your house. Suddenly your street becomes crowded with noisy cars and people. I don't know what I would do if this happened to me. In one or two cases people have been able to effectively protest against the building project. But mostly the municipality wins, because they and the developers make a lot of money out of it. If it happened to me, maybe I would sell at a very good price and buy a flat. It is not easy after all to keep a large house; cleaning is one problem, security is another. Last year a friend of mine was burgled in the middle of the night while all the family were asleep. The burglars had cut the iron bars of the living room window and had taken away his very precious carpet. Some of these high-rise buildings have proper security guards and check all the visitors. Maybe I'd buy one of those flats anyway.

PART THREE

SHAPING THE URBAN LANDSCAPE

9

AGENTS OF TRANSFORMATION

We now have a sense of how a suburban village has become one of the largest cities in the world. We have also outlined some of the main features and processes of urban life in Tehran. Our next step is to investigate the processes which have shaped the urban space. By focusing on the urban development process in Part Three, we analyse the way Tehran's urban environment has been produced, especially during the last 50 years. This process will be analysed through identifying the development agencies, and the resources, rules, and ideas they have used. Chapter 9 first identifies the agencies involved in the urban development process. Chapter 10 looks at land, labour, and capital, i.e. the resources these agencies have used. Chapter 11 analyses the rules and ideas these agencies have employed in the making of the built environment. Chapters 12 and 13 go somewhat further in search of ideas, to find out about the roots of cultural practices and political institutions which have an influence in shaping the urban environment. Therefore, the interaction between the development agencies with resources, rules and ideas, and the impact of this process on urban form is the main concern of Part Three.

Development agencies are those individuals and firms that have been involved in the urban development process, in the creation and transformation of the built environment. To study the development agencies in Tehran, this chapter starts by identifying these agencies, from public and private sectors, and the tensions and frameworks which influence their work. It is essentially through the operations and interrelationships of these agencies that the urban environment has been produced.

WHO BUILDS THE CITY?

The outcomes of Tehran's restructuring, in two phases in the 1870s and 1930s, have been regarded as the "personal creations" of the shahs, the former by Nasser-al-Din Shah (Barthold, 1984), and the latter by Reza Shah (Lockhart, 1960), in the same manner that Isfahan was thought of as the creation of Shah Abbas (Lockhart, 1967). These comments, which regard the state as personified by the ruler, reflect the popular belief which identifies the supreme ruler to be in charge of major undertakings. There is no doubt that it was by the shahs' effort and drive that the city was reformed and that if they were against such schemes, no change would have happened. It is obvious, however, that they were not alone in these attempts and that they shared these ideas and their implementation with some other members of the ruling groups and a large section of the population. The intense power struggles within the ruling groups may be noted (Ladjevardi, 1995) and the effectiveness of the state in these undertakings might be questioned. It is hard, however, to cast doubt on the primary importance of the state in the restructuring of urban space in Tehran. In all phases of urban development, the state was the only agency large and powerful enough to carry out such considerable tasks as the reorganization of space in the capital city. Undertakings such as expanding the city walls, opening up the urban fabric to a new transportation network, and devising a planning system to control the development and channel it to some desired paths were all impossible without a strong state.

The scope of the public sector has been widening during the twentieth century, as consistent with the concentration of political power, the growth of the bureaucracy, and the rise in oil revenue. Many activities which were traditionally carried out by the private sector have been, especially since the First World War, taken over by an ever stronger government. The revolutionary government came to power in 1979 partly in order to counteract this spectacular growth of the state and its relentless intervention in the economy. In its initial stages, however, through vast nationalization programmes, the new government extended the scope of the public sector even more to include banks, large private companies, and the belongings of former rulers across the globe. Many branches of this vast bureaucracy are engaged in some form of development.

In Iran today, public sector development agencies are to be found in a wide range of organizations, from government ministries to post-revolutionary organizations. These agencies, through their hierarchy of central and provincial organizations, operate at national and regional levels. Another tier of development agencies are municipalities which are local organizations with limited geographical areas of involvement. Yet another tier are charities, endowment organizations, and revolutionary foundations, which should be seen as semi-public and might operate at local and national levels.

There are four ministries which are directly involved in the production of infrastructures. The Ministry of Roads and Transportation deals with the development of roads, railways, ports, and airports, although inside Tehran road building is in the hands of the municipality. The Ministry of Energy develops water and electricity, and the Ministry of Posts, Telegraphs, and Telephones deals with the development of communication systems. The one which is most directly related to the urban fabric is the Ministry of Housing and Urban Development (Markaz-e Amar, 1986a). The duties of this ministry include the provision of comprehensive plans for urban areas; provision of buildings for the government's administrative and housing purposes; control over vacant and public land; and provision of building codes and standards (Vezarat-e Maskan, 1977). There are also other ministries which are, each in its own special area of concern, involved in the production of the built environment. The buildings and facilities for military bases, the defence industry, administrative buildings, and servicemen's housing are developed by the Ministry of Defence. The Ministry of Health Care is involved in the development of hospitals, health centres, and related activities. Similarly, the Ministry of Islamic Guidance is responsible for development and maintenance of religious facilities, the Ministry of Education for the development of schools, the Ministry of Higher Education for universities, museums, and research centres, and so on. After the Islamic revolution, new organizations were established in parallel with the existing ministries. The prime objective was to foster the process of change and development with the help of revolutionary organizations which were not stuck within what was thought to be a corrupt and inefficient bureaucratic web. Examples of the post-revolutionary organizations acting as a development agency include the Housing Foundation and Martyrs' Foundations, which are mainly involved in housing provision. Some other organizations were created by nationalization of certain categories of private companies, for example the one responsible for the royal family's belongings. During the course of the last decade, however, some of these organizations have tended either to become new formal ministries or merge into the existing ones.

Some of the ministries have technical offices responsible for the design and supervision of the construction process. Few ministries, however, are directly involved in the process of developing a site. The main method used by all government ministries is to commission private sector consultants and contractors to develop their projects. Even the revolutionary organizations, which were recruiting large numbers of young volunteers and as such were initially able and willing to carry out construction works, have turned to this conventional development procedure. In this sense, the development agencies in the public sector act more as clients which invest in the production of space by public money. They become the channels through which the earnings of the government, mainly from its monopoly over oil production, are transferred into the market-place. A project might be planned and designed by either public or private sectors, but construction is nearly always carried out by the private sector.

CONSTRUCTION SECTOR AND THE NATIONAL ECONOMY

The construction sector has played a major role in the Iranian economy and has expanded more than other sectors of the economy. During the period 1959–83, whereas the gross domestic product (GDP) increased 413.6 per cent in fixed prices, the growth of the value added by construction activities was 706.1 per cent (Bank-e Markazi, 1981, 1983, 1984; Dezhkam, 1985;

TABLE 9.1 Estimated share of building in gross domestic fixed capital formation, 1900–65 (%)

Year	1900–10	1911–20	1925	1930	1935	1940	1945	1950	1955	1960	1965
Housing	44	38	34	12	13	31	38	44	30	19	17
Other	14	13	14	23	30	19	16	23	28	21	38
Total	58	51	48	35	43	50	54	67	58	40	55

Source: Bharier (1971: 54–5).

TABLE 9.2 Share of investment in construction in gross fixed capital formation (GFCF), billion rials at 1982 fixed prices, 1976–93

Year	1976	1981	1986	1989	1990	1991	1992	1993
GFCF in construction	2425	1298	1325	864	918	1161	1227	1270
Total GFCF	3329	1724	1646	1217	1379	1943	2077	2133
Share (%)	73	75	80	71	67	60	59	60

Source: Markaz-e Amar (1996a: 610, 613).

Markaz-e Amar, 1996a). The importance of the construction sector is best reflected in its share in gross fixed capital formation (Lean & Goodall, 1977: 317), which can be studied in an expenditure approach to the GDP (Pass, Lowes & Davies, 1988). Apart from a few intervals, construction has continually made up more than half of the gross domestic fixed capital formation (Table 9.1). During the space of only one decade, 1966–76, capital formation in this sector grew more than sixfold.

During the troubled 1980s, with a dramatic decline in industrial and agricultural activities, the share of construction increased (Table 9.2). This course of events, however, changed with the relative improvement in investment in other sectors.

Construction was encouraged by the government for two main reasons. On the one hand, the growth of this sector, constructing plants, infrastructure, and housing, was regarded as a precondition for the development of other sectors of the economy. On the other, development was easier to achieve in construction than in manufacturing industry and agriculture (Halliday, 1979). The construction industry has been directly related to, and has had an impact on, fluctuations of the national economy. Apart from smaller fluctuations, the periods of recession and boom in construction have been almost the same as those of the national economy. However, a one-year lag is traceable between the two. Whereas the peak of construction activities was in 1976, the national economy continued to grow until 1977. This indicates the effect of this sector on the whole economy, its sensitivity to the decline in the oil revenue as compared to other sectors, and its relative economic instability. The construction sector has had an important impact on other sectors by creating greater demand for their products, both by its strong relationship with other sectors and by generating income which increases the demand for goods and services (Dezhkam, 1985: 169).

KEY ACTORS IN THE DEVELOPMENT INDUSTRY

The development industry is a collection of a variety of agencies involved in the city building process. The main group is formed of those who initiate the projects, mobilize resources, and manage the process. These have included developers, households, and housing co-operatives, who build for sale or for their own use. These agencies have to draw upon the resources needed for the urban development process, i.e. land, labour and capital, which will be discussed in Chapter 10. Other sections of the industry include those who provide the expertise, building materials, and equipment, such as consultants, contractors, and manufacturers, or are engaged in the exchange of the buildings in the market, such as estate agents.

Developers vary according to their size and, subsequently, form of production. The smallest-scale developers are those who acquire a small land parcel to develop and sell. This form of production, which expanded with the rising demand for housing, is usually carried out by an individual, usually a master builder (*mimar*). Nevertheless, the profitability of house building has attracted many others to this trade. At the height of development activities in the 1970s, individual developers could be civil servants, doctors, as well as architects and engineers. The individual developers do not often set up a formal firm, i.e. a registered company with an office in a certain location. Because of the nature of the work, their office is the construction site or their home. Their only contact with formal procedures comes when they intend to buy the land or sell the developed property or when they have to pay tax. In order to reduce the amount of tax, however, they might ask the landowner to transfer the land directly to the buyer of the building some time towards the end of the construction process, as if the land has been developed and sold by the landowner. Because the tax is charged at the time of transaction, the number of transactions and, therefore, the amount of tax is saved. There is also a formal version of the individual developer, which are small construction companies. These firms are comparatively further up-market and their legal status and established office secure them a certain place in the development industry. The individual developer or the small firm supervise a team of skilled and unskilled workers and a number of contractors during the construction process. With an increase in the number of sites and the dimensions of the work, the developer would be able to run the team on a more permanent basis. Construction work, however, is largely seasonal and the workers might have agricultural duties in their villages of origin.

After the Second World War, along with the large-scale increase of Tehran's population, the high demand for the production of dwellings led to a proliferation of developers, who grew in size and scope to reach a peak in the 1970s. The impact of this change of size on the organization of production included the multiplication of the sites under construction by one developer and intensified use of land. Larger developers could build a row of identical houses, a number of identical houses spread in a neighbourhood, or medium and high-rise buildings. In some cases, the size and scope of the developer's work could be larger still, developing entire neighbourhoods. With the growing profitability of development, yet another breed of developers stepped into the development industry. With the help of banks and the royal family, some of them were able to develop new towns in and around the capital city, which provided them with substantial profits. The large number of new towns around Tehran is an evidence of the growth of this breed. The development of new towns often took two forms. In the first, the acquired land was subdivided and provided with some infrastructure. It was then sold to individuals or companies who developed the land, as was the case in Shahrak-e Qods. In the other form, the buildings were also built by developers before being sold, as in Shahrara. In both cases, however, a large portion of the developers' capital came from the considerable deposits which they charged the potential buyers. In a few instances, developers fled with these deposits without even developing a single building. In spite of the inadequate data, it seems that international developers were only beginning to be involved in the production of urban fabric in the 1970s, which remained ill-fated due to the advent of the revolution. Large-scale development has once again been a feature of urban development in the 1990s, when new, favourable economic conditions have allowed major investments in high-rise buildings and large-scale developments. The rising demand for new residential and commercial space and the authorities' emphasis on vertical development of the city have also played a role in this return of large-scale development (Figure 9.1).

The impact of developers on urban form is, therefore, set through their organization and their interaction with the factors of production. The large-scale firms, or those with access to large sums of capital, have often developed large-scale schemes using new technologies and standardized designs. The small-scale developers, however, have only been producing small schemes of lower quality and a wider variety of form. Similar to these small firms individuals and households have been building for their own use. A high proportion of housing is developed for personal consumption, which indicates the importance of individuals who develop their own dwellings. In rural areas and in the poverty-stricken neighbourhoods and shanty towns, the self-help process of housing provision has been dominant. Even in those cases, a few skilled construction workers are often present, who supervise the members of the household working as unskilled workers (Madanipour et al., 1984, 1985). In the majority of cases, however,

FIGURE 9.1 The growing scale of developments has been consistent with the growing scale of development agencies

individuals building their homes have to employ a team of construction workers headed by a master builder. In the more recent developments, the involvement of an architect has also been required. The small scale of investment made by these individuals and households has usually led to the building of a one- to three-storey structure, although the height and density of buildings in the city are rapidly rising. Variation between different locations around the city occurs mostly according to planning regulations and land prices.

Yet another group of developers are housing co-operatives. Housing co-operatives were established in the mid-1960s, in line with the promotion of savings and loan institutions. Until 1974, there were 360 housing co-operatives with 180 000 members, mostly white-collar civil servants, and 180 co-operatives with 11 000 blue-collar members (Dezhkam, 1985). These organizations, however, failed to produce housing in large numbers, due to shortage of capital and land as well as bureaucratic and management difficulties. After the revolution, with support and encouragement of the government to expand the co-operatives, their number increased to 3860 in 1984: 1473 workers' co-operatives with 198 000 members and 2387 other co-operatives with 462 000 members. In Tehran, 83.8 per cent of the co-operatives were formed by public sector employees. In that year, 27.8 per cent of all the co-operatives and 36.3 per cent of their members were concentrated in Tehran (Markaz-e Amar, 1987b). By 1984, however, only

FIGURE 9.2 Development of medium-rise buildings has increased the density of Shahrak-e Qods, which used to be an exclusive new town

12 per cent of the Tehrani co-operatives were able to launch the construction of their dwellings. The failure of other co-operatives was mainly due to difficulties in the provision of land, capital and legal obstacles. In 1984, there was an average number of 98 dwellings in each housing co-operative which had started their buildings. Therefore, the size and the aggregate form of their demand and the shortage of land have had decisive implications for urban form. A good example of this is the already mentioned Shahrak-e Qods (previously Gharb). In attempting to make more use of urban land, and to eradicate the monopoly of the higher income groups over this new town, housing co-operatives were allocated the undeveloped lands, including those meant for green space. They were allowed to aggregate two or three land parcels and build up to four storeys, permissions not available to other applicants for development (Figure 9.2). The result has been numerous medium-rise buildings and a quite high density which has dramatically changed the urban form in Shahrak-e Qods. By winter 1994, there were 1425 housing co-operatives in Tehran province with nearly half a million members (Markaz-e Amar, 1996a: 230).

Contractors are individuals or firms who carry out construction work for clients. At the smallest scale, they are specialized individuals, like electricians, plumbers, etc. who usually work as subcontractors for developers or construction companies. At the next level, there are small construction companies which can be contractors as well as developers. Indeed, a small firm can operate on both bases depending on its capital. An individual master builder (*mimar*) has historically been a builder in charge of the erection of the building as a contractor to the owner. In that role, the *mimar* performed the combined roles of architect, engineer, and master mason. It was after the new division of labour and dramatic profitability of construction work that *mimars* became developers. They have often entered the business as unskilled workers and have progressed to the stage of skilled workers and master builders. The skills of the master builders of this kind, however, are not comparable to those of a traditional *mimar*. At another level, there are large-scale firms of contractors which build large complexes, roads, etc. at a national level. Qualified contractors are those who carry out government commissions in all areas. The size and type of their work require that these firms should have large capital. Foreign contractors have often been employed for technologically advanced schemes. After the revolution, an attempt was made to reorganize the contractors' firms in the form of co-operatives, to give priority to their skills and not to their capital. This attempt, however, led to the bankruptcy of many young companies unable to carry out their commitments as a result of the delays in payments by the bureaucracy or of their own management problems.

An architect or an engineer is required, according to planning regulations, to prepare the plans of the building and to supervise the construction process. This is the area in which most individual consultants or small firms are involved. At a larger scale, there are qualified consultants who are commissioned by the government in nearly all major development projects. In certain instances, depending on the complexity of the project and the technology it requires, international consultants and contractors may be employed. Qualified consultants are also involved in the preparation of comprehensive and guide plans for cities and towns, which mostly take the form of physical planning.

With the expansion of the land and housing market after the Second World War, Tehran's estate agents proliferated to number 1000 in the early 1960s (Naraghi, 1964). Traditionally, these were in the form of small, one-man shops involved in land and property transactions in a limited locality. At no time did this fragmented form of estate agencies develop into an organization operating at the level of the city. Nevertheless, a more recent development of estate agents into more formal firms has resulted in a wider geographical area of interest. This process has expanded after the revolution and estate agents have continued to wield an influence in spite of restrictions from the government and the nationalization of urban land. In the early post-war period, estate agents could even plan how to subdivide the urban land on behalf of the landowners (Naraghi, 1964). In the absence of the required expertise, they provided the kind of skill which the landowners needed. With the proliferation of built environment professionals, however, they have generally retreated from the design process and have focused on transactions.

RELATIONSHIP BETWEEN DEVELOPMENT AGENCIES

Development agencies can be classified according to their access to money as an instrument of production and are subject to structural constraints exerted by the general credit and money system. This commodified link may also be traced in the relationship between development agencies and the rules and ideas which constitute other development factors. Simultaneously, there are areas which are either outside the marketplace, such as certain planning procedures, or have not been touched by the new market operations, such as the persistence of traditional ideas and practices.

In addition to this basic financial link, there are other links which relate the development agencies with each other and with their social and physical environments. These are various networks of relationships whose nature and scope are strongly affected by the extent of the market economy and the persistence of the pre-capitalist systems. For example, contractors and subcontractors relate to each other through formal communication channels as well as through shared family, ethnic, and religious backgrounds. The interrelationships are also affected by the size of development and the legal requirements which might restrict the – often public sector – client. In spite of the presence of institutionalized forms of contact, e.g. advertising, development agencies are often interrelated through personal contacts. It is mostly in the formal, large-scale developments by the government that formal channels of communication are used, although the role of personal contacts cannot be denied.

The size of the development agencies, both in terms of capital and organization, is also another criterion with which to measure interrelationships. Whereas the large private agencies tend to compete with each other, they are more in collaboration with smaller-scale agencies who, in turn, compete with each other. In other words, whereas the horizontal link is competition, the vertical link tends to be collaboration, a mechanism which enables the agencies to work in some form of division of labour. In spite of this broad sketch, however, there may be areas in which competition occurs between large and small agencies, especially during periods of economic recession.

While personal contacts have a critical importance for the interrelationship of private sector agencies, the public sector with its complex organization has various, complicated channels of relationship with the context. Important among these channels are policies which tend to regulate the development agencies, their interrelationships, and their instruments. In addition to this regulatory relationship, there are concepts of space, ideas, and images which relate the agencies to their context and to other agencies in a wider sense.

TENSIONS OF CITY BUILDING: DEVELOPMENT FOR USE OR FOR EXCHANGE

The private development agencies vary depending on their interests, strategies, and roles in the production of the built environment, and the degree to which this process has become an integral part of a market economy. There are agencies that develop land and property for their own use and those that develop for exchange in the market. This difference in purpose can become a major criterion in the classification of development agencies. However, as the process of space making in Tehran has not been monopolized by large organizations, as is the case in some advanced capitalist economies, there is a degree of flexibility for individual developers and householders to play either of these roles at the same time. A single building can have two different values: a place to live in, to satisfy the essential needs of life (use value) and a generator of rent, a commodity for buying and selling (exchange value). The potential conflict between these two values, between residents and entrepreneurs, has a strong influence on the social life and the shape of a city (Logan & Molotch, 1987; Madanipour, 1996a).

As the next chapter will show, private investment has been heavily focused on housing, because of its immediate utility and its profit-making nature. Development for own use has historically constituted the lion's share of the private investment in housing. As house-building activities started to become more integrated into the workings of the market and as working practices have become more specialized, development for sale has increased. Development for own use gradually declined to reach its lowest proportion in 1976, when space production was at its peak. The rate of decline was higher in Tehran, which was the centre of socio-economic change and the building boom. In the same year, there was a large gap between the other urban areas and Tehran, where only 53.7 per cent of new dwellings were developed for own use (Table 9.3).

The statistics show that the dominant form of investment by the private sector has always been made in small-scale developments in response to the basic need of building a dwelling for personal use. Nevertheless, it does not imply that space has not been considered a commodity, as a large proportion of buildings, whatever the initial purpose of development, are ultimately meant for sale. In an economy where urban land prices have almost always been rising, one of the most secure forms of investment has been in land and property. Development for own use, therefore, has usually been seen as a form of investment with a high rate of return, higher than saving in the banks or other forms of investment. At the same time, the large proportion of development for personal use signifies the inability of the construction industry and the banking system, among others, to cope with the growing demand for housing. On the other hand, the expansion of development for sale indicates a dramatic change, from very low proportions at the beginning

TABLE 9.3 The purpose of development in completed dwellings in urban areas, 1975–79 (%)

	Year	Urban areas	Tehran	Large cities	Other urban
Development for own use	1975	78.8	54.5	74.5	86.2
	1976	75.0	53.7	70.7	81.3
	1977	76.1	60.3	76.6	80.0
	1978	82.1	85.4	81.1	81.9
	1979	87.0	85.3	86.1	88.7
Development for sale	1975	17.9	39.7	22.9	10.6
	1976	18.9	44.2	24.8	11.0
	1977	18.8	36.1	19.9	13.0
	1978	13.6	13.3	16.3	12.3
	1979	10.9	13.6	13.4	8.0
Development for rent	1975	3.3	5.8	2.6	3.2
	1976	5.8	2.2	4.2	7.4
	1977	5.1	3.6	3.5	6.6
	1978	4.2	1.3	2.6	6.0
	1979	2.1	1.2	1.5	3.2

Source: Vezarat-e Maskan (1981: 102).

of this century to reach 46.3 per cent of new private developments in Tehran in 1976. Apart from the intensified demand for housing as a result of rapid urbanization, it shows a trend towards more specialization in the production process. Subsequently, it is indicative of the continuous development and increased complexity of a market economy.

Development for sale was widely encouraged by the pre-revolutionary government. It was in line with the specialization of activities and a change in lifestyle signified by higher social and spatial mobility. This higher mobility, and an increasing number of people who cannot afford to become home-owners, are evident in the growing importance of rented accommodation. Even the limited number of years covered in Table 9.3 shows how the proportion of development for rent has been rising to reach a peak in 1976, when it started to decline. The importance of rented accommodation is shown better by statistics from the early 1980s (Table 9.4). In spite of its decline after the Islamic revolution, this still accounted for a quarter of residential occupancy in Tehran urban province, far above the overall rate for all urban areas.

The growing proportion of development for sale until the mid-1970s has been consistent with the growing availability of finance and the increasing size of firms. It signifies a growing dominance of financiers in the marketplace and their impact on urban form, expressed in mass production of dwellings. The process of capital accumulation through large firms was halted by the advent of the revolution which aimed at a level of redistribution of wealth and mistrusted these large establishments, as they were closely associated with the previous regime. The revolutionaries encouraged small

TABLE 9.4 Types of residential occupation in Tehran and other urban areas, 1982–84 (%)

Year	Tehran			All urban areas		
	Owner-occupied	Rented	Other	Owner-occupied	Rented	Other
1984	62.5	26.3	11.2	68.8	16.9	14.3
1985	63.5	25.1	11.4	70.8	16.0	13.2
1986	64.9	22.8	12.3	72.4	14.7	12.9

Source: Markaz-e Amar (1985, 1986b).

firms and housing co-operatives, and, as shown in Table 9.4, promoted home ownership. Also the advent of the war and the following recession in the housing market caused a deterioration in the economic basis of development for sale. In the 1980s, the development for own use once again grew to reach 93.4 per cent of new buildings in urban areas of Tehran province (Bank-e Markazi, 1986). Only 5.7 per cent were developed for sale and a mere 0.8 per cent for rent. Even in the case of non-residential buildings, which constituted 1.2 per cent of new buildings, the development for personal use was 74.5 per cent, sale and rent accounting for 14.5 and 1.6 per cent respectively. It is worth noting that the legal restrictions on land and property transactions may have affected the statistical account, implying that, in reality, there should be a higher rate of production for sale. The decline of the development for sale signified a delay in the further development of the economy in the midst of a war and a revolution. The return to a degree of normality in the 1990s has once again seen a rise in development for sale.

These two major patterns of production for use and production for sale have had far-reaching implications for urban space. The increase in development for sale intensified the competition for space. This was a competition eased by the large-scale redevelopment programmes which opened up the urban fabric from the 1930s onwards. The combination of a unified urban space and the increase in competition led to the major structural characteristics of the urban fabric, as observed in Chapter 6 and as will be expanded upon in the following chapters. Availability of large funds for some and the intensified competition for space have meant that large groups are unable to gain access to land and property. They are pushed out to the south and outer peripheries of the city, creating an atmosphere of tension in urban building with the outcome of an increasingly polarized urban landscape.

Also important are the different rationalities with which these two groups operate: "profitability" in development for sale or "usability" in the development for own use. Traditionally, the former was distinguishable by its lower quality of product, higher intensity in the use of land, and its trend towards standardization and monotony of appearance. An important outcome of the growth of development for sale was a move towards standardization of the built environment, as distinct from the diversity inherent in development for own use. With further development of the production patterns and with the increasing pace of urban development, however, these differences have tended to be minimized. With the escalation of land prices and with the further commodification of land and property, the principle of maximization of floor space in the project is shared between the two groups, as both appear to be ultimately guided by the exchange value of the property they develop.

Development for sale has traditionally been a feature of the private sector, while public sector organizations have been mainly engaged in development for use. This distinction, however, has been challenged by the recent entrepreneurial undertakings of organizations such as the Tehran municipality. The Navab project, in which the municipality acts as a speculative developer, is a major example and shows how the boundaries between public and private sector agencies have become blurred.

TENSIONS OF CITY BUILDING: REGULATION VERSUS SECTORAL INTERVENTION

Another cause of tension in the city building process is caused by the plurality and diversity of the public sector agencies, which at times are engaged in overlapping areas and operate only within their own sectors. This has led to conflicts between them, hence raising the need for a co-ordinating mechanism. At its largest scale, this role is meant to be played economically and spatially by the Plan and Budget Organization. In urban areas, the Ministry of Housing and Urban Development, as well as the Ministry of the Interior, have been responsible for spatial planning and the municipalities for their implementation. This arrangement proved to be inefficient, especially at its weakest point, i.e. the municipalities with their lack of autonomy and shortage of expertise. The sectoral nature of public intervention in the city building process and the absence of horizontal co-ordination between them has had a frustrating effect on the Tehran municipality, which is the only organization with an overview of, and responsibility for, the city (Shahrdari-e Tehran, 1996a).

The conflict between public agencies grew especially in the 1970s when the production of space was at its height of intensity. For example, the Ministry of Defence, which was then called the Ministry of War, was investing huge sums in military projects with almost a free hand. No other authority seemed to have been capable of putting any limit on this process due to the personal interest of the shah in the armed forces. The impact on urban form of the lack of co-ordination between these powerful agencies in the production of the built environment should be seen in the disorder which it created, undermining planning control. Each agency has been pursuing its own projects without an overall interest in or responsibility towards the urban environment. Combined with the nature of the post-1953 governments, which paid little or no attention to the stark social inequality, this conflict and disorder could have done nothing but exacerbate that inequality and its spatial manifestation. In this light, it becomes partially clear why even the location of public institutions, whose development was in the hands of the government agencies, have enhanced the unequal socio-spatial structure of Tehran and its north–south divide. The locations of health care facilities, educational institutions, government offices, banks, post offices, libraries and clubs are all to some extent biased towards the north and central axis, although government agencies are expected to be impartial in their location decisions.

The public sector development agencies can be engaged in two arenas of decision making: direct intervention and regulation. In direct intervention, public sector agencies engage in development of special areas through various stages: to initiate a development, to invest in it, to decide on its location, and to have a powerful stake in the form of the development by determining their needs and preferences. The second form of public intervention is regulation, as manifest in economic and land-use planning systems and the policies which control private development agencies, their instruments, and their interrelationships. These two forms of public intervention, however, often operate independently and have at times created conflict and disarray in the process of space production. In an under-institutionalized market economy, the direct result of disarray between public sector agencies and competition between private sector agencies is pressure on the most vulnerable, who are in danger of marginalization and exclusion.

CONCLUSION: DEVELOPMENT AGENCIES AND URBAN TRANSFORMATION

The development agencies are linked to their social and physical contexts through their role, their purpose, and their relationship with instruments of production. Most of these links are based on the medium of money, due to commodification of space and increasing patterns of capitalist production in construction. Yet there are other forms of personal and communal relationships which put the agencies in contact with each other and with their contexts.

The public sector development agencies are formed of ministries in charge of the production of space, the municipalities, and various intermediate organizations. Their instruments in the process of making the built environment have been direct intervention and regulation through investment of public money, introduction of development policies, and control of the planning system. At times they have operated both on the basis of a social rationality to de-commodify some services and spaces, and an instrumental rationality which pursues the interests of a certain public institution or of some private individuals such as members of the royal family. The increasingly complex and centralized organization of the public agencies has led to the development of large-scale schemes which have had major impacts on the transformation of the city. The conflict between the sectorally involved public agencies, their inefficiency, and their lack of clarity in their relationship with the private sector partly explain the disorder and inequality of Tehran's spatial structure.

Private sector development agencies consist of a whole array of increasingly specializing agencies whose prime motive of development, seeking higher returns on their investments, has led them to focus on housing production. In addition to these agencies, who promote exchange value, there are agencies which develop for their own use, hence focusing on the creation of use value. In the process of developing a market economy, the amount of development for sale was rising, before the revolution and war slowed it down, resulting in an increase in development for own use. As the revolutionary phase gives way to a normalization process, an increase in development for sale can be noted once again.

The private development industry comprises developers, which include a wide range from individuals to housing co-operatives and large-scale firms, those who provide expertise and equipment, including consultants and contractors, and those involved in the exchange process, including estate agents. They can be mainly classified according to their relationship with the resources they control. Therefore, those who invest have a more effective stake in the urban environment than those who work in it. Yet the latter have also had their way of influencing the form of the built environment. The size, organization, and interrelationship of the development agencies have critical effects on the qualities of a development. In general, within a regulatory framework set by the public sector, the development industry shapes the urban space, by mobilizing the factors of development (land, labour, capital), technical know-how, and (imported or inherited) images of built environment. In an under-institutionalized market-place, however, some tensions in city building, such as the one between exchange value and use value or between sectoral intervention and regulation, have led to a social and spatial divide.

10

BUILDING THE CITY: DEVELOPMENT RESOURCES

This chapter explores the dynamics of the main resources involved in the development process, namely land, finance, and labour. These factors are used by development agencies as instruments of production and are subject to, but also constitute, structural constraints which frame the operation of these development agencies. This examination of resources will be supplemented with that of rules and ideas, which will follow in Chapter 11.

LAND

The social and spatial shape of Tehran today is closely intertwined with how urban land has been developed. In this section, the historical evolution of land, its patterns of ownership, supply, demand, price, and the main land policies are discussed. The section starts with the process of commodification of land, from the early, formative stages of land and property development in Tehran to the boom of speculative development after the Second World War, the post-revolutionary nationalization of vacant urban land, and the recent normalization of the land and property market.

Commodification of Land

One of the most important changes in the development of Tehran has been the way land has been turned from a natural resource into a commodity. With the development of capitalism, land has become a pure financial asset, a form of "fictitious" capital (Harvey, 1982, 1989). In the nineteenth century, the categories of land included: private property (*molk*); crown land (*khalesseh*); land immobilized for charitable or other purposes (*vaqf*); vacant land with no owner (*mavat*); and land which had fallen out of cultivation and was abandoned (*bayer*). Apart from conquest and usurpation, private property ownership stemmed from inheritance, gift, purchase, royal grant, and revivification of dead land. Its transmission was by inheritance, gift, and sale (Lambton, 1987: 51–3). This categorization was largely based on Islamic law and has remained in use despite some major alterations which have been introduced in later periods.

Prior to the 1960s land reform, two developments should be regarded as milestones in the changing patterns of landownership. The 1906 revolution abolished a major feature of landownership, a system (*tuyul*) through which the shah allocated the land on a temporary basis in exchange for services or revenue. Its abolition deprived the shah of one of his power bases and paved the way for further change. Another major change was property registration under Reza Shah, which was aimed at the introduction of institutionalized forms of ownership. This trend deprived many peasants of their cultivation rights and helped the landlords, newly emerging merchants, and courtiers to acquire new rights of ownership through registration.

Commodification of land followed the commodification of agricultural products. In urban areas, although exchange of land for money had been practised for a long time, the new surpluses of capital and labour, resulting from the changes in agriculture, found land a marketable commodity. Since the nineteenth century, subsequent waves of monopolization and release of land occurred which intensified this process. Large areas of land which had not attracted any attention for centuries, as they were not arable or were not provided with water, suddenly were in demand. From having no value at all, these lands found some use value and subsequently exchange value, which led to the establishment of a land and property market in the city. In this process, a part of nature had come to be considered as an economic asset for which many would now compete, as its supply was very limited.

Monopolization and Release of Urban Land

As a rare market commodity, land has been subject to consecutive waves of monopolization and release. The first major wave occurred during the nineteenth century, when suburban land was monopolized by members of the royal family and aristocracy, who developed large gardens and palaces outside the city walls. Most of some 77 small and medium-sized rural settlements, which were later incorporated into Tehran, were owned by the crown and aristocratic landowners (Kariman, 1976: 381–449). The first speculations on land were made by these landowners who supplied their land into a new market in search of profit. They were the main beneficiaries of both stages of transformation of the city, when the city walls, as physical barriers separating their land and property from the urban fabric, were removed. These large gardens and the agricultural land around the city were subdivided and sold for development. In the rapidly changing and unstable circumstances of the time, landowners preferred to capitalize their holdings, by working with, or even act as, a developer or by selling them outright. The owners could commission contractors to develop the land, but would not lease the land, as lease-holding often required long-term stability and the development of trust in a very volatile market-place. The only exceptions to this have been the endowment organizations whose constitution prohibits the sale of their land and hence encourages a system of long-term leases. Evidence for the relative absence of rent on land is the very low proportion of cases in which ownership of land and ownership of the building on it are different, only 1.5 per cent in 1984 (Markaz-e Amar, 1986b).

The second wave of monopolization and release of land came after the Second World War, concentrating on vacant and abandoned land. The Civil Code encourages development by attributing the ownership of land to anyone who develops it. Abusing this, many speculators registered and sold vast suburban areas by pretending to develop them, by planting a few trees or enclosing the land by building walls around them overnight. Even the flood relief channels which protected the city were appropriated and sold. The dimensions of this process are best demonstrated by the fact in that just 35 people had appropriated about 4 million m^2 of flood relief channels (Dezhkam, 1985: 200). The devaluation of the currency and inflation which followed the Allies' occupation of Iran on the one hand, and the lack of opportunity to invest in agriculture and industry on the other, encouraged the private sector to consider urban land as a profitable asset. Investments were made in urban land as protection against inflation, for present and future stability of capital, and for the prospect of a secure income. Property development was gaining ground as a result of the growth of the urban population and their demand for housing. Because the supply of land is slow to react to increases in demand for urban land, it is the demand which is the major determinant of property values (Balchin, Kieve & Bull, 1988). Between the end of the Second World War and 1960, 25 000 ha of urban land had been subject to transactions in Tehran, i.e. almost twice the actual urban land area of 13 300 ha (Naraghi, 1964: 11), indicating the intensity of speculative activities on land. Development of infrastructures always lagged behind housing development, hence land prices soared in areas where infrastructures were already in place. From 1940 to 1960, land prices in Tehran increased 23 per cent annually, as compared to a 12 per cent increase in the price of consumer goods and services (Dezhkam, 1985: 200). Before the introduction of the planning system, these lands were freely laid out by landowners or, on their behalf, by estate agents. The new form of the long, narrow land plot was in line with new building forms and street patterns. This new form can be regarded as a "rationalization" of built form; to maximize profit by making this commodity affordable to the newly emerging urban middle class, and to increase accessibility through narrower frontages.

To resolve the land problem, various measures were introduced by the government. State-owned land was allocated to military and civil servants for housing, as exemplified by Yousefabad. Their limited financial resources and high land prices, however, encouraged these new landowners to sell for a good profit. A 1952 Act of Parliament provided for the nationalization of vacant and abandoned land around Tehran, but was brushed aside by the 1953 *coup d'état*. The courts which were set up later in the 1950s to reclaim the appropriated land from speculators ended in failure due to the political influence of the speculators. Tax policies and the economic recession of the early 1960s caused a crash of the land market and decreased prices (Dezhkam, 1985).

The anti-feudal land reform of 1962 encouraged agricultural landowners to leave the countryside and invest in urban land speculation. Together with the economic recovery which followed and tax relaxation, land prices once again soared. The central government in 1960 and municipalities in 1968 acquired the right of compulsory purchase for planning purposes. These rights, however, resulted only in the acquisition of small areas, due to political pressure from landowners (Vezarat-e Maskan, 1981: 93). After the comprehensive plan of Tehran established service boundaries for the city, land prices inside the boundaries increased considerably. They rose even more with the increase in oil revenue in the 1970s and the subsequent property boom. Even the 1975 Act, which prevented more than one transaction on urban land before its development, and various tax policies could not check prices. During the space of one year, 1973, the land prices in Tehran-Pars and Majidiyeh increased by 113.2 and 84.1 per cent respectively (Dezhkam, 1985: 201). Between 1974 and 1977, the land price index in urban areas increased from 100 to 338.6, as compared to the rise in the price of goods and services from 100 to 160.2 in the same period. High land prices have had a negative impact on the agricultural development of the surrounding countryside and have reduced the chance of developing green space, which the city is desperately short of. High land prices have prevented capital from being invested in other sectors of the economy and have increased housing and commercial rents, generating considerable income spent on luxuries, all helping to fuel inflation. Increase in land prices has prevented large sections of the population from gaining access to housing and has accentuated social segregation. It has been detrimental to the development of public facilities and institutions. High land prices have encouraged a more intensive use of land, hence changing the density and height of buildings, and the patterns of land use (Markaz-e Amar, 1985, 1986b; Bank-e Markazi, 1986, 1987; Farmanfarmaian & Gruen, 1968). At the time of the revolution in 1979, the increase of land supply by large landowners, worried about future uncertainties, and by the revolutionary organizations, reduced the urban land prices dramatically to less than half the 1977 prices (Rafiei, 1986). The proportion of land price to total development cost in Tehran fell to 41 per cent in 1978 and further down to 25.2 per cent in 1979 (Vezarat-e Maskan, 1981: 89). At their peak in 1976, land prices in Tehran reached IR250 000 (about US$3570) per square metre, and the proportion of land price to total development cost reached 55.4 per cent (Vezarat-e Maskan, 1981: 89–90). In 1995, the highest land price was 3 205 000 rials (about US$1068) per square metre (*Ettela'at International*,

14 June 1996: 1). In 20 years, although the actual figure in rials had risen 12 times, it could generate only 30 per cent of its previous value in hard currency.

Another major wave of monopolization and release of urban land has been carried out by the post-revolutionary government, which nationalized urban land for the redistribution of landownership (Ghanbari Parsa & Madanipour, 1988). In the context of rising demand for housing, the private ownership of vacant urban land was seen as a barrier to land supply. Land prices were to be curbed and home-ownership was encouraged, the latter seen as the manifestation of the egalitarian notions of the revolution and the only solution to the acute housing problem (Vezarat-e Maskan, 1986). In 1979, transactions on urban land were banned. The policy of the Revolutionary Housing Foundation was to allocate land widely to low-income groups for their housing needs. This, however, led to the intensification of immigration into Tehran, as many people from around the country were attracted to Tehran and other large cities in the hope of free housing and free access to urban services.

As a response to the unintended consequences of land redistribution, the allocation process was stopped in Tehran. It was followed by the 1979 Act by the Revolutionary Council which nationalized urban vacant and abandoned land to be reallocated in accordance with the Comprehensive Plan's requirements. Within two years, the Urban Land Organization, which was set up to implement the Act, was able to allocate 32 million m^2 (59 per cent of which was for housing) at low prices in all urban areas (Dezhkam, 1985). To comply with Islamic laws, the 1981 Act watered down the previous Act by exempting abandoned land from expropriation. It introduced restrictive conditions for allocation, which required the applicants to have been living for 10 years in Tehran, to be financially able to develop the allocated land, and to follow the planning regulations (Sazman-e Zamin, 1985). Every available and eligible parcel of land was regarded as a target for allocation for housing needs. The Comprehensive Plan was disregarded as extravagant and outdated. In some areas, the planned open and green spaces were subdivided and distributed. Public services, due to the financial crisis which made them less viable, were given smaller shares of land. Between 1982 and 1986 in urban areas of Tehran province, a total of 61.9 million m^2 of urban land were appropriated, of which 5.9 million m^2 were allocated to 35 000 households (Table 10.1). The discrepancy between the appropriated and the allocated land has created a potential for future allocation and an opportunity to manage the release of urban land. However, along with the legal prohibition of land transactions, it proved to be crucial in motivating illegal transactions.

A new rise in construction activity caused an increase in the demand for land. Supply, however, was limited mainly due to problems in identification and expropriation procedures as well as to the bureaucratization of supply.

TABLE 10.1 Activities of the Urban Land Organization in Tehran province, 1982–86 (thousand square metres)

	1982	1983	1984	1985	1986	Total
Appropriation	1 007	5 318	16 109	10 493	29 025	61 952
Under discussion	1 827	26 640	25 110	7 139	6 496	67 212
Allocation (total)	441	828	1 490	1 714	1 426	5 899
Non-residential	31	235	31	57	159	513
Residential	410	593	1 459	1 657	1 267	5 386
No. of households	1 912	4 131	11 308	11 869	5 867	35 087

Source: Sazman-e Zamin-e Shahri (Urban Land Organization) (1987).

Land prices rose by 47 per cent in 1982 and 87 per cent in 1983. In 1983, the average land price in urban areas was 63 per cent higher than in 1977 (Rafiei, 1986). In 1984 it rose 14.1 per cent in Tehran, constituting 51.3 per cent of the cost of development (Bank-e Markazi, 1986).

The land allocation programme started with the aim of boosting home-ownership for the low-income urban population. In the beginning, it claimed to provide free land, a policy which later had to be replaced by selling the land at official fixed prices. The use of official land prices, which are several times lower than the real market prices, was regarded as a serious concession. However, the only loan available from the nationalized banks was for those who owned the land, which the banks regarded as the only guarantee for their money. This was in sharp contrast to the financial resources of those who were expected to become home-owners. Therefore, at some stage in the bureaucratic procedure of land allocation, which tended to become highly restrictive by adding more and more controls, the applicant had to, often illegally, sell the land. This was a process which was profitable for the original applicant, due to the difference between the market and the official prices, and led to the change of hands from low-income to middle-income groups who could afford to build. Another problem facing the new landowners was the absence of infrastructure and services, which either prevented them from building or made life in the area very hard. Between 1982 and 1984, the Urban Land Organization allocated 42 million m^2 throughout the country, more than half of which lacked the required infrastructure, making development impractical (Rafiei, 1986: 23).

In 1987, Parliament produced a new Urban Land Act. The government, which in 1988 prepared a framework for its implementation, introduced preferential land prices which would allow low-income groups to benefit from land allocation schemes. Applicants were grouped in two waiting lists for land, if they could develop themselves, and accommodation. Land allocation to housing co-operatives for mass production and the use of local building materials were encouraged. To avoid social segregation, land was not to be allocated to homogeneous income groups or professions in particular areas. Agricultural land was to be protected and, confirming an earlier government decision, creation of satellite towns around big cities was encouraged to prevent suburban sprawl (*Me'mari va Shahrsazi*, No. 1, October–November 1988: 9–11).

Most interpreters of Islamic law maintain that it strongly protects private property, hence fierce opposition was raised against the nationalization of land. The ruling clergy, therefore, had to find religious justification for this and similar radical programmes, which were often introduced as necessary but temporary measures, as a permanent change of Islamic principles was impossible. It is no wonder that restrictions on landownership had to be renegotiated later. As the country has undergone a process of normalization in the 1990s, many restrictions on ownership and transaction of land have been relaxed. The government controls large amounts of land and supplies them at subsidized prices to housing co-operatives and some low-income households. The early 1990s saw a slowdown in the economy and a recession in the land and property markets. This trend, however, has changed in the mid-1990s and land prices have started to rise again. As before, high land prices cause a more intensive use of land, both in terms of faster recycling and higher densities (Figure 10.1). The land and property market has become relatively more stable compared to the post World War II days of absence of regulation or the post-revolutionary days of uncertainty. Outside the city's official boundaries, where the development process is at its peak and municipal control is absent, however, the land market is still very volatile and far from regulated. It is on these margins that the metropolis is growing fast and uncontrollably.

Land and Spatial Structure

The first transformation of Tehran in the nineteenth century set the present pattern of a polarized spatial structure for the city, where the north and south are distinctively divided. Once established, it expanded on the same basis, somewhat similar to the classic sectoral model of urban structure as developed by Hoyt in 1939. According to this model, "if one sector of the city first develops as a high, medium, or low rental residential area, it will tend to retain that character for long distances". Through the process of the city's growth, the sectors extend from the city centre along the main transportation axes (Hoyt, in Nelson, 1971: 79). The emergence of the north–south divide developed along this principle. What sustained this polarized socio-spatial structure was the mechanism of land price. This mechanism, based on the commodification of land, has been a vehicle which has maintained social stratification and its spatial manifestation through the creation of barriers to low-income groups. The land price mechanism, therefore, has institutionalized the supremacy of the north by referring to both its physical and social qualities. After the establishment of this

FIGURE 10.1 Higher land prices mean land is being developed in shorter cycles and at higher densities

supremacy, land prices have consistently reflected the difference. In autumn 1995, the cheapest residential land price in Tehran was recorded as IR185 000 per square metre in district 20, the southernmost part of the city. In comparison, the most expensive land was in district 1, the northernmost part of Tehran, at IR3.205m. per square metre, i.e. 17 times higher, reflecting the dimensions of price differentiation and social polarization in the city (*Ettela'at International*, 14 June 1996: 1).

Land price mechanisms also sustain another spatial relationship: that between the core and periphery. As we have seen earlier, Tehran's spatial structure bears a limited resemblance to the earliest classic model of urban structure as developed by Burgess in 1925 (Scargill, 1979; Herbert & Thomas, 1982). There is a central business district (CBD) in Tehran, the bazaar and the north-central areas, which now form the traffic restriction zone. We can identify a "zone in transition" comprising areas of residential deterioration resulting from the encroachment of the CBD, exemplified by the Oudlajan quarter. There is also a "commuter zone" of dormitory suburbs, such as Tehran-Pars and Gharchak. Other zones, however, are hardly identifiable, basically due to social and economic circumstances which differ from those of industrialized countries.

This concentric pattern is supported by urban land theory which assumes that the differential accessibility reflected in land values leads to a competition for sites in the centre (Alonso, 1971), a competition which reflects social and wage stratifications within society (Harvey, 1989). The second transformation of the city in the 1930s dismantled the fragmented, parochialist structure of the urban space and created a unified space in which it was easier to compete. The general transformation of society was made possible through removing the social and physical barriers to this competition. We know, however, that in Tehran the north–south divide overrules the core–periphery relationship and that therefore the differential accessibility is not merely a matter of distance from the centre. As Abedin Dorkoosh reminds us (1991), the north and south of the CBD have different patterns of land price. In the affluent north, prices increase by moving away from the centre, while in the poor south they fall, as clearly the southerners are less mobile.

A pattern which the case of Tehran does not validate is that of intra-urban population density, described as a negative exponential decline of density with distance from the city centre (Korcelli, 1982). Although Tehran has been subjected to deconcentration processes, the north–south divide is also reflected in residential density, where the centre and south have higher densities. Furthermore, the density in the south, as opposed to the north, increases with some distance from the centre. More resemblance to Tehran, however, is found in the third classic model of urban structure, the multiple nuclei model, which was developed by Harris and Ullman in 1945. With the growth of Tehran engulfing the city of Ray and many small settlements, the city now has a number of centres to grow around them. Despite the persistence of the old core and its northward extension as the main centre of activity, the metropolis is increasingly developing new nuclei for its ever-growing population.

FINANCING THE URBAN DEVELOPMENT PROCESS

In a market economy, money is the major medium through which development agencies relate to each other, to their contexts, and to their factors of development. Availability of financial resources enables development agencies to have access to land, to acquire the building materials and technology, and to employ the workforce. At the same time, they are subject to the dynamics of the market and the rules which regulate the process.

Construction activities seem to have been always associated with the existence of some form of surplus of resources. When there has been political stability, this surplus has grown and could have been used in construction. This was the case in the sixteenth-century walls of Tehran, as part of the vast construction programmes of the Safavids, and has also been the case in later periods. As opposed to this are the periods of war, political instability, and economic decline, when few buildings are built and less attention paid to the existing urban fabric. In the second half of the nineteenth century, the increase in foreign trade and agricultural production provided new sources of revenue for the government, as its main income was from tax on trade and agriculture. The building of new walls and moats for Tehran and palaces inside the royal compound, as well as the ceremonial events and European trips of the shahs and their entourage were financed in this way (Amirahmadi & Kiafar, 1987). Between the world wars, two periods of growth of the gross domestic fixed capital formation are identified, 1926–30 and 1931–8, whose rates of growth are higher than the first quarter of the century but similar to the post-Second World War growth periods (Bharier, 1971). These are periods marked by the availability of funds for urban development projects. The first growth period owed much to the reorganization and centralization of financial administration. The trough between the two was caused by the great world-wide depression and the government's attempt to put the economy on a strict, centrally controlled basis. The transformation of Tehran, as well as a number of other well-publicized government enterprises, were carried out in the second growth period in the 1930s. These were funded by new taxes, increased oil royalties, a fluctuating customs surcharge, and some savings by inflation (Bharier, 1971).

After another trough caused by the Second World War, the construction boom of 1946–49 was partly financed by spending the funds built up by Allied expenditure in the country. During the period 1953–58, capital formation which had slowed down due to the nationalization of the oil industry in the early 1950s, rose as a result of the financial backing which the resumption of oil revenue and a certain amount of deficit finance provided. The crisis of the early 1960s and the fall in capital formation was reversed in the period 1963–77, when the rapidly rising oil revenue and reliable banking facilities supported capital formation (Bharier, 1971: 49–53). This period, which is especially marked by the dramatic increase in the oil price in 1973, ended with another economic crisis and a revolution. Another rise in capital formation in the early 1980s was due to the increase in oil revenue and came to an end because of the falling oil revenue and the disastrous effects of the war with Iraq. The end of the war with Iraq and the injection of borrowed money into the economy provided a new source of surplus to find its way to the construction sector before a new recession hit the sector in the early 1990s. In this way, the urban landscape of Tehran is clearly a product of the periods of upturn in economic cycles of boom and bust which characterize market economies.

Banks and Financial Institutions

Before the establishment of modern banks in the late nineteenth century, it was the merchants who dealt with money lending and credit. Until the 1920s, two foreign banks, which belonged to the two rival British and Russian powers and had been established in 1889 and 1890, dominated the fiscal and financial affairs of the country. The inter-war years witnessed the establishment of a number of Iranian banks, especially Bank-e Melli-e Iran (National Bank of Iran) in 1928, which became the core of the banking system with the right to issue money. The duties of this bank were taken over by Bank-e Markazi-e Iran (Central Bank of Iran) in 1960. Until 1952, six banks had been launched of which four were owned by the state. After this period, however, private banks grew considerably. Between 1952 and 1973, 19 new banks were established of which only three were entirely state-owned. The rest were developed by foreign and Iranian private capital or by their partnership with the state. This process intensified after 1973 so that, by 1977, the number of banks increased to 36, only 8 of them owned by the state and one a partnership with the private sector. During this period, the turnover of the banks grew sixfold. Foreign capital made up 23.6 per cent of half of the private banks' capital. In 1978, the 36 banks had 8374 branches around the country, 26 per cent of which were concentrated in Tehran; 95 per cent of the branches belonged to commercial banks (Razzaghi, 1988: 218–25). After the large-scale flight of capital during the revolution and bankruptcy of the private banks, all banks were nationalized. Apart from a few, they were aggregated into five major banks devoted to mining and industry, housing, agriculture, and commerce.

The private banks, during their period of rise and fall, were widely involved in crediting both supply and demand sides in building, thus having direct impacts on producers and consumers of built space. Sometimes, as was the case in a new town development (Shahrak-e Gharb), a bank (Bank-e Omran) was itself the development agency. Relying on the vast sums of money it controlled, as it belonged to the royal family, this bank was able to develop an entire new town. Even after their nationalization, the private banks continued to have an important impact through the public sector, especially within the framework of the Ministry of Treasury and Economic Affairs.

From the mid-1960s, a number of private financial institutions called Saving and Loan for Housing were established. They were encouraged by the government through tax holidays. These institutions grew rapidly during the 1970s, their number reaching 16 before the revolution, 3 of them based in Tehran. In 1977, they were able to provide about a fifth of the credit for construction, as compared to a third by the major public bank, Rahni. Their high interest rates (14–15 per cent) enabled them to make huge profits, e.g. the Kourosh Company was paying an annual 40 per cent profit to its shareholders during 1974–77 (Vezarat-e Maskan, 1981; Dezhkam, 1985).

Another form of financial institution for housing was the Housing Saving Fund, which was first established in 1958 by the public Rahni Bank. After the success of the Saving and Loan for Housing institutions, other public and private banks followed them. These financial institutions were all nationalized after the revolution and incorporated into the banking system. The new private financial institutions, which now rival the nationalized banks, are the charitable funds which attract large sums of money.

Public and Private Sectors' Investment in Construction

Knowing how much the public and private sectors have invested in the production of the built environment, in what areas, and in what forms has crucial implications for our understanding of urban space. Historically, it appears that the contribution of the public sector in the construction industry has formed a smaller, but more important, part than that of the private sector. A comparison between the expenditure on buildings by government ministries during the period 1926–65 (Bharier, 1971: 233) with that by the private sector (p. 235) shows the difference. Even when public expenditure figures have included construction of roads, the public sector has spent far less than the private sector. This course of events, however, changed after the rapid economic development of the mid-1960s (Table 10.2). From 1967, the government's investment in construction surpassed that of the private sector and, by 1976, increased sixfold in fixed prices, when up to two-thirds of the investment in construction was by the government.

This changed once again in 1979 when a 54.9 per cent decline in public investment occurred. Because of the long war in the 1980s, the share of public sector investment in construction was reduced to almost half that of the private sector. With the end of the war, however, the 1990s have witnessed a return to an equal share between public and private sector investment in construction (Table 10.3), a pattern that was predominant in the 1950s.

Areas of Involvement

In the nineteenth century, the government was seldom engaged in development of the urban environment. Housing, commercial, and industrial buildings were all developed by the private sector. Most public facilities such as public baths, water reservoirs, wells, mosques, and schools were built by private individuals, usually wealthy merchants, endowment

TABLE 10.2 Investment in construction by public and private sectors, 1959–71 (billion rials at 1974 fixed prices)

Year	1959	1961	1966	1971
Private sector	29	47	61	87
Per cent	50	61	51	37
Public sector	29	30	58	146
Per cent	50	39	49	63

Source: Bank-e Markazi (1981, 1983, 1984); Dezhkam (1985).

TABLE 10.3 Share of public and private investment in construction in gross fixed capital formation, billion rials at 1982 fixed prices, 1976–93

Year	1976	1981	1986	1989	1990	1991	1992	1993
Private sector	909	707	842	550	535	643	637	663
Per cent	37	45	64	64	58	55	52	52
Public sector	1516	591	483	314	383	519	590	607
Per cent	63	55	36	36	42	45	48	48

Source: Markaz-e Amar (1996a: 614).

institutions, or members of the ruling aristocracy. The government's share was confined to development of palaces and a few prestige mosques and shrines. It has been, however, by centralization of the political authority and some improvement in economic performance that the government has sought to interfere in the production of urban space. Restructuring the walls and moats in the 1870s reflects such a move. Another large-scale urban development scheme in Tehran, erecting the 1553 walls, had also been carried out by a strong, centralized government.

These interventions in urban development have been intensive activities over short periods and relatively small in size when compared to the private sector's involvement over long periods. They have, however, set frameworks for urban change. The walls and moats of the 1870s and the transportation network of the 1930s were both framing the growth of the urban environment. The same is true of the post-war construction of new roads, infrastructure, and major public buildings. These have acted as frameworks to which the private sector producers of urban space have had to adapt.

Having the largest single share in the urban fabric (more than 40 per cent in the 1960s) (Farmanfarmaian & Gruen, 1968), housing has traditionally been the main area of the private sector's involvement. With the sudden rise in oil revenues and, subsequently, construction activities, the share of housing in private investment in construction rose even further. Between 1973 and 1985, the share of housing never went below 83.4 per cent of all private investment in construction (Bank-e Markazi, 1986, 1987; Rafiei, 1986;

Dezhkam, 1985). In 1985, 97.4 per cent of the private investment in new buildings in urban areas of Tehran province was made in the production of housing (Bank-e Markazi, 1986, 1987). Even in the 1970s, at the peak of public sector involvement in the development process, its share in housing provision never surpassed 24 per cent (Dezhkam, 1985: 205; Rafiei, 1986: 43). After the revolution, its share declined even further, down to only 6.7 per cent in 1983. In the early 1990s, the main form of housing in which the public sector has been involved has been the reconstruction of the war-damaged areas and the provision of housing for public employees (Central Bank, 1993: 148).

The private sector's involvement in housing development has been essentially motivated by high returns on investment and by development for personal use. That is why private investment has been mainly concentrated in urban areas, where demand has been at its highest (Bank-e Markazi, 1981, 1983, 1984; Dezhkam, 1985). Within urban areas, it has been Tehran and the large cities which have accounted for the largest portion of investment (Dezhkam, 1985: 210; Vezarat-e Maskan, 1986). During the 20 years before the revolution, 47.3 per cent of private investment in construction was made in Tehran, 26.1 per cent in the large cities, and only 26.6 per cent in other urban areas. The level of investment in Tehran reached its peak of 62.8 per cent in 1969. After that, there has been a general decline in the share of Tehran, which has been in line with the patterns of population growth due to large-scale suburbanization with the help of buses and motor cars. This decline in investment intensified with the decentralization policies of the revolutionary government, to reach the level of 19.3 per cent in 1984 (Dezhkam, 1985: 205; Rafiei, 1986: 43).

As compared to housing which is dominated by the private sector, most other construction works are initiated by the government. These have included the provision of infrastructure, development of ports and airports, public facilities, and government buildings, both civil and military, mostly undertaken at the times of political stability and economic prosperity. As Table 9.1 shows, in the 1930s, capital formation in non-residential buildings has been more than that in housing. This is the period of the second restructuring of Tehran as well as of many other public works such as the development of the Trans-Iranian Railway. Another period with a higher share of non-residential construction works, which is also identified with rapid economic development, started in the mid-1950s and ended in 1978 (Tables 9.1 and 9.2). The first of these two periods ended with the outbreak of the Second World War and the second with the revolution and the Iraqi War, phases in which the government was politically and economically paralysed. In broad terms, therefore, it is these historical, destabilizing events, which have given rise to a decline in investment in the production of the built environment by both public and private sectors. Similarly, the stable periods between these focal points have witnessed the intensification of the production process by both sectors. The built environment is therefore essentially a product of these cycles of growth, and itself is a major sign of these periods.

Distribution: Patterns and Policies

Since the private sector has been mainly involved in the production of housing, the bulk of the credit has been devoted to house building (Bank-e Markazi, 1984). Until the end of the 1970s, the housing credit system increasingly favoured the higher- and middle-income groups concentrated in Tehran and other large cities (Dezhkam, 1985; Rafiei, 1986; Vezarat-e Maskan, 1977). After the revolution, serious attempts were made to offset this policy. Nevertheless, low-income groups have continued to be deprived of credit facilities. This is mainly due to the increase in land and housing prices, decline in purchasing power of the population, and the large gap between the amount of loans and the costs of constructing or buying a dwelling.

Since the late 1950s, the building of large-scale housing schemes and high-rise buildings has been encouraged by the credit system. The increasing size of the credits was directly associated with the increasing size of the developments. The willingness of the banks and the encouragement of the government led to the development of many housing estates and high-rise buildings by private developers. Even after the revolution, in the early 1990s, credits were mainly paid by the Housing Bank to the developers of large housing projects (Central Bank, 1993). Companies such as Sherkat-e Nosazi va Tose'eh-ye Tehran, which was set up in 1974 and developed Ekbatan new town with its 14 800 dwellings, are once again seen as the way forward (*Abadi*, No. 14, Autumn 1994: 72–4).

Nevertheless, a large proportion of house-building activities have been carried out without the help of the institutional credit system. For small-scale builders, credit has become available through relying on the resources of the potential buyers and on the high and rapid rate of return from their investment. For the consumers, however, it has been the heavy burden of the house price which they have to carry by relying on transformation of the family assets, aid from relatives, and loans from informal financiers. The latter might be charitable foundations, which do not usually charge an interest rate but offer small loans, or money-lenders, whose rate of interest is very high indeed.

LABOUR

Rapid urbanization and unprecedented expansion of the city have dramatically changed the size and scope of the construction labour market. These changes have had far-reaching impacts on wages, training systems, and the exchange of ideas and skills. The transformation of the old agricultural structure from the second half of the nineteenth century and the rapid growth of population have created a surplus of labour, which has needed to be absorbed in new activities. The construction sector has been one of the most important employers of unskilled workers, mostly supplied by the rural population. Because of the seasonal nature of both construction activities and agriculture, and their dramatic difference in wages, there has been competition between the two, increasingly in favour of construction work, although some workers continue to be engaged in both.

The country's relatively young population and rural–urban migration have caused a steady flow of newcomers into the urban labour markets. The emphasis on high-technology manufacturing industries and the neglect of, and limited employment opportunities in, agriculture led the job-seekers to be absorbed into construction or services, where special skills were not required. Major characteristics of employment in the construction sector have been the predominance of private sector employees and the relatively low proportion of employers to a large number of employees (Razzaghi, 1988: 123). No form of labour organization can be mentioned in the construction sector, as governments have been suspicious, if not frightened, of trade unions and any form of social organization which would threaten their authority. Even in a more relaxed political environment, the seasonal nature of work and the agricultural links of the construction workers would work against any prospect of large-scale collaboration between them.

During the period 1956–86, the number employed in agriculture declined from more than a half to less than a third of the workforce (Razzaghi, 1988: 117). The share of construction in employment rose from 5.7 per cent in 1956 to 13.5 per cent in 1976, which, together with the related industries and services, reached 25 per cent (Vezarat-e Maskan, 1981: 150–1). These sectors, however, have not been capable of absorbing all the new workforce. Even at the peak of economic activities in 1976 in Iran, more than 10 per cent of the population were unemployed. After the revolution, employment in construction, like all other sectors of the economy apart from the service sector, fell. In 1986, employment in construction was reduced to 11 per cent and in 1991 to 10.5 per cent (Markaz-e Amar, 1996a: 67).

Because of the rapid expansion of building activities in the 1970s, the demand for labour surpassed the supply, which, along with inflation, led to an increase in wages. Wages of construction workers, which during 1961–71 had grown at an average annual rate of 7.2 per cent, nearly quadrupled between 1973 and 1977. Afterwards, in spite of the general recession, the wages continued to grow due to inflation, although at a lower rate, e.g. 15.3 per cent in 1979 (Dezhkam, 1985; Vezarat-e Maskan, 1981). Between 1982 and 1992, average wages in construction grew fourfold, but at only half the rate of growth in the cost of building materials (Central Bank, 1993: 152). The cost of construction has increased partly as a result of increases in wages, reducing the chance of certain forms of development taking place and creating a barrier for the low-income groups to gain access to housing and facilities. The higher wages, however, were offset by the seasonal and unstable nature of employment in construction.

The increase in numbers of the workforce and rising wages in the construction sector have reduced the chance of training for many unskilled workers with a rural origin. The demand for the production of space, however, has remained high, suggesting an intensified demand for skilled workers. Many brighter unskilled workers, therefore, were urged, after a short period of being engaged in construction work, to identify themselves as skilled. This process, which resulted from the rapid pace of production, together with problems in methods and management of construction projects, has undoubtedly led to a decline of the quality of the built space.

Before the land reform of the early 1960s which mobilized the rural populations and gave rise to large-scale migration into urban areas, the construction labour market was entirely dependent on local human resources. Construction workers in Tehran and other cities came from the surrounding countryside, where they were mainly engaged in agriculture. With improvement of communication, development of a national market, and restructuring of agricultural landownership, Tehran grew as the largest concentration of job opportunities, high wages, and urban facilities. Increasingly, therefore, workers were attracted from the provinces. Initially, those from the northern regions constituted the larger proportion of the workforce. Later, the less developed areas of the south, east, and west, and even neighbouring Afghanistan, entered this market. In the 1970s there were hundreds of thousands of foreign workers in Iran from many different countries, many of whom were involved in construction.

At the time when the local labour force could sufficiently support local construction activities, building was carried out by a limited number of skilled workers who lived in the city. The unskilled seasonal workers lived and cultivated for most of the year on the urban fringe or in the nearby villages. The relative similarity of building materials and construction technology in the city and the village, apart from the more complex urban buildings of mosques, palaces, etc., eased this collaboration. The familiarity of rural workers with these materials and techniques indicated their capability in undertaking construction works in the city as well as in the building of their own houses in the village. With the introduction of new materials and technology in the city, a gap was created between the skills found in the town and countryside (Figure 10.2). There was also a skills gap between Iranian skilled workers and their Western counterparts. A 50 per cent difference in productivity of Iranian workers with those from advanced

FIGURE 10.2 New building materials have had a major impact on urban form

industrialized countries has been identified (Vezarat-e Maskan, 1981: 152). This has inevitably led to a loss of quality in the application of these new techniques and materials, especially in the more complex cases.

Because of the practical absence of formal training programmes, informal contacts and the exchange of ideas have proved to have a limited effect on the skills and concepts of the production of space. This is best exemplified by the observation of the built form in remote rural areas of the country in which, especially through migrating workers, new concepts, materials, and techniques are introduced. These are sometimes not well understood and badly implemented, at times with more negative consequences in the waste of resources and undermining of local architectural traditions. Nevertheless, these should be seen as the manifestation of diffusion of the patterns of production and ideas, resulting from the return of migrant workers as well as from other forms of communication, with strong impacts on the built form.

CONCLUSION: FLOW OF RESOURCES INTO THE BUILT ENVIRONMENT

The shape of the city is largely dependent on the way urban land has been managed. Through various waves of restructuring the urban fabric and the increasing demand for space, the surrounding countryside became appropriated, subdivided, and developed. The pattern of this development has been institutionalized through the establishment of the land market, which has determined a new spatial structure for the city, where competition for land and the access to resources are its main features. The gap between supply and demand and the existence of powerful players in the land market have caused a continuous rise in land prices, depriving large sections of the population of access to housing and the city as a whole of public utilities and infrastructure. The post-revolutionary state interventions to control the supply and price of land were attempts to confront these social barriers. They have, however, failed, as the post-revolutionary normalization processes have accompanied a change in public policy and a reassertion of the land and property markets.

The pattern which the flow of resources into the built environment takes is of crucial importance for urban form. Surpluses of capital and labour, resulting from the commodification of the countryside, increase in oil revenue, and population growth, were switched into the production of space by state and financial institutions. The increasing intervention of the state in space making, either directly through transformation of the urban environment or indirectly through channelling the flow of resources, has provided physical and social frameworks within which the private sector has operated.

A review of the periods of urban development activities shows their direct relationship with the periods of economic growth and political stability. In these periods, surpluses of labour and capital have been absorbed by the construction sector, hence integrating this sector into the national economy as a major component part. After the Second World War, the public and private sectors had an equal share in their investment in construction. With the rising oil revenues, the government's development ambitions changed the balance. In the 1960s and 1970s, the share of public investment grew, before the instabilities of the 1980s caused a dramatic fall in its role. In the 1990s, however, a new balance appears to have emerged.

Historically, the public sector's intervention in the making of the built environment was limited to short but intensive periods of transformation, which had a major, structural significance for urban development activities. The private sector's investment, motivated by high returns and by development for personal use, has been mainly involved in urban housing. The public sector has controlled the flow of oil revenue and has channelled it partly to the construction sector through the banking system's credit schemes, which were often biased towards middle- and higher-income groups. The way credits are provided follows a government policy of focusing on mass production by large-scale developers, a policy pursued in the 1970s and the 1990s alike, i.e. before and after the revolution. The small-scale development of the built environment, however, has continued without much assistance from formal channels of credit.

Dramatic changes in agricultural relations and the rapid growth of the population have created a surplus in the workforce. The construction industry has absorbed many unskilled workers and has accelerated the urbanization process. However, the industry's ability to provide employment for a constant flow of job-seekers has fluctuated with economic and political cycles. In the periods of economic growth and political stability, the construction sector has flourished, as against periods of decline and uncertainty when its capacities have been limited. In a fast-growing city, the shortage of skills and the demands of new patterns of production have led to the abandonment of traditional forms of training, reliance on a workforce from various regions and countries, and a more formal education of the experts, all affecting the quality, nature, and scope of urban development.

11

BUILDING THE CITY: RULES AND IDEAS

Development agencies use resources in the making of the urban space. But what are the ideas they employ? What are the regulatory frameworks of their operation? What rules and ideas have shaped the city of Tehran? In this chapter, we look at the stages of urban transformation in Tehran, looking for the evolution of the planning system in the city and the influences on the concepts of space used in the process of change. In the following chapters, we will complement the discussion of these concepts and practices, which are mainly borrowed from the West, with those inherited from previous generations.

THE CITY WALLS OF THE 1870S

The first major attempts to reshape the city of Tehran occurred in the 1860s and 1870s, when the city was enlarged and new walls were built. The need for security has historically been a major concern in shaping cities, especially in a land where sedentary life was under a constant threat from invading armies and nomadic tribes. Many characteristics of the Middle Eastern cities reflect the defensive measures taken against the mounted invaders: walls, moats, and gates of the city; walls and gates of segregated neighbourhoods; narrow, twisting streets with overhangs and bridges; and introverted buildings whose external face is formed of a blank wall and a gate (Hourani, 1970; Frye, 1965). It appears that Tehran's neighbourhoods never had walls and gates. The narrow streets and blank façades, however, existed but apparently lost their defensive value with changing circumstances. The 1553 walls of Tehran were built to enclose and protect a growing town. The physical barrier, which the walls created around the settlement, resulted in the development of a high-density urban fabric by the second half of the nineteenth century.

The perfect octagonal shape of Tehran in its first transformation is known to have been mainly designed by the Frenchman, General Bohler, who was a military teacher in the newly established polytechnic of Dar al-Fonun. With the implementation of this plan, as well as the construction of new streets and buildings inside the city, westernization and modernization of Tehran started. General Bohler was inspired by the old fortifications of Paris before the Franco-Prussian War (Barthold, 1984), which had been designed by Vauban (Lockhart, 1960). Vauban was the dominant figure in military architecture in France and had designed fortifications for many French cities during the late eighteenth century (Lavedan, 1959: 224–8). The transformed Tehran resembled his typical works, which in turn resembled the Renaissance ideal cities. The polygonal, star-shaped, massive fortifications of the Renaissance ideal cities (Argan, 1969; Rosenau, 1974) were designed for the new defensive requirements in a time of increasing importance of firearms. The new walls of Tehran, however, were not considered as being of a high defensive value (Curzon, 1892). They were so designed to relate the citadel and the city in a new way, placing the royal compound in the centre of the city, as distinct from its peripheral location in the previous urban structure. What Tehran shared with Renaissance cities was the rule of a despot. In the Renaissance city, the apparently perfect political and social arrangement was reflected by designers in the perfect form of the physical fabric (Argan, 1969). Despite its social and political imperfection, Tehran's new walls shared with Renaissance cities a geometric regularity. In the Renaissance cities, this stemmed partly from a concern for the exterior, which resulted in the design of buildings and cities being carried out from outside in (Vance, 1977: 227–29). It also stemmed from concepts of symmetry and proportion through revival and interpretation of the classical Vitruvian theory (Argan, 1969). Whereas this concern in the Renaissance period was a part of the revival of ancient approaches to built form, in Tehran it was not linked to the ancient Iranian geometric forms. In other words, it was the first in a series of imported concepts to give the city a European image. Rather than a revival, it was a rupture, a break with the past.

Many features of the transformation of Tehran recall those of Paris in different periods. One of these similarities was the building of wide streets in the place of old walls. In Paris under Louis XIV (1643–1715), the old walls were demolished and replaced by new boulevards (Couperie, 1970). In Tehran, under Nasser al-Din Shah the walls of the citadel, and under Reza Shah the city walls were pulled down to be substituted by wide avenues. The most influential transformation of Paris was that of the Second Empire. The 1868 reform of Tehran was immediately after the period of transformation of Paris by Baron Haussmann under Napoleon III (1850–70), setting a pattern which spread around the world. The presence of French nationals in the Qajar court and the increased European contacts of Iranians suggest that there should have been an immediate, although limited, impact. What the 1868 reform of Tehran shared with the transformation of Paris was the enlargement of the city boundaries and the introduction of new, wide streets. In Paris, the old tax boundaries were abolished and the city was enlarged to be divided into 20 *arrondissements*. This extended the municipality's income from dues paid on consumer goods entering Paris (*octroi*) (Sutcliffe, 1970). A decade later in Tehran, the extension of the city walls was extending the basis of gate tax which was charged on incoming goods (Curzon, 1892). A century later, Tehran was also divided into 20 districts.

The transformation of Paris was essentially in the form of new, wide streets cutting through the old fabric of the city. In Britain, the concern for public health had led to the demolition of courtyards and the building of by-law houses in straight streets (Bayley, 1975). However, the building of new streets in Tehran was small in scale, leaving the old fabric intact. It was more an introduction of a new typology of wide, straight streets, which was a contemporary feature of European cities. The pattern of the Chahar-Bagh Boulevard from sixteenth-century Isfahan seems to have been of minor influence in the building of new streets in Tehran. Nevertheless, the typology of Safavid squares kept its influence. The presence of a strong tradition of urban squares, the low level of mobility, and the demand for security resulted in the new streets of Tehran being treated somewhat as the squares, i.e. as enclosed urban spaces. Western influence can also be noted in the architecture of Qajar villas, which replaced the old courtyard houses (Faghih, 1988), and the landscape design of the aristocratic gardens (Alemi, 1985).

The outcome of the transformation of Tehran in the late 1860s and the 1870s was the beginning of a duality in social and physical morphology, in which new and old coexisted. This stage is portrayed by George (later Lord) Curzon:

> "We are in a city which was born and nurtured in the East, but is beginning to clothe itself at a West-End's tailor's. European Tehran has certainly become, or is becoming; but yet, if the distinction can be made intelligible, it is being Europeanised upon Asiatic lines . . . Though often showy, . . . it has not bartered away an originality of which the most modern would not wish to deprive it" (Curzon, 1892: 307).

THE OPEN MATRIX OF THE 1930S

The establishment of the central government's authority and its monopoly over the means of violence caused the final destruction of the city walls in the 1930s (Figure 11.1). The second transformation of Tehran was part of Reza Shah's strategy to establish his authority after his accession to the throne which followed the revolution of 1906–11. It included the fragmentation of the old royal compound, destruction of large areas of the city, such as Sangeladj, and opening up of other areas, which gave the troops easy access to these quarters. His capital was to become a unified space with a modern framework for development, an open matrix, where goods and services could flow easily.

It is well known that in most areas conquered by Islam after the seventh century, wheeled vehicles were replaced with considerably cheaper camels

FIGURE 11.1 Darvazeh Shemiran, where wide straight roads have replaced the city walls and gates

and other beasts of burden. It has seemed logical that the circulation system that became the common feature of the cities in these areas would result from entirely different demands in the absence of wheeled vehicles (Abu-Lughod, 1983). In Iran, the change of the rectilinear layout of ancient cities to the organic layout of the Islamic period, of which old Tehran is an example, can be seen as evidence. Similarly, the increased use of wheeled vehicles, from the nineteenth century onwards, should be seen as one of the prime causes of the demand for wide, cobbled streets. It started with widening the streets of the royal compound for carriage access, followed by several urban streets around the citadel. This trend was intensified with the introduction of motor cars, which later became almost the sole determinant of the street size and form, and eventually the criterion with which to evaluate the urban fabric. During the 1930s, when the streets of Tehran found the form of a transportation network, there was a rise in the import of cars. This is also the case in the post-war period in which the city grew with unprecedented speed (Bharier, 1971: 197–8).

The increase in the number of cars has had a direct relationship with the gradual disappearance of narrow streets and culs-de-sac in the new developments. New legislation was introduced to foster this process. The first modern planning law in Iran, the Act Concerning Building and Widening of Streets and Alleys, was passed in 1933 by Parliament (Vezarat-e Maskan, 1982). In 1941, it was revised as the Street Widening Act, which was subject to amendments in the 1966 Municipality Act. It was abolished in 1968 when the Urban Development and Redevelopment Act was introduced. As the title of these early laws show, they were basically produced to ease the process of imposition of new road networks on the old fabric of the cities. Therefore, in the 1930s, Tehran's mayor, General Karim Bouzarjomehri (Zaka, 1970), was legally enabled to carry out vast redevelopment schemes to build a new transportation network. The new streets had to be wide and the overhangs and bridges removed. In addition to the city walls, many Qajar edifices such as the city gates and royal palaces, some of them considered as parts of the cultural heritage, were destroyed. This was a process followed immediately in the major cities and later in the smaller urban areas (Clarke, 1963; Clarke & Clark, 1969).

The shape and orientation of the street pattern were partly influenced by the topography, which set the pattern of irrigation. In Persian and Islamic gardens, the patterns of irrigation were idealized in their geometry and layout and water was shown as the physical and symbolic source of life (MacDougall & Ettinghausen, 1976; Wilber, 1962). During the Qajar period, the supply of water to Tehran was by *qanats*, whose number gradually increased. The *qanat* is a system which collects ground water along the descent of terrain and leads it to the settlement and its fields. Typically, it comprises a mother-well, a number of shafts, and an underground aqueduct which connects them. By the 1960s, 34 *qanats* had survived in Tehran, each with lengths of usually between 5 to 10 and even as long as 24 km, bringing water from different directions (de Planhol, 1968: 452). The *qanat* system originated in the Iranian highlands in the first half of the first millennium BC and its introduction made many piedmonts habitable (Gaube, 1979). It has had a significant impact on the morphology of settlements in Iran (English, 1966). The subterranean aqueduct led to a canal and was distributed through ditches bordered by plane and poplar trees. So it could affect the location of the social strata: the rich near the mouth of the *qanat*, where they could use fresh and clean water, and the poor further away. The form and orientation of the street system of Tehran are clearly influenced by its *qanats* and canals. A number of *qanats*, mostly from the north and the west, converged in the city and led to a distribution system of open canals and ditches by means of gravity. Therefore, the network of streets and alleys which was laid out in the 1930s matched the distribution of water in the city, with the main streets running parallel to the slope and from them alleys branching off at right angles (Gaube, 1979: 6). Since the development of a pipeline network in the 1950s, the importance of the old water distribution system in urban form has almost disappeared.

The transformation of Paris by Haussmann had a limited impact on the early reforms of Tehran. It was, however, the second stage of reforms of Tehran in the 1930s which bore more resemblance to it. Reza Shah and Napoleon III both represented the establishment of an absolute power after a revolutionary period. Many have attributed the opening up of new streets in Paris as measures to make the military control of working-class quarters possible (Chapman & Chapman, 1957). This was also the case with Reza Shah who wanted to safeguard his newly established dynasty against the strong democratic movements of the time. The street developments of Reza Shah were very similar to those in the French Second Empire: imposing a degree of geometrical regularity by carving out new streets through densely built areas; concern with monuments and with architectural uniformity in the façades of the new streets; and loss of individuality of different areas which blended into each other (Benevolo, 1980: 798). Tehran resembled Paris in treating the urban space as a totality in which a working whole was to be created through interrelationships of different quarters and different functions (Harvey, 1985: 74). Both were comprehensive town planning programmes produced within a short period of time. The Paris of Louis Napoleon and Haussmann was a post-liberal city which was superimposed on the earlier city, tending to destroy it (Benevolo, 1980). Many characteristics of this city were distinguishable in the Tehran of Reza Shah in which the old city was to disappear through the imposition of new structures. The interests of landowners were quite clearly privileged and it was they who, especially during the building boom of the post-war period, mostly benefited from the expansion of the city and retained this benefit. In its transformation, Tehran was similar to Paris which had become "a vast discriminatory apparatus, which confirmed the dominion of the strong over the weak" (Benevolo, 1980: 787).

The transformations of the Tehran of Reza Shah and the Paris of Louis Napoleon were both a response to processes already in motion, and the framework around which these processes could cluster. The processes were those of industrial and commercial development, of housing investment and residential segregation and so on. In this sense, the shaping of urban space found an active rather than passive role in the urban process. The transformed urban space had a clear effect on improving the capacity for the intra-urban circulation of goods and people. Moreover, it improved the circulation of capital whose surplus, and that of labour, had to be absorbed through large-scale public works (Harvey, 1985: 76).

The impact of the developments of Paris on Tehran should be seen in the context of a wide range of cultural contacts with the French (Young, 1948). This was a country whose imperial power had never reached the Iranian borders, hence being more favourable to the rising tide of nationalism. As regards the concepts of space, these were introduced by French architects who worked in Iran, such as Maxim Siroux and André Godard, and the

Iranian architects who had studied at the Ecole des Beaux Arts in Paris (Wilber, 1986).

In addition to the French cultural connection, Reza Shah had developed strong economic ties with Germany, which ultimately led to the Allied occupation of Iran during the Second World War. In the inter-war years, German town planners and architects were employed by the Technical Bureau of the Ministry of the Interior (Vezarat-e Maskan, 1982). It is not surprising, therefore, that the redevelopment programmes of inter-war Europe were transferred to Iran through these consultants. They appeared to be using ideas from the transformation of central Berlin by Shinkel (Pundt, 1972) to the Bauhaus movement and the neo-classicism of Nazi Germany. The neo-classical style which was used in Iran, however, was combined with the revival of the ancient Iranian and Islamic architectural styles (Wilber, 1986), but with Western-style interiors (Lockhart, 1960).

FOUNDATION OF URBAN PLANNING IN THE 1960S

Since its emergence in the 1960s, town planning in Tehran has mainly focused on physical change, as did the earlier forms of planning, in the 1870s and 1930s. This trend of keeping town planning as a technical and apolitical process concentrating on growth management and physical planning has continued even after the revolution. The main characteristics of the modern urban planning in Iran have been that forward planning and development control have been carried out by two different, sometimes disconnected, agencies. Whereas forward planning has been undertaken by central government agencies and their consultants, development control has been the responsibility of the municipality. This division of labour has inevitably brought about conflicts and disorders. Whereas the Ministry of Housing and Urban Development and the Town Planning High Council are responsible for the production and approval of comprehensive plans, the Ministry of the Interior has been in charge of guide plans for smaller towns, and the Plan and Budget Organization for development and spatial planning at the national scale (Mofid, 1987; Bostock & Jones, 1989). As already mentioned, vertical and horizontal interventions in urban areas have often been unrelated. These conflicts, which are built into the centralized system of administration, have continued to exist after the revolution, which in practice has left its essence almost intact. The conflicts and disorders of the planning system are also built upon a major duality arising from a government willing to promote the private sector and at the same time trying to control it. The gap between these two aims, between regulation and development, has been too wide to overcome.

The 1966 Municipality Act for the first time provided a legal framework for the formation of the Town Planning High Council and for the establishment of land-use planning in the form of comprehensive plans. The Urban Development and Redevelopment Act of 1968 introduced a new property tax and the procedures through which compensation and improvement were dealt with in redevelopment schemes. It also enabled municipalities to practise, according to comprehensive plans, a strict control over new developments. The 1972 Act of Establishment of the Town Planning High Council and the 1973 Law of Supervision over the Expansion of Tehran were both produced to provide legal bases for planning procedures. A 1974 Act changed the name of the ministry to Housing and Urban Development and put forward a clearer definition of comprehensive plans, detailed plans, and guide plans. Its 1976 regulations set the definitions of the city boundaries and the development process in suburban areas. The regulations concerning land subdivision, planning permission, and development control were set out by the consulting engineers who produced comprehensive plans, mainly aimed at managing the rapid expansion of cities. The main theme in urban development schemes was the problem of dealing with private interests, hence the tendency to reinforce the government with compulsory purchase powers. After the revolution, with some initial decline in the government's authority, this conflict grew, especially with reference to Islamic laws which respect the private rights of ownership. Planning authorities had to seek religious leaders' ruling (*fatwa*) to be able to implement town planning schemes. It was argued that the ownership of land is ultimately held by the Muslim community, and that the religious government was therefore responsible for using it in the interests of all the community. However, the controversy over the state's rights to take precedence over private property rights has not been completely settled. As the revolutionary phase has gradually passed, private property owners have reasserted their rights.

The strengths and weaknesses of the planning system in Iran have come to be known and documented (Mozayeni, 1974; Mantagheh, 1976; Vezarat-e Maskan, 1977; Clark, 1981). The initial post-revolutionary reactions to comprehensive plans were very critical, calling them unacceptable or even opposed to the public interests and the principles of the revolution. For a while, in the atmosphere of mistrust of the previous regime, some pressure groups advocated a complete demise of the planning system. But gradually the benefits of a revised planning system and the long-term, undesirable consequences of uncontrolled urban development were appreciated (Vezarat-e Maskan, 1981, 1982; Hashemi, 1993). The pre-revolutionary urban planning system might have favoured a small, well-connected minority. However, it had, to some extent, introduced some form of control over the operations of landowners, speculators, and developers, which was beneficial for large sections of the population. The redesign of the planning process, however, was halted, mainly due to the advent of the almost decade-long Iran–Iraq War.

Tehran Comprehensive Plan

The most important document in Tehran's post-war development was the Tehran Comprehensive Plan (TCP). The rapid, unprecedented, post-war growth of Tehran, in which the population grew fourfold in 20 years, was mostly carried out by landowners and speculators who determined the layout and land use of new developments. The municipality was not legally and financially capable of interference in this process. In 1962, participants in a seminar on social problems of Tehran asked for an updated map of the city, provision of a comprehensive plan, and reinforcement of the municipality (Naraghi, 1964; Shur, 1964; Ghaffari, 1964; Behnam, 1964). In 1964, the preparation of the TCP was jointly commissioned to Aziz Farmanfarmaian Associates of Iran and Victor Gruen Associates of the United States under the direction of Fereydun Ghaffari, an Iranian town planner (Ardalan, 1986). The plan was legislatively approved by the government in 1968.

The TCP identified the problems of the city as including high density, especially in the city centre, expansion of commercial activities along the main roads, pollution, inefficient infrastructure, widespread unemployment in the poorer areas, and the continuous migration of low-income groups to Tehran. The solution was seen as a modification of the physical, social, and economic fabric of the city (Farmanfarmaian & Gruen, 1968). The proposals were nevertheless mostly physical, attempting to impose a new order on the existing physical fabric. The envisaged future form of the city was a linear one which, stretching towards the west, reduced the concentration of activities in the city centre. The city would be formed of 10 large urban districts, each with about 500 000 population, a commercial and an industrial centre with high-rise buildings. Each district (*mantagheh*) would be subdivided into a number of areas (*nahyeh*) and neighbourhoods (*mahalleh*). An area, with a population of about 15 000–30 000, would have a high school and a commercial centre and other necessary facilities. The neighbourhood with its 5000 population would have a primary school and a local commercial centre. These districts and areas would be linked by a transportation network whose two main features are a rapid transit route and a bus route. The stops in the rapid transit route would be developed as the concentration of activities with a high residential density. The existing city fabric would be subject to redevelopment and improvement schemes which necessitate a resettlement of up to 600 000 townspeople out of central areas.

Almost all these measures can be traced back to the fashionable planning ideas of the time, transposed on to the city of Tehran. The idea of the linear city, which had stemmed from the proposal of Soria Y Mata for Madrid in 1882 and from Tony Garnier's project for an industrial city, was proposed for the reconstruction of London after the Second World War (RIBA, 1943). It was applied later in the designs of the new towns Cumbernauld and

Hook (Osborn & Whittick, 1963; London County Council, 1963) and led to numerous debates and a lasting influence (Jencks, 1973: 355; Llewelyn-Davies, 1972: 104; Chermayeff & Tzonis, 1971: 225; Chadwick, 1971: 121; Krier, 1979). After the TCP, a linear administrative centre for Tehran was designed by Lord Llewelyn-Davies who had designed Washington and Milton Keynes new towns in Britain with a gridiron pattern of primary streets (Holley, 1983; Llewelyn-Davies et al., 1966; Walker, 1982; Llewelyn-Davies, 1972).

The influence of the British new towns movement, which had been of great international interest, was paramount. In his book, *The Heart of Our Cities*, Victor Gruen (1965) had proposed how the metropolis of tomorrow would be comprised of a central city surrounded by 10 cities each with its own centre, a proposal resembling the "social cities" of Ebenezer Howard (1960: 142), which were formed of a cluster of garden cities grouped around a central city. Victor Gruen's proposal for Tehran was a linear version of this concept. One aspect of linear design, which the TCP shared with new towns such as Redditch, Runcorn, and Irvine (Wilson & Womersley, 1966; Ling, 1967; Irvine New Town Corporation, 1971), was the importance of a public transport route as the spine of the town, with its stopping points serving as the foci of the town. Another point was the use of neighbourhood units of limited population focused on a neighbourhood centre and a primary school. This idea had been developed in the 1920s in the United States by Clarence Perry and was based on the catchment area of a primary school (Mumford, 1954; Hall, 1975), advocating the creation of intimate communities through juxtaposition of a small number of people in physically separated areas. The idea was widely used in the first generation of the British new towns and, after being criticized about its social objectives (Goss, 1961), remained in use as a means of provision of facilities (Schaffer, 1972) and of organization of urban space.

Yet another design concept was the Radburn idea of superblocks inwardly ramified into culs-de-sac. Culs-de-sac had been used in the late-nineteenth-century design of London's New Earswick garden suburb by Raymond Unwin (Bayley, 1975: 18). Developed in the inter-war period in the United States, the Radburn idea, which was widely used later in new towns, integrated culs-de-sac into superblocks with central parks to create a separation of pedestrian from car (Stein, 1966). The TCP's use of neighbourhoods and culs-de-sac resulted from a transfer of ideas from the West, unrelated to the actual shape of Iranian cities at the time, which actually included close-knit neighbourhoods and culs-de-sac but had been discarded in recent times as outdated.

The TCP used the design concepts of the British new towns without pursuing their social objectives. Howard's ideas have been regarded as the midpoint in the line between the nineteenth-century Utopians and the twentieth-century planners (Camhis, 1979: 27). He proposed garden cities as

FIGURE 11.2 Modernist design has essentially shaped Tehran

a "real path to reform" which would combine the benefits of town and country and be free from the disadvantages of either (Howard, 1960: 46–7). The two generations of post-war British new towns (Champion et al., 1977) were planned and developed as alternatives to city overgrowth and congestion and to urban sprawl (Osborn & Whittick, 1963: 7). They were proposed to be "self-contained" and socially "balanced" communities for working and living (Cresswell & Thomas, 1973: 14). Nevertheless, these two objectives seemed to have remained out of reach: the balanced communities of all classes and ages were not achieved (Wirz, 1975; Cresswell & Thomas, 1973), and self-containment was eroded by increasing mobility and heterogeneity of employment (Aldridge, 1979). In the development of satellite towns for Tehran, which have continued to this day, the main aim has been management and containment of urban growth, rather than achieving social and Utopian goals.

Another source of influence for the TCP was the modernist ideas of the time. The principles of the Modern Movement, although utilized by individual architects who had studied in the West (Pakdaman, 1983), had not found a wide appeal before the early 1960s. At this time, when the disorderly, rapid, post-war growth of Tehran had made its disastrous effects felt, a need for urban planning as advocated by the Charter of Athens began to be emphasized (Moayed, 1964) (Figure 11.2). In this 1933 document, modern planning and modern technology were seen as offering unlimited possibilities for the reconstruction of cities. Densely populated districts and their street system with insufficient widths were relics of past eras, and were to be replaced with high-rise residential blocks set in parks and served by a new access system. It was argued that, "adaptation to the past should not be tolerated in any case" (Sert, 1944: 242–9). For the post-war generation, large-scale slum clearance and urban redevelopment was a way of reshaping the cities and towns. This was especially the case where apparently two major problems were faced: traffic congestion and worn-out structures. It was argued that, "if we are to have any chance of living at peace with the motor car, we shall need a different sort of city" (Buchanan, 1963: 41–2). In Iran, following the inter-war trends, large sections of the urban fabric were subject to redevelopment and imposition of new roads. In the early master plans (Kocks et al., 1961), the old fabrics of the towns were targets of redevelopment schemes meant to bring them into "order". Nevertheless, many of the social objectives of the Western programmes were not adopted by the Iranian development agencies. High-rise buildings were being built in the north city for housing the middle classes, rather than reducing the congestion of the centre. Urban motorways served the affluent suburbs, rather than giving easier access to the CBD. In other words, images were borrowed without their purpose and contents. This could be an alienating process, in which an image was divorced from its original context and was employed with some new intentions.

The economic recession in the West, which had created a decline in redevelopment schemes, reached Iran in the mid-1970s, when demand for conservation was rising (Falamaki, 1978). The post-revolutionary government claimed to revive many traditional forms and practices. In relation to the built environment, however, it shows strongly modernist tendencies. Redevelopment has remained as a strong force in the transformation of urban space. New schemes for urban motorways and large-scale redevelopment of the central and decayed areas continue to be prepared and implemented without evaluating the social and cultural impacts of similar schemes previously applied.

The TCP had asked for social *and* physical transformation of the city. However, the modification of the physical fabric was not extended to the social and economic fabric of the city. The north–south social divide was not only recognized but also enhanced. The north was meant to be occupied by higher-income groups associated with a low density of up to 150 persons per hectare. As opposed to this, the south would be the living place of the low-income groups in densities of up to 500 persons per hectare. The proposed industrial areas were planned to be next to the low-income areas of the south. The effects of the TCP for the inner areas of the city was the imposition of a blight. For example, Oudlajan has been one of the areas which the TCP suggested be entirely redeveloped. The complexities of landownership and the financial requirements of such an undertaking made the proposed, large-scale redevelopment improbable.

Meanwhile, planning permissions for improvement and renewal were refused. This created a long-term blight which led to gradual deterioration of a large and old part at the heart of the city (Rahmani & Hafeznia, 1988).

The large-scale proposals of TCP proved impossible to be implemented. It set, however, planning regulations which, although changed through the years, have been most effective in the creation of a new townscape. These regulations have controlled the floor ratio, height of buildings, and their use. The other main concerns with building form have been expressed in restriction on overhangs, open spaces, and parking (Shahrdari-e Tehran, 1986). The essential requirements of devoting at least 40 per cent of a residential land parcel to open space and to take into account the neighbours' building location have created terraces and courtyards. Also the requirement of the provision of parking space within the development has encouraged a widespread application of pilotis, supporting pillars, in residential areas, which have dramatically changed the street scene. In this way, the doors and windows of houses are replaced with the doors and bars of ground-floor garages, depriving the street level of its liveliness and diversity.

The TCP came under numerous attacks after the revolution, as it was seen to have been unable to cope with the pace of change in the city. In 1988, Tehran's mayor criticized the plan in that it was mainly a physical development plan, that it was rooted in the political framework of the previous regime, and that it did not pay enough attention to the problems of implementation (Mashhadizadeh Dehaghani, 1995: 487).

City Boundaries

The TCP which was approved in 1968 determined a 230 km² service boundary, better known as the 5-year boundary (5YB) and the provision for future expansion within a 630 km² 25-year boundary (25YB). A hinterland was also identified beyond the 25YB. The service boundary was the area in which the municipality was required to provide urban services and infrastructure. It was expected to be revised in five-year intervals so that it would expand to reach the 25YB. In order to control the expansion of the city, development was prohibited beyond the 5YB (Vezarat-e Maskan, 1977; Kariman, 1976).

The second 5YB, however, was never introduced. It was argued that there was enough undeveloped land within the present boundary. Moreover, the municipality seemed unable to cope with the rising demand of new developments for infrastructure. This led to an increase in land prices both within and without the 5YB and, subsequently, a higher rate of redevelopment, higher density and traffic congestion, and a reduction of open space.

In 1973, a group of cabinet ministers formed the Supervisory Council for the Expansion of Tehran. The council was to contain the expansion of the city by controlling the development in the area between the 5YB and the 25YB. This was expected to put an end to the period in which various and sometimes contradictory decisions were made for the inter-boundary area. Apart from procedural ambiguities, the main shortcomings of the council were the exclusion of members of the city council from it, as was also the case earlier in the approval of the TCP (Vezarat-e Maskan, 1977). It also disregarded the areas beyond the 25YB which were already linked to Tehran and formed a metropolitan region. Initially, the council blocked any new development. From 1976, however, it agreed to grant permissions for large-scale developments: townships larger than 300 000 m^2 and residential complexes larger than 30 000 m^2. The 1973 law asked the municipality to comply with the council and to demolish any development in this area which took place illegally. With even faster rates of population growth in Tehran, however, new shanty towns were being built in this area. The demolition of one of these shanty towns led to bloodshed and was one of the early events which marked the beginning of the revolution. Even with this background, scenes of demolition and conflict were repeated after the revolution, as the municipality attempted to prevent illegal development. The relaxation of control during the revolution led to an influx of illegal development in the inter-boundary area. Immediately after the revolution, the government was forced to announce the 25YB as the present service boundary in which development through planning permission was allowed. The rate at which these suburban areas developed afterwards has been unprecedented indeed.

After the Second World War, with an increase in mobility and a changing pattern of landownership, many small satellite settlements grew around the cities, constituting one of the major forms of urban development in Tehran and other large cities in Iran. One of the first townships which was developed in 1951 was Tehran-Pars. These were large housing estates without any provision for jobs or local facilities. It has only been with the passage of time that a high street with some shops and services has evolved in these suburban townships. The development of these townships was under no form of planning control before the 1966 law, which required the development process to be based on consent from the Ministry of the Interior. It was the 1974 law and its 1976 subsequent by-law which set the regulatory framework for this form of development, requiring the townships to apply for planning permission. After the enlargement of the municipal boundaries, many satellite towns are now annexed to the city. Since the 1950s, 108 rural settlements have been incorporated in the 25YB. Some of these settlements have kept a separate identity and have grown considerably. Depending on their location, they have attracted immigrant workers or suburbanizing middle classes. There are also 40 new towns which have been developed through various mechanisms. These satellite towns often receive very limited services from the municipality, although they have been formally integrated into the city (Nazarian, 1991).

TEHRAN MUNICIPALITY'S STRATEGIC PLAN IN THE 1990S

The first development plan after the revolution (Vezarat-e Barnameh, 1987a) summarized the structural problems of urban development. These included: the lack of necessary mechanisms to mobilize non-governmental resources; lack of comprehensive national and regional planning for housing and urban development, incorporating urban planning; ambiguities in identification of urban land; and legal contradictions between the agencies involved. Other problems included weakness of municipalities; imbalance in the urban system; inefficiency in laws and regulation; and lack of implementation of comprehensive plans. The policies which the plan adopted for the following five years were, therefore, to provide a long-term national and regional spatial plan; updating the comprehensive plans of Tehran and other large cities; reinforcing municipalities; improving public transport; completion and privatization of the half-built buildings; and giving priority to the redevelopment of old neighbourhoods in order to control urban expansion. These policies have been used largely in the preparation of a new strategic plan by the Tehran municipality (Shahrdari-e Tehran, 1996a). The Minister of Housing and Urban Development, in his address to a conference on physical planning in Iran, stressed the need that all aspects of town planning should be undertaken by the municipalities. He also emphasized the need to enlarge the service boundaries of the municipalities and to set up a single authority for urban regions (*Abadi*, No. 3, Winter 1993: 4–5).

The 1968 TCP's 25-year period came to an end in 1993. The new TCP (Tarh-e Jame'-e Samandehi-e Shahr-e Tehran), which was prepared by a firm of private consultants (A-Tec), however, could not secure Tehran municipality's approval. The municipality disagreed with the new plan's priorities and the way various activities have been evaluated and inter-related. So it set out to prepare a strategic plan of its own, as it is the municipality which is mainly responsible for implementing it. The plan has been prepared by bringing together a set of evaluations and proposals from the municipality's various departments (Shahrdari-e Tehran, 1996a, b). It has been called the Tehran Municipality's First Plan (Barnameh-ye Avval-e Shahrdari-e Tehran) or "Tehran 80", covering the period 1996–2001 (AH 1375–1380).

The plan identifies the city's main problems under six groups of issues:

1. *Shortage of investment.* The gap between the demand and supply of employment and services has been growing as a result of a lack of necessary investment. The central government has reduced its investment in the city and the municipality has difficulty in generating revenue. As a result the city cannot meet the increasing demands of its citizens for services and for new jobs.

2. *Growth of the city*. The pace and pattern with which the city has grown have made the provision of services a very difficult task.
3. *Plan implementation*. The 1968 TCP's policies for density, land use, road networks, etc. have not been fully implemented.
4. *Environmental pollution*. The particular natural physical environment of the city is such that environmental pollution in Tehran has become a major problem.
5. *Public transport*. The absence of effective public transport has caused too much reliance on private vehicles. This has led to atmospheric pollution, traffic congestion, health threats, and problems for the national economy.
6. *Bureaucracy*. The inefficiency of the bureaucracy and the absence of information systems have caused an increase in intra-urban trips.

The plan predicts that in 2001 Tehran will have 7 million inhabitants in the city and 5 million in the suburbs. The population during the day, therefore, will be 8.5 million, for whom the city will have to provide services. There will be a need to extend the city's jurisdiction from the west, to include new areas for housing development. The plan also promotes the policy of decentralization and enhancement of local government, which is one of the goals of the country's second, post-revolutionary development plan. It then outlines its vision of the city in 2001 along with the problems it has identified and establishes the priorities for investment. The municipality's vision of the ideal city has been elaborated to include six major characteristics:

1. *A clean city (shahr-e pak)*. By allocating 8.8 per cent of the investment in the plan period (IR693.7bn), it is aimed to improve the environmental quality of the city by reducing the atmospheric pollution by half, continue working on a sewerage system, manage and recycle waste, and pay attention to noise pollution.
2. *A moving city (shahr-e ravan)*. Around 38.2 per cent of the available funds (IR3020.3bn) will be invested in ensuring ease of movement in the city. Completion of the motorway networks, redesign of roads and junctions, completion and use of a metro and improvement of public transport, to account for 80 per cent of the urban trips, are among the means of resolving the problem of traffic congestion and reaching the aim of doubling the speed of travel in the city.
3. *A green city (shahr-e sabz)*. Creation of urban parks and green spaces would contribute to the improvement of air quality, environmental improvement of the city, and provision of places for entertainment. The aim is to increase the city's green space to 189 million m^2 by 2001, i.e. 26.6 m^2 per person. This means an allocation of 12.9 per cent of municipal investment (IR1022.9bn) over five years.

4. *A cultural city (shahr-e ba farhang-e ghani)*. Around 15.4 per cent of the resources (IR1219.9bn) will be used in developing cultural, sports, entertainment, educational, health, and tourist facilities. The aim is to provide a cultural centre for every 3400 persons, by developing libraries, tea houses and restaurants, women's cultural centres, art galleries, zoo, hotels and tourist centres, and conservation of the urban heritage.
5. *A dynamic city (shahr-e pouya)*. Around 2.2 per cent of the funds (IR170.7bn) will be invested in organizational reforms to solve the problem of inefficient bureaucracy and lack of information systems. This will be invested in information centres, decentralization and municipal administrative reforms, establishment of the Islamic city council, collection of data, welfare services for municipal personnel. As a result, citizens will not have to approach several organizations for their needs, saving time and reducing the pressure on traffic.
6. *A traditional and modern city (shahr-e ba baft-e sonnati va modern)*. The aim is to improve the physical fabric of the city by allocating 22.4 per cent of investment (IR1771.9bn) in the plan period (Figure 11.3). This will be spent on the preparation of comprehensive and detailed plans for conservation of parts of the urban fabric, management of land use, creation of open spaces, reduction of density in central areas, distribution of commercial and administrative land uses, evaluation of earthquake threat, improvement of river beds and flood relief channels, and improvement of fire-fighting capacities.

Following its predecessors, the plan does not intend to deal with the difficult social and political challenges of the city. It does not aim to address the stark social and spatial divide which keeps the city on the verge of instability. It does not include *a democratic city* and *a just city* as its other aims, as these are seen to be the problem of central government, falling outside the remit of the municipality. City planning in Tehran deals mainly with physical and environmental improvement, with some attention to social and cultural development in the city.

CONCLUSION: RULES AND IDEAS THAT TRANSFORMED THE CITY

Despite contradictions between private and public interests and disorder and conflict between the agencies involved, the planning system has been able to practise a degree of control over the development of urban space. Despite the absence of urban autonomy, this has been carried out through a set of planning laws and an expanding municipal bureaucracy associated with the expansion of the state authority. It started with the imposition of road networks on the old city and was followed by the TCP. These stages

FIGURE 11.3 Attempts at re-creating Tehran in the image of the West have not been abandoned even after the advent of a traditionalist revolution

facilitated and enhanced the north–south social and physical divide, attempted to create an open urban space, initiated a new street system, encouraged large-scale suburbanization and certain building forms, and set the patterns of land use and city boundaries.

The main transformations of Tehran have been based on planning frameworks developed by the government. From the 1870s' and the 1930s' wholesale redevelopments to the 1960s' establishment of legal frameworks and the development of a comprehensive plan for the city, the state has provided mechanisms to deal with the physical fabric of the city. At first, the size and scale of the city allowed the government to plan and implement at the same time. Later interventions, however, have been moving towards developing a regulatory framework. The emphasis has moved to include concern for environmental issues in the city, although social concerns are not part of the planning process.

These interventions have largely shaped the urban fabric of Tehran. At the same time, a combination of causes, such as the weakness of municipalities, have limited the effectiveness of the regulatory framework. There has been a gap in the institutional relationships, between forward planning from development control, between vertical intervention and horizontal management. Now, Tehran municipality has taken the planning of the city in its hands, putting forward its vision of the city for the year 2001. The integration of forward planning and development control under the management of the municipality should inevitably be seen as a step forward for urban planning in Tehran, although the role and nature of the urban governance are still in need of urgent reform.

The transformation of Tehran during the last century has occurred largely by importing and using the images of the West. As Iran had felt humiliated in the nineteenth century by the might of industrializing Europe, it aimed to re-create itself in the image of the West. Through direct contacts and employment of Western or Western-educated architects and planners, Tehran was being reshaped. Paris has been a continuous source of influence, but there were also ideas borrowed from other Western countries, mainly Germany, Britain, and the United States. The transfer of the concepts of space in the course of the transformation of Tehran shows that these have been essentially adopted in accordance with the new, emerging social and economic formation of Iran. At the same time, their implementation has exerted a stimulating effect upon the process of capitalist development of the country. On the other hand, the belated entry of the country into the world market has implied that many of the initiatives were used as merely prestigious spatial concepts dissociated from their social and economic contexts.

12

INHERITED CONCEPTS OF SPACE AND POLITICAL INSTITUTIONS

A major feature of the transformation of Tehran, its society and its space, is the duality stemming from the juxtaposition of old and new. The gradual, and belated, integration of the economy into the world market has not always been associated with a change of forms of culture, politics, and social norms. In many instances, pre-capitalist, traditional norms have resisted the change and have therefore survived, able to shape and transform the new norms and create synthetic outcomes. In other instances, however, they have been doomed to disappear under the pressure for modernization.

In spite of the fundamental changes that Tehran has undergone, some key social, political, and cultural contexts, which have remained from the past, have continued to practise different levels of impact on urban form. This chapter discusses some of the main patterns of urban form which have been characteristic of Iranian cities for millennia and traces their presence in the city of today. These include the separation of the citadel from the city, the axiality of the urban structure, and the various approaches to geometry of the city. These are explored in their relationship with the main form of political rule and the way political and social institutions mediate between various groups. The discussion of the inherited concepts of space will be followed in the next chapter by focusing on cultural practices.

POLITICAL AUTHORITY AND URBAN STRUCTURE

The importance of the monarch in Iranian politics was such that it is crucial to concentrate on his actions and positions (Halliday, 1979: 54). It was this characteristic of the state, the monarchy, which signified a continuity with the long history of previous rulers, the so-called 2500 years of imperial rule in Iran. The absolute power of the monarch, his distance from his subjects, and his personal domination over and intervention in daily affairs were among the features which the Pahlavis shared with their predecessors.

The historical continuity of the main political institution, the executive monarchy, suggests that it should have had critical impacts on other social institutions, one of which is the management and spatial arrangement of the urban environment. Although the relationship between the institution of monarchy and the urban space has not yet been subjected to any form of analysis, it is possible to trace certain links. To do so, we can start from some points of similarity between the urban structure of contemporary Tehran and that of the nineteenth-century city, mainly the existence of a main urban axis leading to the royal quarters. Another shared feature is that in both cases, the living and working places of the ruler were distinguishably separated from the rest of the population. Because of the influence of the ruler in the social life of the country, his location in the city was one of the major constituent parts of the urban structure. Other parts were so arranged to show a clear relationship with the royal quarter, hence development of an urban axis which linked the royal quarter with the city and beyond.

CITADEL AND CITY

A major characteristic of nineteenth-century Tehran, also to be found in some other Iranian cities of the time, was the duality of the citadel-city, both enclosed in walls and moats. This is a characteristic continuously present in the cities of this area for the last 5000 years. Indeed, the separation of the ruler and the ruled seems to be as old as the city itself and the urban civilization with which it emerged (Figure 12.1).

Urban settlements started to flourish in the lands of present-day Iran in the third and the second millennia BC, although rural settlements are found to have existed there from the eighth millennium BC (Sajjadi, 1986). A level of "urban revolution" seems to have taken place after 3000 BC in the Elamite civilization in the Khuzestan plain, neighbouring Sumerians in the Euphrates valley. Increase in food production led to a division of labour in society, as handicraftsmen separated from agriculturalists, and concentration on priestly, military, judicial, and administrative tasks became possible. A class-based civilization emerged here in several city-states, the most important of which was Susa (Diakonoff, 1985a: 4–5), now Shush in southwest Iran.

The form of Mesopotamian cities clearly reflected the new social stratification and power relationships. The palace and the temple, as the seat of government and the centre of religious and intellectual life, were joined together in the citadel. This was a walled precinct situated on a raised platform in the middle or on one side of the city. Around the citadel was an inner city, walled and protected by rivers and moats. The inner city was surrounded by an outer city which often had walls and moats of its own. Inherent in this hierarchical arrangement was a residential segregation according to social stratification, in which the highest ranks lived in the innermost areas. The markets were situated either within or without the walls, while workshops were often related to the temple (Benevolo, 1980; Gaube, 1979; Morris, 1979).

FIGURE 12.1 Walls and gates separated the royal compound from the rest of Tehran (Arg's southern gateway)

When Aryan nomads moved from the north into the Iranian plateau in the second millennium BC, they interacted with the neighbouring, long-established, Mesopotamian civilization. This was intensified by the occupation of Babylon in 539 BC by Cyrus and the political unification of Iran and Mesopotamia which lasted for the following 15 centuries. From about 700 BC, autonomous city-states, which had a powerful council of elders and a popular assembly, and which were governed by the "lord of the township", united to form the Median kingdom. Their cities, as depicted by the Assyrian reliefs, were formed of a citadel in the middle of several concentric fortifications, up to seven in the capital Ecbatana (now Hamadan) (Diakonoff, 1985b; Ghirshman, 1964).

The foundation of a world-wide empire by the Achaemenians (559–331 BC) led to an increase in the power of the king and hence the widened social divide (Cook, 1983). The distance and the striking disparity between the royal town and the people's town are best exemplified by Susa (Amiet, 1986; Perrot, 1986; Berghe, 1966), and Persepolis (Colledge, 1977; Porada, 1985). The Greek cities, as in Knossos in Crete and later in Athens, were also typified by the distinction between the religious and government precinct, the acropolis, and the surrounding residential areas enclosed within the city walls. As such, the acropolis was seen by Aristotle as suitable for oligarchy and monarchy, as opposed to level ground for democracy (Vance, 1977).

The Macedonian conquest (330–250 BC), which was followed by a Hellenized period in Iran (Schlumberger, 1983), witnessed the estalishment of a number of polis-type cities by Alexander and the Seleucid monarchs (Lukonin, 1983). The Seleucid cities, such as Dura-Europos (Perkins, 1973), Merv (Colledge, 1977), Ai Khanum (Schlumberger, 1983), and Taxila (Colledge, 1977), were all built with a raised citadel within a walled city. The Parthian dynasty (250 BC–AD 224), which succeeded the Greek Seleucids, had a more or less feudal structure through dependence on the loyalty of hereditary great families (Brown, 1978). Apart from the raised citadel, some Parthian towns were divided into two walled parts accommodating the nobility and the townspeople separately (Kiani, 1986).

In the context of a feudal economic structure (English, 1966), the Sassanian dynasty (AD 224–641) built a more centralized political system with many new royal cities as its administrative headquarters (Lukonin, 1983). The first Sassanian kings established and improved the old cities: 8 cities by the first and 15 by the second king. They settled migrants to secure the development of agriculture and industry throughout the empire. The apex of city plantation and urbanization was the second half of the third century and the fourth century. A second but less important wave of foundation of new settlements occurred in the sixth century. On the verge of the Islamic conquest, Iranian towns often had a citadel (*quhandezh*) on a high level, a walled town (*sharestan*), and sometimes an outer town (*birun, rabaz*). The society was formally divided into four estates (Perikhanian, 1983), but only some of the cities were internally subdivided by walls (Huff, 1986). The markets were located in the suburbs (von Grunebaum, 1981), whose walls were sometimes erected to protect the food supply (Huff, 1986), to enclose the town expansion (Taqavi-Nezhad, 1985), or to protect a whole area with its rural settlements (Frye, 1965).

Between the Arab conquest in the seventh century and the appearance of the general physical pattern of the Islamic city in the eleventh century (Lapidus, 1973), lay a period of transformation and modification of the society and the cities. Seeking control over the conquered as well as over the migrating Arabs, the conquerors settled down in garrison camps located either in the suburbs of the existing towns or near to them (von Grunebaum, 1981; Cahen, 1970; Lapidus, 1973). Thus the ancient towns were confronted by Arab-founded or Arab-settled places, which gave rise to a double city tradition (Lapidus, 1973). In some places, like Merv and Bukhara in eastern Iranian lands, large numbers of Arabs settled in cities to keep control of the Silk Route (Frye, 1979a), while many of them chose to settle down in villages throughout Iran (Wagstaff, 1980). The establishment of garrison camps outside the towns gradually resulted in the creation of large urban areas, attracting the rural population freed from the former strict class divide. Naturally, the ancient cities did not have the capacity to accommodate rapid population growth. The suburbs, therefore, became where the bazaars were built and where the tradesmen and craftsmen resided alongside the conquerors. The camp towns became the foci of cultural fusion and in many spheres of life new distinctions of class, status, and power came into being along with new commercial, political, and religious ties (Ashtor, 1976; Lapidus, 1973). This implied, in some cases deliberate, a drain of the ancient towns' livelihood by shifting the town centre (Gaube, 1979) or abandonment of the citadel and the walled city (Barthold, 1984; Streck, 1978).

Inheriting the centralized administrative system of the Sassanians, the Abbasid empire created a unified political and economic unity with a money economy at a pre-capitalist stage (Ashtor, 1976). By the time this empire disintegrated following the revolutionary upheavals of the tenth and eleventh centuries, the cities of Islamic lands had acquired their similar urban form. In the period before the rise of the Safavid and Ottoman empires, Islamic cities and cities with pre-Islamic origins need no longer be distinguished (Lapidus, 1973).

In Iran, the period between the two flourishing stages of the tenth and the fourteenth centuries (Frye, 1979b, c; Hodgson, 1974; Grabar, 1968), witnessed the political instability and disastrous invasions of Moguls and Turks (Lambton, 1978). While the eastern cities like Bukhara expanded in the first flourishing stage in the tenth century (Frye, 1965), the fourteenth century is a period in which the cities and even villages in west, south-west, and centre of Iran reached their quasi-permanent architectural setting (Grabar, 1986). The pattern of the cities which emerged during the Islamic period no longer shows a hierarchy of inner and outer towns. Nevertheless, the duality of citadel-city was retained (Wagstaff, 1980; Gaube, 1979; Tavassoli, 1982). The hilltop citadels remained in use but in new cities the ruler's quarter was built at ground level separated by walls. This was mostly located on one side of the town to be protected from both internal and external dangers.

In Isfahan, the capital of the Safavids (1502–1722) under whom re-emerged the old centralized administrative system, a new royal quarter was built. Being added to the old city, it has been called a "Persian garden suburb" (Wagstaff, 1980: 29) and seems to have reduced substantially the city–citadel duality. Nevertheless, other cities, including Tehran, Kerman (English, 1966), Kermanshah (Clarke & Clark, 1969), Bam (Gaube, 1979), and Yazd (Tavassoli, 1982), as well as Herat (English, 1973) continued to have this structural duality until the end of the nineteenth century and well into the twentieth.

After the First World War, with the establishment of a strong, centralized government, the Iranian city walls were demolished and the citadels abandoned or redeveloped. Without undermining the advance of destructive firepower which reduced the defensive effectiveness of city walls, their disappearance has been seen as the most tangible expression of discontinuity which occurred in the city with the advent and maturation of capitalism (Giddens, 1981: 146–9). The two dominant features of the non-capitalist, class-divided cities were the monopoly of the centre by ceremonial and administrative buildings and the presence of city walls. The city was the dominant power container and its walls represented the physical enclosure of this power. Apart from the economic transformation in land use, the obsolescence of the walls signified major alterations in the control and deployment of military power. This was made possible by increasing the consolidation of the means of violence in the hands of the nation state.

The concentration of power in the hands of the state also resulted in a change in the relationship between the government buildings and the rest of the city. The extension of effective authority over the national territory by the new, strong, and integrative central government implied the obsolescence of the physically segregated seat of power. The new royal residential quarter which was developed under Reza Shah was not separated by a single wall from the city. As a result of specialization of functions and places, royal palaces were separated from the military and administrative buildings. The high walls which now enclosed the royal palaces and military bases were not comparable to those of the citadel's. Nevertheless, under the monarchy of the Pahlavis (1924–79) as in the nineteenth century, the seat of the ruler was located on one side of the city, its northernmost area. It was surrounded by the living areas of the upper classes to create a social barrier, rather than a physical one, which separated it from the rest of the city.

With the disappearance of monarchy, the idea and practice of a ruler who is above the law have not been abandoned. The leaders of the revolution have filled the power vacuum left by the abolition of monarchy, despite the establishment of a republic and an elected Parliament. Even though Ayatollah Khomeini did not rely on the upper classes of the northern city to protect him from the rest of the citizens, he resided in an area not very far from Mohammad Reza Shah's Niavaran Palace on the slopes of the northern mountains. His resting place, however, now lies at the southernmost part of the city.

AXIALITY AND CENTRALITY IN URBAN SPACE

The city of Tehran in the nineteenth century had an axial structure, a characteristic of Iranian towns which is traceable at least back to the middle of the first millennium BC. Urban space in nineteenth-century Tehran centred on a square which linked the citadel with the main artery, the bazaar, leading to the main city gate. This axial pattern has been in use for long periods in Iran with similarities in some other parts of the world.

An excavated residential area of the Mesopotamian city of Ur shows a rudimentary form of bazaar, where along a main intra-urban communication axis were located religious buildings, schools, hostels for foreign merchants, shops, and nearby craftsmen (Gaube, 1979). A settlement pattern, which had a considerable influence on the development of Iranian towns and villages, started to develop in the middle of the first millennium BC in Khurasan in eastern Iran. These settlements, now called *qaleh* (castle), had an external rectangular form and an internal axial layout. It was formed by a main street, stretching from the single gateway and flanked by houses, and a central square as the communal park of the cattle. Individual courtyard houses were all attached to each other and scattered against the inner face of the habitable defensive wall which was a quadrangle with corner towers (de Planhol, 1968: 425–8).

A similar pattern can be found in the city of Athens in the fifth century BC, which, like other unplanned Greek cities of the time, had a main path, leading from the main gate to the acropolis, along which an agora evolved from a market and a meeting place (Morris, 1979: 25–6). In the Hippodamian principles, however, a gridiron was centred on an agora and the pattern of a main street was not used. Therefore, the axial layout of Selinus in Sicily by the Greeks has been regarded as unusual (Morris, 1979). Nevertheless, the Hellenistic cities in the East had axial layouts. In Dura-Europos, the main street of the grid stretched from the main gate through a ravine, above which on both sides stood the citadel and the palace of the city's chief magistrate, and led to the river gate. The agora, an open square surrounded by shops, was situated at the intersection of the main street with the other axis of the grid on which temples were located (Perkins, 1973; Colledge, 1977). The cities of Merv (Colledge, 1977) and Herat (Gaube, 1979; English, 1973) were square-shaped settlements with two main axes intersecting at right angles leading to four gates. This is a pattern which Herat has kept until the twentieth century, and which has been known as a major characteristic of Iranian cities.

The principle of a square-shaped city oriented to the cardinal points of the compass with four gates in the middle of its four sides and two main axes is also found to have traces in Indian thought (Gaube, 1979). The combination of biaxiality and gridiron pattern in a square-shaped settlement might also be found in Roman cities. The Romans applied the Hippodamian principles in a simplified and standard way and added to it a biaxiality inherited from the Etruscan past (Benevolo, 1980; Vance, 1977). The two main axes, *decumanus maximus* and *cardo maximus*, were laid down towards the cardinal points of the compass. In the Parthian cities, the trades and crafts were placed along the streets which led to the gates (Kiani, 1986). The Sassanian cities were mostly quadrangles oriented to the cardinal points of the compass with four gates in the middle of each side, from which two intersecting axes stemmed to form the internal layout of the city. This biaxial layout was also present in circular cities like Firuzabad (Huff, 1986).

It appears that with the abandonment of the gridiron pattern in the internal layout of the cities, the principle of biaxiality was also abandoned in some cities in favour of the old monoaxial layout. The city of Aivan-e Karkheh, which was built in the fourth century, is evidence of the return to the monoaxial layout. It was a 4×1 km rectangle, divided into three parts by walls but linked with an off-centre longitudinal street (Huff, 1986). The biaxial pattern in quadrangular settlements was kept in most cities at least until the tenth century (Barthold, 1984: 126, 139). Based on existing urban forms, the pattern of an Islamic city which emerged had both monoaxial and biaxial patterns (Wagstaff, 1980: 22; Gaube, 1979: 20; Tavassoli, 1982: 44). According to a historian in the Islamic period, the Sassanians believed that the world has four sides and the city gates should be opened to them (Ibn Isfandiar, in Ashraf, 1974), a characteristic also found in the architecture of major buildings. It has been said that the addition of new gates to the four existing ones in the Islamic period was a symbolic confrontation of the values of the ancient non-Muslims who had built them. This clearly shows the symbolic value of the geometry of urban space for Iranians.

Axiality of the urban structure also had an obvious functional importance, as it allowed the concentration of public life and commercial activities. The position of the ruler was defined in relation to this symbolic and functional order. The main street or streets of the Islamic city were roofed and flanked by shops and workshops to constitute the bazaar. It was the backbone of the physical fabric on which the street pattern centred. In larger cities, the bazaar was a network of shopping streets stretching from the city centre or from the citadel towards the gates along the main intra-urban axes with, moving towards the periphery, a pattern of gradual decrease in prosperity and importance of each branch of trade. Even in this network, a shopping street which was more important was considered as the main bazaar.

The Safavids introduced a new form of street, a wide boulevard with trees, streams, and pools called Chahar Bagh (Four Gardens) (Honarfar, 1984a). The patterns that they set were repeated in Kerman (Hillenbrand, 1986b), Shiraz (Arberry, 1960), and followed by the developments of the Zand dynasty in the second half of the eighteenth century (Clarke, 1963). In Mashhad, the old city was cut by the Safavids to provide access to the shrine of Imam Reza through two broad avenues which had a water canal running down their middle (Paganini Alberti, 1971).

Twentieth-century Tehran, in spite of dramatic social and economic changes and a much larger population, also has an axial structure. In this city, the ruler lived in the northernmost area and a main axis linked him with the rest of the city, leading to what was for a time meant to be the new city gate, the railway station. Along this axis developed a concentration of many new land uses not unlike a bazaar. Certain aspects of the nineteenth-century city, however, disappeared. The fact that the ruler's quarter was not enclosed in a citadel and that movement was not based on a pedestrian scale led to the disappearance of the linking square. Also the sheer size of the city and the use of motor cars, among other factors, would appear to be contrary to the development of a single street as the main axis. However, it is true that the main north–south axis, now called Vali Asr but previously Pahlavi, has continued to have the highest land prices in the city.

The continuity in axiality of urban structure signifies the power relations focused on the shah, as the highest authority who was far above any other member of the administration and played a personal key role in most important affairs of the country. The despotic monarchy, which had been in practice for nearly all the history of Iran, in spite of the recent development of a market economy, continued to dominate the political arena. This contradiction between the political needs of a developing market economy and the exclusion of society from decision making was what the revolution was partly aiming to resolve unsuccessfully.

The idea of biaxiality has also survived to this day in Tehran. Tehran has a secondary axis at right angles with the main north–south axis. Enghelab and Vali-Asr streets therefore show a biaxial structure for the city, not dissimilar to the old city of Herat. The biaxial layout was superimposed on the old fabrics of many towns across Iran by Reza Shah (Saidi Rezvani, 1992). Even the new metro system is to have the shape of a cross. More than the influence of the political authority, biaxiality appears to show the cultural significance of the four directions in Persian thought, symbolizing an order amidst the chaos of the outside world.

NODES OF URBAN SPACE: PUBLIC SQUARES

The evolution of streets and squares in Iranian cities reveals the continuous presence of axiality in urban structure. The streets were, in gridiron pattern or in distributional pattern, forming a network, whose main street was elaborated, functionally and architecturally, as the backbone of the urban social and physical fabric. The square in this arrangement was often a part of the main axis which linked it with the ruler's quarters in the citadel.

It is known that the early rectangular settlements of north-eastern Iran had, apart from a main street, a central square. But, due to the lack of information, there is no clear trace of squares in subsequent periods, apart from the agora in Hellenistic cities. Ferdowsi mentions that a legendary king, Lohrasp, had built in the city of Balkh places in the streets, bazaars, and quarters "to hold the Feast of Sada, round a Fane of Fire" (quoted in Boyce, 1983: 793). Gaube (1979) refers to an open market-place inside the walls in front of the northern gate of the Sassanian city of Jayy (Isfahan) in which the farmers could take refuge from danger. There are also reports about the urban squares in which polo was played.

In the Islamic period, there existed a public square in some cities. In medieval Isfahan, a square was in the middle of the city surrounded by mosques, madrasas, palaces, bazaar and Qaysariyeh, and a royal music pavilion (Gaube, 1979: 76–7). This square was used as a racecourse as were the squares in the outskirts of many Iranian cities, which were also used for commercial purposes. In some cities, like Bukhara, a square linked the citadel and the city, where it was possible for the town and the ruler to meet. It became the administrative centre of the city with official buildings and palaces of amirs around it. This square was also used for festivals (Frye, 1965: 42, 92, 94). The pattern of a main square in the middle of the city remained a typical component of many Iranian cities. It reached its most sophisticated form in the Safavid Isfahan in which the main square (Maydan-e Shah, King's Square) was flanked by monumental buildings of a royal palace and two mosques as well as by the entrance of the main bazaar. Symbols of political power, religious and intellectual life, and economic activities were all present. The square itself was used as a marketplace as well as a place to play polo (Honarfar, 1984b). This square predated the Place Royale (Faghih, 1984), which was completed in 1615, the first great public square in Paris and the model for squares in London and other Western cities (Vance, 1977: 237). Isfahan's Maydan-e Shah was renowned in the England of Shakespeare's time and by the middle of the twentieth century was still the largest public square in the world (except for Red Square in Moscow) (Groseclose, 1947: 8).

Another form of urban square may be seen in the courtyards of religious buildings. *Takiyeh*, a place for religious ceremonies, and the mosque both provided enclosed squares in the middle of the urban fabric with access to different routes. Although the main mosque was situated along the main bazaar, it has been sometimes separated from the secular square which linked the citadel with the city. Rather than the temporal power of the ruler, these open spaces represented the spiritual power of the clergy. Small spaces which almost incidentally were left open at the intersection of the streets should also be noted as another form of square.

INTERMEDIATE GROUPS

Another argument which supports the spatial arrangements of axiality and centrality is the concept of intermediate agents. Lapidus (1967, 1969, 1973) has argued that in Islamic cities the parochial groups which constituted society were linked together through intermediate groups such as religious leaders. In spatial terms, this has been reflected by the location of the Friday mosque in the city centre and numerous other mosques and religious institutions in the local centres as focal points of the urban fabric (Figure 12.2).

FIGURE 12.2 Religious institutions were the focal points of the old settlements (Shrine of Imamzadeh Slaeh, Tajrish, north of Tehran)

As the layout of the nineteenth-century city suggests, the central location of the citadel and the bazaar also reveals intermediate roles for economic and political agencies. The Friday mosque and the bazaar are both the meeting points of different, and sometimes rival, sections of society. As for the government, it is true that it practised an absolute power over the people, but it is also true that it had to consider the segregation of these sections and play an intermediate role to be able to rule.

It is this intermediary role of the state which has been reflected in the location of the citadel and the axial structure of the urban space. With the increasing power of the state in the contemporary period, the previous balance of power collapsed. The secular power of the state, which was in a form of balance with other intermediate groups, changed radically to undermine them. Therefore, if the religious leaders initially lost their intermediary role, the state, as personified by the shah, had an increasing importance, hence the reproduction of the axial pattern in an urban structure in which the mosque had no effective importance.

Undermining the religious leaders led to a secularization of urban space, in which religious institutions were not among the favoured new public institutions. As the development of Tehran since the second half of the nineteenth century shows, the number of mosques and other religious buildings declined (Ettehadieh, 1983) (Figure 12.3). Nevertheless, after the Islamic revolution of 1979, the religious leaders regained their powerful social role combined with a political one. This new combination, together

FIGURE 12.3 In the secular city, it was not the mosque which flanked the major squares (Imam Hussein Square)

with the abolition of the monarchy and the disappearance of the communal social structure, will have a new, and potentially more complex, spatial manifestation.

AUTONOMY AND URBAN FORM

There have been many arguments about the absence of urban autonomy in the cities in Islamic lands, which followed the centralized pattern of Byzantine and Sassanian empires, as compared to the communes in medieval Europe which came into being in underorganized states (Cahen, 1970: 521). The typical characteristic of the Islamic city has been the looseness of its structure and the absence of corporate municipal institutions, derived from the absence of corporate institutions in general in Islamic society (Stern, 1970). The apparently irregular street pattern of the Islamic city, therefore, is argued to have been closely related to this feature (Eisenstadt & Schachar, 1987).

Islamic cities had fortifications, markets, and, to some extent, corporate institutions, lacking two of the five features which Weber (1960) identifies as the main features of an urban community: autonomous law, due to the fact that Islamic law does not recognize privileges for one group of believers over others, and urban autonomy, except in a few cases, were absent. The most important social groups whose interests were put forward by Islamic law were family and neighbours, and not state or province or city

(Schacht, 1970). The Muslim is a citizen of the community of believers, but a mere resident of his town (von Grunebaum, 1981).

The new forms of city management in Iran show that urban autonomy, in spite of various legal provisions and attempts, has not been achieved. Yet this experience also shows that a complex bureaucratic organization, such as the Tehran municipality, would be capable of controlling urban form without having any real degree of autonomy. Even before any development of municipal institutions, it was possible to create a planned built form in Isfahan of the seventeenth century or Tehran of the nineteenth. The interwar reform of Tehran should also be seen as belonging to this category.

It should be stressed, however, that different forms of urban government, i.e. different degrees of the contribution and participation of the townspeople in the running of their settlement, might have different impacts on the built form. The experience in Iran shows how the development of the built environment has suffered from the absence of public participation (Madanipour, 1988a, b, 1989b). The evidence from Tehran, however, clearly implies that, in the creation or modification of urban space, the ability to control is more crucial than the form from which this ability has derived its legitimacy. In other words, in order to constitute a planned urban development, the presence or absence of autonomy of municipal government has been less important than the presence or absence of an authority politically and economically capable of implementing its decisions. This conclusion, however, is incomplete since it does not enter two important discussions: the relationship between autonomy and the stability and capability of the authority, and the different nature and quality of planning in the presence or absence of autonomy. As the municipal authority's capacity to implement schemes diminishes, due to the scarcity of resources, the question of involving the citizens in urban management becomes ever more crucial.

GEOMETRICAL REGULARITY AND RATIONALITY

Geometric forms in urban space have been associated with rationality and, hence, planning. On this basis, the urban form of Islamic cities has been criticized as "an anarchic maze" (de Planhol, 1970: 454) in sharp contrast with what was idealized as the beautiful orderliness of ancient towns (Cahen, 1970). This has been in line with the criticisms made of the medieval urban form in Europe. Le Corbusier (1971: 11) reveals his contempt for the latter in associating it with "pack-donkey's way". According to him, "Man walks in a straight line because he has a goal and knows where he is going." This is against the pack-donkey which "meanders along, meditates a little in his scatter-brained and distracted fashion". This reflects the difference between medieval people who accepted the leading of the pack-donkey in their urban forms, and modern people who strive towards straight lines. "Where the orthogonal is supreme, there can be read the height of a civilization." On the other hand, it has been argued that the non-orthogonal spatial forms of the past resulted from the disposition of the units of social and productive organization (family, clan, tribe) rather than by theoretical systems imposed directly on to the structures (Guidoni, 1978: 5). The rationality at work here was one which has been described as a conservationist principle which concentrated on the minimum space required (Vance, 1977).

Geometrical regularity seems always to have been present in certain categories of urban buildings, such as palaces, temples, and mosques. We need to look at the presence or absence of geometric regularity in the evolution of urban form to find out about its relationship with the form and extent of concern and willingness of the political authority to produce urban space. Rectilinearity, as a form of geometrical regularity, was introduced into the physical fabric of Tehran in the two phases of reform in the 1870s and 1930s. This was against the main characteristics of urban form of the immediate past. However, geometrical regularity, in the shape of walls and street patterns, might be traced back in ancient cities. The street pattern of nineteenth-century Tehran was very similar to that of Ur in the third millennium BC, both with twisting streets leading to dead-end alleys and courtyard houses. In both cities, geometrically ordered forms were absent from the form of city walls and urban space but present in the ceremonial and administrative buildings as well as in the houses.

In the ancient world, however, the rectilinear forms were a sign of temporal and symbolic order, separating the cities from the chaos of the outside world. The city of Babylon, founded in about 2000 BC, had an inner town laid out in a geometrical pattern. It was a rectangle bisected by the Euphrates river and streets crossing at right angles. The same pattern was found in Khorsabad which, founded after 720 BC, was a square-shaped settlement with intersecting rectilinear streets (Benevolo, 1980). In the Achaemenian capitals of Susa and Persepolis, grandiose rectangular patterns of royal palaces contrasted significantly with the irregular layout of towns surrounding them (Perrot, 1986; Porada, 1985). Townships and villages with a rectangular external shape, with high walls, corner towers, and a single gateway controlled by a watchtower, started to develop in the middle of the first millennium BC to become a common feature in Central Asia by the time of Alexander (de Planhol, 1968: 425–6). This form of settlement enclosed in rectangular walls, which has survived to this date in some parts of the country, was the basis of a more or less standard form for Iranian cities until the beginning of the Middle Ages.

The Macedonian conquest introduced the strict geometrical forms which were also used by Hippodamus of Miletus in the fifth century BC for the rebuilding of towns devastated by wars (Vance, 1977; Benevolo, 1980). The Hippodamian plans of Miletus and Pirene show a gridiron network of streets within irregular city walls. Whereas the Greeks used this pattern in the building of Dura-Europos on the Euphrates river (Perkins, 1973; Colledge, 1977), they seem to have built Merv and Herat in Central Asia on another pattern. In the building of these cities, the Greek Hippodamian style of gridiron networks of streets was combined with the Central Asian tradition of rectangular city walls. This pattern, which was also widely used in Roman cities, was to become one of the main characteristics of the towns laid out in Iran, especially during the Sassanian period.

In the castles and towns in the Parthians' birthplace in Gorgan plain, south-east of the Caspian Sea, which were built or repaired from the third century BC, a move towards stricter geometric forms might be seen, from polygonal to circular and rectangular city walls (Kiani, 1986). The circular form which developed under the Parthians has been said to be derived from the defensive value of reduction in the length of city walls compared to rectangular forms (Colledge, 1977: 34). The first Sassanian king (AD 224–240) built as his capital a circular city based on detailed calculations with much greater accuracy than its Parthian prototypes (Huff, 1986). The cities built by the Sassanian emperors, however, were mostly quadrangles with an internal gridiron pattern.

The use of the gridiron pattern seems to have come to an end by the fourth century (Huff, 1986). Nevertheless, the external shape of the cities continued to be rectangular. In the second period of Sassanian city building in the sixth century, the main stress was on the building of palaces, castles, and temples. Less attention was now paid to urban residential areas, which appears not to be unrelated to the introduction of the formal stratification of society in the mid-Sassanian period (Perikhanian, 1983). As in Roman towns after the apex of that empire in the second century (von Grunebaum, 1981), the transformation of the gridiron pattern seems to have started in Iran in the late Sassanian period.

After the Muslim conquest in the seventh century, in spite of the highly sophisticated use of geometry in architectural space and detail, no trace could be found of geometric regularity in street patterns or city walls. An exception such as the round city of Baghdad is, following the late Sassanian cities, significant of concern for the external shape rather than the internal patterns of streets. In Iran, in the Islamic period as in pre-Islamic times, highly sophisticated geometric forms were used in the gardens, houses, palaces, and religious and public buildings. The only exception which extended geometric forms to urban space was in the developments in Isfahan and other major cities in the sixteenth and seventeenth centuries. In Tehran of the nineteenth century, as in most cities of the Islamic period, geometric forms were present in buildings and absent in the layout of the streets and city walls.

Considering the fact that, throughout the history of urban development in Iran, geometric forms have almost always been used in buildings. However, only some periods have witnessed the use of geometric forms in urban

FIGURE 12.4 Wide, straight streets representing power and order

form, as exemplified by street patterns and city walls. Therefore, it seems hard to believe in the presence of rationality in some periods and its absence in others. If geometric forms are to be taken as a sign of rationality, it is not the presence of rationality which should be doubted. It is the extent of the application of rationality which should be investigated. In other words, individual arenas and private spheres have benefited from an instrumental rationality, which is goal-oriented and seeks self-interest, while the public domain has suffered from the absence of a social rationality, which seeks public interest. On the other hand, it might be possible to refer to geometric form as merely an indicator of some form of order, whether rational or not. This would represent the presence of an authority politically and economically capable of imposing that order on the built space. In this case, the geometric form in single buildings would refer to the presence of an authority in the individual agency's private realm. In the case of city walls, whose presence in the first place reflects the presence of political power, geometric forms indicate a higher form of authority. When this authority is extended to the internal arrangement of the city, it will be the ultimate representation of authority over the townspeople (Figure 12.4).

Separation of order, as the rule established by an authority, from rationality might simply change the way rationality and reason are defined. In this case, the geometrically irregular street pattern of an Islamic city like nineteenth-century Tehran, as the outcome of thousands of small-scale consultations and adjustments, might be seen as orderly and rational. Indeed, there has been a strong belief that the street system's hierarchical distributional pattern has been the most rational solution possible, given the state of the economy and technology. However, it would not be a straightforward task to make a judgement between this collective, bottom-up rationality and the top-down one carried out later to impose a new order on the old structures. The dichotomy between these two forms of action implies that neither of them has been able to take advantage of the positive dimensions of the other, an inability to negotiate between the private and public domains.

CONCLUSION: POWER, INSTITUTIONAL CONTINUITY, AND URBAN FORM

The city of Tehran has been heavily influenced by Western ideas and trends. It also reveals the influence of the concepts of space inherited from the past. Although the impact of new concepts of space have undermined the centuries-old concepts used in the production of space, many of these concepts have survived. These are basically the concepts which are associated with the continuing political and social institutions, symbolic significance, or with a combination of the old and new. Capitalism, because of its belated arrival, has failed to transform many of the social institutions and spatial practices. The continuation of the monarchy had a direct impact on the reproduction of the segregation of the royal quarters from the rest of the city, albeit in a new way. It also partly caused the re-emergence of a gigantic intra-urban axis which led to the royal quarters. The absolute power of the ruler, the intermediary role of the religious and economic institutions, and the symbolic notions of order and direction have all had direct implications for urban form, implications which can be traced in today's Tehran as well as in the supposedly long-forgotten past. Axiality of urban structure, separation of the ruler from the ruled and his influence over the spatial structure, the location and character of the nodes in urban space, and the necessity of a powerful authority for spatial change are all among aspects of urban form that Tehran has inherited from its historic predecessors.

13

CULTURAL PRACTICES AND URBAN FORM

In this chapter, we continue our exploration of the inherited concepts of space, as discussed in Chapter 12. Here we will look at the patterns of residential differentiation in urban space throughout history and whether they are relevant to the urban form today. This will be followed by an analysis of how some cultural beliefs and practices have had a direct impact on urban form and its evolution. The chapter concludes with a discussion of the relationship between tradition and modernity in the social and spatial environments of Tehran.

DIFFERENCE AND RESIDENTIAL SEGREGATION IN URBAN SPACE: NEIGHBOURHOODS

The north–south divide in the city of Tehran shows a very clear social and spatial segregation across economic lines. Access to resources shapes the city and determines its patterns of differentiation. But has the city always been structured in this way? How different was the way cities were subdivided in the past? How far have these patterns survived? What does the spatial subdivision of the city tell us about the way people live their lives and relate to each other?

Before the arrival of the modern era, the cities of the Middle East were subdivided into identifiable urban quarters. Parochiality of social structure in the form of ethnic and religious segregation was a feature of the factionally divided cities of the region. With the expansion and transformation of Tehran, the pattern of distinguishable urban quarters, which had structured the city until the nineteenth century, was dismantled. It was replaced by a new form of residential segregation along the lines of access to resources rather than location within social groups. This section, by a brief historical survey, tries to show how the subdivision of urban space has changed and how urban quarters have evolved.

The most distinguishable subdivision of urban space has been the separation of the citadel from the rest of the city. As shown in the previous chapter, this was combined in the pre-Islamic periods with the subdivision of cities into inner and outer towns. This constituted a subdivided urban space to accommodate a class-divided society. The size of the subdivision was also a witness to the hierarchical subdivision of society: the citadel was smaller than the inner town and the inner town smaller than the outer town. The gridiron pattern, and its associated subdivision of space into blocks, was introduced with the Macedonian conquest and, until its abandonment in the fourth century AD (Huff, 1986), remained in use for almost eight centuries. The Greek urban designer and political theorist, Hippodamus, had envisaged the townspeople as three classes of artisans, farmers, and warriors (Vance, 1977). In the Hellenistic cities of Iran and those laid out later on the gridiron pattern, blocks formed the units of the urban fabric. However, the ancient, historical subdivision of urban space into citadel–inner town–outer town continued. This hierarchy was not always manifest in a concentric urban structure. In the Parthian cities of the Gorgan plain with their gridiron pattern of streets (Kiani, 1986), the urban space was subdivided into a citadel and two other parts by walls. In the Sassanian town of Aivan-e Karkheh (Huff, 1986), the three subdivisions of the town, which was in the form of a very long rectangle, were aligned along a longitudinal axis.

The roots of the formal stratification of society in Iran have been traced back to the Sassanian period (Varjavand, 1984; Lambton, 1980). Sassanian society was stratified by estates and classes, and was composed of agnatic groups. According to a reform, introduced not later than the fifth century AD, society was divided into four estates: the priests, associated with judges; the warriors; the scribes, the members of the bureaucracy; and the cultivators, craftsmen, and merchants. Membership of each estate was hereditary and movement from one estate to another was extremely difficult. Slave labour was extensively used, but it was the work of the free population that mainly sustained the economy. The most important structure within the civic community was the agnatic group, a community of kinsmen consisting of several dozen extended patriarchal families with the same origin from the father's side going back three or four generations, which had a head and a council formed by the heads of families. This organization, which replaced the previous clan and tribal system, existed in the same form in ancient Greece and Rome and its members, in addition to kinship, were united in economic, political, and religious aspects of life (Perikhanian, 1983: 633–44). The lack of information about the relationship between this social organization and the urban form could lead us to surmise that both physical and social barriers have been used to keep the estates apart.

After the Muslim conquest, a dramatic change in social organization seems to have taken place. The Arab garrison settlements were organized on tribal principles so that various tribes were settled in their own quarters which, under the tribal chief, were coherently preserved for some time (Stern, 1970: 30). With the passage of time, through connection with the native Persians, an urban character appeared and the way of life in Arab camps became civil rather than military. With the intermixture of elements from different tribes and the increasing importance of the urban way of life, the tribal life pattern of the conquerors was transformed and at times reduced to a sentimental link (Cahen, 1970).

The fusion of the Sassanian strict formal classes and the Arab tribal structure in the cities resulted in a new form of social organization represented by the new subdivision of urban space. The inner–outer town arrangement was abandoned. Residential areas of the Islamic city were divided into quarters, geographical entities as well as homogeneous communities which were closely knit, forming the basic unit of society. The solidarity between the small group of people living in each quarter was based on family, clientage, common village origin, ethnic or sectarian religious identity, in some cases probably strengthened by common occupation. There is no evidence to show the homogeneity of social groups on the basis of economic structure since they were communities of both rich and poor. These village-like communities within the urban whole, with relatively few institutions connecting them to each other, were administrative units represented on city-wide political or ceremonial occasions, by a head who was selected by the governor (Lapidus, 1967: 85–95; 1969: 49–51).

On many occasions, the quarters of a town showed endless hostility towards each other. The disputes between the quarters of a city, between neighbouring towns and villages, between different religious sects, or between tribal loyalties were causing an ever-present strife in the cities. With the establishment of Shiism by the Safavid dynasty as the state religion in the sixteenth century, the strife between Sunnis and Shiites was transformed. Now there was an open, national tension between the Shiite Iranians and the Sunni Ottomans. The urban strife continued in the form of rivalry between two Sufi sects of Heydari and Ne'mati. The conflict between these factions, which continued in some cases until the early twentieth century, caused much violence and bloodshed. This conflict often ruined the commercial life of a town or at least kept it in a state of continuous instability (Lambton, 1980).

The quarters were self-contained, with their own mosque, bazaar, and public baths, which were usually located around the central core and were surrounded by semi-urban areas. Their location was in general determined by the availability of vacant land (Greenshields, 1980: 123). In some cities, quarters were separated from each other by undefined stretches of land or by ruins (Cahen, 1970: 521), whereas in others they were walled and protected by strong bars and gates (Arberry, 1960: 54; Lambton, 1980: 8). The walls provided security and made the quarters "manageable component parts" of the city (Brown, 1973: 32).

The number of quarters, being the basic unit of the city's social and physical fabric, could often suggest the size and importance of a city, e.g. the large and prosperous Nishapur had 47 quarters (Frye, 1979d). The number of inhabitants of the quarters was relatively small, which permitted closer communication. In the late medieval period, Damascus had 70 quarters of

500 population and Aleppo had 50 quarters of 1200 (Lapidus, 1967: 85). The quarters were different in status. Hia was known to be the best quarter in Nishapur and its fully roofed bazaar was the largest in the city (Frye, 1979d). The quarter to the north-west of the central square in Bukhara (Frye, 1965) and the Avval quarter in Herat, which was the first to receive water in an open water distribution system (English, 1973), were also considered to be superior to the other quarters.

The quarter system in the Islamic cities, as in medieval Europe (Vance, 1977), might be seen as an outcome of feudalism, even though the forms of feudalism in the Middle East and Europe have been different (Lambton, 1987). The fragmentation and parochiality (Lapidus, 1967, 1969, 1973) of the feudal society, therefore, have been reflected in the form of quarters so unrelated that the Islamic city has been regarded as "an assemblage of disparate elements" (de Planhol, 1970: 454). It has also been seen as resulting from the alienation of the administration from the mass of the population through seizure of power by alien groups (Wagstaff, 1980: 22–3).

It is, however, possible to cast doubt about a direct relationship between feudalism and the quarter system, since feudal disintegration, along with a centralized imperial power, is known to have been at work in Iran both before and after the advent of Islam. Nevertheless, shortage of information about the quarter system in the pre-Islamic period prevents any general conclusions being made. It seems more plausible, however, to associate the erosion of the quarter system with the disappearance of feudalism in Iran and with the coming of capitalism and integrative nationalism, which tended to introduce new patterns of stratification in social and physical environments.

In the melting pot of Tehran and other large cities, to which people migrated from all over the country, separate sects and groups did not produce any geographical conglomeration at an urban scale. Across the country, the two sects of Heydari and Ne'mati faded away, and the different ethnic groups, such as Azeris and Kurds, sought new forms of national identity and autonomy at a regional scale. The urban space witnessed another form of conglomeration of groups. This was according to the possession of money which had now increasingly become the basis of social relationships as distinct from communal bonds. Nevertheless, despite the change in communal structure and nuclearization of family, some spatial manifestations of communal bonds have remained in practice.

In Tehran of the nineteenth century, the living quarters were not physically separated from each other and apparently no formal factional strife existed. The only loosely identifiable geographical segregation was that of the Jewish quarter to the east of Oudlajan. In the twentieth century, however, this quarter has not kept its identity due to the intermingling of various groups in the new neighbourhoods. Nevertheless, a level of geographical segregation by minority groups has been present throughout this

FIGURE 13.1 Sarkis Church is a landmark for the Armenian community

century. Armenians, the largest Christian minority, have tended to dwell in certain urban areas which have eventually found a degree of Armenian identity. These areas, such as Naderi, Bahar, and Majidiyeh, are now located in the centre and the north of the city. The living places of other minority groups, such as Afghani and Iraqi refugees and the more established immigrants from the Indian subcontinent, may be identified in pockets in the city centre.

None of these segregations, however, created ghettos. None have been so clearly defined as to prevent minority groups from living elsewhere or majority groups from living in these areas, nor that the segregation has been physically expressed, other than, in Armenian quarters, by the presence of a church or the casual use of the Armenian alphabet (Figure 13.1). The main difference of this communal segregation in space from that of the nineteenth century is that now the minority groups are themselves split according to the stratifications of the new market economy. Instead of a single concentration of the members of a community, they are now living as individual households or in relatively small or medium concentrations spread across the city, each accommodating different social strata. So the affluent members of a religious or ethnic minority tend to be separated from the poor members of the same minority, in the same way that the majority of ethnic and religious groups have split along their lines of access to resources. In other words, the group identity and social cohesion of different communities have been redefined along monetary lines.

The poor immigrants to the city tend to group together for support in an alien environment. In particular people from the same town or village create informal networks for finding jobs and housing. This explains the concentrations of people of similar origin in the same areas. These are much more traceable in the newly growing settlements around the city, which are often the first port of call for many poor immigrants. This pattern is very similar to the way in which the urban quarters had historically developed. These concentrations in the metropolis, however, appear to be small or temporary. As the city demands physical and social mobility, these concentrations tend to be dismantled or weakened by the movement of their members.

Many new neighbourhoods, which were developed with the rapid expansion of the city, have mostly accommodated the members of the salaried middle class. The modern, westernized lifestyle of many of these groups was more or less consistent with the physical fabric in which they lived. The objection of the traditional middle classes to the new lifestyles, which were mostly manifest in the new quarters, has been shown in their reluctance to move into these areas. Some areas of the old city, such as Iran Street, where the incoming leaders of the revolution arrived in 1979, are still occupied by the traditional middle classes. Some other areas, however, have gradually lost their status and, due to the high density, congestion, and pollution, have been abandoned by their original inhabitants. In line with this, there has been a migration to specific points in the north, especially to the village of Gholhak, which has thus found a traditional character but has now been integrated into the urban whole. This segregation has by no means embraced all the members of traditional groups. They have been increasingly living in the new quarters, although tending to show a preference for their lifestyle by erecting higher walls around their dwellings. With the increasing religious tendencies which were associated with the Islamic revolution, this practice of building high, light walls seems to have found more appeal, suggesting the emergence of new building forms.

CULTURAL TRADITIONS AND URBAN FORM

The urban form of Tehran in the nineteenth century was more or less a typical manifestation of what has been called the Islamic city. The concept of the Islamic city was developed by the earlier generations of students of the Middle East, who tried to show how Islam was essentially urban in character and to explain the Islamic urban form by referring to the religious beliefs of Muslims. Coexistence of sedentary life in the oases and pastoral nomads was the characteristic of the birthplace of Islam. A few years after the introduction of the new faith in the town of Mecca, the relationship between the two groups was established in favour of the townsmen, creating a coalition which unified the peninsula and conquered large areas outside it. This combination of the groups has been chosen by some to explain the twofold nature of the Islamic expansion in which the most complete expression of the religion, at the first instance being spread by nomads, appears in an urban setting (de Planhol, 1970: 443–7).

Migration to the cities from the desert or from villages was known as a "hegira", an entry to Islam which asked the believers to gather in communal prayer. The Friday prayer, the most significant religious meeting of the whole community (*umma*) demands a fixed and permanent place. The Friday mosque, fixed, roofed, and fully walled as defined by theologians, is to be built in cities. According to some law schools, the Friday prayer is valid when 40 persons participate. The mosque, being the characteristic symbol of the presence of a Muslim community, makes the settlement defined as a city, the only place in which could be lived out to the full the correct life as prescribed by the book of God and the Prophet's tradition (von Grunebaum, 1981: 143). The rhythm of Muslim practices and the installations this demands are regarded as designed for town dwellers: the pool of the mosque for ablution, the five daily prayers, the call of the muezzin, the active nights of the Ramadan fast are seen to be urban in character (de Planhol, 1970: 446). Furthermore, town life is necessary for the dignified life which Islam demands. The sacred character of cities like Mecca, Medina, and Jerusalem, and the holy cities by virtue of the presence of shrines and graves of scholars and saints, suggest the importance of the city in Islam.

On the other hand, it has been argued that, rather than on religious principles, the association of Islam with cities has been more based on historical circumstance, in which Arab Muslims mostly settled in a few cities during the conquest. This is because what is essential in Islam are communities of persons and not cities or physical settlements. For an Islamic community what is required is a small number of Muslims who adhere to the faith, rather than persons who belong to any particular territory or space. In this sense, a Muslim community may be a bedouin group, a village, a sect, a law school, or a Sufi brotherhood (Lapidus, 1973: 59). The view that Islam was essentially urban has been challenged on the grounds that an Islamic city or an Islamic system of city building has never existed if the term refers to "a common set of architectural building blocks generated by a common process and combined according to a common set of rules into a common composite urban pattern" (Abu-Lughod, 1983: 64). A cultural diversity can be identified in Islamic countries, which essentially stems from their pre-Islamic traditions and from their different geographical location which has caused continuous contact with neighbouring civilizations. It has been argued that this diversity has obstructed the development of a homogeneity and unity in Islamic architecture or urban form and has characterized Islamic culture with a plurality of forms and styles (Kuban, 1983).

Despite the striking diversity, however, there is a remarkable similarity between idioms which recur all around the Islamic areas, and the areas which came under the influence of Islam (Guidoni, 1978), which make them distinguishable from Roman or Hindu cities. These include a street pattern of narrow, twisting alleys leading to culs-de-sac, courtyard houses, bazaars, mosques, and minarets. Several religious and cultural factors have often been used to explain this similarity. These factors can also explain some of the main features of the present-day built form in Tehran.

Prayer

The Islamic prayer is required to be made towards Qibla, the house of Kaaba in the holy city of Mecca, i.e. towards the south-west of Tehran. This religious requirement has had important implications for building form. Traditionally, the dwellings have been so laid out to face Qibla, implying that large sections of the urban fabric have had a general orientation towards the south-west and, in the absence of detailed measurement, the south. This has also been strengthened with the climatic desirability of facing south. This general orientation is manifest in both the old and new neighbourhoods of Tehran.

Privacy

The demand for privacy, as enhanced by Islam (Llewellyn, 1983), seems to be a key factor in the organization of space in the Islamic city, as best reflected in the residential cell and in the circulation system. The demand for privacy is largely consistent with, and inspired by, the pattern of male–female segregation. It is, however, true that this pattern has existed in other cultures, with quite different physical expressions. Abu-Lughod (1983) attempts to find the difference between Islamic and Hindu cultures, which both shared this pattern, in their different definitions of female modesty.

The courtyard house is usually seen as an example of the importance of privacy. The house finds an introverted layout centred around a courtyard, which restricts the relationship between the interior and exterior of the dwelling. With no windows to the street and its twisted entrance, the house plan ensures a controlled contact with the outside world. The interior of the large houses is also sometimes divided according to the male and female domains. This characteristic, which nineteenth-century Tehran shared with the rest of the Islamic lands, stretched back through time, is to be found in many houses in the older neighbourhoods.

The principle of privacy led to a threefold organization of space in which the private realm was separated from the public by a semi-private realm (Abu-Lughod, 1983). The public realm was the main arteries and the bazaar, mosques, baths, and other public institutions. The semi-private was the blind alley which was merely shared by a few houses to which it led. The control of this cul-de-sac, therefore, remained mainly in the hands of its users, and its form, sometimes supported with gates and bridges, discouraged outsiders from entering it. The semi-private realm could be extended inside the house in the entrance areas and, in larger houses, in the guest quarters.

In Tehran, the new house form, which emerged after the modernizations of the urban environment, was an extroverted one, opening its windows on to the streets. The pattern of a central courtyard was abandoned. However, the need for privacy survived. Like its predecessor, the new house was enclosed within high walls. The courtyard remained the area in which women could move without being seen from outside. The windows to the street were mostly covered with curtains and the balconies left underutilized or annexed to the rooms. In some areas, even the entrance doors were covered, from within the house, by curtains. In the built forms which later emerged, however, privacy found less and less ground. The use of flats and condominiums meant that a courtyard was used by more than one household, especially in the case of the plots with an entrance through the courtyard. The shared courtyard thus lost its previous uses and increasingly became the parking place of the dwellings. In a city with an ever-increasing density, multi-occupancy has become a common practice in the poor areas of immigrants. Each household lives in a room, as exemplified in some areas adjacent to the bazaar, with very low levels of privacy and comfort.

Nevertheless, privacy has remained a priority in housing development. Since the 1960s and 1970s, the use of pilotis was widespread in the new developments, allowing the ground floor to be used as parking space. This turned out to be especially popular due to the fact that living on the first floor meant the occupants were not overlooked. It was a clear departure from the emphasis on the street which was predominant in the early transformations, depriving the street-level façades of much of their livelihood.

In earlier stages of transformation, culs-de-sac were still being used. The presence of semi-private space in the city, however, reduced dramatically with the gradual disappearance of blind alleys. These were now replaced with streets which were channels of transportation, flanked by building façades. In the later developments, the sense of privacy has been far less than the earlier, post-transformation areas in which the residue of a distributional access system is at work. The cul-de-sac system has been deliberately used in some of the new developments to re-create the sense of privacy in a semi-public space, which seems to be far less successful.

The need for privacy has found a manifestation in the resistance of the central areas of the urban blocks to non-residential uses. This has effectively reduced the level of intrusion by outsiders in these central areas, creating, in some cases, islands of peace and quiet within the disturbing noise of the city. Especially in the older areas, the street pattern has been a major barrier to intrusion, despite deterioration of the urban fabric. After the revolution, the demand for privacy in dwellings has been enhanced by planning regulations. According to the new regulations, windows on the northern sides of the buildings which had a potential sight of the neighbouring courtyards were to be built higher than a limit. However, it remained largely an unused regulation.

External Modesty

The exterior of a house in nineteenth-century Tehran was formed of blank walls pierced only with a portal. Although the portal of a large house was different from that of a small one, they were both relatively modest when compared to their interior. This tendency has continued to exist in contemporary Tehran, especially within the traditional middle classes. Although the external façades of buildings are now much more elaborate, and they reveal the economic status of the inhabitants, a tendency to conceal the owners' wealth has survived.

A number of different explanations are given for this phenomenon. Most medieval mosques were built on irregular sites in the midst of bazaars, sometimes on the site of earlier buildings. Hillenbrand (1983: 18) argues that these contextual constraints sometimes resulted in haphazard plans, discouraged carefully designed external façades, and may explain the Islamic architects' preference for inner façades. One viewpoint argues that the sense of religious equality before God, as proclaimed by Islam, has been crucial in determining the interiority of the Muslim city (de Montequin, 1983). The presence of this notion has given rise to a demand for modesty as a sign of respect to fellow Muslims. Therefore, interiors are kept invisible to prevent disclosure of the economic affluence or prestigious social status of the owners. However grand the interior of a house or a palace, it finds no reflection in the external façades which are usually blank walls.

Contrasting with this viewpoint is the argument that this exterior modesty and interior grandiosity could have stemmed from the insecurity felt by the better off, resulting from the arbitrary nature of governments and from the fragility of urban life against the threat of nomadic invaders. Another explanation of this modesty might be the existence of a form of social rationality, a strong sense of conformity to the prevailing social norms, which required a certain extent of modesty. This was predominant in the nineteenth century and, to a lesser extent, continued to be respected in the twentieth. Modesty was one of the mechanisms which supported and reproduced the communal bonds which were so essential to the maintenance of the social structure. As against this developed, with the spread of capitalism, an individualism which led to a more open spatial expression. Now there were some social groups who had broken their ties with the prevalent social norms of modesty and, with the change from introverted to extroverted building forms, found it legitimate to express their individuality in the exterior of the buildings they built. The outcome has been buildings that are symbolic representations of an emerging individualism, especially by the *nouveaux riches*. Expressive decorations, expensive building materials, and anti-contextual designs are among the mechanisms through which this individualism has been expressed.

TRADITION AND MODERNITY: CULTURAL CHALLENGE AND RESPONSE

During the last 150 years, the political and economic contact of the country with the West has found a dual response in Iranian society, as best reflected in two distinctive strata: modern intelligentsia and traditional middle classes (Abrahamian, 1982). These formed both nationalist movements opposed to foreign political interference and economic dominance, and to the country's rulers whom they saw as responsible for the humiliating effects of such dominance. The two forces usually confronted each other, opposition reaching its peak during periods of political freedom such as the 1940s (Young, 1948). However, in two instances in the recent history of Iran, these two groups formed alliances, which led to the advent of revolutions in both 1906 and 1979.

The modern intelligentsia were those intellectuals who, through travel, translations, and new educational establishments, had adopted modern ideas, aspirations, and values along Western lines. Initially, they came from different strata, from the aristocracy as well as from the bazaar, and were too few to form a social class. In the twentieth century, however, resulting mainly from the expansion of the bureaucracy and the armed forces, they developed into a salaried middle class (Abrahamian, 1982).

The constituent parts of the traditional middle classes were the clergy and the bazaar community of merchants and artisans who, before the impact of the West, practised a large degree of control over economic and social affairs. The traditional privileges of this group were lost through the establishment of new economic orders and the predominance of foreign interests and their associates, and through secularization of the society by the government. Integration of the country into the world economy somewhat marginalized this group, which turned into a propertied middle class.

The modern intelligentsia, who gained the upper hand in the first revolution, believed that, to break the chains of royal despotism, clerical dogmatism, and foreign imperialism, the solutions were liberalism, secularism, and nationalism. They argued that, to have a modern, strong, and developed Iran, a radical transformation of society was required. To pave the way for a capitalist development, the country needed to be restructured in the image of the materialized example of industrial development, the West.

Against this approach were the traditional middle classes, who gained the upper hand in the second revolution. They believed in a nationalism in which the political and economic independence of the country was sought through a return to the traditional values, as idealized in the Islamic culture of society, and through the least possible contact with Western forces and values.

Against this background, it is not surprising that the two phases of restructuring of Tehran were encouraged, or carried out, by the modern intelligentsia as a part of the process of re-creation of society in a new image. The outcome of this transformation of society was to have no relationship with its predecessors, as traditions and everything associated with them were thought to indicate backwardness. This sharp break with the past meant that the new forms – of urban environment as well as of economic activities and social norms – could not develop out of the existing ones. The existing institutions and practices were totally disregarded and a process of heavy borrowing from the West started. The new institutions and structures which were imported, therefore, were imposed on or juxtaposed to the existing social practices and physical environments, creating an uneasy coexistence of sometimes antagonistic entities. Iran had experienced this juxtaposition of old and new in various invasions of different cultures and armies, as best exemplified in the dual city tradition after the Arab conquest, when the new and old were first put together and were integrated later. The speed of change in our time, however, could not allow the combination to gradually develop into a new cultural tradition.

Unlike many other countries of the Third World, these new forms were not directly introduced by Westerners, since Iran was never colonized. Instead, the agents of transformation here were the group that came into existence as a result of contacts with those powers. However, like many other colonized countries, the imposition of new institutions led to a crisis of cultural identity, and was partly instrumental in causing economic failure and political breakdown. Nevertheless, the coexistence of the new and old institutions resulted in the apparently permanent establishment of the new and the relative disappearance of the old. This was made possible by the direct intervention of the state in the creation and support of new institutions for most of the twentieth century. It was also supported by the apparent success of the similar forms of institutions elsewhere, especially in the West. Urban form, especially in Tehran, whose transformation predates other Iranian cities and whose old parts are proportionately smaller, appears to be the product of, and a contributor to, these new institutions.

The coexistence and duality of the old and new, of two modes of production and two cultures, found spatial manifestation in numerous aspects. The most obvious one was the rivalry of two city centres: a new city centre to the north of the old one. Whereas the new centre, housed in the new urban space, was encouraged by the state as a sign of modernity, the old centre, with the bazaar as its focus, was undermined and threatened by destruction. The outcome was hoped to be a unity and homogeneity of urban space. Nevertheless, as in many other cases, this threat did not materialize, leading to the coexistence of old and new, as the old was strong and deeply rooted enough to wage a war against the new. The battle between the old and new continues even after the apparent victory of the traditional values and forms. With the establishment of a religious government and the role of the clergy in judicial, legislative, and executive branches of the government, it would appear that traditionalism has now won the battle. The reality, however, is that at all times and under any regime in the country, the battle between tradition and modernity has been fought, as both tendencies can be clearly traced in both the modern intelligentsia and the traditional middle classes. The integrative nationalism of the Pahlavis was associated with the ancient political form of executive monarchy, as is now the republic associated with the ancient institution and traditionalism of the clergy. These contradictions are signs of tension inside both camps and a continuing struggle between tradition and modernity. The new approaches to economic development and spatial transformation signify a rising strength of modernity. In Tehran today, a return to modernization tendencies by a clerical government is observable. The development of new motorways, threatening the old core of the city with redevelopment, and some grandiose schemes (such as the crossing of the Alburz mountains by a straight motorway to link Tehran with the Caspian Sea) are all modernizing the capital. The concepts of space used are once again modern, rather than traditional, images, although some attempts are being made to reconcile the two (Figure 13.2). At the same time, there are strong reactions to these developments, which in due course may reverse the trend once again.

INDIVIDUALISM OR CONFORMITY

The development of a capitalist economy has introduced new social relations. The communal bonds of small communities have been eroded in favour of relationships defined by individuals' access to money. As is the case with all such transitions, old communities began to be replaced by the community of money (Harvey, 1989). In the old communities, an action was justifiable and rational if it was in line with communal beliefs and traditions.

FIGURE 13.2 Juxtaposition of old and new finds a comfortable home in postmodernism

Communal bonds included various religious, ethnic, and cultural relations which had developed over long periods of time and linked a group of individuals together. Conforming to these relations and the norms which were based on them constituted a form of social rationality for individual actions. Social rationality was in close relationship with environmental rationality, as sustainable ways of dealing with nature had been tested for millennia. Therefore, before the dramatic transformations since the nineteenth century, the basis of a rational action, including the production of urban space, was to take these dual rationalities into consideration.

All this started to change after the nineteenth century, as a new form of rationality emerged: an instrumental rationality that urges individuals to aspire for personal gain. Increasingly, an action would seem rational if it led to a material gain. This has had a major impact on the social and spatial fabric of the city. In Tehran, where uprooted immigrants gathered together, the predominance of instrumental rationality over social and environmental rationality was very clear. The city building process is perhaps the arena in which this conflict of rationalities is most visible.

This, however, did not mean that no form of social rationality has been at work after these societal transformations. On the one hand, a new set of social and cultural bonds have been created which have established the platforms of a new, socially rational behaviour. These were either enforced by the government through laws and regulations or spread informally along with the gradual integration of the country into the Western-centred world system. Although the advent of the Islamic revolution has shown that rationality of the new social and cultural norms has been less deep-rooted and so less resistant to change, a large number of these new norms continue to be valued. On the other hand, many of the old social and cultural, and especially religious, patterns showed resilience. Although these were increasingly undermined in a coexistence of different forms of rationality in which the newer forms have been gaining ground, the Islamic revolution has proved how the old forms can survive and exert a powerful influence on social processes.

Challenging the power of the social context, of the reign of tradition and custom, has been a hallmark of the modern era (Gellner, 1992), and has freed individuals from the tyranny of the past. The main challenge, however, has been to find ways in which these individuals could live together and develop meaningful and civilized social relations. In the transformation of Iranian society, there has been an adverse relationship between these two rationalities. In an increasingly capitalist economy and society, personal gain, especially economic gain as a bridge to other material gains, has established the foundation of a new instrumental rationality according to which most social codes have been, or are being, adjusted. Although the drive for personal gain is as old as humanity itself, it appears that at no time throughout history has it been so predominant in social relationships, as previously it was mostly controlled by some form of social bond. More difficult to achieve has been a stable framework, in the form of an institutionalized legal system which would regulate the relationship among these individuals. A century of legislation had failed to offer an effective framework for social relationships. This explains the emerging attractions of Islam, which offered a framework historically tested and already accepted by many as legitimate and capable of regulating social relations. The new challenge was now to interpret it for the new demands of a market economy.

The impact of the conflict between instrumental and social rationalities on urban form has been very important. The physical development process, as a social process, was one in which the individual development agencies had to operate within a set of social rules and ideas as evolved over long periods of time. The strength of these rules and ideas ensured that personal action, and subsequently the form of the built environment produced, conformed to what the community saw as acceptable. The whole community was involved in the development of an urban development project. As personal profit seeking, which became the motivation of speculative developments of the modern period, undermined this presence, it resulted in a built environment full of disorder, conflicts, and inequalities.

CONTEXT AND MODERNIZATION

Every new addition to or modification of the urban environment has to be carried out with some consideration of the existing context. Whatever the viewpoint and the outcome of these considerations, enhancing or disregarding the existing context, it has some impact on future developments. During the first 300 years of Tehran's urban life, from the building of the 1553 walls to the restructuring of 1868, the main approach, as regards the context of built space, leant towards consensus and conformity. Throughout this period, no large-scale transformation of the city had occurred. Because of various constraints which limited the agents of production, every act of development had to be carefully set against its context, and the outcome was usually adaptable to it.

This contextualism, however, could not survive the two major phases of transition in the 1870s and 1930s. During the 1870s, attempts were made to create a balance between the old and the new. Therefore, new neighbourhoods were juxtaposed to old ones without attempting to transform them. Here, a degree of respect for and adaptation to the past was at work. However, the extent of conformity to the old city was diminished. The new patterns of streets and buildings in the new quarters were put forward as a rival as well as a complement to the old ones. The break with contextual conformity, which created a dualism in the typology of the physical fabric, was consistent with the break in social structure which was on the way. This cautious attempt at modernization still paid respect to tradition and the old urban environment. The fierce attack on these two, however, came with the major attempts of the 1930s which, with a total disregard for the old city, tore it apart. The new networks of streets, which were imposed on it, were to build new façades as soon as possible to hide whatever remained of the old environment. The long-term trend was to eliminate the latter to replace it with a modern fabric. The new was to have no relationship with the old (Figure 13.3).

CULTURAL PRACTICES AND URBAN FORM / **251**

FIGURE 13.3 The modern urban fabric has no relationship with what it has replaced

The framework which this cry for modernity established provided the basis for the future development of the city. The sheer size of post-war urban development, in which the principle of minimal relationship with the past was maintained, reduced, and virtually nullified, the proportion of the old fabric to, and its impact on, new developments. In the latter, a position had to be taken towards the existing context. In most cases, however, this context was itself a newly developed part of the city, due to the rapid pace of urban expansion (Figure 13.4).

The twentieth century has witnessed a new contextualism alongside a vigorous modernization process. On the one hand, market forces and the new planning system have ensured that the social status of the new development and its occupiers match their context, hence emphasizing the sectoral development of urban structure and its north–south socio-spatial divide. On the other hand, the nature of the developing agencies and their limited abilities and instruments, combined with the rapid pace of urban development, have had enormous impacts on the built form. They paid respect to short-lived fashions and architectural styles which, once established, spread very rapidly throughout the city, and led to the development of entire urban quarters with a large degree of physical uniformity. Whereas now this new contextualism is still strongly at work, a change of approach has started to develop since the 1970s. The necessity of total disregard of the older buildings and neighbourhoods is less stressed and some attempts have been made to revitalize parts of them. This confirms the continuing

FIGURE 13.4 A new urban context is emerging (north of Ferdowsi Square)

impact of the old traditions on future developments, even if their physical presence has been considerably reduced. It should be noted that, at a stage where the physical presence of a form is diminished, has disappeared, or even has never materialized, it becomes a concept of space, capable of influencing the built form in various ways.

CONCLUSION: THE TENSION BETWEEN OLD AND NEW

The juxtaposition of the inherited and the borrowed concepts of space represents, as much as stimulates, the uneven coexistence of the traditional, pre-capitalist life forms with the modern, capitalist ones. A tense coexistence of the old and new, in which they constantly struggle for domination, is a hallmark of the modern history of Iran and its capital, Tehran. Different social groups tended to resist or be associated with the incoming change, which created a cultural duality expressed even in their separated places of living and working, to be gradually lifted only by the passage of time and the revolution. Although ethnic and religious communities are no longer segregated formally in space, they have maintained a form of communal spatial manifestation. Islamic traditions and norms of conduct, the demand for privacy and the forms of prayer, have had critical implications for urban form, which have guaranteed certain points of similarity between the new and old urban environments.

14

CHALLENGES OF THE TWENTY-FIRST CENTURY

Even until a generation ago, many Tehranis used to sleep at nights on rooftops and in the courtyards of their houses. After a long hot day, the cool breeze from the snow-capped Alburz mountains offered a refreshing change. During the day, the city of plane trees would offer promising opportunities to many of its citizens. A major industrialization drive was on the way, oil prices were rising, and women and rural populations had found new freedoms, which were among the reasons for the city to attract large numbers of newcomers from towns and villages around the country and from around the world. By the mid-1960s, Tehran's population had reached 2.7 million and was rising. People could not participate in decision making, and social polarization was quite manifest in the city. A new middle class, however, felt at home in a city whose infrastructure, roads, parks, schools, museums, and dwellings were all new. It would have been impossible for Tehranis to imagine that within a relatively short period of time an entirely new picture would emerge.

Now, through the continued increase of population, Tehran has spread across the countryside in all directions to become a metropolis with 11 million inhabitants. Women and the young are on the margins of the labour market and the elderly have little protection. The demise of the extended family has deprived individuals of a strong source of support in response to social and economic difficulties. The city's economic growth has been disrupted by falling oil prices, a revolution and a war. It suffers from inner-city decay and social and environmental problems. The physical stock is dilapidated, inflation rates are constantly growing, the gap between rich and poor has intensified, transport problems appear to be insoluble and Tehran has become one of the most polluted cities on earth. The city's acute shortage of water is combined with the rise of underground water tables, which are being polluted by the city's growing waste. For two-thirds of the year, a dome of hot air hangs above the city, trapping the poisonous pollutants which threaten the health of the citizens. Indeed, sleeping on the rooftops and in the courtyard is no longer a safe option.

Where will the city be in another generation? Will it have a population of more than 25 million living in far worse social and environmental conditions? Or will it give up dealing with its problems and start shrinking and disappearing, as happened to the ancient city of Ray whose ruins are near by? Or can it start to heal its wounds and become a better place? There are some promising signs that the latter is not an impossible alternative. Population growth has slowed down and the family continues to be a strong social and economic unit, despite the major changes that it has gone through. The economic pressure on local authorities to seek support from the public signifies the possibility of a more democratic local governance. The city is trying to integrate itself more into the global economy and is relying on advanced and environmentally friendly technologies to deal with its problems. Tehran municipality's efforts in reducing carbon monoxide emissions and enlarging the city's green space, from 2.5 to 10 m^2 per person, have won the city international recognition. Tehran (alongside 24 other cities) has been identified by the United Nations' 1996 Habitat Conference as a best practice city, offering models for future programmes in cities world-wide.

More, however, needs to be done. The city's environmental problems cannot be solved without addressing its social problems, which pose a serious challenge for the future. A major challenge is accommodating the future population growth of the city. While the city centre is suffering from decay and lack of attention caused by suburbanization, many have seen the solution to lie in the fragmented addition of new satellite settlements around the city. This policy, however, tends to contribute further to the existing socio-spatial fragmentation of the city, as these new settlements are left on the margins of infrastructure provision and municipal management. Space becomes an even greater barrier for the marginalized and the challenges of creating sustainable development become more daunting.

The enormous problem of the social and spatial divide threatens the city's stability, as it has done before. To confront social polarization and exclusion, what is needed is to confront the existing socio-spatial barriers and to create possibilities for integration. Attempts at social integration have often been forceful here, as difference has caused fear of fragmentation and loss of control. Forceful social integration, however, always leads to discrimination and new forms of social exclusion. The ability to create social integration, on the contrary, should provide the opportunity for people to have access to material resources through access to work; to have access to decision making through political participation; and to have access to common narratives and identities through communication and socialization. What the city needs is the development of arenas, public spheres, in which these channels of integration are negotiated rather than imposed. The recent debates in Tehran about the necessity of developing a strong civil society is one indication of this need. It is one of the platforms on which the new president of the republic was elected in 1997, the latest step in a century-long struggle for democratic governance.

Closely related to the challenge of involving the citizens in decision making is the challenge of a secure economic foundation for the city and the municipality. The city finances are now largely dependent on speculative property development. For the city government to have a more reliable financial basis, there is a need to find ways in which the urban region as a whole can contribute to its management and maintenance. The municipality is not alone in having to rely on a narrow financial base. The entire city's economy is facing a major challenge to find a more secure future. Its reliance on public sector employment, itself dependent on the fluctuations of the oil prices in the global economy, makes the city's economy vulnerable. To lessen this vulnerability, a major challenge for the city is to diversify its economy.

But diversification is not the only challenge in the global context. Another is the continuous political challenges of globalization. Ever since the Islamic revolution two decades ago, the city has been engaged in responding to the challenges of globalization by performing symbolic gestures. However, there must be a time when symbolism should give way to a real consolidation of the city's position in the global space. This will only be possible through social and economic development, rather than an endless continuation of symbolic contest.

Tehran has grown from a small village to a giant metropolis. It is the largest concentration of people and wealth in a vast country and plays the role of a peripheral partner in the world system of capitalist economies, exerting a degree of political, economic, and cultural influence in international affairs. Each stage of this transformation has often been painful, as the city has had to cope with enormous problems, especially in the twentieth century. The city in this century has been marked by two revolutions, one at the beginning and the other towards the end. On the surface, the first revolution was a point of entry into the realm of modernity and the second an exit from it into a postmodern era. Within a broader, historical context, however, both revolutions have marked the tensions of dealing with modernity, the city's struggle to cope with its role in the global space and to aspire to a better future. Both revolutions and many more social upheavals signify the struggles of a people searching for a stable, and yet dynamic, framework to redefine their relationships with each other and with the outside world. Although the nature of the city, populated with the young and undergoing rapid change, has denied its people any such stable framework, the elusive search continues. A major challenge of the future therefore is to find an institutional framework, a paradigm which would allow the city to define its place in the global space and to establish cohesive and meaningful social relations among its citizens. For a while, a combination of nationalism, secularism, and modernization was seen to provide the answer. In reaction to its failure, the paradigm was to be found in religion and tradition. The complexities of the social world, however, have shown that the answer cannot be found readily available either in another place or another era, in the West or in the past. Any such answers will have to be adapted to the complex realities of the contemporary city and as such they have to evolve out of the lived experiences of the citizens.

Tehran is often seen to lack continuity, as the bulk of its people and places have come together in the last 50 years. It is a place of transition and as such people's attachment to each other and to their places is rather limited. The city's space is thus open and fluid, even though it acts as a barrier to those who lack the means of crossing it. A major challenge for the city is to combine this sense of fluidity with a sense of belonging and of permanence. Constant social change, as best exemplified by two revolutions, and spatial transformation, as best seen in the process of urban change, are the main features of the city's life this century. The challenge of the next century will therefore be to combine the need for change and the need for security. Part of this challenge would mean allowing the city to find a degree of maturity, where a degree of trust in people and places can be established, to counterbalance the constant flow of change. As expressed in a revolution earlier this century, it is true that the city has embraced, and has benefited from, the money economy, freeing its citizens from the tyranny of the customs and traditions of the past, when position in relatively rigid social networks could be the last word in determining an individual's future. As exemplified by a second revolution this century, however, it is also true that the city rejects the disenchantment associated with the tyranny of instrumental reason.

Iran, and its capital city Tehran which houses more than a fifth of its population, have undergone considerable transformation in the modern period, a change whose dimensions and, especially, pace have been beyond control, creating tensions and political, economic, and cultural difficulties. For too long, however, this change has been seen as beyond control, managed by powers from outside and causing unforeseen consequences. This has often caused widespread cynicism among the citizens, who have felt powerless and have found no way to intervene in the restless flow of change, despite frequent and often honourable attempts. What is needed now is to abandon the legacy of victimization and of being overwhelmed by change. What is needed is to develop a confidence with which it is possible to appreciate the necessity of change as well as the need for continuity, to realize that it is not impossible to be in charge of change, despite its unintended consequences, and to devise ways of collectively managing this change and its balance with the continuity of the socio-spatial world.

BIBLIOGRAPHY

Abedin Dorkoosh, S. 1991, "Takhmeen-e tabe'e gheymat-e vahed-e maskooni dar shahrha-ye koochak-e Iran", *Abadi*, No. 1, Summer 1370, pp. 38–44.
Abedin Dorkoosh, S. 1993, *Daramadi Beh Eghtessad-e Shahri (An Introduction to Urban Economics)*, 1372, Iran University Press, Tehran.
Abercrombie, P. 1945, *Greater London Plan 1944*, HMSO, London.
Abrahamian, E. 1980, "Kasravi: the Integrative Nationalist of Iran", in E. Kedourie & S. Heim, eds, *Towards a Modern Iran*, Frank Cass, London, pp. 96–131.
Abrahamian, E. 1982, *Iran between Two Revolutions*, Princeton University Press, New Jersey.
Abrahamian, E. 1993, *Khomeinism: Essays on the Islamic Republic*, University of California Press, Berkeley.
Abu-Lughod, J. 1983, "Contemporary Relevance of Islamic Urban Principles", in A. Germen, ed., *Islamic Architecture and Urbanism*, King Faisal University, Dammam, Saudi Arabia, pp. 64–70.
Afary, J. 1994, "Social Democracy and the Iranian Constitutional Revolution of 1906–11", in J. Foran, ed., *A Century of Revolution*, University of Minnesota Press, Minneapolis, pp. 21–43.
Afshar, H. ed. 1985, *Iran: A revolution in turmoil*, Macmillan, London.
Ahmadi, F. & Ahmadi, N. 1995, *Iranian Islam and the Concept of the Individual: On the non-development of the concept of the individual in the ways of thinking of Iranians*, Uppsala University, Uppsala.
Ahsan, M. 1995, "Tamarkoz ya tamarkoz-zodaii va asar-e kalbodi-e an", *Abadi*, No. 15, Winter 1373, pp. 54–9.
Alavi, B. 1983, "Critical Writings on the Renewal of Iran", in E. Bosworth & C. Hillenbrand, eds, *Qajar Iran, Political, Social and Cultural Change 1800–1925*, Edinburgh University Press, Edinburgh, pp. 243–54.
Aldridge, M. 1979, *The British New Towns, a Programme without a Policy*, Routledge & Kegan Paul, London.
Alemi, M. 1985, "The 1891 Map of Tehran, Two Cities, Two Cores, Two Cultures", *Journal of the Islamic Environmental Design Research Centre*, 1985, No. 1, pp. 74–84.
Alonso, W. 1971, "A Theory of the Urban Land Market", in L. S. Bourne, ed., *Internal Structure of the City*, Oxford Unversity Press, New York, pp. 154–9.
Ambrose, P. 1986, *Whatever Happened to Planning?*, Methuen, London.
Amiet, P. 1986, "Elamite Urbanization in Susa" (Persian translation), in M. Y. Kiani, ed., *Nazari Ejmali beh Shahrneshini va Shahrsazi dar Iran (A General Study on Urbanization & Urban Planning in Iran)*, Homa, Tehran, pp. 95–8.
Amirahmadi, H. 1990, *Revolution and Economic Transition: The Iranian experience*, State University of New York Press, Albany.
Amirahmadi, H. & Kiafar, A. 1987, "Tehran: Growth and Contradictions", *Journal of Planning Education and Research*, Vol. 6, No. 3, pp. 167–77.
Arberry, A. J. 1960, *Shiraz: Persian City of Saints and Poets*, University of Oklahoma Press, Norman.

Ardalan, N. 1986, "Architecture viii. Pahlavi, after World War II", in *Encyclopaedia Iranica*, vol. II, 4, Routledge & Kegan Paul, London, pp. 351–5.
Ardalan, P. 1992a, "Motale'at-e jame'e haml va naghl va terafik-e Tehran", *Bulletin*, No. 7, Azar 1371, pp. 31–5.
Ardalan, P. 1992b, "Sherkat-e vahed: bar-e geran-e yek vazifeh-ye doshvar", *Bulletin*, No. 9, Esfand 1371, pp. 32–7.
Ardalan, P. 1995a, "Shahrdari-e Tehran va oughat-e faraghat", *Bulletin*, No. 37, 5th Mordad 1374, pp. 20–6.
Ardalan, P. 1995b, "Baghha va shahrdari-e Tehran", *Bulletin*, No. 36, 5th Tir 1374, pp. 10–16.
Ardam, Consultant Engineers, 1986, *Ghassemabad Project*, Vezarat-e Maskan va Shahrsazi, Tehran.
Argan, G. 1969, *The Renaissance City*, Studio Vista, London.
Ashraf, A. 1974, "Vizhegi-ha-ye Tarikhi-e Shahrneshini dar Iran-e Doureh-ye Eslami (Historical Specificity of Iranian Cities in Islamic Era)", *Olum-e Ejtemai (Social Sciences)*, Vol. I, No. 4, June 1974, Tehran University Press, Tehran, pp. 7–49.
Ashraf, A. 1993, "The crisis of national and ethnic identities in contemporary Iran", *Iranian Studies*, Vol. 26, Nos 1–2, Winter/Spring 1993, pp. 159–64.
Ashtor, E. 1976, *A Social and Economic History of the Near East in the Middle Ages*, Collins, London.
Aslani, M. R. 1992, "Tehran shahr-e bidefa", *Ketab-e Tehran*, Roshangaran, Tehran, pp. 30–5.
Aslani, M. R. 1993, "Parkha-ye in kaj aiin-e gharn", *Ketab-e Tehran*, Roshangaran, Tehran, pp. 72–93.
Avery, P. & Simmons, J. 1980, "Persia on a Cross of Silver", in E. Kedourie & S. Haim, eds, *Towards a Modern Iran*, Frank Cass, London, pp. 1–37.
Azhdari, A. 1964, "Prozheh-ye Shahrsazi-e yek Bakhsh-e Ghadimi, Oudlajan", in *Masael-e Ejtemai-e Shahr-e Tehran*, a colloquium by the Institute of Social Research and Study, University of Tehran, Tehran University Press, Tehran, pp. 198–201.
Badi', M. 1964, "Elal-e Peydayesh-e Kuyha-ye Tazeh", in *Masael-e Ejtemai-e Shahr-e Tehran*, a colloquium by the Institute of Social Research and Study, University of Tehran, Tehran University Press, Tehran, pp. 210–18.
Bahram Soltani, K. 1994, "Andazehgiri-e aloodegi-e hava-ye shahr-e Tehran", *Abadi*, No. 12, Spring 1373, pp. 72–5.
Balchin, P., Kieve, J., & Bull, G. 1988, *Urban Land Economics and Public Policy*, Macmillan, London.
Bank-e Markazi-e Iran (Central Bank of Iran), 1981, *Hesab-ha-ye Melli-e Iran 1338–1356*, BMI, Tehran.
Bank-e Markazi-e Iran, 1983, *Baravord-ha-ye Avvaliye-ye Towlid va Hazineh-ye Melli-e Keshvar dar Sal-e 1362*, BMI, Tehran.
Bank-e Markazi-e Iran, 1984, *Barrasi-e Tahavvolat-e Eghtessadi-e Keshvar Ba'd az Enghelab*, BMI, Tehran.
Bank-e Markazi-e Iran, 1986, *Gozaresh-e Mashrooh-e Fa'aliyat-ha-ye Sakhtemani- e Bakhsh-e Khossussi dar Manategh-e Shahri-e Ostan-ha-ye Mokhtalef-e Keshvar, 1363*, BMI, Tehran.
Bank-e Markazi-e Iran, 1987, *Barrasi-e Amari-e Fa'aliyat-ha-ye Sakhtemani-e Bakhsh-e Khossussi dar Manategh-e Shahri-e Keshvar be Tafkik-e Ostanha, 1364*, BMI, Tehran.
Barnett, J. 1982, *An Introduction to Urban Design*, Harper & Row, New York.
Barthold, W. 1984, *An Historical Geography of Iran*, Princeton University Press, New Jersey.

Bayley, S. 1975, *The Garden City*, The Open University Press, Milton Keynes.
Behazin, D. 1994, "Masa'el-e zist mohiti dar ravand-e tose'eh-ye Tehran", *Ketab-e Tehran*, Roshangaran, Tehran, pp. 112–24.
Behnam, J. 1964, "Natijehgiri", in *Masael-e Ejtemai-e Shahr-e Tehran*, a colloquium by the Institute of Social Research and Study, University of Tehran, Tehran University Press, Tehran, pp. 85–8.
Bell, G. 1928, *Persian Pictures*, Ernest Benn, London.
Benevolo, L. 1980, *The History of the City*, Scolar Press, London.
Berghe, L. V. 1966, *Archéologie de l'Iran Ancien*, E. J. Brill, Leiden.
Bharier, J. 1971, *Economic Development in Iran 1900–1971*, Oxford University Press, London.
Blowers, A. 1973, "Planning Residential Areas", in *Planning and the City* (Prepared by the Course Team), Urban Development Unit 29, The Open University Press, Milton Keynes, pp. 91–139.
Bostock, F. & Jones, G. 1989, *Planning and Power in Iran: Ebtehaj and economic development under the shah*, Frank Cass, London.
Boyce, M. 1983, "Iranian Festivals", in E. Yarshater, ed., *The Cambridge History of Iran*, Vol. 3(2), *The Selucid, Parthian, and Sasanian Periods*, Cambridge University Press, Cambridge, pp. 792–818.
Bradway Laska, S. & Spain, D. 1980, *Back to the City*, Pergamon Press, New York.
Briggs, A. 1968, *Victorian Cities*, Penguin, Harmondsworth.
Brown, L. C. 1973, "Introduction", in L. C. Brown, ed., *From Madina to Metropolis*, Darwin Press, Princeton, New Jersey, pp. 15–46.
Brown, P. R. L. 1978, "Parthians and Sasanians", in J. A. Boyle, ed., *Persia, History and Heritage*, Henry Melland, London, pp. 24–30.
Browne, E. G. 1926, *A Year amongst the Persians*, Cambridge University Press, Cambridge.
Buchanan, P. (Ministry of Transport), 1963, *Traffic in Towns*, HMSO, London.
Burns, W. 1963, *New Towns for Old*, Leonard Hill, London.
Cahen, C. 1970, "Economy, Society, Institutions", in *The Cambridge History of Islam*, Vol. 2B, *Islamic Society and Civilization*, Cambridge University Press, Cambridge, pp. 511–38.
Camhis, M. 1979, *Planning Theory and Philosophy*, Tavistock, London.
Cazerooni, S. 1988, "Mosahebeh ba Vazir-e Maskan va Shahrsazi", *Me'mari va Honar-e Iran (The Iranian Art and Architecture)*, No. 4. pp. 43–5.
Central Bank of the Islamic Republic of Iran, 1993, *Economic Report and Balance Sheet 1371 (1992–93)*, Economic Research Department, Central Bank of the Islamic Republic of Iran, Tehran.
Chadwick, G. 1971, *A System View of Planning*, Pergamon, Oxford.
Champion, A., Clegg, K., & Davies, R. 1977, *Facts about the New Towns*, Retailing and Planning Associates, Corbridge, Northumberland.
Chapman, J. M. & Chapman, B. 1957, *The Life and Times of Baron Haussmann, Paris in the Second Empire*, Weidenfeld & Nicolson, London.
Chermayeff, S. & Tzonis, A. 1971, *Shape of Community*, MIT Press, Cambridge, Massachusetts.
Clark, B. 1981, "Urban Planning in Iran", in J. I. Clarke & H. Bowen-Jones, eds, *Change and Development in the Middle East*, Methuen, London, pp. 280–8.
Clarke, B. 1973, "Urban Renewal", in *Planning and the City* (Prepared by the Course Team), Urban Development Unit 28, The Open University Press, Milton Keynes, pp. 41–90.
Clarke, J. & Clark, B. 1969, *Kermanshah, an Iranian Provincial City*, Centre for Middle Eastern and Islamic Studies, Durham.

Clarke, J. I. 1963, *The Iranian City of Shiraz*, Department of Geography, University of Durham.
Clawson, P. 1993, "Knitting Iran Together: The Land Transport Revolution, 1920–1940", *Iranian Studies*, Vol. 26, Nos 3–4, Summer/Fall 1993, pp. 235–50.
Clay, P. 1979, *Neighborhood Renewal*, Lexington Books, Lexington, Massachusetts.
Colledge, M. 1977, *Parthian Art*, Paul Elek, London.
Cook, J. M. 1983, *The Persian Empire*, J. M. Dent & Sons, London.
Costello, V. 1977, *Urbanization in the Middle East*, Cambridge University Press, Cambridge.
Cottam, R. 1964, *Nationalism in Iran*, University of Pittsburgh Press, Pittsburgh.
Couperie, P. 1970, *Paris through the Ages*, Barrie & Jenkins, London.
Cresswell, P. & Thomas, R. 1973, *The New Town Idea*, The Open University Press, Milton Keynes.
Crosby, T. 1967, *Architecture: City sense*, Studio Vista, London.
Curzon, G. 1892, *Persia and the Persian Question*, Longmans Green, London.
Daneshvar, S. 1994, *Jazireh-ye Sargardani*, Kharazmi, Tehran.
De Montequin, F. A. 1983, "The Essence of Urban Existence in the World of Islam", in A. Germen, ed., *Islamic Architecture and Urbanism*, King Faisal University, Dammam, pp. 43–63.
De Planhol, X. 1968, "Geography of Settlement", in W. B. Fisher, ed., *The Cambridge History of Iran*, Vol. 1, *The Land of Iran*, Cambridge University Press, Cambridge, pp. 409–67.
De Planhol, X. 1970, "The Geography of Setting", in *The Cambridge History of Islam*, Vol. 2B, *Islamic Society and Civilization*, Cambridge University Press, Cambridge, pp. 443–68.
Dezhkam, Zh. 1985, Mas'aleh-ye Maskan dar Iran, Unpublished PhD Thesis, Department of Economics, University of Tehran.
Diakonoff, I. M. 1985a, "Elam", in I. Gershevitch, ed., *The Cambridge History of Iran*, Vol. 2, *The Median and Achaemenian Periods*, Cambridge University Press, Cambridge, pp. 1–24.
Diakonoff, I. M. 1985b, "Media", in *The Cambridge History of Iran*, Vol. 2, *The Median and Achaemenian Periods*, Cambridge University Press, Cambridge, pp. 36–148.
Ehlers, E. and Floor, W. 1993, "Urban change in Iran, 1920–1941", *Iranian Studies*, Vol. 26, Nos 3–4, Summer/Fall 1993, pp. 251–76.
Ehteshami, A. 1995, *After Khomeini: The Iranian second republic*, Routledge, London.
Eisenstadt, S. & Schachar, A. 1987, *Society, Culture, and Urbanization*, Sage, Newbury Park, California.
EIU, 1995, *Country Profile: Iran 1995–96*, The Economist Intelligence Unit, London.
Elwell-Sutton, L. P. 1941, *Modern Iran*, George Routledge & Sons, London.
English, P. 1966, *City and Village in Iran*, The University of Wisconsin Press, Madison.
English, P. 1973, "The Traditional City of Herat, Afghanistan", in L. C. Brown, ed., *From Madina to Metropolis*, The Darwin Press, Princeton, New Jersey, pp. 73–89.
Ettehadieh, M. 1983, "Patterns in Urban Development; the Growth of Tehran (1852–1903)", in E. Bosworth & C. Hillenbrand, eds, *Qajar Iran, Political, Social and Cultural Change 1800–1925*, Edinburgh University Press, Edinburgh, pp. 199–212.
Faghih, N. 1984, "Esfahan, Shahri baraye Aber-e Piadeh", in A. Javadi, ed., *Me'mari-e Iran*, Vol. II, Mojarrad, Tehran, pp. 663–9.

Faghih, N. 1988, "Tarikhcheh-ye Mokhtasari az Naghshaeh-ye Shahr-e Tehran", *Me'mari va Honar-e Iran (Iranian Art and Architecture)*, No. 4, pp. 38–42.
Falamaki, M. 1978, *Seiri dar Tajareb-e Maremmat-e Shahri: az Veniz ta Shiraz*, Vezarat-e Maskan va Shahrsazi, Tehran.
Falamaki, M. 1988, "Tehran, Masaleh ya Moamma?", *Sakhteman*, No. 3, pp. 56–65.
Farmand, R. & Rafiei, M. 1991, "Malekiyat-e otomobil-e shakhsi va daramad-e khanevar dar Tehran", *Abadi*, No. 2, Autumn 1370, pp. 56–67.
Farmanfarmaian, A. & Gruen, V. 1968, *Tarh-e Jame-e Tehran*, Sazman-e Barnameh va Budgeh, Tehran.
Fathy, H. 1986, *Natural Energy and Vernacular Architecture*, University of Chicago Press, Chicago.
Ferrier, R. 1986, "Trade from the Mid-14th Century to the End of the Safavid Period", in P. Jackson, ed., *The Cambridge History of Iran*, Vol. 6, *The Timurid and Safavid Periods*, Cambridge University Press, Cambridge, pp. 412–90.
Fisher, W. 1968, "Physical Geography", in W. Fisher, ed., *The Cambridge History of Iran*, Vol. 1, *The Land of Iran*, Cambridge University Press, Cambridge, pp. 3–110.
Fleming, J., Honour, H. & Pevsner, N. 1984, *The Penguin Dictionary of Architecture*, Penguin, Harmondsworth.
Foran, J. ed. 1994, *A Century of Revolution: Social movements in Iran*, University of Minnesota Press, Minneapolis.
Frye, R. 1965, *Bukhara, the Medieval Achievement*, University of Oklahoma Press, Norman.
Frye, R. N. 1979a, "The Iranicization of Islam", in R. N. Frye, *Islamic Iran and Central Asia (7th–12th Centuries)*, Variorum Reprints, London, pp. 1–7.
Frye, R. N. 1979b, "Notes on the Renaissance of the 10th and 11th Centuries in Eastern Iran", in R. N. Frye, *Islamic Iran and Central Asia (7th–12th Centuries)*, Variorum Reprints, London, pp. 137–43.
Frye, R. N. 1979c, "The New Persian Renaissance in Western Iran", in R. N. Frye, *Islamic Iran and Central Asia (7th–12th Centuries)*, Variorum Reprints, London, pp. 225–31.
Frye, R. N. 1979d, "City Chronicles of Central Asia and Khurasan, The Tarix-i Nishapur", in R. Frye, *Islamic Iran and Central Asia (7th–12th Centuries)*, Variorum Reprints, London, pp. 405–20.
Frye, R. N. 1993, "Iranian Identity in Ancient Times", *Iranian Studies*, Vol. 26, Nos 1–2, Winter/Spring 1993, pp. 143–6.
Ganji, M. H. 1968, "Climate", in W. Fisher, ed., *The Cambridge History of Iran* Vol. 1. *The Land of Iran*, Cambridge University Press, Cambridge, pp. 212–49.
Gans, H. 1968, *People and Plans*, Basic Books, New York.
Gates, D. 1972, *Man and His Environment: Climate*, Harper & Row, New York.
Gaube, H. 1979, *Iranian Cities*, New York University Press, New York.
Gellner, E. 1992, *Reason and Culture: The historic role of rationality and rationalism*, Blackwell, Oxford.
Ghaffari, F. 1964, "Moassesat-e Konooni va Zaroorat-e Hamahangi dar Fa'aliyat-e an-ha", in *Masael-e Ejtemai-e Shahr-e Tehran*, a colloquium by the Institute of Social Research and Study, University of Tehran, Tehran University Press, Tehran, pp. 74–80.
Ghanbari Parsa, A. & Madanipour, A. R. 1988, "A Review of Methods of Public Land Ownership and Allocation for Housing in Iran", *Planning Outlook*, Vol. 31, No. 2, pp. 110–15.
Ghirshman, R. 1964, *Persia, From the Origins to Alexander the Great*, Thames and Hudson, London.

Gibson, M. & Langstaff, M. 1982, *An Introduction to Urban Renewal*, Hutchinson, London.
Giddens, A. 1981, *A Contemporary Critique of Historical Materialism*, Macmillan, London.
Giddens, A. 1984, *The Constitution of Society: Outline of the theory of structuration*, Polity Press, Cambridge.
Gilbar, G. 1976, "Demographic Developments in Late Qajar Persia, 1870–1906", *Asian and African Studies*, Vol. XI, pp. 125–56.
Gilbar, G. 1979, "Persian Agriculture in the Late Qajar Period, 1860–1906: Some Economic and Social Aspects", *Asian and African Studies*, Vol. XII, pp. 312–65.
Gilbert, A. & Healey, P. 1985, *The Political Economy of Land: Urban development in an oil economy*, Gower, Aldershot.
Golestani, D. 1964, "Proje-ye Yek Haste-ye Markazi Baraye Gharb-e Tehran", in *Masael-e Ejtemai-e Shahr-e Tehran*, a colloquium by the Institute of Social Research and Study, University of Tehran, Tehran University Press, Tehran, pp. 189–97.
Goss, A. 1961, "Neighbourhood Units in British New Towns", *Town Planning Review*, Vol. 32, pp. 62–82.
Grabar, O. 1968, "The Visual Arts, 1050–1350", in J. A. Boyle, ed., *The Cambridge History of Iran*, Vol. 5, *The Saljuq and Mongol Periods*, Cambridge University Press, Cambridge, pp. 626–58.
Grabar, O. 1986, "Architecture, V. Islamic, Pre-Safavid", in E. Yarshater, ed., *Encyclopaedia Iranica*, Vol. ii, Fascicle 4, Routledge & Kegan Paul, London, pp. 339–41.
Graham, R. 1979, *Iran, the Illusion of Power*, Croom Helm, London.
Greenshields, T. H. 1980, "Quarters and Ethnicity", in G. H. Blake & R. I. Lawless, eds, *The Changing Middle Eastern City*, Croom Helm, London, pp. 120–40.
Groseclose, E. 1947, *Introduction to Iran*, Oxford University Press, New York.
Gruen, V. 1965, *The Heart of Our Cities*, Thames and Hudson, London.
Grunwald, K. & Ronall, J. 1975, *Industrialization in the Middle East*, Greenwood Press, Westport, Connecticut.
Guidoni, E. 1978, "Street and Block, from the Late Middle Ages to the Eighteenth Century", *Lotus International*, No. 19, June 1978, pp. 4–19.
Habermas, J. 1987, *The Theory of Communicative Action: Lifeworld and System: Critique of Functional Reason*, Polity Press, Cambridge.
Hafizi, F. 1980, The Housing Problem in Iran, Unpublished M. Phil Dissertation in Town Planning, University College, London.
Hall, P. 1975, *Urban and Regional Planning*, Newton Abbot, London.
Halliday, F. 1979, *Iran, Dictatorship and Development*, Penguin, Harmondsworth.
Harvey, D. 1982, *The Limits to Capital*, Basil Blackwell, Oxford.
Harvey, D. 1985, *Consciousness and the Urban Experience*, Basil Blackwell, Oxford.
Harvey, D. 1989, *The Urban Experience*, Basil Blackwell, Oxford.
Hashemi, S. R. 1993, "Ghalamro-ye roo beh gostaresh-e nezarat-e kalbodi", *Abadi*, No. 8, Spring 1372, pp. 2–5.
Healey, P., Cameron, S., Davoudi, S., Graham, S. & Madanipour, A. 1995, *Managing Cities: The new urban context*, John Wiley, Chichester.
Herbert, D. & Thomas, C. 1982, *Urban Geography*, John Wiley, Chichester.
Hesamian, F. 1987, "Sarshomari-e 65, Tasviri Mobham az Jam'iyat-e Tehran", *Adineh*, No. 13, pp. 20–1.
Hillenbrand, R. 1983, "Some Observations on the Use of Space in Medieval Islamic

Buildings", in A. Germen, ed., *Islamic Architecture and Urbanism*, King Faisal University, Dammam, Saudi Arabia, pp. 17–30.

Hillenbrand, R. 1986a, "Architecture, VI. Safavid to Qajar", in E. Yarshater, ed., *Encyclopaedia Iranica*, Vol. ii, Fascicle 4, Routledge & Kegan Paul, London, pp. 345–9.

Hillenbrand, R. 1986b, "Safavid Architecture", in P. Jackson & L. Lockhart, eds, *The Cambridge History of Iran*, Vol. 6, *The Timurid and Safavid Periods*, Cambridge University Press, Cambridge, pp. 759–842.

Hodgson, M. G. S. 1974, *The Venture of Islam*, Vol. 3: *The Gun Powder Empires and Modern Times*, The University of Chicago Press, Chicago.

Holley, S. 1983, *Washington: Quicker by quango, the history of Washington new town 1964–1983*, Washington Development Corporation, Washington, Tyne and Wear.

Holliday, J. 1973, *City Centre Redevelopment*, Charles Knight & Co., London.

Holliday, J. 1983, "City Centre Plans in the 1980s", in R. Davies, & A. Champion, eds, *The Future of the City Centre*, Academic Press, London, pp. 13–28.

Honarfar, L. 1984a, "Chahar-Bagh-e Esfahan", in A. Javadi, ed., *Me'mari-e Iran*, Vol. II, Mojarrad, Tehran, pp. 527–39.

Honarfar, L. 1984b, "Meidan-e Naghsh-e Jahan-e Esfahan", in A. Javadi, ed., *Me'mari-e Iran*, Mojarrad, Tehran, pp. 577–610.

Hourani, A. H. 1970, "Islamic City in the Light of Recent Research", in A. Hourani & S. Stern, eds, *The Islamic City, a Colloquium*, Bruno Cassirer, Oxford, pp. 9–25.

Howard, E. 1960, *Garden Cities of To-Morrow*, Faber & Faber, London.

Huff, D. 1986, "Sasanian Cities" (Persian Translation), in M. Y. Kiani, ed., *Nazari Ejmali beh Shahrneshini va Shahrsazi dar Iran (A General Study on Urbanization & Urban Planning in Iran)*, Homa, Tehran, pp. 176–204.

IMO (Iranian Meteorological Organization), 1974, *Meteorological Yearbook 1970*, IMO, Tehran.

Irvine New Town Corporation, 1971, *Irvine New Town Plan*, Irvine New Town Corporation, Irvine, Scotland.

Issawi, C. 1971, *The Economic History of Iran 1800–1914*, University of Chicago Press, Chicago.

Issawi, C. 1982, *An Economic History of the Middle East and North Africa*, Columbia University Press, New York.

Istakhri, A. I. 1961, *Masalek va Mamalek* (Anonymous Persian Translation from v/vi century AH), ed., Iraj Afshar, BTNK, Tehran.

Jacobs, A. & Appleyard, D. 1987, "Towards an Urban Design Manifesto", *Journal of American Planners Association*, Winter 1987, pp. 112–20.

Jencks, C. 1973, *Modern Movements in Architecture*, Penguin, Harmondsworth.

Kariman, H. 1971, *Asar-e Bazmandeh az Ray-e Ghadim*, Iran's National University Press, Tehran.

Kariman, H. 1976, *Tehran dar Gozashteh va Hal*, Iran's National University Press, Tehran.

Kasraian, N. & H. Zolfaghari, 1995, *Tehran*, Kasraian, Tehran.

Kasravi Tabrizi, A. 1965, *Tarikh-e Mashrooteh-ye Iran*, Amir Kabir, Tehran.

Katouzian, H. 1981, *The Political Economy of Modern Iran, Despotism and Pseudo-Modernism 1926–1979*, Macmillan Press, London.

Katouzian, H. 1995, "Problems of Political Development in Iran", *British Journal of Middle Eastern Studies*, Vol. 22, Nos 1&2, pp. 5–20.

Kaviani, S. 1988, "Foroudgah-e bein-al-melali-e jadid-e Tehran (Haftom-e Tir)", *Me'mari va Honar-e Iran (Iranian Art & Architecture)*, No. 4, Summer 1367, pp. 26–37.

Keddie, N. 1981, *Roots of Revolution*, Yale University Press, New Haven.
Keeble, L. 1961, *Principles and Practice of Town and Country Planning*, The Estate Gazette, London.
Kermani, Nazem-al-Islam, 1967, *Tarikh-e Bidari-e Iranian*, edited by Saidi Sirjani, Bonyad-e Farhang-e Iran, Tehran.
Khalili Araghi, M. 1988, *Shenakht-e Avamel-e Mo'asser dar Gostaresh-e biraviyeh-ye Shahr-e Tehran*, Tehran University Press, Tehran.
Kharrat Zebardast, E. & Moezzeddin, P. 1992, "Shenasaii-e manategh-e kam fa'aliyat-e keshvar az lahaz-e san'at", *Abadi* , No. 5, Summer 1371, pp. 84–7.
Khatam, A. 1993, "Kondi-e roshd-e jam'iyat-e paitakht, paian-e yek kaboos", *Ketab-e Tehran*, Vol. 3, Roshangaran, Autumn 1372, Tehran, pp. 94–107.
Kiani, M. Y. 1986, "Shahr-ha-ye Ashkani", in M. Y. Kiani, ed., *Nazari Ejmali beh Shahrneshini va Shahrsazi dar Iran (A General Study on Urbanization & Urban Planning in Iran)*, Homa, Tehran, pp. 105–75.
Knapp, W. 1977, "1921–1941: The Period of Riza Shah", in H. Amirsadeghi, ed., *Twentieth Century Iran*, Heinemann, London, pp. 23–52.
Kocks, F., Pfeil, F. & von Behr, P. (Consulting Engineers), 1961, *Esfahan Master Plan*, United States Operation Mission to Iran, Public Administration Division, Tehran.
Korcelli, P. 1982, "Theory of Intra-urban Structure: Review and Synthesis", in L. S. Bourne, ed., *Internal Structure of the City*, Oxford University Press, New York, pp. 93–110.
Krier, L. 1979, "The Cities within the City, II, Luxembourg", *Architectural Design*, Vol. 49, No. 1, pp. 18–32.
Kuban, D. 1983, "The Geographical and Historical Bases of the Diversity of Muslim Architectural Styles: Summary of a Conceptual Approach", in A. Germen, ed., *Islamic Architecture and Urbanism*, King Faisal University, Dammam, Saudi Arabia, pp. 1–5.
Ladjevardi, H. ed. 1995, *Khaterat-e Ali Amini (Memoirs of Ali Amini)*, Iranian Oral History Project, Centre for Middle Eastern Studies, Harvard University, Cambridge, Massachusetts.
Lambton, A. 1978, "Iran, to the Turkoman Invasions", in E. van Donzel, B. Lewis, & Ch. Pellat, eds, *The Encyclopaedia of Islam*, Vol. IV, E. J. Brill, Leiden, pp. 13–33.
Lambton, A. 1980, "Islamic Society in Persia", in A. Lambton, *Theory and Practice in Medieval Persian Government*, Variorum Reprints, London, pp. 3–32.
Lambton, A. 1987, *Qajar Persia: Eleven studies*, I. B. Tauris, London.
Lapidus, I. 1967, *Muslim Cities in the Later Middle Ages*, Harvard University Press, Cambridge, Massachusetts.
Lapidus, I. 1969, "Muslim Cities and Islamic Societies", in I. Lapidus, ed., *Middle Eastern Cities*, University of California Press, Berkeley, pp. 47–79.
Lapidus, I. 1973, "Traditional Muslim Cities: Structure and Change", in L. C. Brown, ed., *From Madina to Metropolis*, The Darwin Press, Princeton, New Jersey, pp. 51–69.
Lavedan, P. 1959, *Histoire de l'Urbanisme, Renaissance et Temps Moderne*, Henri Laurens, Paris.
Lean, W. & Goodall, B. 1977, *Aspects of Land Economics*, The Estate Gazette Limited, London.
Le Corbusier, 1971 (first published in 1924), *City of Tomorrow*, Architectural Press, London.
Lefebvre, H. 1991, *The Production of Space*, Blackwell, Oxford.
Ling, A. 1967, *Runcorn New Town Master Plan*, Runcorn Development Corporation, Runcorn.

Llewelyn-Davies, L. 1972, "Changing Goals in Design: The Milton Keynes Example", in H. Evans, ed., *New Towns: the British Experience*, Charles Knight, London, pp. 102–16.

Llewelyn-Davies Weeks & Partners, 1966, *Washington New Town Master Plan and Report*, Washington Development Corporation, Washington, Tyne and Wear.

Llewellyn, O. 1983, "Shari'ah Values Pertaining to Landscape and Design", in A. Germen, ed., *Islamic Architecture and Urbanism*, King Faisal University, Dammam, Saudi Arabia, pp. 31–42.

Lockhart, L. 1939, *Famous Cities of Iran*, Walter Pearce & Co., Brentford, Middlesex.

Lockhart, L. 1960, *Persian Cities*, Luzac, London.

Lockhart, L. 1967, "Shah Abbas's Isfahan", in A. Toynbee, ed., *Cities of Destiny*, Thames and Hudson, London, pp. 210–25.

Logan, J. & Molotch, H. 1987, *Urban Fortunes: The political economy of place*, University of California Press, Berkeley.

London County Council, 1963, *The Planning of a New Town*, LCC, London.

Looney, D. 1975, *Income Distribution Policies and Economic Growth in Semi-industrialized Countries*, Praeger, New York.

Looney, D. 1982, *Economic Origins of the Iranian Revolution*, Pergamon, New York.

Lukonin, V. G. 1983, "Political, Social and Administrative Institutions: Taxes and Trade", in E. Yarshater, ed., *The Cambridge History of Iran* Vol. 3(2), *The Selucid, Parthian and Sasanian Periods*, Cambridge University Press, Cambridge, pp. 681–746.

MacDougall, E. & Ettinghausen, R. eds, 1976, *The Islamic Garden*, Dumbarton Oaks, Trustees for Harvard University, Washington DC.

McLean, D. 1979, *Britain and Her Buffer State, The Collapse of the Persian Empire, 1890–1914*, Royal Historical Society, London.

Madanipour, A. 1988a, "Design and Change, the Case of Rural Settlements of Iran", *Open House International*, Vol. 13, No. 4, pp. 29–35.

Madanipour, A. 1988b, "Design and Change in Reconstructed Rural Settlements of Iran", in *Settlement Reconstruction Post-War*, Institute of Advanced Architectural Studies, University of York.

Madanipour, A. 1989a, "Redistribution of Urban Land and the Quality of Environment: a Post-revolutionary Experience in Iran", in *Quality in the Built Environment, Public and Private Responsibilities in Housing Design and Settlement Planning*, Conference Proceedings July 1989, Urban International Press, Newcastle upon Tyne, pp. 115–19.

Madanipour, A. 1989b, "Postwar Reconstruction and Participation of the Public", *Paper presented at Settlement Reconstruction after War Conference*, The Institute of Advanced Architectural Studies, University of York, 16–18 May 1989.

Madanipour, A. 1995, "Postwar Reconstruction in Southwest Iran: New Settlements or New Identities?", in Eric Watkins, ed., *The Middle Eastern Environment*, St Malo Press, Cambridge, pp. 209–19.

Madanipour, A. 1996a, *Design of Urban Space: An inquiry into a socio-spatial process*, John Wiley, Chichester.

Madanipour, A. 1996b, "Urban Design and the Dilemmas of Space", *Environment and Planning D: Society and Space*, Vol. 14, pp. 331–55.

Madanipour, A. 1997, "Ambiguities of Urban Design", *Town Planning Review*, Vol. 68, No. 3, July 1997, pp. 363–83.

Madanipour. A., Cars, G. & Allen, J. eds, 1998, *Social Exclusion in European Cities: Processes, experiences, responses*, Regional Policy and Development Series, Series

Editor Ron Martin, Jessica Kingsley Publishers (with Regional Studies Association), London.

Madanipour, A., Davoudi, S., Mahmoodi, M. & Mojtabavi, J. (Akhir Consultant Engineers), 1984, *Guneh Shenasi-e Maskan-e Roustai Khuzestan, Dafter-e Sevvom: Masaleh va Sistem-ha-ye Sakhtemani*, Markaz-e Tahghighat-e Sakhteman va Maskan, Tehran.

Madanipour, A., Davoudi, S., Mahmoodi, M. & Mojtabavi, J. (Akhir Consultant Engineers) 1985, *Guneh Shenasi-e Maskan-e Roustai Khuzestan, Dafter-e Panjom: Baft*, Markaz-e Tahghighat-e Sakhteman va Maskan, Tehran.

Madanipour, A., Davoudi, S., Mahmoodi, M. & Mojtabavi, J. (Akhir Consultant Engineers), 1986, *Guneh Shenasi-e Maskan-e Roustai Khuzestan, Dafter-e Dovvom: Vahed-e Maskooni*, Markaz-e Tahghighat-e Sakhteman va Maskan, Tehran.

Mantagheh (Consultant Engineers), 1976, *Barrasi-e Tarh-ha- ye Jame'-e Shahri*, Mantagheh Consultants, Tehran.

Markaz-e Amar-e Iran (Iran Statistical Centre), 1981, *Natayej-e Amargiri-e Tehran 59*, 21 volumes, Markaz-e Amar-e Iran, Tehran.

Markaz-e Amar-e Iran, 1985, *Barrasi-e Vaz'iyat-e Maskan-e Khanevar-ha-ye Nemooneh-ye Shahri va Roustaiy-e Keshvar dar Sal-ha-ye 1361 va 1362*, Markaz-e Amar-e Iran, Tehran.

Markaz-e Amar-e Iran, 1986a, *Salnameh-ye Amari, 1363*, Markaz-e Amar-e Iran, Tehran.

Markaz-e Amar-e Iran, 1986b, *Barrasi-e Vaz'iyat-e Maskan-e Khanevar-ha-ye Nemooneh-ye Shahri va Roustaiy-e Keshvar dar Sal-e 1363*, Markaz-e Amar-e Iran, Tehran.

Markaz-e Amar-e Iran, 1987a, *Sarshomari-e Omumi-e Nofus va Maskan 1365, Natayej-e Moghaddamati-e Shahr-ha-ye Keshvar*, Markaz-e Amar-e Iran, Tehran.

Markaz-e Amar-e Iran, 1987b, *Natayej-e Tafsili-e Sarshomari az Sherkat-ha-ye Ta'avoni-e Maskan, 1364*, Markaz-e Amar-e Iran, Tehran.

Markaz-e Amar-e Iran, 1990, *Natayej-e Amargiri az: Daramad va Hazinehha-ye Shahrdariha-ye Keshvar dar Sal-e 1366*, Markaz-e Amar-e Iran, Tehran.

Markaz-e Amar-e Iran, 1993, *Amar-e Kargahha-ye San'ati-e Keshvar, Sal-e 1367*, Markaz-e Amar-e Iran, Tehran.

Markaz-e Amar-e Iran, 1994, *Natayej-e Amargiri-e Jari-e Jam'iyat 1372*, 1373, Markaz-e Amar-e Iran, Tehran.

Markaz-e Amar-e Iran, 1995, *Amar-e Kargahha-ye Bozorg-e San'ati-e Keshvar, Sal-e 1372*, Markaz-e Amar-e Iran, Tehran.

Markaz-e Amar-e Iran, 1996a, *Salnameh-ye Amari-e Keshvar 1373 (Iran Statistical Yearbook 1373: March 1994–March 1995)*, Markaz-e Amar-e Iran (Statistical Centre of Iran), Tehran.

Markaz-e Amar-e Iran, 1996b, *Amargiri-e Vizhegiha-ye Eshteghal va Bikari-e Khanevar, Sal-e 1373*, Markaz-e Amar-e Iran, Tehran.

Markaz-e Amar-e Iran, 1996c, *Natayej-e Amargiri az Khanevarha-ye Dara-ye Fa'aliyat-e San'ati, Sal-e 1373*, Markaz-e Amar-e Iran, Tehran.

Markaz-e Amar-e Iran, 1996d, *Natayej-e Tafsili-e Amargiri az Hazineh va Daramad-e Khanevarha-ye Shahri, Sal-e 1373*, Markaz-e Amar-e Iran, Tehran.

Markaz-e Amar-e Iran, 1996e, *Taghiirat-e Gheimat-e Kalaha va Khadamat-e Masrafi-e Khanevarha-ye Shahri-e Keshvar, Mehr 1374*, Markaz-e Amar-e Iran, Tehran.

Markaz-e Amar-e Iran, 1996f, *Taghiirat-e Gheimat-e Kalaha va Khadamat-e Masrafi-e Khanevarha-ye Shahri-e Keshvar, Aban 1374*, Markaz-e Amar-e Iran, Tehran.

Markaz-e Amar-e Iran, 1996g, *Taghiirat-e Gheimat-e Kalaha va Khadamat-e Masrafi-e Khanevarha-ye Shahri-e Keshvar, Azar 1374*, Markaz-e Amar-e Iran, Tehran.

Markaz-e Amar-e Iran, 1996h, *Taghiirat-e Gheimat-e Kalaha va Khadamat-e Masrafi-e Khanevarha-ye Shahri-e Keshvar, Dey 1374*, Markaz-e Amar-e Iran, Tehran.

Markaz-e Motale'at va Barnamehrizi-e Shahr-e Tehran, 1994, *Barrasi va Shenakht-e Vaz'e Mojood-e Jam'iyat-e Shahr-e Tehran*, Markaz-e Motale'at va Barnamehrizi-e Shahr-e Tehran, Tehran.

Markaz-e Motale'at va Barnamehrizi-e Shahr-e Tehran, 1995, *Motale'at-e Eghtesadi-e Shahr-e Tehran*, two volumes, Shahrdari-e Tehran, Tehran.

Martin, L. 1975, "The Grid as Generator", in L. Martin & L. March, eds, *Urban Space and Structure*, Cambridge University Press, Cambridge, pp. 6–27.

Mashhadizadeh Dehaghani, N. 1995, *Tahlili Az Vizhegiha-ye Barnamehrizi-e Shahri Dar Iran (An Analysis of Urban Planning Characteristics in Iran)*, Elm va San'at University Press, Tehran.

Milani, M. 1993, "The Evolution of the Iranian Presidency: From Bani Sadr to Rafsanjani", *British Journal of Middle Eastern Studies*, Vol. 20, No. 1, pp. 82–97.

Ministry of Housing, 1962, *Town Centres, Approach to Renewal*, HMSO, London.

Minorsky, V. 1934, "Teheran", in M. Th. Houtsma, A. J. Wensinck, H. A. R. Gibb, W. Heffening, & E. Levi-Provencal, eds, *The Encyclopaedia of Islam*, Vol. IV, E. J. Brill, Leyden & Luzac & Co., London, pp. 713–720.

Moayed, M. 1964, "Tanzeem va Tanseegh-e Omur-e Shahr", in *Masael-e Ejtemai-e Shahr-e Tehran*, a colloquium by the Institute of Social Research and Study, University of Tehran, Tehran University Press, Tehran, pp. 37–46.

Mofid, K. 1987, *Development Planning in Iran: From monarchy to Islamic republic*, Middle East & North African Studies Press, Wisbech, Cambridgeshire.

Mojabi, J. 1993, "Lahjeh-ye tehrooni", *Ketab-e Tehran*, Roshangaran, Tehran, pp. 160–6.

Morgan, D. 1988, *Medieval Persia 1040–1797: A history of the new East*, Longman, Harlow.

Morris, A. E. J. 1979, *History of Urban Form*, George Godwin, London.

Motamani, M. 1964, "Enhetat-e Bakhsh-e Ghadimi-e Shahr-e Tehran", in *Masael-e Ejtemai-e Shahr-e Tehran*, a colloquium by the Institute of Social Research and Study, University of Tehran, Tehran University Press, Tehran, pp. 331–6.

Mousavi, N. 1992, "Tehran ghorbani-e nahamgooni-e farhangha", *Ketab-e Tehran*, Roshangaran, Tehran, pp. 123–6.

Mousavi, S. Y. 1998, Urban neighbourhoods of Tehran: the social relations of residents and their living place, Unpublished PhD thesis, University of Newcastle, Newcastle upon Tyne.

Mozayeni, M. 1974, "City Planning in Iran: Evolution and Problems", *Ekistics*, Vol. 38, No. 227, pp. 264–7.

Mumford, L. 1954, "The Neighbourhood Unit", *Town Planning Review*, Vol. 24, pp. 256–70.

Munn, R. E. 1966, *Descriptive Micrometeorology*, Academic Press, New York.

Nafisi, A. 1964, "Shahrdari-e Tehran", in *Masael-e Ejtemai-e Shahr-e Tehran*, a colloquium by the Institute of Social Research and Study, University of Tehran, Tehran University Press, Tehran, pp. 424–34.

Najmi, N. 1984, *Iran-e Ghadim va Tehran-e Ghadim*, Janzadeh, Tehran.

Naraghi, E. 1964, "Motale'at va Tahghighat-e Ejtema'i", in *Masael-e Ejtemai-e Shahr-e Tehran*, a colloquium by the Institute of Social Research and Study, University of Tehran, Tehran University Press, Tehran, pp. 9–12.

Nazarian, A. 1991, "Gostaresh-e fazaii-e shahr-e Tehran va peydayesh-e shahrakha-ye aghmari", *Faslnameh-ye Tahghighat-e Joghrafiaii*, No. 20, Spring 1370, pp. 97–139.

Nelson, H. J. 1971, "The Form and Structure of Cities: Urban Growth Patterns", in L. S. Bourne, *Internal Structure of the City*, Oxford University Press, New York, pp. 75–83.

Olson, W. 1980, "The Genesis of the Anglo-Persian Agreement of 1919", in E. Kedourie & S. Heim, eds, *Towards a Modern Iran*, Frank Cass, London, pp. 96–131.

Osborn, F. & Whittick, A. 1963, *The New Towns, the Answer to Megalopolis*, Leonard Hill, London.

Owens, S. 1986, *Energy, Planning and Urban Form*, Pion, London.

Paganini Alberti, M. P. 1971, *Strutture Commerciali di una Citta di Pellegrinaggio: Mashhad (Iran Nord-Orientale)*, Del Bianco, Udine.

Pakdaman, B. 1983, *Yadnameh-ye Vartan Hovanesian*, Jame'eh-ye Moshaveran-e Iran, Tehran.

Parsa, M. 1989, *Social Origins of the Iranian Revolution*, Rutgers University Press, New Brunswick and London.

Pass, C., Lowes, B. & Davies, L. 1988, *Dictionary of Economics*, Collins, London.

Perikhanian, A. 1983, "Iranian Society and Law", in *The Cambridge History of Iran*, Vol. 3(2), Cambridge University Press, Cambridge, pp. 627–80.

Perkins, A. 1973, *The Art of Dura-Europos*, Oxford University Press, London.

Perrot, J. 1986, "Achaemenid Urbanization in Susa" (Persian translation), in M. Y. Kiani, ed., *Nazari Ejmali beh Shahrneshini va Shahrsazi dar Iran (A General Study on Urbanization & Urban Planning in Iran)*, Homa, Tehran, pp. 99–104.

Peterson, J. 1969, *The Climate of Cities: A Survey of Recent Literature*, US Department of Health, Education, and Welfare, Raleigh, North Carolina.

Piran, P. 1988, "Aloonak neshini dar Tehran", *Ettela'at-e Syasi-Eghtesadi*, No. 6, pp. 46–7, No. 7, pp. 32–5, No. 8, pp. 50–2, No. 9, pp. 30–31 and 61, No. 10, pp. 51–5, No. 11, pp. 56–8.

Porada, E. 1985, "Classic Achaemenian Architecture and Sculpture", in *The Cambridge History of Iran*, Vol. 2, Cambridge University Press, Cambridge, pp. 793–827.

Pundt, H. 1972, *Schinkel's Berlin, A Study in Environmental Planning*, Harvard University Press, Cambridge, Massachusetts.

Rafiei, M. 1986, *Maskan-e Shahri*, Jame'eh-ye Moshaveran-e Iran, Tehran.

Rafiei, M. 1991, "Tamarkoz-e eghtessadi dar Tehran", *Abadi*, No. 1, Summer 1370, pp. 45–57.

Rafiei, M. 1989, *Maskan Va Daramad Dar Tehran: Gozashteh, hal, ayandeh (Housing and Income in Tehran: Past, Present, Future)*, Urban Planning and Architecture Research Centre, Ministry of Housing & Urban Development, Tehran.

Rahbari, A. 1986, *Meteorological Yearbook*, Meteorological Station, Building and Housing Research Centre, Tehran.

Rahimi Farzan, H. 1991, "Gozaresh-e Suferto darbareh-ye haml va naghl-e shahri-e Tehran", *Me'mari va Shahrsazi (L'Architecture et L'Urbanisme)*, Vol. 3, Nos 13–14, Mehr 1370, pp. 5–12.

Rahmani, A. & Hafeznia, M. 1988, "Barrasi-ye Tahavvolat-e Ecolozhiki va Zendeghi dar Bakhsh-e Markazi-ye Shahr-e Tehran", *Faslname-ye Tahghighat-e Joghrafiai (Geographical Research Quarterly)*, No. 8, Islamic Research Foundation, Mashhad, pp. 58–76.

Razzaghi, E. 1988, *Eghtessad-e Iran (Iran's Economy)*, Nashr-e Nay, Tehran.
RIBA, 1943, *Rebuilding Britain*, RIBA, London.
Richards, A. 1995, "Economic Pressures for Accountable Governance in the Middle East and North Africa", in Augustus Richard Norton, ed., *Civil Society in the Middle East*, E. J. Brill, Leiden, pp. 55–78.
Richards, J. M. 1945, *English House*, Architectural Press, Surrey.
Rosenau, H. 1974, *The Ideal City, Its Architectural Evolution*, Studio Vista, London.
Ross, D. 1931, *The Persians*, Clarendon Press, Oxford.
Rowe, C. & Koetter, F. 1978, *Collage City*, MIT Press, Cambridge, Massachusetts.
Safamanesh, K. 1993, "Baft-e tarikhi-e Tehran va nahveh-ye barkhord ba an", *Abadi*, No. 8, Spring 1372, pp. 6–17.
Safamanesh, K. 1994, "Negahi beh siyasatha va ravesh-e tarrahi dar behsazi va bazsazi-e badanehha-ye khiyaban-e Nasser Khosro", *Abadi*, No. 12, Spring 1373, pp. 27–30.
Safamanesh, K. and Monadizadeh, B. 1993, "Zavabet-e sakhtemani baray-e ijad-e hoviyat va hamahangi dar sima-ye shahrha", *Abadi*, No. 9, Summer 1372, pp. 22–5.
Saffari, S. 1993, "The Legitimation of the Clergy's Right to Rule in the Iranian Constitution of 1979", *British Journal of Middle Eastern Studies*, Vol. 20, No. 1, pp. 64–81.
Saidi Rezvani, N. 1992, "Shahrneshini va shahrsazi dar doreh-ye bist saleh-ye 1300–1320 H. Sh. (Doran-e hokoomat-e Reza Khan)", *Faslnameh-ye Tahghighat-e Joghrafiaii*, Vol. 7, No. 2, Summer 1371, pp. 140–65.
Saidnia, A. 1994, "Devistomin sal-e paitakhti-e Tehran", *Ketab-e Tehran*, Roshangaran, Tehran, pp. 8–15.
Sajjadi, M. 1986, "Shahr-e Sukhteh", in M. Y. Kiani, ed., *Nazari Ejmali beh Shahrneshini va Shahrsazi dar Iran (A General Study on Urbanization and Urban Planning in Iran)*, Homa, Tehran, pp. 51–77.
Sazman-e Zamin-e Shahri (Urban Land Organization), 1985, *Majmoo'e-ye Kamel-e Ghavanin, Mogharrarat, va Ayinname-ha-ye Marbout be Zamin dakhel-e Mahdoode-ye Shahri*, Sazman-e Zamin-e Shahri, Tehran.
Sazman-e Zamin-e Shahri, 1987, *Amar-e Fa'aliyat-ha-ye Sazman-e Zamin-e Shahri*, Sazman-e Zamin-e Shahri, Tehran.
Scarce, J. 1983, "The Royal Palaces of the Qajar Dynasty; a Survey", in E. Bosworth & C. Hillenbrand, eds, *Qajar Iran, Political, Social and Cultural Change 1800–1925*, Edinburgh University Press, Edinburgh, pp. 329–51.
Scargill, D. I. 1979, *The Form of Cities*, Bell & Hyman, London.
Schacht, J. 1970, "Law and Justice", in Hott, P. M., A. K. S. Lambton, & B. Lewis, eds, *The Cambridge History of Islam*, Vol. 2B, *Islamic Society and Civilization*, Cambridge University Press, Cambridge, pp. 539–68.
Schaffer, F. 1972, *The New Town Story*, Paladin, London.
Schlumberger, D. 1983, "Parthian Art", in E. Yarshater, ed., *The Cambridge History of Iran*, Vol. 3(2), Cambridge University Press, Cambridge, pp. 1027–54.
Searle, J. 1995, *The Construction of Social Reality*, Penguin, London.
Sedaghat Kerdar, A. 1985, *Barrasi-e Vazi'yat-e Maskan dar Sal-e 1363*, Ministry of Plan and Budget, Tehran.
Seger, M. 1978, *Tehran, eine stadtgeographische Studie*, Springer-Verlag, Vienna.
Semsar, M. 1986, "Shahr-e Tehran", in M. Y. Kiani, ed., *Nazari Ejmali beh Shahrneshini va Shahrsazi dar Iran (A General Study on Urbanization and Urban Planning in Iran)*, Homa, Tehran, pp. 349–70.
Sert, J. 1944, *Can Our Cities Survive?*, Harvard University Press, Cambridge.

Shahrdari-e Tehran (Tehran Municipality), 1978, *Gozaresh-e Ejmali darbareh-ye Tehran*, Shahrdari-e Tehran, Tehran.
Shahrdari-e Tehran, 1985, *Nashriyeh-ye Amari*, Shahrdari-e Tehran, Tehran.
Shahrdari-e Tehran, 1986, *Zavabet-e Me'mari va Sakhtemani-e Bana-ha-ye Maskooni*, Shahrdari-e Tehran, Tehran.
Shardari-e Tehran, 1995, *Tehran dar Yek Negah (Tehran at a Glance)*, Public Relations Office and International Affairs Department, Tehran Municipality, Tehran.
Shahrdari-e Tehran, 1996a, *Barnameh-ye Avval-e Shahrdari-e Tehran, 'Tehran 80', 1375–1380, Ketab-e Barnameh*, Markaz-e Motale'at va Barnamehrizi, Shahrdari-e Tehran, Tehran.
Shahrdari-e Tehran, 1996b, *Mostanadat-e Ketab-e Barnameh-ye Shahrdari-e Tehran "Tehran-80", 1375–1380*, Markaz-e Motale'at va Barnamehrizi-e Shahr-e Tehran, Shahrdari-e Tehran, Tehran.
Shahri, J. 1978, *Tehran-e Ghadim: Goosheh-i az tarikh-e ejtema'i*, Amir Kabir, Tehran.
Shur, A. 1964, "Marahel-e Seganeh Shahrsazi-e Shahr-e Tehran", in *Masael-e Ejtemai-e Shahr-e Tehran*, a colloquium by the Institute of Social Research and Study, University of Tehran, Tehran University Press, Tehran, pp. 19–30.
Smith, K. 1975, *Principles of Applied Climatology*, McGraw-Hill, London.
Stein, C. 1966, *Towards New Towns for America*, MIT Press, Cambridge, Massachusetts.
Stern, S. M. 1970, "The Constitution of Islamic City", in A. Hourani & S. Stern, eds, *The Islamic City, a Colloquium*, Bruno Cassirer, Oxford, pp. 25–50.
Streck, M. 1978, "Istakhr", in E. van Danzel, B. Lewis, & Ch. Pellat, eds, *The Encyclopaedia of Islam*, Vol. IV, E. J. Brill, Leiden, pp. 214–22.
Sutcliffe, A. 1970, *The Autumn of Central Paris, The Defeat of Town Planning 1850–1970*, Edward Arnold, London.
Sykes, P. 1902, *Ten Thousand Miles in Persia, or Eight Years in Iran*, John Murray, London.
Taleghani, M. ed., 1990, *Maskan (Le Logement)*, Tehran: The 200–year Old Capital of Iran, Sociological studies, Tehran, The Tehran Studies Research Group, Cultural Studies and Research Institute.
Taleghani, M. ed., 1992, *Jam'iyat (Population)*, Tehran: The 200–year Old Capital of Iran, Sociological Studies, The Tehran Studies Research Group, Cultural Studies and Research Institute, Tehran.
Taqavi-Nezhad, M. 1985, *Me'mari, Shahrsazi va Shahrneshini-e Iran dar Gozar-e Zaman*, Yassavoli, Tehran.
Tavassoli, M. 1982, *Sakht-e Shahr va Memari dar Eghlim-e Garm va Khoshk-e Iran (Urban Structure and Architecture in the Hot Arid Zone of Iran)*, Tavassoli, Tehran.
Taylor, C. 1989, *Sources of the Self: The making of the modern identity*, Cambridge University Press, Cambridge.
Teymoori, S. 1992, "Yaddashthaii parakandeh baray-e Tehran", *Ketab-e Tehran*, Roshangaran, Tehran, pp. 113–17.
Toumeh, A. 1994, "Moshkelat-e harekat dar mohit-e shahri", *Abadi*, No. 14, Autumn 1373, pp. 52–6.
Touraine, A. 1995, *Critique of Modernity*, Blackwell, Oxford.
Towfighi, S. 1993, "Gami besooye san'ati kardan-e sakhteman", *Abadi*, No. 8, Spring 1372, pp. 81–7.
Tuan, Y. F. 1977, *Space and Place*, Edward Arnold, London.
United Nations, 1996, *Habitat Press Release: Urban problems mushrooming*, United

Nations Centre for Human Settlements, http://www. un. org/Conferences/habitat/unchs/press/bestpr. htm.
Vahedi, M. 1989, "Tehran va masa'el-e zist mohiti", *Kholaseh Maghalat: Seminar-e tadavom-e hayat dar baft-e shahrha-ye ghadimi-e Iran*, Tehran, Elm va San'at University Press, 1368, pp. 155–76.
Vance, J. E. 1977, *This Scene of Man*, Harper's College Press, New York.
Varjavand, P. 1984, "Estemrar-e Honar-e Me'mari va Shahrsazi-e Iran-e pish as Eslam dar Dowran-e Eslami", in A. Javadi, ed., *Me'mari-e Iran*, Vol. I, Mojarrad, Tehran, pp. 163–71.
Vezarat-e Barnameh va Budgeh (Ministry of Plan and Budget) 1987a, *Roshd-e Tehran va Shahrak-ha-ye Aghmari*, Vezarat-e Barnameh va Budgeh, Tehran.
Vezarat-e Barnameh va Budgeh, 1987b, *Eslahiyeh-ye Barnameh-ye Avval-e Towse'eh-ye Jomhouri-ye Eslami-ye Iran*, Vezarat-e Barnameh va Budgeh, Tehran.
Vezarat-e Maskan va Shahrsazi (Ministry of Housing and Urban Development), 1977, *Barrasi-e Ghavanin va Mogharrarat va Ravesh-ha-ye Mowred-e Amal dar Omur-e Shahri, Shahrsazi, Zamin, Sakhteman va Maskan*, 2 volumes, Vezarat-e Maskan va Shahrsazi, Tehran.
Vezarat-e Maskan va Shahrsazi, 1981, *Barnamehrizi-e Maskan, Barrasi-e Moghaddamati*, Vezarat-e Maskan va Shahrsazi, Tehran.
Vezarat-e Maskan va Shahrsazi, 1982, *Fehrest va Ettela'at-e Jam'a Avary Shodeh-ye Shahrak-ha dar Sath-e Keshvar*, Vezarat-e Maskan va Shahrsazi, Tehran.
Vezarat-e Maskan va Shahrsazi, 1986, *Nezam-e Estijar*, Vezarat-e Maskan va Shahrsazi, Tehran.
Vezarat-e Maskan va Shahrsazi, 1992, *Bulletin-e Eghtessad-e Maskan*, No. 6, Summer 1992, Vezarat-e Maskan va Shahrsazi, Tehran.
Von Grunebaum, G. E. 1981, *Islam, Essays in the Nature and Growth of a Cultural Tradition*, Greenwood Press, Westport, Connecticut.
Von Hertzen, H. & Spreiregen, P. 1971, *Building a New Town, Finland's New Garden City Tapiola*, MIT Press, Cambridge, Massachusetts.
Wagstaff, J. M. 1980, "The Origin and Evolution of Towns: 4000 B.C. to A.D. 1900", in G. H. Blake & R. I. Lawless, eds, *The Changing Middle Eastern City*, Croom Helm, London, pp. 11–33.
Wagstaff, J. M. 1985, *The Evolution of Middle Eastern Landscapes: An outline to A.D. 1840*, Croom Helm, London.
Walker, D. 1982, *The Architecture and Planning of Milton Keynes*, Architectural Press, London.
Weber, M. 1960, *The City*, Heinemann, London.
Wilber, D. 1962, *Persian Gardens and Garden Pavilions*, Charles E. Tuttle, Rutland, Vermont and Tokyo.
Wilber, D. 1963, *Contemporary Iran*, Thames and Hudson, London.
Wilber, D. 1986, "Architecture, vii. Pahlavi, before World War II", in E. Yarshater, ed., *Encyclopaedia Iranica*, Vol. II, 4, Routledge & Kegan Paul, London, pp. 349–51.
Wilson, H. & Womersley, L. 1966, *Redditch New Town, Planning Proposals*, Redditch Development Corporation, Redditch.
Wirz, H. M. 1975, *Social Aspects of Planning in New Towns*, Saxon House, Westmead.
World Bank, 1995, *The World Bank Atlas 1996*, The World Bank, Washington DC.
Yapp, M. 1977, "1900–1921: The Last Years of the Qajar Dynasty", in H. Amirsadeghi, ed., *Twentieth Century Iran*, Heinemann, London, pp. 1–22.
Yarshater, E. 1983, "Observations on Nasir al-Din Shah", in E. Bosworth & C.

Hillenbrand, eds, *Qajar Iran, Political, Social, and Cultural Change 1800–1925*, Edinburgh University Press, Edinburgh, pp. 3–13.

Young, T. C. 1948, "The Problem of Westernization in Modern Iran", *The Middle East Journal*, Washington, No. 2, 1948, pp. 47–59.

Zaka, Y. 1970, *Tarikhche-ye Sakhtemanha-ye Arg-e Saltanati-e Tehran*, The Institute of National Heritage, Tehran.

LIST OF TABLES

3.1	Employment in the main sectors of Tehran's economy	57
3.2	Retail price index for goods and services in Tehran	62
5.1	Tehran's population between the first and the last census, 1867–1991	83
5.2	Annual growth rate of population, 1956–91	84
5.3	The change in the main age groups, 1966–91	87
5.4	The main reasons for, and the conditions before, immigration	89
9.1	Estimated share of building in gross domestic fixed capital formation, 1900–65	166
9.2	Share of investment in construction in gross fixed capital formation, 1976–93	166
9.3	The purpose of development in completed dwellings in urban areas, 1975–79	174
9.4	Types of residential occupation in Tehran and other urban areas, 1982–84	175
10.1	Activities of the Urban Land Organization in Tehran province, 1982–86	184
10.2	Investment in construction by public and private sectors, 1959–71	191
10.3	Share of public and private investment in construction in gross fixed capital formation, 1976–93	191

LIST OF FIGURES

1.1	Tehran is located at the foot of Mount Damavand, the highest peak in the land	6
2.1	Tehran in 1858 had an axial layout and a functional structure	30
2.2	Tehran in 1890, after its first transformation which laid the foundations of a socio-spatial divide	32
2.3	Nasseriyeh was one of the new, wide streets that surrounded the royal compound, which included Shams al-Emareh Palace	35
2.4	Sepahsalar (now Motahari) mosque used to be regarded as Tehran's most imposing building	36
2.5	Tehran in 1937, after the second transformation which turned it into an open matrix	38
2.6	Golestan Palace is now a museum	39
2.7	The city expanded in all directions	41
2.8	Baharestan Square today, where the memories of the Constitutional Revolution and many political activities afterwards linger on	44
2.9	Shohada (Martyrs') Square was the site of the first major clash between the people and the state in the Islamic Revolution	45
3.1	Tehran is the largest concentration of wealth in the country (Modarres motorway)	52
3.2	Tehran's old bazaar is still a centre of the city's wholesale and retail activities (Hajeb al-Dowleh Arcade)	56
4.1	Before its demolition to ease traffic, the Tehran municipality building flanked the city's central square (Tup-Khaneh, now Imam Khomeini Square)	68
4.2	The city is now divided into 20 districts each managed by a municipality	71
4.3	Financial dependence on property development makes the municipality vulnerable	80
5.1	Annual rate of population growth, 1956–91. Ever since the mid-1950s, the rate of population growth in Tehran has been declining	84
5.2	Annual rate of population growth, 1980–91. Many central districts have started to lose population while outer districts have grown	85

5.3	Average age of population, 1991. The central and northern districts have older populations than the peripheral areas	87
5.4	Literacy, 1991. There is a clear north–south divide	88
5.5	Tea houses provide a focal point in social networks and job markets for new immigrants	90
5.6	Household size, 1991. Central and northern districts have smaller households	92
5.7	Tup-Khaneh (Imam Khomeini) Square, "the best known destination for any stranger"	98
6.1	Tehran sits on the southern slopes of the Alburz mountain range	104
6.2	The street system is adjusted to the landform (Africa Avenue)	105
6.3	The better climate of the northern foothills has attracted the better-off	107
6.4	Tehran's urban fabric	110
6.5	Land prices in the north and south show a sharp contrast, 1991	112
6.6	Population density is higher in the central and southern districts, 1991	112
6.7	Higher densities and lower quality of environment in the southern parts of the city	114
6.8	Two main axes can be identified in the spatial structure of the city	118
6.9	Enghelab (formerly Shah-Reza) Avenue is the main east–west axis of the city	119
6.10	The narrow, twisting streets leading to culs-de-sac were an integral part of the old urban fabric	120
6.11	Evolution of the street system, from a hierarchy of narrow, twisting streets to a network of wide, straight roads	121
6.12	Distribution of land use shows a degree of specialization in the urban space, 1992	124
6.13	The changing pattern of building form, from (1) an inward-looking, low-rise courtyard house to (2) an outward-looking, medium-rise house with a courtyard, to (3) high-rise apartment buildings	125
6.14	The courtyard houses of the old core have been neglected	126
6.15	The increasingly dominant building form in the city	127
7.1	Traffic is a major problem in the city	129
7.2	The urban motorway network continues to be the centre of attention	132
7.3	The city suffers from atmospheric pollution for most of the year	133
7.4	Urban development has destroyed the city's green spaces	137

7.5	Some gardens have survived in the northern suburbs	139
7.6	Housing conditions are poorer in the south and west (residential space, 1991)	142
7.7	The old buildings suffer from decay and lack of maintenance	145
8.1	Nine in the morning at Imam Hussein Square, the eastern gate to the city	148
8.2	Despite their name, coffee houses (*ghahveh khaneh*) serve tea	149
8.3	An Achaemenian pillar in Iran Bastan Museum	150
8.4	The fruit market in Amin al-Sultan Square	153
8.5	A shop in the coppersmiths' market	155
8.6	Dizin ski slopes are not far from the city	157
8.7	The 13th day of the Persian New Year (Nowrooz) is spent outdoors	158
9.1	The growing scale of developments has been consistent with the growing scale of development agencies	169
9.2	Development of medium-rise buildings has increased the density of Shahrak-e Qods, which used to be an exclusive new town	170
10.1	Higher land prices mean land is being developed in shorter cycles and at higher densities	186
10.2	New building materials have had a major impact on urban form	196
11.1	Darvazeh Shemiran, where wide straight roads have replaced the city walls and gates	202
11.2	Modernist design has essentially shaped Tehran	209
11.3	Attempts at re-creating Tehran in the image of the West have not been abandoned even after the advent of a traditionalist revolution	216
12.1	Walls and gates separated the royal compound from the rest of Tehran (Arg's southern gateway)	220
12.2	Religious institutions were the focal points of the old settlements (shrine of Imamzadeh Slaeh, Tajrish, north of Tehran)	228
12.3	In the secular city, it was not the mosque which flanked the major squares (Imam Hussein Square)	229
12.4	Wide, straight streets representing power and order	233
13.1	Sarkis Church is a landmark for the Armenian community	239
13.2	Juxtaposition of old and new finds a comfortable home in postmodernism	248
13.3	The modern urban fabric has no relationship with what it has replaced	251
13.4	A new urban context is emerging (north of Ferdowsi Square)	252

PHOTOGRAPH CREDITS

Figures 3.1, 3.2, 5.5, 5.7, 6.2, 6.3, 6.7, 6.14, 7.7, 8.4 and 12.2 are from *Tehran* (Kasraian and Zolfaghari, 1995), used with kind permission of the photographer and publisher Nassrollah Kasraian. Figures 1.1, 2.3, 2.4, 2.6, 4.1, 6.15, 8.2, 8.3, 8.5, 8.6, 12.1, 13.1 and 13.4 are from *Tehran at a Glance* (Shahrdari-e Tehran, 1995), used with kind permission of the publisher, Tehran Municipality's Public Relations Office and International Affairs Department. The author wishes to thank Abdolhussein Abarghouei for Figures 2.8, 2.9, 6.9, 8.1, 11.1 and 12.3, Jafar Mojtabavi for Figures 4.3, 7.1, 7.2, 7.3, 7.5, 9.1, 9.2, 10.1, 10.2, 11.3 and 13.2, and Babak Zirak for Figures 6.10 and 13.3.

INDEX

A'zam al-Dowleh (Saghafi), Khalil 66
Abali 136
Abbas Mirza 12
Abbasids 4
Abedin Dorkoosh 141, 187
absolute power 12
accessibility 119
Achaemenians 150, 220, 231
acropolis 220, 224
Afghanistan ix, 29, 89, 147–9, 195, 239
Africa Avenue 105
Afsariyeh 150
Agha Muhammad Khan 5, 29
agriculture 7, 14, 17, 18, 19, 23, 24, 26, 36, 51, 56, 81, 109, 117, 135, 166, 180, 181, 182, 185, 188, 189, 194, 198, 219, 221
Ahmadi 93
Ahura Mazda 3
Ai Khanum 221
air pollution 109, 111, 130, 133–5, 214
airport 131, 132, 136, 164, 192
Aivan-e Karkheh 225, 236
Ala al-Dowleh street 34
Alburz 3, 28, 38, 102, 103, 104, 105, 106, 108, 135, 247, 254
Aleppo 238
Alexander 221, 231
alienation 97
Allies 16, 17, 181, 188, 205
Amin al-Sultan square 153
Amir Kabir 12, 31
Amiriyeh 151
Anglo-Iranian agreement 13
Anglo-Iranian Oil Company 17
Anglo-Persian Oil Company 15
Anglo-Russian agreement 13
Arabic language 67
Arabs 4, 77, 96, 221, 236, 237, 241, 246
architects 170, 171, 204, 205, 209, 217
architecture 144, 200, 201, 204, 225, 232, 241, 251

Arg gate 29, 220
Aristotle 220
Armenians 153, 239
Aryans 3
Asia 102, 201
Assyria 220
Athens 220, 224
Avesta 3
Avval 238
axiality 30, 31, 37–8, 43, 117–9, 127, 218, 219, 223–6
Ayatollah (Imam) Khomeini 23, 24, 151, 223
Azerbaijan xii, 88, 89, 96, 238

Babylon 220, 231
Baghdad 232
Bahar 239
Baharestan 121
Baharestan Square 43, 44
Baladiyeh 65, 66, 67
Balkh 226
Baluchis 96
Bam 222
Bank-e Markazi-e Iran 189
Bank-e Melli-e Iran 187
Bank-e Omran 189
Bank-e Rahni 190
banks and financial institutions 113, 116, 125, 143, 164, 168, 177, 184, 188, 189–90, 197
Bauhaus 205
bayer 179
bazaar 4, 11, 21, 29, 30, 31, 33, 34, 37, 39, 43, 56, 65, 115, 116, 117, 119, 123, 141, 144, 154, 222, 223, 225, 226, 227, 228, 237, 242, 244, 245, 247
bazaarcheh 31
Behjatabad 34
Belgium 130
Berlin 205
birun 221

black market 51, 61
blood ties 93
Bohler, General 32, 199
Bolshevik revolution 13
boulevards 200, 201, 225
Bouzarjomehri, General Karim 37, 67, 203
Britain 8, 10, 13, 25, 43, 51, 122, 189, 201, 208, 209, 217
British Petroleum 17
building form 123–6, 211, 216
building materials 113, 125, 126, 140, 167, 184, 187, 195, 196, 245
built environment 20, 28, 44, 103, 111, 144, 145, 163, 165, 171, 173, 175, 176, 192, 193, 197, 210, 230, 250
Bukhara 221, 222, 227, 228
bureaucracy 164, 214, 215
Burgess 186
Buwaih, House of, 4
Byzantine 229

Café Naderi 153
California 159
capital 20, 22, 26, 40, 50, 51, 53, 79, 109, 111, 113, 166, 167, 168, 169, 170, 171, 172, 174, 178, 179, 180, 182, 192, 197, 204
capital city 3, 5, 13, 18, 21, 23, 29, 31, 35, 52, 78, 82, 84, 88, 96, 100, 109, 115, 120, 135, 164, 188
capitalism 8, 18, 21, 22, 26, 50, 109, 111, 113, 172, 173, 177, 179, 217, 218, 222, 223, 234, 238, 245, 247, 249, 252, 256
caravanserais 35
cash crops 8, 9
Caspian Sea ix, 14, 96, 102, 106, 135, 155, 159, 232, 247
Caucasus 25
census 10
Central Asia ix, 25, 51, 231, 232
chahar-bagh 29, 201, 225
Charter of Athens 209
chenarestan 29
children 90
Christians 86, 239
citadel 28, 29, 30, 32, 34, 38, 103, 111, 117, 200, 202, 218, 219–23, 224, 226, 228, 235, 236 (*see also* royal compound)
citizenship 97

city boundaries 42, 68, 74, 75, 81, 82, 83, 85, 103, 109, 115, 182, 200, 206, 211–2, 216
city centre 42, 86, 105, 117, 123, 127, 130, 142, 145, 148, 185, 186, 187, 207, 210, 215, 223, 227, 239, 247, 255
city council 66, 67, 68, 69, 70, 72, 74, 76, 77, 212, 215
city gates 28, 29, 30, 32, 33, 34, 37, 117, 118, 199, 202, 220, 223, 237
city moats 29, 30, 32, 34, 35, 37, 39, 83, 188, 191, 199, 219
city planning 40, 73, 74, 79, 113, 115, 120, 123, 129, 144, 164, 169, 171, 177, 178, 181, 182, 183, 199, 203, 204, 205–15, 217, 230, 244, 251
city quarters 4, 28, 30, 31, 33, 37, 38, 39, 40, 111, 113, 116, 120, 122, 123, 201, 204, 226, 235–40, 251 (*see also* neighbourhoods)
city size 109, 111, 115, 123
city walls 4, 28, 29, 30, 32, 33, 34, 35, 37, 39, 83, 115, 164, 180, 188, 191, 199–201, 202, 203, 219, 220, 221, 222, 223, 224, 225, 231, 232, 233, 237, 250
Civil Code 181
civil society 97, 100, 101, 255
Clavijo 4
clergy 11, 12, 21, 23, 95, 185, 227, 245, 246, 247
climate 102, 103, 106–9, 111, 126, 242
coach terminals 131
coalition 49
coffee house 149, 154
collective action 96
collective identity 94, 95
collective loyalty 93
collective memory 101, 118
commodification 36, 40, 95, 101, 109, 115, 172, 176, 177, 179, 180, 185, 197
communal bonds 7, 113, 245, 247, 248, 249
competition 122, 177
competition for sites 115, 117, 123, 126, 175, 180, 187, 197
concepts of space 117, 172, 199ff, 204, 247, 252
conformity 94, 244, 247–50
conservation 144–5, 210, 215

conservatives 11, 12,
Constitutional Revolution xi, 11–13, 22, 23, 43, 44, 64, 71, 75, 97, 179, 201
construction 20, 21, 32, 33, 56, 62, 88, 90, 111, 113, 116, 125, 131, 136, 158, 165-7, 170, 171, 183, 188, 190, 192, 193, 194, 195, 198
consultants 167, 171, 178, 205, 215
contextualism 250, 251, 252
contractors 167, 170, 171, 178
co-operatives 51
core–periphery 114–6, 117, 123, 126, 186, 187
cost of living 61, 91, 100, 128
coup d'etat 11, 17, 27, 182
courtyards 07, 108, 123, 125, 126, 127, 134, 137, 141, 150, 152, 154, 156, 159, 201, 211, 224, 231, 241, 242, 243, 244
credit 193, 198
Crete 220
cultural centres 215
cultural divide 99, 252
cultural identity 95–9, 101, 145, 246
cultural practices 235ff
cultural traditions 240
Cumbernauld 207
Curzon, Lord (George) 28, 201
Cyrus 220

D'Arcy, W. 15
dam 135, 136
Damascus 237
Damavand 28, 102, 103
Dar al-Fonun 32, 199
Dari 148
darugheh 65
Darvazeh Shemiran 202
decentralization 115, 116, 130, 131, 145, 192, 214, 215
della Valle, P. 29
democratic governance 70, 75, 76–7, 100, 255
density 36, 37, 42, 79, 80, 85, 96, 107, 109, 111, 112, 114, 115, 116, 125, 128, 130, 134, 136, 137, 138, 141, 169, 170, 182, 185, 187, 199, 207, 209, 210, 214, 215, 240, 243
deprivation 24
deregulation 50, 51
desert 103, 106, 107, 109, 126, 136, 241

design 165, 168, 172, 199, 201, 207, 208, 209, 214, 236, 245
despotic rule 117
developers 167, 168, 170, 171, 178, 180, 206
development agencies 113, 115, 116, 117, 163–78, 187, 199, 210, 215, 250
development industry 143, 167ff, 178
development plan 23, 53, 57, 58, 74, 143
difference 97, 98, 100, 235–40
differentiation 235
diffusion of ideas 196
districts 70, 71, 72, 73, 81, 84, 86, 92, 112, 139, 141, 186, 201, 207, 209
divorce 91, 92
Dizin 157
domes 31, 105
Dowlat gate 29
duality 201
Dura-Europos 221, 224, 232

East 50, 96, 201, 224
East Asia 6, 25
Ecbatana 220
Ecoles des Beaux Arts 205
economic concentration 52ff
economic sectors 55ff
Ehtesabiyeh 65
Ekbatan 193
Ekhtiyaiyeh 81
Elahiyeh 159
Elamites 219
elitism 99
Elwell-Sutton, 37
employment 9, 16, 19, 20, 24, 50, 53, 54ff, 61, 62, 63, 89, 91, 93, 111, 143, 194, 195, 207, 209, 256
energy 59, 74
Enghelab square 98, 156
Enghelab street 37, 43, 80, 117, 118, 119, 226
England 227
English language xi
environmental pollution 128 132–7, 145, 207, 214, 240, 254 (*see also* air pollution, water pollution, noise pollution)
environmental problems 25
environmental quality 116, 128, 137, 138, 139, 214

environmental rationality 108, 122, 248, 249
estate agents 167, 171, 178, 181
ethnic groups 96, 97, 114
Etruscan 224
Euphrates 219, 231, 232
Europe 7, 8, 10, 11, 12, 15, 17, 31, 33, 34, 51, 102, 153, 188, 200, 201, 205, 217, 224, 230, 238
exchange value 144, 173–6, 178

facades 108, 126, 158, 199, 204, 243, 244, 250
factional strife 4, 8, 49, 237, 238
factionalism 40, 120
family (see household)
famine 9
Farmanfarmaian, Aziz 207
farrash 65
Fath Ali Shah 29
fatwa 206
Ferdowsi 96, 226
Ferdowsi square 252
feudal 7, 10, 13, 238
financial independence 77–81
financial resources 187–93
firms, 55, 56, 60, 62, 82, 123, 167, 168, 170, 171, 174, 178
First World War 12, 13, 39, 164, 222
Firuzabad 224
floods 105, 106, 111, 136, 181, 215
foreign debts 100
foreign trade 6, 8, 10, 11, 15, 57, 188
France 32, 131, 199, 200, 204, 205
Franco-Prussian war 200
Fraser 31
Friday mosque 30, 43, 227, 228, 241
fruit and vegetable markets 81, 131, 153
Fujiyama 28

gardens 32, 34, 107, 108, 119, 137–40, 145, 159, 180, 201, 203, 232
Garnier, Tony 207
gate tax 33, 66, 70, 201
Gaube 226
gazmeh 65
Gemeinschaft 94
General Gardane 5
geometrical regularity 108, 200, 203, 204, 218, 225, 230–4
Germany 15, 16, 122, 205, 217
Gesellschaft 94

Ghaffari, Fereydun 207
Ghar 28
Gharchak 135, 149, 150, 187
Gholhak 240
global economy xi, 9, 24, 25, 26, 101, 109, 113, 245, 255, 256
globalization x, xi, 256
Godard, André 204
Golestan palace 37, 39
Gorgan 232, 236
Gowd 71
Greeks 96, 220, 221, 224, 231, 232, 236
green space 107, 109, 111, 124, 128, 137–40, 146, 170, 182, 183, 214, 255
Gregorian Calendar xi
growth management 115, 205, 208
Gruen, Victor 207, 208

Hafez 96
Hajeb al-Dowleh arcade 56
Hamadan 220
Hanafi 4
Harris 187
Haussmann, Baron, 200, 204
Hazrat Abd al-Azim 4, 30, 43
Heart 222, 224, 226, 232, 238
Hellenistic 224, 226, 236
Hellenization 221
Herbert, Sir Thomas, 29
Heydari 237
Hia 238
High Council for Resettlement of Squatters 71
High Council for Town Planning and Architecture 68, 69, 205
high rise buildings 79, 125, 127, 139, 160, 168, 193, 207, 210
high streets 42, 117, 123, 212, 224
High Technical Council 38
Hillenbrand 244
Hindu 242
Hippodamus 224, 231, 232, 236
home ownership 141, 174, 183
homogenization x, 40
Hook 208
households 55, 61, 91–3, 99, 100, 111, 140, 141, 254, 255
housing 20, 61, 74, 88, 91, 115, 125, 128, 140–44, 145, 164, 165, 166, 171, 173, 174, 178, 181, 182, 183, 189, 190, 191, 192, 193, 195, 197, 204, 214, 243

Housing Bank   193
housing co-operatives   167, 169, 170, 174, 178, 185
Housing Foundation   165, 183
Howard, Ebenezer   208
humanism   94, 95

identity   237, 240, 255
Ilkhanids   10
image   200, 210, 216, 217, 246
Imam Hussein square   229
Imam Khomeini square   68, 98 (see also Tup-Khaneh)
Imam Reza   151, 225
Imamzadeh Saleh   228
Imperial Bank of Persia   33
income distribution   21
India   148, 224, 239
individualism   91, 93–5, 101, 113, 122, 126, 245
Indo-Europeans   94, 96
industrialization   14, 15, 17, 22, 27, 51, 88, 109, 254
industry   24, 42, 50, 56, 57, 59, 85, 122, 133, 134, 135, 136, 166, 181, 189, 190, 198, 204, 207, 210, 221
inflation   16, 61, 62, 80, 100, 128, 143, 181, 182, 188, 194, 254
informal economy   60, 61
infrastructures   36, 37, 78, 115, 164, 166, 168, 181, 184, 192, 197, 207, 211, 254, 255
institutions   246, 247
instrumental rationality   94, 113, 122, 177, 233, 249, 250, 257
intelligentsia   11, 245, 246, 247
intermediate groups   227–9
International Monetary Fund   18
investment   20, 78, 173, 177, 182, 187–93, 197, 204, 213, 214, 215
Iran Bastan Museum   150
Iran Street   240
Iran's Statistical Centre   60
Iraq   ix, 23, 24, 50, 56, 57, 58, 76, 89, 100, 131, 188, 192, 206, 239
Iron Curtain   25
Irvine   208
Isfahan   4, 5, 31, 58, 72, 88, 140, 163, 201, 222, 226, 227, 230
Islam   4, 201, 238, 240, 241, 242, 249
Islamic architecture   205, 242, 244

Islamic city   221, 222, 225, 227, 229, 230, 233, 238, 240, 242, 244
Islamic culture   242, 246
Islamic gardens   203
Islamic lands   222, 229, 243
Islamic law   65, 94, 142, 179, 183, 185, 206, 229
Islamic period   29, 202, 225, 227, 232
Islamic prayer   131, 242
Islamic Republic   50, 53, 93
Islamic revolution   ix, xi, xii, 22–4, 43, 67, 70, 71, 72, 85, 86, 88, 91, 95, 118, 144, 165, 228, 240, 249, 256
Islamic society   64, 229
Islamic traditions   126, 253
Islamist movements   ix
Islamshahr   24, 83
Israel   25

Jahad-e Sazandegi   51
Jajrood   135, 136
Japan   28
Jayy   226
Jerusalem   241
Jews   86, 238

Kaaba   242
Kabul   147
kadkhuda   65
Kahrizak   135, 136
Kakh-e Marmar (Marble palace)   37
kalantar   65
Karaj   24, 42, 82, 103, 135, 157
Kavir   103
Kennedy, J.   18
Ker Porter   5
Kerman   222, 225
Kermanshah   222
khalesseh   179
Khatami, M.   25, 100
Khorsabad   231
Khurasan   3, 150, 224
Khuzestan   89, 219
Kinnier   5
Knossos   220
Kourosh Company   190
Kurds   96, 97, 238
Kuwait   23

labour   20, 21, 26, 40, 50, 53, 54, 92, 93, 109, 111, 116, 125, 167, 178, 180, 193–7, 204, 254

Lalehzar street   34
land   9, 18, 26, 74, 95, 102, 103, 107, 108, 109, 115, 125, 139, 142, 165, 167, 168, 169, 170, 176, 178, 179–87, 197, 206, 211, 213
land and property development   17, 74, 80, 173, 181
land and property market   40, 81, 113, 143, 171, 175, 182, 185, 197
land and property ownership   14, 125, 167, 171, 179, 180, 181, 182, 183, 184, 204, 206, 207, 210, 212
land contamination   136
land prices   79, 91, 111, 112, 113, 115, 117, 137, 138, 140, 141, 144, 169, 173, 176, 181, 182, 184, 185, 186, 193, 197, 211
land reform   18, 19, 26, 27, 109, 179, 182, 195
land use   34, 116, 122–3, 124, 127, 131, 135, 177, 182, 206, 207, 214, 215, 216, 223, 225
Lar   135
Latian   135
Le Corbusier   230
liberalism   246
liberalization   51, 56, 58, 62, 72
literacy   86, 88, 90, 111
Llewlyn-Davies, Lord   208
Lockhart   5
Lohrasp   226
London   99, 207, 208
Louis XIV   200
Lurs   96

Macedonians   221, 231, 236
madraseh   31
Madrid   207
Majidiyeh   182, 239
manufacturing industry   14, 17, 19, 23, 26, 53, 55, 58ff, 62, 166, 194
marginal space   34
marginalization   34
market economy   36, 40, 50, 95, 113, 172, 173, 178, 187, 189, 226, 239, 249
marriage   91, 92, 93
Martyrs' Foundation   165
maseel   105, 106
Mashhad   5, 140, 151, 225
mass production   143, 174, 184, 198

master builder   167, 169, 171 (see also mimar)
mavat   179
Maydan-e Arg   30
Maydan-e Shah   227
mayor   66, 67, 68, 69, 72, 73, 75, 76, 78, 80, 203, 211
Mazandaran   135
meaning   147
Mecca   122, 241, 242
Medians   3, 220
Medina   241
Mehrabad   132
melting pot   97
Mer'at al-Boldan   5
Merv   221, 224, 232
Mesopotamia   219, 220, 223
methodology   x
metropolitan region (see urban region)
Middle Ages   8, 231, 238
middle class   13, 21, 22, 93, 98, 99, 111, 113, 125, 141, 181, 184, 193, 198, 210, 212, 240, 244, 245, 247, 254
Middle East   ix, x, 7, 11, 25, 64, 77, 107, 115, 199, 235, 238, 240
migration/migrants   10, 20, 22, 51, 85, 86, 87–91, 93, 94, 95, 96, 98, 99, 100, 109, 113, 116, 140, 142, 143, 183, 207, 212, 221, 238, 239, 240, 241, 243, 249
Miletus   231
Milton Keynes   208
mimar   167, 171 (see also master builder)
minarets   105
Ministry of Defence   176
Ministry of Economic Affairs   74, 189
Ministry of Education   74
Ministry of Energy   74, 164
Ministry of Finance   37
Ministry of Health   74
Ministry of Higher Education   74
Ministry of Housing and Urban Development   74, 164, 176, 205, 206
Ministry of Interior   66, 67, 74, 70, 76, 176, 205, 212
Ministry of Islamic Guidance   74
Ministry of Justice   37
Ministry of Posts, Telegraphs and Telephones   74, 164

Ministry of Roads and Transportation 164
Ministry of Trade 74
Ministry of War 176
Minorsky 5, 28
Mirza Issa 32
mobility 40, 44, 90, 94, 106, 119, 142, 174, 201, 209, 212, 240
Modarres motorway 52
Modern Movement 122, 209
modernism 144, 209–10
modernity x, 114, 122, 126, 245–7, 251, 256
modernization xi, 11, 15, 18, 22, 37, 50, 91, 101, 199, 218, 243, 247, 250–52, 256
modesty 244, 245
Moguls 4, 96, 222
Mojabi, J. 98
molk 179
monarchy ix, 12, 17, 33, 49, 68, 95, 118, 144, 218, 219, 220, 223, 226, 229, 234, 247
monopolization 20, 27, 64, 180–85
Moscow 227
Mossadegh, M. 17, 67
Mostowfi al-Mamalek 32
mountains 3, 38, 102, 103, 104, 105, 106, 108, 109, 126, 132, 133, 134, 135, 136, 139, 154, 223, 247, 254
Mowlavi 96
Muhammad Reza Shah 16, 67, 223
Muhammad Shah 29
muhtasib 64, 65
municipal organization 66, 71, 120
municipal revenue 78, 79
municipality 64ff, 93, 99, 123, 129, 130, 131, 138, 139, 143, 145, 146, 159, 164, 176, 177, 185, 200, 203, 205, 207, 211, 213–5, 217, 229, 230, 255, 256
municipality's strategic plan 73, 131, 134, 140, 213–5
Muslims 86, 206, 230, 232, 236, 241, 244
mysticism 93, 94, 156, 157 (*see also* Sufi)

Naderi 153, 239
Napoleon III 200, 204
Narmak 42
Nasser al-Din Shah 12, 31, 163, 200
Nasseriyeh street 34, 35

nation state 97
national assembly 43
national bourgeoisie 9
national economy 49–52, 59, 62, 111, 165–7, 197
national identity 97, 238
national space 13, 16, 52, 96
nationalism, 13, 95, 97, 120, 204, 238, 245, 246, 247, 256
nationalization 17, 19, 23, 53, 56, 57, 164, 165, 171, 181, 183, 184, 185, 188, 189
natural space 102
Navab street 79, 176
Nazis 205
Ne'mati 237
neighbourhoods 34, 117, 152, 154, 159, 168, 199, 207, 208, 213, 235–40, 242, 250, 251 (*see also* city quarters)
neo-classicism 205
New Earswick 208
new towns 144, 168, 170, 189, 193, 207–9 (*see also* satellite towns)
Niavaran palace 223
Nishapur 237, 238
noise pollution 136, 214, 244
nomadic tribes 7, 16, 19, 96, 220
normalization 24–5, 62, 178, 179, 197
north–south axis 8, 37, 108, 117–9, 177, 226
north–south divide 34, 40, 88, 101, 109, 111–4, 115, 117, 177, 185, 187, 210, 216, 235, 251
Nowrooz 5, 155, 158

oil economy ix, x, 15, 17, 26, 50ff, 60, 62, 77, 88, 95, 99, 109, 141, 165, 188
Oil Ministry 74
oil revenue 15, 17, 19, 21, 22, 23, 26, 27, 50, 51, 53, 58, 79, 100, 109, 111, 116, 164, 166, 182, 188, 191, 254
old city 32, 39, 103, 114, 115, 122, 123, 144–5, 187, 204, 215, 247, 256
Olivier 29
OPEC ix, 50
open matrix 39, 119, 120, 201–5
open space 43, 76, 79, 211, 215
Orient ix, 37
orientation 103, 108, 122, 126, 203, 242
ostan 92
Ottomans 96, 222, 237

Oudlajan 121, 144, 147, 187, 210, 238
Ouseley 5, 29
overcrowding 128

Pahlavi street 37, 226 (*see also* Vali Asr street)
Pahlavis 22, 96, 97, 218, 223, 247
Pakistan 25
Paris 99, 122, 199, 200, 201, 204, 205, 217, 227
Park-e Shahr 106
parks 39, 81, 134, 138, 140, 158
Parliament 23, 39, 65, 66, 74, 130, 181, 184, 203, 223
Parthians 3, 221, 224, 232, 236
Pasdaran 154
pedestrians 119, 128, 208, 226
Perry, Clarence 208
Persepolis 220, 231
Persian culture 96, 226
Persian empire 7, 8, 82, 96
Persian Gulf 14, 25
Persian landscape 28, 137, 203, 222
Persian xi, 5, 67, 96–8, 137, 148, 149, 155, 157, 222, 236
Philippines 151
Piran 142
Pirene 231
Place Royale 227
Plan and Budget Organization 74, 176, 205
pluralism 93, 98
political authority 218ff
political centralization 10, 11, 13, 26, 27, 33, 53, 64, 67, 75, 81, 88, 97, 109, 111, 113, 164, 191, 215, 221, 222
political institutions 144, 218
political participation 22, 99, 100
political suppression 16
popular culture 100
population 9, 10, 11, 15, 16, 17, 18, 19, 20, 23, 24, 26, 31, 32, 36, 37, 40, 42, 44, 53, 54, 57, 62, 79, 82–7, 100, 109, 115, 135, 137, 140, 181, 207, 214, 221, 225, 238, 254, 255
postmodern xi, 248, 256
privacy 79, 126, 242–4
private sector 14, 16, 18, 20, 23, 24, 51, 53, 56ff, 76, 7, 125, 131, 144, 145, 163, 172, 178, 189, 190, 191, 192, 193, 194, 197, 205
private sphere 233

private vehicles 129, 134
privatization 16, 50, 51, 72, 78, 213
production of space 115, 125, 145, 165, 173, 176, 177, 191, 192, 195, 196, 197, 231, 234, 248
property tax 79, 206
public participation 75, 76, 81, 100, 230, 254
public sector 14, 18, 20, 42, 56ff, 62, 75, 76, 78, 82, 125, 138, 143, 145, 163, 164, 172, 176, 177, 190, 192, 197, 256
public space 43, 44, 59, 107, 122, 138, 243, 244
public sphere 95, 97, 101, 255
public squares 15, 30, 31, 33, 34, 37, 43, 45, 76, 98, 117, 120, 201, 224, 226–7
public transport 128, 130, 131, 135, 208, 213, 214

qadi 64, 65
Qajars 5, 6, 13, 29, 31, 96, 200, 201, 203
qaleh 224
qanats 122, 135, 203
Qaysariyeh 227
Qazvin 5
Qibla 242
Qom 43
quhandezh 29, 221
Qur'an 28

rabaz 29, 221
Radburn 208
radicalism 49
Rafsanjani, A. 50
Raga 3
railway station 131
rainfall 106
Rajaiishahr 83
Ramadan 150, 241
rationing 90–1, 151
rationality 230–4
Ray 3–4, 5, 26, 28, 82, 103, 105, 187, 254
Red Square 227
Redditch 208
redevelopment 37, 39, 210, 211, 213, 216
refinery 59
reform 11, 12, 13, 15, 18, 19, 50, 58, 61, 62, 72, 200, 217, 230, 236
regeneration 144

regionalism 16
religious institutions 35
religious internationalism 97
religious minorities 10, 86, 114
religious nationalism 97
religious populism 95
Renaissance 122, 200
republic 23, 95, 101, 144, 223, 247 (*see also* Islamic Republic)
Resalat motorway 129
retail 55, 60, 63, 79, 80
revolution 3, 11, 26, 43, 49, 50, 53, 57, 61, 62, 65, 70, 76, 77, 78, 79, 85, 90, 91, 93, 94, 95, 97, 99, 100, 109, 114, 129, 130, 131, 134, 143, 151, 152, 159, 168, 169, 171, 174, 175, 182, 183, 189, 190, 192, 193, 198, 204, 205, 206, 211, 212, 223, 240, 244, 245, 246, 253, 254, 256, 257
Reza Shah 13–16, 37, 39, 66, 163, 180, 200, 201, 204, 205, 223, 226
Romans 96, 224, 232, 242
Rome 236
royal compound 30ff, 200, 201, 202, 219, 220, 222, 223, 225, 226, 234 (*see also* citadel)
royal despotism 246
royal dictatorship 17, 21
royal family 21, 38, 165, 168, 178, 189
Runcorn 208
Russia 8, 10, 13, 25, 43, 189

Sa'dabad palace 38, 106
Sa'di 96
Sabzeh Maydan 30
Sada 226
Saddam Hussein 89, 151
Safavids 4, 5, 10, 28, 29, 30, 31, 32, 97, 188, 201, 222, 225, 227, 237
Saidnia 23
Salman Rushdie 25
Sangeladj 38, 201
Sarkis church 239
Sassanians 4, 221, 222, 224, 225, 226, 229, 232, 236, 237
satellite towns 40, 42, 86, 90, 116–7, 127, 185, 209, 212, 255 (*see also* new towns)
Saudi Arabia 25
Savejbolagh 82
Saving and Loan for Housing 189, 190

Second Empire 200, 204
Second World War xi, 16, 28, 38, 40, 43, 44, 67, 114, 115, 167, 171, 179, 181, 185, 188, 192, 197, 205, 207, 212
sectoral management 73ff, 176–7, 178
secular space 114, 228, 229
secularism 245, 246, 256
security 201
Selinus 224
Seljuk 4, 10
Selucids 221
Semnan 24
Sepahsalar (Motahari) mosque 34, 36
services 55, 56, 60, 61, 62
sewage 106, 136, 214
Shafii 4
shah 7, 12, 14, 17, 49, 51, 68, 75, 97, 117, 163, 180, 188, 226, 228
Shah Abbas 29, 163
Shah mosque 30
Shah Suleiman 29
Shah Tahmasb 4, 28, 29
Shahrak-e Qods (Gharb) 168, 170, 189
Shahrara 42, 168
Shahrdari 67
shahrestan 83
Shah-Reza street 37, 38
Shahri, J. 34
Shahryar 82
Shahyad 43
Shakespeare 227
Shams al-Emareh 34, 35
shanty towns 99, 117, 142, 143, 163, 212 (*see also* squatters)
sharestan 29, 221
shari'a 65
Shemiran 109, 153
Shemiranat 82
Shiism 97, 237
Shinkel 205
Shiraz 5, 99, 140, 151, 225
Shohada (Martyrs') Square 44, 45
Shush 219
Shush Square 156
Sicily 224
Silk Route 3, 6, 25, 221
Siroux, Maxim, 204
social cohesion 240
social control 94
social development 96
social divide 21, 31, 126, 141, 142, 178, 182, 215, 220, 221, 235, 255

social exclusion 34, 99, 100, 101, 143, 177, 255
social fragmentation 95, 96
social integration 97, 99
social movements 12, 22, 26, 42ff, 99
social networks 90, 92, 99, 100, 117, 257
social norms 91, 94, 95, 101, 126, 244, 245, 246, 249
social polarization 15, 25, 27, 33, 61, 86, 99, 100, 114, 184, 185, 186, 254, 255
social rationality 177, 233, 244, 248, 249, 250
social relations 95, 101, 249
social space 102
social stratification 8, 10, 33, 45, 103, 113, 120, 126, 177, 185, 187, 219, 232, 236, 238, 239, 245
socialism 50
socialization 93, 99
Soria Y Mata 207
Soviet Union ix, 17, 25, 50, 89
space and social movements 42–4
space x, xi, 26, 28, 33, 34, 36, 37, 39, 40, 43, 45, 102–27, 139, 141, 163, 164, 175, 177, 178, 187, 189, 190, 201, 204, 208, 210, 215, 216, 219, 228, 230, 232, 237, 247, 257
spatial behaviour 43
spatial segregation 33, 40, 199, 204, 215, 219, 234, 235–40
spatial structure 33, 34, 37, 45, 86–7, 113, 114, 117, 127, 175, 185–7, 197
spatial structure, classical models of 115, 185–7
specialization 173, 174, 223
speculative development 17, 18, 42, 106, 125, 136, 138, 142, 167, 176, 180, 181, 182, 206, 207, 250, 256
squatters 71, 117 (*see also* shanty towns)
standardization 175
strangers 95–9, 101
strategic location 3, 4, 5, 8, 25, 35
street system 37, 79, 103, 105, 108, 119–22, 126, 127, 203, 210, 214, 216, 226, 231, 232, 242, 243, 250
streets 15, 34, 35, 37, 39, 40, 45, 76, 99, 107, 108, 115, 120, 129, 148, 151, 158, 199, 200, 201, 202, 203, 211, 225, 226, 236, 250

subsidies 57, 61, 85, 152, 158, 185
suburbanization 84, 85, 90, 109, 114–6, 192, 212, 216, 255
suburbs 10, 24, 32, 33, 34, 39, 40, 42, 15, 83, 84, 91, 100, 103, 106, 109, 116–7, 139, 157, 180, 181, 206, 208, 210, 212, 214, 221, 222
Sufi 156, 237, 241 (*see also* mysticism)
Sumerians 219
Sunni 97, 237
Supervisory Council for the Expansion of Tehran 68, 69, 211
Susa 219, 220, 231

Tabriz 5
Tajrish 153, 228
takyeh 31, 227
Taleghan 135
Taxila 221
technology 187, 195, 196
Tehran Comprehensive Plan 68, 82, 116, 182, 183, 207–11, 215, 217
Tehran University 38, 156
Tehran's economy 42ff
Tehrani accent xi, 98
Tehran-Pars 182, 187, 212
territorial structure 7
Third World 246
Timur 4
To-Chal 103
Toghril Beg 4
topography 102–6, 122, 134
trade unions 194
traditionalism 11, 114, 216, 245–7
traffic congestion 85, 116, 130, 210, 211, 214, 240
traffic management 85, 116, 131, 139, 186
Trans-Iranian Railway 13, 37, 192
transport 56, 72, 111, 128–32, 164
transportation network 14, 37, 39, 42, 164, 191, 202, 203, 207, 214, 215
trees 29, 34, 39, 111, 134, 136, 137–40, 181, 203, 225, 254
tribal territories 5, 29
Tup-Khaneh Square 31, 33, 68, 98 (*see also* Imam Khomeini Square)
Turkey 25, 77
Turkish language 96
Turkmans 96
Turks 222
tuyul 180

ulama 64
Ullman 187
umma 241
unified space 39, 120, 187, 201ff
uniformity 107, 204
United Nations 139, 255
United States 15, 17, 22, 25, 51, 100, 122, 207, 208, 217
Unwin, Raymond 208
Ur 223, 231
urban autonomy 66, 67, 69, 72, 75, 120, 176, 215, 220, 229–30,
urban blocks 116, 122, 127, 236, 244
urban culture 99
urban development process x, xii, 13, 37, 39, 40, 42, 43, 74, 115, 117, 123, 137, 138, 163, 176, 187, 188, 197, 212, 230, 232, 250, 251
urban expansion 32, 33, 34, 35, 37, 40, 41, 68, 103, 105, 114, 115, 116, 117, 123, 132, 136, 137, 138, 144, 193, 206, 211, 213, 221, 235, 240, 251
urban governance 73ff
Urban Land Organization 183, 184
urban land theory 187
urban region 24, 81, 84, 85, 87, 212, 213, 256
urban transformation 31ff, 199ff
urbanization 17, 20, 23, 24, 75, 173, 193, 198, 221
use value 144, 168, 173–6, 178

vacant land 34, 124, 165, 179, 237
Vali Asr Square 153
Vali Asr street 37, 117, 118, 153, 226 (*see also* Pahlavi street)
vaqf 179
Varamin 4, 82, 106, 135
Vauban 200

Victorian 31
visibility 105
Vitruvian theory 200

war ix, xii, 22–4, 26, 50, 54, 56, 57, 58, 59, 60, 61, 62, 72, 76, 78, 85, 86, 90, 100, 114, 129, 131, 151, 152, 154, 174, 175, 188, 192, 200, 206, 254
Washington 208
waste disposal 136, 214
water distribution 106, 135
water pollution 135, 136
Weber, M. 229
West 6, 8, 9, 11, 12, 15, 19, 22, 25, 45, 50, 93, 94, 95, 96, 122, 125, 159, 195, 199, 201, 205, 209, 210, 216, 217, 245, 246, 256
White Balloon 98
White Revolution 18, 23
winds 108, 122, 134
women and employment 54, 57, 60, 62
women and literacy 86
women and migration 89
women and space 86, 242, 243
working class 15, 16, 21, 204
World Health Organization 133
world market 8–11, 24, 26, 36, 44, 51, 52, 63, 81, 217, 218

Yaqut 28
Yazd 222
Yousefabad 34, 42, 121, 152, 153, 181

Zagros 102
Zand, Karim Khan 5, 29
Zands 225
Zhaleh Square 43
Zoroastrians 3, 86, 137

```
HT 384 .I652 T446 1998
Madanipour, Ali.
Tehran
```